Writing at the Kitchen Table

Also by Artemis Cooper

Cairo in the War 1939–1945

Mr Wu and Mrs Stitch:
The Letters of Evelyn Waugh and Diana Cooper (ed.)

Watching in the Dark

Paris after the Liberation 1944–1949 (with Antony Beevor)

ARTEMIS COOPER

Writing at the Kitchen Table

* * * * * * * *

THE AUTHORIZED BIOGRAPHY OF

Elizabeth David

MICHAEL JOSEPH
LONDON

MICHAEL JOSEPH

Published by the Penguin Group
Penguin Books Ltd, 27 Wrights Lane, London w8 5tz, England
Penguin Putnam Inc., 375 Hudson Street, New York, New York 10014, USA
Penguin Books Australia Ltd, Ringwood, Victoria, Australia
Penguin Books Canada Ltd, 10 Alcorn Avenue, Toronto, Ontario, Canada m4v 3b2
Penguin Books (NZ) Ltd, Private Bag 102902, NSMC, Auckland, New Zealand

Penguin Books Ltd, Registered Offices: Harmondsworth, Middlesex, England

First published 1999
1 3 5 7 9 10 8 6 4 2

Set in 11.75/15.5pt Monotype Ehrhardt
Typeset by Rowland Phototypesetting Ltd, Bury St Edmunds, Suffolk
Printed in Great Britain by Clays Ltd, St Ives plc

A CIP catalogue record for this book is available from the British Library

ISBN 0-718-14224-1

Contents

	List of Illustrations	vi
	Family Tree	viii
	Introduction and Acknowledgements	xi
1.	The Gwynnes	1
2.	The Gwynne Girls Grow Up	10
3.	Paris and Munich	28
4.	Acting it Out	35
5.	Norman Douglas	60
6.	The Loss of the *Evelyn Hope*	70
7.	Alexandria	84
8.	Tony David	98
9.	Indian Interlude	117
10.	Back in Blighty	124
11.	*Mediterranean Food*	139
12.	*Italian Food*	161
13.	Friends, Editors and Other Enemies	183
14.	On the Road in Provincial France	194
15.	The Year of Betrayal	208
16.	Farewell to P. H.	227
17.	The Shop	235
18.	Salt and Spice	256
19.	Baking Bread	275
20.	Omelette and Ice	291
21.	Brave New World	316
	Epilogue	334
	Notes and Sources	337
	Selected Bibliography	350
	Index	353

List of Illustrations

Section one

1. Stella Gwynne, Elizabeth's mother
2. Rupert Gwynne MP, Elizabeth's father
3. Wootton Manor
4. Portrait of Elizabeth by Ambrose McEvoy
5. Family group at Wootton, 1924
6. Stella and her daughters, late 1920s
7. Elizabeth as an actress
8. Charles Gibson Cowan
9. Peter Laing
10. Norman Douglas
11. Elizabeth, 1944
12. Tony David, 1944
13. Elizabeth at her desk in Cairo, *c.*1943
14. Tony David in Cairo, 1943
15. Cairo friends, 1944
16. Renée Fedden

Section two

17. Elizabeth and George Lassalle, early 1950s
18. Lesley O'Malley at Halsey Street
19. Elizabeth, early 1950s
20. Diana Gwynne's wedding to Christopher Grey, 1941
21. Elizabeth with John Lehmann, early 1950s
22. Elizabeth in her kitchen at Halsey Street, mid 1950s
23. Elizabeth in the kitchen, 1956 or 1957

24. Elizabeth, 1956 or 1957
25. Elizabeth by Anthony Denney, 1964
26. Peter Higgins
27. Elizabeth in the shop, mid 1960s
28. Anthony Denney
29. Elizabeth David Ltd in Bourne Street, Pimlico
30. Elizabeth in France, c.1971
31. Elizabeth's sister Felicité
32. Elizabeth in old age, late 1980s

Photographic Acknowledgements

The author wishes to thank the following for their permission to reproduce the above photographs; those not listed below all come from the Elizabeth David Archives:

Steve Grey: 4

Mrs Aileen Gibson Cowan: 8

Islay Lyons: 10

Hassia, Cairo: 11

Jean Weinberg, Cairo: 12

Jane Blakemore: 15, 18

Doreen Thornton: 19

Mrs Anthony Denney: 25, 27

Georgina Tritton: 26

Piggott: 32

John Carels = Indonesian ranee

Anna Carels = Theunis In'tveld

John GWYNNE
(d. 1855)
m. Agnes
Anderson

Cornelia = William Purvis
In'tveld

James Gwynne = May
(1832–1915)   (1841–1923)

Matthew = Mary
White,   (d. 1899)
1st Viscount
RIDLEY
(1842–1904)

Evelyn
(1865–1935)

Reginald
(1863–1942)

Nevile
(1868–1951)
m. Bluebelle
Wake

Violet
(1871–1948)
m. (1894)
Gordon
Woodhouse

Dorothy
(1877–1958)

Roland
(1882–1971)

Rupert = Stella
(1873–1924)   (1884–1973)
m. 2nd (1933)
John Hamilton
(d. 1952)

Kathleen
(1897–1989)

Veronica

Mary

John
m. Patricia
Morrison-Bell

Priscilla
(b. 1909)
m. (1933)
Richard
Barnes-
Longland

ELIZABETH
(1913–92)
m. (1944)
Lt Col. Anthony
David (1911–67)

Martin
(b. 1942)

Jessica
(b. 1944)

Sabrina
(b. 1939)

Julia
(b. 1941)

FAMILY TREE SHOWING THE GWYNNES, RIDLEYS, MARJORIBANKS, HOGGS AND PALMERS

Introduction and Acknowledgements

On 22 February 1994, two years after Elizabeth David's death, the contents of her two kitchens at 24 Halsey Street, Chelsea, went on sale at Phillips auction rooms in Bayswater. The press had taken up the story as soon as the forthcoming sale was announced, showing photographs of pots and pans, spoons and storage jars, all displayed on her scrubbed-pine kitchen table. Cookery writers and chefs were invited to choose items they coveted or might bid for. From the moment viewing began, a steady stream of people made their way to the showrooms. They were private individuals, not professional dealers, and they spent hours poring over cheese graters and ramekins which could have come from a junk shop.

The day itself took everyone by surprise. The saleroom was packed by nine-thirty in the morning, and the auction, scheduled to take place at midday, was delayed by the crush. 'We brought in every chair we could,' said one of the saleroom staff, 'but the crowd was unbelievable. They were out in the corridor and all the way down the stairs. There must have been three hundred, perhaps four hundred people ... and there was this sense of excitement, of electricity. I've never seen anything like it.'

When the proceedings finally began, the auctioneer was almost overwhelmed by the sheer volume of bids. People wanted something, anything, even if they didn't know what it was. 'I don't know exactly what I've bought,' said one woman after paying £75 for a lot. 'I just wanted to have some keepsake.' One of Elizabeth's friends recalled how odd it was to see little things that he had given her go for fifty to a hundred pounds. Some people had their eyes on certain pieces: Prue Leith was determined to buy the kitchen table, and a roar of approval went up from the crowd when the table went to her for £1,100. Leith rose to her feet with a whoop of delight, and took a little bow amidst a round of spontaneous applause. 'I'm going to cook on it just like she did, and think of her,' said Prue Leith afterwards. 'She was the most important cookery writer this century. That's why I wanted her table. I can't believe I've got it.' By the end of the afternoon the sale had made £49,000 – more than three times its estimated value. The bidders had not bought pots and wooden spoons, but relics: fragments from someone they had never met, but who had had such an effect on their lives that they wanted to keep a little piece of her for ever.

Elizabeth David's reputation rests primarily on her first five books. *A Book of Mediterranean Food* appeared in 1949 while England was still in the grip of rationing. Her aim was 'to bring a flavour of those blessed lands of sun and sea and olive trees' into English kitchens. At a time when aubergines, lemons and olive oil were almost unobtainable, the book's success amazed both her and her publishers. What Elizabeth had managed to do, in this book and those that followed, was to describe food in such a way as to make people dream of it and want to cook it.

Timing was with her. After the dismal years of war and post-war austerity, the world was opening up. People started travelling as never before, and they were not afraid of garlic and wine sauces as their parents' generation had been. At the same time, new transport systems were established which brought foreign food hitherto unavailable in English shops. Some of Elizabeth David's staunchest supporters declare that it is due to her alone that we can now find Italian olive oil, red peppers and Israeli avocados in every supermarket. This must be an exaggeration, but there is an argument for saying that, in her quiet way, she was the most influential cookery writer of her time. There is scarcely a professional cook of any distinction in these islands who does not acknowledge her as an inspiration. She also taught a whole generation of people how to think about food in ways they never had before, and how to cook the simple, authentic dishes she described. Elizabeth never approached cooking as a chore. It was hard work, certainly, but her writing made cooking a creative act to be enjoyed for its own sake, not something to be got out of the way.

There was also something compelling about her writing. On the surface, it seemed admirably spare, straightforward and to the point. But behind those crisp sentences, one can feel the pressure of her loves and hates, her enthusiasm and her passion. The reader becomes acutely aware of these emotions, although they are never mentioned. This is what makes her prose so powerful, and why she inspired a whole generation not only to take up cooking, but to plunge into it with her own kind of serious enjoyment. 'I think,' she wrote, 'that the ideal cookery writer is one who makes his readers *want* to cook as well as telling them how it is done; he should also leave something, not too much perhaps, but a little, unsaid; people must make their own discoveries, use their own intelligence, otherwise they will be deprived of part of the fun.'

About her private life, Elizabeth left everything unsaid. She hated publicity of any kind, and revealed very few clues about the sort of person she might be. The photographs in the press showed an elegant, rather beautiful woman with clever, cat-like eyes. She wore well-cut, classical clothes, and emphasized her long neck with white shirts open at the throat. Sometimes there was a photograph of her crowded kitchen, with its French armoires and bowls of eggs and lemons on the dressers; but that was as close as the public ever got to her private life. 'Everything I want to say is in my books,' she maintained. She gave out nothing else, and anyone foolish enough to ask an impertinent question would shrivel up in the frozen silence that followed.

*

Fortunately for the biographer, the crockery and kitchen equipment sold at Phillips had not been the only things she left behind. In her house in Halsey Street, books spilled out of every available bookshelf. They had taken over the sitting room to such an extent that the floor was an obstacle course and there was nowhere to sit down. They had advanced up to the first floor in little piles on each stair. Her bedroom contained more bookshelves, also full to bursting; and there was a subsidiary library in her kitchen. She had never been able to acquire them on an expensive scale, but her books made a magnificent collection on the history of cookery and gastronomy in English, French and Italian. First choice went, as she had instructed, to the Warburg Institute. The rest went to the Guildhall Library.

There were also, in every room, innumerable files and cardboard boxes of papers, notebooks, correspondence and catalogues. Elizabeth had appointed her long-time editor and friend Jill Norman to be her literary executor, and before the house in Halsey Street was sold, Jill and her husband Paul Breman moved the archive to their house in Hampstead.

I never met Elizabeth David, although I did talk to her once on the telephone. I was just beginning a book about Cairo during the Second World War when a friend gave me her telephone number. She was a considerable name. I had two of her books and was very keen to meet her, but I had also been told that she could be difficult. While I summoned up the courage to dial, I wrote out what I wanted to say on a piece of paper.

'Hello?' The voice was cold, absent-minded. I threw myself into my introductory patter. By about the third sentence I realized I was getting none of those encouraging little noises that most people make, although I knew she was listening. I rambled on nervously, and finally managed to ask whether I might come and see her. There was a long silence, and then the single word, 'No.' My heart sank. 'But,' she said, 'you can talk to me now if you like.' I was totally unprepared for an interview, and was at that embarrassing stage of

xiv

very early research when one knows almost nothing. Elizabeth realized this at once, but decided to take pity on me. She told me about her *suffragi* (cook-housekeeper) Suleiman, and the little restaurants on the edge of the Nile where one went to eat freshly grilled pigeon. She also told me a very complicated story which featured a general, several people I had never heard of and the revolving door of the Continental Hotel.

It was not a very satisfactory interview. I tried to find out more, especially about her marriage, which I knew had taken place during the war; but while I talked to a number of people who knew her, they all seemed very vague about her activities. I looked up her own descriptions of Egypt, in *An Omelette and a Glass of Wine*. They were redolent of the time and place, but gave no clues as to what was happening in her life.

Two years later, when my book was nearly finished, I happened to meet Jill Norman and asked if she thought Elizabeth might be willing to talk to me again. Jill thought it unlikely. Elizabeth was not well. A sister to whom she was devoted had recently died, and she herself was in hospital with a broken leg. A few days later Jill rang to say that she had tried to put in a good word for me, but Elizabeth was really not interested. That, I thought, was that. I assumed I would never find out what had happened to her in Cairo.

Ten years later, out of the blue, I received a telephone call from Eleo Gordon of Penguin Books. She wanted to know if I was interested in writing Elizabeth David's authorized biography. My instinct was to say yes at once because I longed to know more about her, but the word 'authorized' made me nervous. What did it mean? If it meant censorship in any form, then my answer would have to be no. However, I was reassured by Jill Norman, and Jenny Dereham of Michael Joseph, who had edited Elizabeth's posthumous book *Harvest of the Cold Months*. Both agreed that what I wrote would be up to me. As far as they were concerned, the word authorized simply meant that I would have full access to Elizabeth David's papers.

Jenny Dereham became my editor when I accepted the commission.

The papers stood in a series of sixty cardboard filing boxes in the studio of Jill's house in Hampstead, taking up two rows of a long set of bookshelves that ran the length of the room. To my immense relief, they had already been meticulously catalogued: an enormous task undertaken by Jill's husband Paul Breman, to whom I am immensely grateful. On that first morning I stood in front of them, awestruck. Here was an impressive collection of papers, but would there be enough material to put together both sides of her life? A swift glance at the contents of each box, neatly labelled on the outside, confirmed that most contained papers to do with her work; but in the course of a morning of mounting excitement, I realized that her private life was here too. There were letters from Sybille Bedford, Mark Boxer, Lawrence Durrell, John Lehmann and Hilary Spurling, not to mention cookery writers such as Jane Grigson and Julia Child. There were albums, photographs, several boxes of family papers and correspondence. Best of all was the discovery that Elizabeth had kept handwritten drafts of almost all the most important letters she sent.

There were also treasures, such as a little blue writing case (smelling faintly of old leather and cumin seeds) that contained bills and snapshots and fabric swatches dating from the 1940s. I found her wartime passport, which charts her passage from France to Italy, the Balkans, Greece and Egypt. Elizabeth's godson, David Watkins, lent me the collection of letters from Norman Douglas that she had given to him. They were kept in a small handbag covered in rust-coloured cloth, and with the letters was an Egyptian leather purse, with another little cache of photographs, papers, letters and old invoices from her days in Egypt.

In the months that followed I began to talk to her friends and family, and piece her life together with the help of the archive. The image that emerged was of an extraordinarily enigmatic woman who was very difficult to pin down. She could be open-hearted but utterly unforgiving. She laughed a lot and was very funny, while taking herself and her work very seriously indeed. Her conversation was challenging, unpredictable and even spiky, yet she was also very shy and reserved. She was utterly without pretension and could sniff out the bogus and pretentious in others with devastating accuracy, but she also played the great lady who expected to be treated as such.

As I immersed myself in her life, the archive that had looked so daunting at first began to seem more manageable. I also began to collect photocopies of long letters she had written to friends and family. And yet, rather like Elizabeth's writing on cookery, what was omitted was as intriguing as what she recorded. In all the thousands of pages of notes, of letters to friends, of drafted articles, there was so little about herself. Sometimes she described what was happening to her, in very funny set pieces: a disastrous trip to Morocco, six weeks of frantic driving all over France for a series of articles in *Vogue*. The only revealing glimpses came indirectly, in letters or articles that seem to have been written in a state of controlled rage.

This was why it was so particularly exciting to read the one long letter in the archive – perhaps the only such letter she ever wrote in her life – which describes the end of an affair with a man she still loved. I had come across it early on, and realized its importance. But since it was part of the second half of her life and I was then concentrating on the first, I did not spend much time on it. When I read it again several months later, I had that eerie sensation of finding the key I had been looking for, while knowing it had been under my nose all along. At that moment, a series of jumbled thoughts that had been clattering around in my head suddenly fell into place. This moment of illumination could never have happened had I not, simultaneously, been talking to and mulling things over with people who had known Elizabeth for years.

The following people have made all the difference in helping me to understand Elizabeth David and her life: Jack Andrews, Sybille

Bedford CBE, April Boyes, Johnny Grey, Rosi Hanson, Veronica Nicholson and Elizabeth Savage. The prolonged conversations I had with them were all crucial to me, because it was only by talking things through with the people who knew her best that I was able to put what I found in the archive into perspective. They have been unfailingly generous with their time and, best of all, they allowed me to feel that I could ring them up whenever I needed help and advice – which I frequently did. I must also at this point mention my husband, Antony Beevor. Quite apart from his constant encouragement and his initial work on the text, he has provided that inestimable asset to any biographer: an outsider's perception.

I was also exceptionally lucky in receiving so much help, and hospitality, from Elizabeth's nephews Rupert, Johnny and Steven Grey. This book is immeasurably richer for the help and support of the Grey brothers and their unfailing honesty in answering my most awkward questions.

I would also like to acknowledge my gratitude to Gerald Asher, Paul Bailey, Ann Balfour-Fraser, Ann Barr, Alan and Olivia Bell, Jane Blakemore, Emma Bolland, Gordon Bowker, Arabella Boxer, Lady Anne Brewis, Nathalie Brooke, Sir Bernard and the late Lady Burrows, Julia Caffyn, James Chandler, Janet Clarke, Patricia Clarke, Derek Cooper, Simon Courtauld, Josette d'Amade, Antony Daniels, Anne Davies, Alan and Jane Davidson, Michael Day, Celia Denney, Jessica Douglas-Home, Barbara Doxat, Roger Eland, George Elliott, the late Roger Ellis, Priscilla Esslin, Frances Fedden, the late Eunice Frost, Christopher Gibbs, Aileen Gibson Cowan, Lady May Gore, The Earl of Gowrie, Antonia Graham, Henrietta Greene, Professor N. G. L. Hammond CBE, DSO, Anthony Hanson, Sabrina Harcourt-Smith, Frances Harper, John Hatt, Lady Dorothy Heber-Percy, Stephanie Hoppen, Anne Higgins, Derek Hill, Michael Holroyd C.B.E., John and Ellen-Ann Hopkins, Simon Hopkinson, Professor Richard Hosking, Laurette Hugo, Kate Hunloke, Molly Izzard, Rosalind Jenkinson, Hugh and Judy Johnson, John King, Kathleen Laing, Heidi Lascelles, Caroline and the late George Lassalle, Roger

Latham, Richard Leech, Paul Levy, Patrick and Joan Leigh Fermor, Patrick Lewin, Jeremy Lewis, Jenny Lo, Priscilla Longland, Hitch Lyam, Lady Maynard, Jean McAuliffe, Victor Morrison, Patrick O'Connor, Marguerite Patten, OBE, Burnet Pavitt, Neville Phillips, the Countess of Ranfurly, Liz Ray, The Viscount Ridley, Jancis Robinson, Lady Sibell Rowley, John Ruden, John Sandoe, Anne Scott-James, Hilary Spurling, Ann and Franco Taruschio, Doreen Thornton, Peter Trier, Georgina Tritton, Katharine Whitehorn, Audrey Withers, Patrick Woodcock and Michael Zyw.

Lastly I would like to say how hugely indebted I am to Jill Norman. Jill put up with me in her house for what must have seemed far too long, and her help and guidance have been invaluable – as were the powerful espresso coffees and impromptu lunches with which she and Paul Breman kept me going. Jenny has been a wonderfully supportive editor. She has given me every possible encouragement, and has saved me from several mistakes. Any that remain, needless to say, are mine alone.

* * * * * * *

CHAPTER ONE

The Gwynnes

Elizabeth David's family, the Gwynnes, originally came from Wales. Their fortune was founded in the 1840s by John Gwynne, an engineer who developed the first centrifugal pump for land drainage. With the banker and tea trader Herbert Twining, he also bought up plots of land in London south of the Strand, which became prime sites for development with the completion of the Thames Embankment in 1870.

Like all the best family histories, that of the Gwynnes contains a love match, a secret, a tyrannical patriarch and an intractable will. John Gwynne married Agnes Anderson, who came from a family of well-to-do Scottish professionals. Their first son was James Eglinton Anderson Gwynne, Elizabeth's paternal grandfather, and he is the most important figure in this brief family history. Tall and domineering, with pale eyes, sandy hair and a patrician beard, James inherited his father's engineering firm. He became a good manager and an excellent businessman, but his younger brothers resented the fact that they were given no authority in the family business.

While James's position as head of the family was unquestioned, home life was ruled by their widowed mother Agnes, a strict Presbyterian. On Saturdays she would go round the house putting away every book and paper that was not a sermon, and on Sunday – a day of unmitigated gloom – most of the blinds in the house were kept down.

In 1859, the peace of Mrs Gwynne's family was shattered when

James Gwynne met and fell in love with an eighteen-year-old girl called May Purvis. On one level, the match looked suitable enough: he had met May when visiting his mother's cousins in Edinburgh, and the Purvises were respectable. They were merchants with connections to the Dutch traders of the East Indies. Yet what the Purvises did not like to mention was that May Purvis's Dutch great-grandfather, John Carels, had married a Sumatran 'ranee' (a term that covered every rank from chieftain's daughter to princess), by whom he had had children. The ranee's name has not survived, but she had a considerable effect on the looks of her descendants: for while May was an accomplished young woman with musical talent and a spirited disposition, her Indonesian genes had given her a fragile, exotic beauty that was distinctly un-Scottish.

Right from the start old Mrs Gwynne was suspicious of May Purvis and violently opposed the match. She probably guessed from May's appearance that there was something other than Scottish and Dutch blood in her veins, and she did everything she could to break off the engagement. She nearly succeeded, but James managed to persuade May that their union was only a matter of time if they both stood firm. They were eventually married in 1862. The wedding took place in the house of May's brother in Edinburgh, the Gwynnes and the Andersons being conspicuous by their absence. At the time of her marriage, May's health was not considered good: her doctors feared that she might develop tuberculosis, and one of James's wedding presents to his bride had been a respirator. Yet she proved strong enough to bear nine children, seven of whom survived: Reginald, Evelyn (Eva), Nevile, Violet, Rupert, Dorothy and Roland.

Rupert Gwynne, Elizabeth's father, was born in 1873. He and his brothers and sisters were brought up at Folkington (pronounced Fowington), a large property at the foot of the Sussex Downs near Eastbourne, complete with lodges and a park, a farm, a church and a rectory. The main house was a neo-Jacobean mansion with gabled roofs and tall chimneys, and in James Gwynne's day it made up in comfort what it lacked in architectural distinction. The drawing room was furnished with the most generous sofas and armchairs, every bed-room was well-stocked with books and had a blazing fire in winter, and the greenhouses were filled with heavily scented flowers and Muscat grapes. It was a curious feature of Folkington that, although James Gwynne had been one of the pioneers of electricity supply in London in 1882, his house was lit by oil lamps. There was no plumbing either; though thanks to the teams of servants and fires in every room, a morning bath was hardly a Spartan experience.

The household staff was so huge and well-run that May could claim that she had never been into her own kitchen. She was an affectionate mother, who loved music and riding and entertaining, but her life was lived in the threatening shadow of her husband. As he grew older James became more and more stern and authoritarian, and he could explode into terrifying rages. May, who could not bear rows, became psychologically his prisoner, living in perpetual fear of his temper.

The children grew up in a world of shoots and hunts and point-to-points. Rupert was admired for his reckless courage on a horse, as were Nevile and Dorothy. Violet, on the other hand, developed an exceptional talent for music, which her mother recognized. May saw to it that her daughter had the best teachers, and took her to as many concerts and recitals as she could. Violet was the darling of both her parents, who spoilt her and indulged all her caprices. She and Rupert were curiously alike: both were very dark, with deep-set eyes, and both were endowed with a dazzling and confident charm. May's youngest son Roland was born in 1882, and had the most curious upbringing. His mother doted on him in a way that was almost unhealthy, and insisted that he never leave her side. For once, James gave in to her wishes: the boy was educated entirely at home, first by governesses and then by the rector of Folkington.

Once settled at Folkington, James Gwynne set about turning himself into a country gentleman. It seemed a classic example of British industrial decadence. He allowed the family firm to fall behind, and made no effort to install new equipment or keep up with the rival engineering firm established by his younger brother John. Instead, he turned his attention to land and housing speculation, in London and Sussex. He bought several country estates around Folkington, and members of the local hunt used to say that one could ride all day without ever leaving Squire Gwynne's land.

As James Gwynne's children grew up, their father grew ever more jealous and mistrustful, as if he suspected them all of trying to steal his money and usurp his power. To keep them under his control they were kept on the most miserable allowances, which they overspent at their peril. James's retribution was severe and long-lasting, and he never forgot a grudge. His eldest son Reginald was cut out of his will for reckless extravagance at Eton and Oxford. He fled to Canada, settled there, and eventually prospered, though he and his father were never reconciled. The second son, Nevile, took a degree in engineering at Cambridge and then joined 'the works', as the family firm was known. James treated him in the same way he had treated his younger brothers: Nevile was kept overworked, underpaid and without authority in the firm, despite the fact that James had all but lost interest in it.

Elizabeth's father Rupert was also expected to live on a pittance. Having been to school at Shrewsbury he went to Pembroke College, Cambridge, where he studied history with enough energy to get a degree, but little enthusiasm. Hunting, shooting and social life in general proved far more attractive. One of his closest friends was a shy, good-natured boy called Gordon Woodhouse. Rupert introduced Woodhouse to his musical sister Violet, and they were married in the summer of 1894. Thus began one of the most celebrated and eccentric marriages of Edwardian England, in the course of which Violet acquired three subsidiary 'husbands' without ever losing the devotion of her first.

Having no particular aptitude for engineering, Rupert read for the Bar. He managed to exist on his small allowance thanks to Violet and Gordon, with whom he lived while he was doing his articles in London. At the same time, he spent every day he could at Folkington: not only to keep down his expenses, but also to enjoy the days of hunting, shooting and point-to-point racing at which he proved so skilful.

For those pleasures, there was another, grimmer price to pay, for Rupert had a weak heart. The doctors told him that if he gave up all his active pursuits, he might live as long as most men; but that if he continued with them, he might not survive beyond middle age. Rupert decided that he could not change. He went on riding and racing as hard as ever, and adding to his collection of trophies and silver cups.

Another pleasure in Rupert's life was the exercise of his considerable charm. He talked and laughed easily, danced well, and women blossomed in his company. On one occasion, he exerted a rather stronger spell than he intended. A family friend fell desperately in love with Rupert, going so far as to follow him to his room one night – she might have forced her way in had he not locked the door. She fled the following day accompanied by her mother, leaving Rupert profoundly relieved. He preferred brief, light-hearted affairs with actresses or married women.

Rupert was called to the Bar in 1898, though it did not take him long to realize that he would never rise to the top of his profession. Politics interested him, but he lacked the means to stand for Parliament, and there was not a hope that his father would back such an ambitious venture. Rupert would still have to depend for many years on his small allowance, counting every penny, an austerity only relieved by the rural pleasures provided free at Folkington. Like most young men of his upbringing he loved the country-house world of Edwardian masculinity with its smells of leather, dubbin, Turkish cigarettes and gun oil; the sound of hooves on cobble, as tired hunters were led by stable boys across the yard to their loose boxes to be rubbed down; the reverberation of the dressing gong for dinner, and the prospect of a very hot bath.

Rupert Gwynne was thirty when his father and his older brother Nevile had a quarrel that was to have far-reaching consequences, not least for Rupert himself. Over the years, Nevile had begged his father again and again to invest in new plant and up-to-date technology, essential if the firm were to hold its own in the market; and each time his father had refused. Nevile's final attempt to make his father see reason took place one evening in August 1903. Their discussion started calmly enough, but tempers rose and the quarrel ended in blows and unforgivable words. Nevile was banished from his father's house for ever.

Nevile was stunned by what had happened, but Rupert promised his brother that he would do all he could to heal the breach and reinstate him in their father's affections (and, at least by implication, restore him to his inheritance). Nevile's daughter, Katharine Ayling, had no doubt that Rupert meant what he said at the time. But Rupert, who had seen his two elder brothers banished and treated like outcasts, was now in line to inherit the bulk of his father's fortune – provided he did not repeat their mistakes.

Rupert's position as heir-presumptive grew stronger on 3 May 1905, when he made a most advantageous match. 'A crowd of relatives and guests assembled in St Margaret's Westminster,' wrote one social gazette, 'when Mr Rupert Gwynne ... was married to the Hon. Stella Ridley, elder surviving daughter of the late Viscount Ridley, sister of the present peer, a granddaughter of Dudley Coutts (first Lord Tweedmouth), and niece of the Countess of Aberdeen ... Viscount Ridley gave away the bride, a tall, fine-looking girl of twenty-one, with beautiful colouring, who looked extremely well in her long-trained gown of ivory-tinted, rich, soft, corded silk.'

There had been Ridleys in and around the Tyne valley since the twelfth century, although the bulk of the family fortune was founded on coal mining in the early eighteenth century. They had ties by marriage with another well-established local family, the Whites; and when in 1763 Sir Matthew White died unmarried, his baronetcy and the estate of Blagdon were inherited by his Ridley nephews. The arms of the Ridleys were added to those of the Whites over the neoclassical portico of Blagdon Hall, and from then on the eldest son of the family has always been called Matthew White Ridley – right up to the present day. Ridleys had for generations been mayors of Newcastle, and had represented the city in Parliament; but the family's political influence reached a new peak with Stella's father, the fifth baronet. He became Home Secretary under Lord Salisbury in 1895, and was made a viscount in 1900.

Rupert could not have chosen better. He had married a rich woman, whose money would free him from his dependence on his father – and her family's position in the Conservative Party meant that he now had the means and the contacts to enter Parliament. Meanwhile Stella's family and guardians had been allowed to understand that although he had two older brothers, it was Rupert who would inherit Folkington and his father's fortune.

With the help of his wife's connections Rupert now became the Conservative candidate for Eastbourne, which was then held by the Liberals. He fought the 1910 election on the platform of 'Unionism, Empire and Tariff Reform'. He won, and held Eastbourne for the rest of his life. His daughter Elizabeth was very proud of her father. In later life she sought out and collected his election cards and addresses, and kept his photograph in a leather frame beside her bed.

To the surprise of his family, the choleric patriarch James Gwynne began to mellow as his health failed. He became reconciled to his disgraced son Nevile, who was devoted to the old man during his last weeks. Yet when James died in March 1915, Nevile was astounded to discover that neither he, nor his son John (the only grandson James and May Gwynne were to have), were mentioned as beneficiaries in his father's will. It was a disastrous testament: any imagination, caution or foresight James Gwynne might have used when drafting his will was evidently blinded by a desire to control his fortune from beyond the grave.

The future Elizabeth David later described her grandfather's will as 'a document which two generations of lawyers and counsel without number have failed to unravel'.[1] The problem was that it set out a rigid line of inheritance. He stipulated that his money must be passed on through the sons he had not disinherited, their grandsons, and their male heirs in the order he set out. Yet all this depended on there being male heirs at crucial points in the line of succession. When these failed to materialize, the family was inevitably thrown into an unseemly squabble over inheritance, which only expensive court cases could decide. For the immediate future, however, all was clear: Rupert and his younger brother Roland were left in possession of the family fortune.

It was the cosseted young Roland, not Rupert, who took over the huge family house at Folkington after their mother's death. Rupert and Stella had already settled into the far more attractive manor house at Wootton, where they set to work on an ambitious programme of extensions. Rupert had never shown much interest in literature and music; but he did have a feel for architecture, and for the work he employed one of the best architects of Edwardian England: Detmar Blow. Blow identified firmly with the principles of the Arts and Crafts movement, and was much used by the Souls, the political and intellectual coterie that clustered around Arthur Balfour (who was prime minister from 1902 to 1905).

To the original building, a compact Jacobean manor dating from the 1670s, Blow added a large staircase and a wing that doubled the size of the house. The lower level of the new wing became the nursery, consisting of a series of rooms opening on to a long corridor. Above it was a library, the largest and most beautiful room in the house. The predominant colours are the rich tones of gold-tooled, leather-bound books, contrasting with the cool grey-painted walls. It is lit by a huge Venetian window overlooking the Sussex Downs, and – unlike many libraries – it gives a feeling of airiness and space.

Detmar Blow also built a gatehouse and two cobbled courtyards connected by a handsome archway. The courtyards were surrounded by a complex of stables, barns and outhouses which, thanks to Blow's sensitivity to texture and his insistence on the very best traditional materials, look as if they had grown out of the centuries.

Stella and Rupert both had a very good eye, and their taste was in harmony with that of their architect. Every object in the house was chosen with care, and was well-made and unpretentious: a taste which profoundly influenced their daughter Elizabeth.

* * * * * * *

CHAPTER TWO

The Gwynne Girls Grow Up

Initial impressions of Rupert's wife were mixed when she first came and settled in Sussex in 1905. At a time when young women were largely judged by their looks, Stella was considered more handsome than beautiful. Tall and broad-boned, she had a creamy complexion, and her thick chestnut hair was ideally suited to the abundant, swept-up hairstyles of the day. But a heavy jaw and prominent nose gave her face more character than was fashionable. She was proud of being a Ridley, proud of her political connections, and a certain reserve contrasted unfavourably with the warmth and gregariousness of her husband.

As time went on Stella's talents unfolded, and admiration for her grew. She was a keen gardener, became an excellent botanical painter and she developed a real love and knowledge of antiques. Her taste was sure and confident, and she could juxtapose apparently unrelated objects to great effect – a gift that reflected her personality: a close friend and relative described her as 'a high Tory with a strong streak of the rebel'.[1]

Stella was one of a family of four surviving children, with two older brothers, Matthew and Jasper, and a younger sister Grace. She had been born with a powerful and determined character, and when her mother died when Stella was fifteen, she and her sister were put under the care of her aunt Ishbel, Countess of Aberdeen. Lady Aberdeen found her less tractable than her more gentle and obedient sister Grace.

It was said that Stella had come perilously close to a rash marriage before she met Rupert. Some said her first love was her cousin, the Hon. Dudley Gordon, who became Elizabeth's godfather and later 3rd Marquess of Aberdeen. Some even whispered about one of the grooms at Blagdon. There can be no doubt, however, that Stella was very much in love with Rupert when she married him. Their first child, Priscilla, was born in 1909. Their second was Sackville, the only son Stella was ever to bear; but he was still-born.

Her next child, Elizabeth, was born on Boxing Day, 1913. She was christened on 22 January 1914, in the beautiful crypt chapel of the House of Commons, in a family christening robe of fine Irish lace. Her godmothers were May Gwynne and Mrs Detmar Blow, the wife of the architect of Wootton. Her godfathers were Dudley Gordon and the Hon. Alfred Lyttelton.

Diana was born in 1915, and Felicité two years later. As girl followed girl, Stella and Rupert saw their hope of leaving Wootton to a male heir fade away. James Gwynne's will had started to exert its obduracy over them. Stella resented her daughters and grieved for them at the same time. She thought it preposterous that Wootton would pass into the hands of Rupert's sybaritic, childless brother Roland, who already owned Folkington. Rows often developed between husband and wife on the subject. Stella thought they must be able to find some legal loophole – while Rupert told her, with equal force, that there was nothing to be done.

In Parliament, Rupert was noticed more for his performance in debate than for his skills as an orator. Known for being on the extreme right wing of the party, he fought every move towards a relaxation of imperial rule, whether in Ireland, Egypt or India, and he was implacably opposed to women's suffrage. When in London he lived at 47 Catherine Place, which had been given to Stella by her family when she married. It consisted of two Queen Anne houses converted into one, and it boasted a division bell. This useful device rang about eight minutes before a division in the Commons took place, and many private houses around Westminster had them.

The house was also useful for Rupert's occasional illicit afternoons.

The most serious affair of Rupert's life had begun while Stella was pregnant with Elizabeth. A couple called the Cecils came to live in Sussex with their schoolboy son. Vera Cecil was very pretty in a blonde, feminine way; and while she was perhaps not as intelligent as Stella, she made up for it with a lively mind and a warm, light-hearted nature. By 1914 Mrs Cecil and Rupert Gwynne were constantly in each other's company, at hunt balls and race meetings, and they were seen riding together in the early mornings. Mr Cecil did not seem to mind: it was even said that he was rather relieved, since he had a long-standing mistress of his own and it suited him very well that his wife had someone to amuse her.

For Stella, however, the situation was deeply humiliating. At first, Rupert had upheld the conventions of their class: the affair had been conducted discreetly, and he had continued to treat his wife with consideration and respect. However, as time went on his infatuation became more flagrant. Mrs Cecil was often invited over to Wootton, and her son was sent to play with Stella's daughters. Stella did not throw scenes, that was not her style; but one witness to these developments recalled that Stella made no attempt to hide her distaste for Vera Cecil, and that not many women could have supported the freezing looks that Stella gave her rival.

While the pace of life at Wootton remained decorous enough, the children were aware of the tensions: not only between their parents, but with other members of the family. Violet Gordon Woodhouse still adored her brother Rupert, but never got on with Stella: mostly from jealousy, for Violet did not like to see herself displaced in anyone's affections. They saw little of their Uncle Nevile, who never forgave Rupert for failing to intercede with their father. Aunt Dorothy disliked Stella, and some years later she and Rupert fell out once and for all. Roland was disliked and mistrusted by his brothers and sisters, and Dorothy could not forgive him for turning her out of her childhood home. At the heart of all these eruptions was the temper that James Gwynne had passed on to his children, along with his impossible will. 'As children we had had enough of the bitter quarrels,'[2] Elizabeth wrote many years later.

All these tensions and struggles, however, were mere rustles and whispers in the background. In the forefront of everyone's mind was the war.

Rupert attended and spoke at a great many recruiting rallies for the newly formed battalions of the Sussex Regiment, including one at Seaford, where he 'appealed to the employers of labour to make it as easy as possible for their workmen to enlist, by promising that their situations would be kept open for them, and their wives and dependents looked after'.[3] At the same time he never lost sight of his constituency duties, and his assiduous attendance at the meetings of the Eastbourne Rural District Council and the East Sussex District Council was evidently much appreciated.

Stella was to have two more babies before the war was over, but she did not neglect her duty either. She was involved in the League of Mercy and the Eastbourne branch of the Red Cross, for which she organized a matinée in December 1914 at the Devonshire Park Theatre. This consisted of patriotic songs, and tableaux with people representing Glory, Britannia, France, Russia, and Belgium. It was considered a great success, and raised over £121. Stella also chaired the committee of ladies which founded Eastbourne's Union Jack Club, which was a social centre for the wives and children of men on active service. The Club was officially opened in March 1915 by Lady Jellicoe, who was presented with a bouquet by Stella's eldest daughter Priscilla, then aged five. By the following year, Stella was president of the Soldiers and Sailors' Families Association.

Rupert's brother Nevile wanted to join up, but it was decided that his engineering skills were of more use at home making aeroplane engines. Roland joined the Sussex Yeomanry in 1914, though he was not posted to France until September 1916. No one in the family had a high opinion of his courage, whether moral or physical, so it was a great surprise when Roland was awarded the DSO in February

1917 for 'conspicuous gallantry and judgement': he had led a successful daylight raid into enemy trenches. A few months later he returned to France, and was badly wounded in the knee during the Third Battle of Ypres. For some time he was in danger of losing his leg. It healed eventually, but he had a stiff knee and a limp ever afterwards.

Nothing was the same after the First World War, yet while it was going on the pace of change at Wootton was barely noticeable. Sometimes, they might just catch the distant thunder of the guns a little more than a hundred miles away in France. A man was arrested outside Polegate for shouting abuse at a group of women – it was said he had been 'shell-shocked'. Hemlines rose dramatically, from ankle-length in 1914 to mid-calf by 1918. Everyone ate bread made of Standard flour, and Stella no doubt felt obliged to encourage cook to experiment with some of the nutritious recipes using maize, lentils and barley-meal which were supposed to save the country from the high cost of imported wheat. Yet for the children there were still eggs and milk, honey and home-made jam. Elizabeth was five when the war ended, and seems to have had no recollection of it at all.

Stella was not a very demonstrative or affectionate mother. One cousin described her as 'the most unmaternal woman I have ever met'.[4] There was in Stella an inner core of rock-solid, egocentric self-certainty which was rare, at a time when all a woman's cultural conditioning was focused on devotion to husband and family. Stella did not care. She had done her duty during the war and in public she was very much Mrs Gwynne, but after 1918 she led an independent life based on her own interests and pursuits. The result was that from their earliest years, her daughters were starved of motherly affection.

Since they received so little love from their mother, the girls turned to their father instead. The fact that they did not see much of him made him even more of a godlike figure, and it seemed that all the warmth and laughter that they enjoyed as children came from him rather than their mother. He had the gift of making each of them feel especially loved, though he was not above playing a daughter off against his wife. A cousin noticed it happening with Priscilla in particular; but when she mentioned it years later to Elizabeth, she bristled and said, 'He did that with all of us!'[5]

As soon as they were old enough, the girls were put on horseback. Priscilla, the eldest, took to it easily, as did Diana and Felicité. The only one who never really enjoyed being on a horse was Elizabeth. Since riding was Rupert's passion, he followed this aspect of his daughters' education with some interest. As Elizabeth saw her younger sisters catch up and surpass her own half-hearted efforts on horseback, she felt at a disadvantage in the fierce competition between the sisters for his affection. This was bad enough; but worse was the feeling that she had disappointed her father.

Priscilla, inevitably known as Pris, never allowed her sisters to forget that she was the eldest and exerted her authority whenever possible. Elizabeth, who inherited a great deal of her mother's stubborn integrity, found this profoundly irritating; and her response was to forge a bond of close complicity with her wild, scatty sister Diana. Elizabeth was known as Liza, a diminutive that was linked to the word 'lizard'. Like the animal, Liza seemed to combine both agility and laziness. Until she was two, Diana was known as Bulgie but when Felicité was born, this baby-name devolved on to her. Sadly for Felicité, she enjoyed none of the other indulgent attentions usually lavished on the youngest in a family. Her mother gave her no more love than she gave her other daughters, and Felicité was left with the impression that she was always last, and that however hard she ran she would never catch up.

Although Elizabeth played with the golden retrievers and elk-hounds that lolled about the yard, she developed a particular fondness for cats. She romped and squabbled with her sisters, teased the governess by putting salt in her tea, and made secret houses in the garden; yet very early on Elizabeth began to resist what one of her nieces called 'the wellington-boot side of country life'. At the same time, Wootton and Folkington were the only worlds she knew.

The only escape was reading, which luckily her mother had always encouraged. Elizabeth read everything she could. In later life she recalled 'a childish memory, of primitive coloured pictures and sheets of brightly uniformed soldiers, the Images d'Epinal, which have the same primitive charm as our penny-plain twopence-coloured prints'.[6] Elsewhere she mentions Walter de la Mare's *Come Hither*, an anthology of poetry that made a profound impact on her. The books she returned to again and again were Lewis Carroll's *Alice in Wonderland* and *Through the Looking-Glass*: stories about a curious and intelligent little girl trying to make sense of very peculiar worlds in which she did not belong.

One place where she would have liked to spend more time was the kitchen, which Elizabeth remembered as a centre of bustling activity. Dining room, servants' hall, nursery and schoolroom all had meals of varying quality at different times of day, though it was all cooked on the same coal-burning range. At the same time it was a sociable place, full of laughter and gossip. Throughout the day, 'a massive black iron kettle was kept with water on the simmer for the cups of tea to be administered to any outdoor staff such as the gardener bringing fruit and vegetables, or a stable-boy who might drop in. There would also be a succession of van drivers delivering groceries and household stores . . . the baker and the butcher bringing bread and meat . . . the postman with parcels, a telegraph boy with telegrams from the village post office. All would be offered tea, biscuits, bread and cheese, cake.'[7] The only people who were not welcomed into the warm and busy kitchen were the children.

Instead they had to put up with the horrible food that came out of it, which gave the defiant and provocative Elizabeth something to rebel against at least once a day. Food for the nursery was not made by the cook, but by the kitchen maid, who had much else to do besides. However, she did not have to waste time on making nursery food appetizing. All the emphasis was on nourishment. There was a lot of mutton and beef, and potatoes which had been put through an implement called a ricer, so they appeared in dry, flaky mounds. Like most children Elizabeth hated vegetables, which tended to be boiled yellow marrows and overcooked turnip tops and parsnips. She even hated puddings: 'junket was slippery and slimy, jam roly-poly greasy, something called ground-rice pudding dry and stodgy, tapioca the most revolting of them all . . .'[8] The gastronomic miseries were even worse on fish days. 'The food,' she wrote, 'looked so terrifying even before it was on your plate. Egg sauce didn't do much to compensate for the black skin and monstrous head of a boiled cod; fish pudding, a few spiteful bones inevitably lying in wait in that viscous mass, and whitings biting their own tails, were frightening dishes for children, and often painful too . . .'[9]

All children complain about the food they are given, but when Elizabeth was young there was no avoiding it. Either the child was forced to sit at table until the plate was clean, or, if that became impractical, they would have it served up cold for tea. Elizabeth must have either gone to bed hungry or swallowed the congealed food; but whatever the result, these early battles did more to strengthen her resolve than to break her spirit.

The only pleasant memory was Nannie's illicit cooking over the nursery fire. There was a sort of sticky fudge called 'stuff', scooped up in spoonfuls out of saucers or soap-dishes. In high summer there were gooseberries, red currants and raspberries which Nannie used to throw into a saucepan and heat quickly with sugar: this hot fruit salad embodied, for Elizabeth, the very essence of summer. Best of all, there were mushrooms: real field mushrooms gathered at dawn by Elizabeth and her sisters and carried back to Nannie, who cooked them with fresh thick cream, stolen, Elizabeth surmised, from the kitchen. 'As in most households, Nannie and the cook thoroughly disapproved of each other, and had she known this private cookery was going on upstairs in the nursery, the cook would have made a blistering row. We must have been aware of this, as children always are of tensions between grown-ups, because Nannie's mushrooms had the charm of the forbidden. We must never be caught eating them . . .'[10] It is interesting that her first taste of something really delicious should be associated with naughtiness, complicity, a secret.

The days passed, and a succession of governesses (some more tolerant of being teased than others) came and went. As England returned to the peacetime routine in the early 1920s, the seasons were once more punctuated by hunts and point-to-points, and holidays by the sea with their cousins, the Palmers. Stella's youngest sister Grace had married Roundell Cecil Palmer, Viscount Wolmer (later 3rd Earl of Selborne) in 1910, and had six surviving children; and since she knew her sister Stella was not a motherly woman, Grace would scoop up the four Gwynne girls and, together with her own brood, take them all off to the seaside. One of Grace's daughters, Anne, remembers a sunburnt Liza, aged seven, on holiday with them on Hayling Island. With her shock of dark hair cropped short at the back and with a fringe in front, and a square, determined look about her face, she looked 'just like a little red Indian'.

As they grew older Anne and Elizabeth became closer. They both hated sports, and were not very physically coordinated: Anne remembered one occasion when her father took them all boating in Regent's Park. He took the younger children, while Elizabeth and Anne were given a boat of their own. They got stuck in the middle of the lake because, with one oar each, Anne could not get Elizabeth to row properly; so they went round in circles until rescued by the boatman.

Anne was passionately interested in natural history, and wanted to become, as she put it, 'a female Gilbert White'. When Anne came to stay at Wootton Elizabeth was very happy to go along with this new hobby, looking for plants and examining wild flowers as they walked on the Downs. Their friendship might have blossomed further, but as a pair they were considered a bad influence on each other – a suspicion confirmed after an incident in which the French governess's cardigan was hidden under a pile of weeds. Anne was not invited again.

Whether Elizabeth was bored, frustrated or merely seeking attention, she began to see Wootton as a place to escape from, not to come back to. Several times she ran away from home: 'It was the usual thing,' she once told a friend, 'walking down the drive with your suitcase. You must have done it.' On one occasion, however, the scene was played out with rather more drama than usual. Elizabeth got up at dawn, and whispered goodbye to Diana before setting off once again down the long drive. This time, she seems to have gone further than usual, or her parents had finally had enough. There was all hell to pay when she was finally brought back home. Her father was informed when he came back from London. He stormed into the bathroom where the girls were being bathed. Elizabeth was told that she was a wicked, selfish girl who had put her family to considerable anxiety, and while delivering the lecture he slapped her as she tried to hide behind the towel horse.

When the girls were considered old enough, tea was taken with their mother; and at this point Elizabeth discovered that the food served in the world beyond the nursery was considerably more appetizing. Stella presided over the long tea table, with the silver teapot and the hot-water urn set over a spirit lamp. There was a jug of cream, but that was for guests only. Once her girls were out of the nursery, they were expected to take their tea with lemon. There was always a selection of delicious, elegant food: thin bread and butter, scones, home-made quince or apple jelly, and a sponge cake. For special occasions, there was a cake with orange-flavoured icing. Stella was very fond of chocolate, and sometimes there was chocolate cake too. There was an uproar when one of the golden retrievers found its way into the larder and demolished an entire chocolate cake. 'Who had left the larder door open? Recriminations and arguments raged for days, the younger children fell, as always, under suspicion and the kitchen regions were more strictly than ever out of bounds.'[11]

By 1922, Rupert's health was beginning to cause concern. Although he was an abstemious man who drank little and never smoked, all those years of racing and riding were beginning to take a toll on his weak heart, just as his doctors had warned him. A series of pillboxes and medicine bottles now stood beside his plate at every meal. Yet for Rupert perhaps the greatest worry was that, when he died, everything would go to his younger brother Roland.

The strict provisions of James's will, insisting on the male line of succession, appeared ever more self-defeating. Rupert had only daughters, Roland was what was known as 'a confirmed bachelor' and their sisters were childless. Stella would have a life interest in Wootton, and she was independently rich; but his daughters would inherit nothing of James Gwynne's fortune. Rupert at last took legal advice to try and circumvent his father's will, and a scheme was put forward by which the brothers and sisters who stood in the line of succession would waive their claim in return for a financial settlement. Everyone was agreed, until Rupert quarrelled with his sister Dorothy. In revenge she refused to sign away her birthright, and the plan – which depended on all the siblings acting in unison – fell apart.

In 1923, Rupert was appointed Financial Secretary to the War Office in Stanley Baldwin's government; and to mark the event, the local Conservative Association declared that they would like to give Mr and Mrs Gwynne a handsome present. This consisted of a silver inkwell, an illuminated album containing the signatures of over 9,000 subscribers, and – at Stella's request – a set of portraits of their four daughters. The painter she chose was Ambrose McEvoy, somewhat to the dismay of the Association: McEvoy's painting was energetic and articulate, and he was considered rather too 'modern' for most people's taste.

For some reason Elizabeth was done first, and she remembered being taken to his studio in Grosvenor Road. Elizabeth was then nine years old, and McEvoy was evidently very good with children. 'I was entirely beguiled by your father and his studio,' she wrote to McEvoy's daughter in 1974, 'and it was all the greatest possible excitement for me. It was your father who was responsible I think for giving me what became a very great and permanent interest in painting (although I can't paint at all) . . .'[12] Ambrose McEvoy came down to paint Priscilla, Diana and Felicité in the summer of 1924, and the girls found his company quite delightful. Then Rupert's health took a sudden turn for the worse. McEvoy finished the portraits more hurriedly than he had intended, and returned to London.

Rupert's illness had been brought on by his increased workload. His doctors insisted that he should rest as much as possible, yet he seems to have been particularly restless and anxious that summer, pacing up and down the ballroom when he could not sleep.

He suffered a severe heart attack, after which he needed two nurses around the clock. Once his kidneys failed, it was merely a question of time – although there was little the doctors could do to relieve his agonizing pain. The one person who might have brought him some comfort was Vera Cecil, but she was no longer allowed in the house. Stella argued that it was out of the question for Rupert to see her on the grounds that any emotional excitement was bad for him.

Rupert died on 12 October, aged fifty-two. The local newspaper could be relied on to deliver a respectful eulogy on the occasion, but it also reflected a genuine warmth and sense of loss felt by his constituency. 'It is doubtful if the borough has ever been more moved by the passing of one of its public men,' wrote the *Eastbourne Chronicle*.[13] 'Mr Gwynne occupied a warm place in the hearts of the inhabitants, all the more remarkable in view of his tenacious allegiance to the advanced wing of the Conservative Party.' His coffin of unpolished oak was put on a farm wagon lined with evergreens, and drawn by two horses to St Peter's ad Vincula, Folkington. Stella and Priscilla, attended by Rupert's brothers and sisters and a great crowd of mourners, attended the funeral, but Elizabeth and her younger sisters were not present.

Elizabeth was almost eleven years old. The girls were put under the joint guardianship of their Uncle Top (Aunt Grace's husband Lord Wolmer), and Douglas Hogg, the 1st Viscount Hailsham: a relation of Stella's and a Sussex neighbour. His son Quintin, Elizabeth's cousin, later became Lord Chancellor.

Although Stella had put a great deal of herself into Wootton and its gardens, the animating spirit of the place had been Rupert's. After his death, there were fewer visitors and there was less money. The years that followed were difficult ones for Stella. Roland, who had entertained on a lavish scale since inheriting Folkington, was rapidly dissipating his fortune. He desperately needed money, and by the terms of James Gwynne's will, he had now inherited Wootton. While he could not throw Stella out, he used his position as her effective landlord to make life as difficult as possible.

Stella decided to send her daughters to boarding school. Priscilla, who was still getting over her father's death, was quite unprepared for life at Wycombe Abbey and reacted violently against it. After one term she came home with whooping cough, and then persuaded her mother to let her stay at home to help nurse Felicité, desperately ill with peritonitis. She flatly refused to go back to school after that.

In September 1925, Elizabeth was sent to Godstowe Preparatory School near High Wycombe. According to a fellow-pupil, 'she appeared to be a very solitary being',[14] but she seems to have enjoyed it. In later life she described it as 'a charming, lovely school', and she remembered the history teacher with particular fondness. The records show that she left Godstowe in April 1927, probably due to illness. She was then sent to St Clare's Ladies Private School in Tunbridge Wells. She never had the company of Diana or Felicité at school, since Stella sent her youngest daughters to Moira House in Eastbourne.

Elizabeth herself gave very few details of her schooldays, although she was good at history. In 1929, aged fifteen, she had attended a course of ten lectures on European history in the nineteenth century, culminating in an exam which she passed with distinction. Her cousin Anne remembers Elizabeth mentioning that her interest in the theatre began at school, and that at Godstowe she had had a row with the drama teacher when she was not given a coveted part in the school play. The only thing Elizabeth recorded in later life were her memories of 'limp fried plaice, followed by tinned apricots and custard'.[15]

In Elizabeth's immediate world, the separation from her sisters was the biggest change in her life; but the fact that it had been imposed by her cold and autocratic mother increased her sense of loss from the death of the father she adored. Stella was far from happy herself and was beset with worries; but she took no comfort from her daughters, and gave them none either. Instead, she travelled abroad whenever she could – which was surprisingly often, considering how much she complained of her financial problems. Elizabeth told a friend in later life that 'Mummy always had better things to do than look after us.'[16] She and her sisters began to build up resentment against their mother. In the loveless atmosphere of Wootton and the noisy regimentation of school, Elizabeth soon learned emotional self-reliance.

During the holidays when their mother was abroad, the girls were farmed out to relatives. Sometimes they stayed with their Uncle Jasper Ridley and his wife Nathalie, where they played endless card games. (Nathalie was a Benckendorff, daughter of the last Imperial Russian Ambassador to Britain.) Most often they stayed with their Aunt Grace and her great romp of Palmer children. The four Gwynne girls spent the winters of 1924 and 1925 at Blackmoor, the Palmers' house in Hampshire. They skated on Flash Pond, made a house of snow and – on one occasion – found an old sleigh which had not been used since 1825. In the New Year, Grace's extended family would take the train to Adelboden in the German Alps. If there was not enough snow for skiing they went skating, although Anne, still a keen naturalist, and Elizabeth, who liked winter sports no better than summer ones, often preferred to go walking.

Stella would make periodic visits during the holidays: but it was obvious to the children that she viewed them with a faint distaste, and was relieved when they were all sent off to play. Had she noticed, Stella might have been pleased at how close her daughters were to each other; but at the heart of their complicity was their sense of existing on the margins of their mother's life.

Elizabeth enjoyed being a part of the great clan of cousins, although there was an intense, concentrated streak in her. One holiday, marked by a great many booby traps, ambushes and apple-pie beds, polarized the boys into one camp and the girls in another. It was all quite good-humoured until Liza arrived. She took it all terribly seriously and before long it turned into a veritable battle of the sexes.

Elizabeth was about twelve when she spent one of the happiest holidays of her childhood at Wolcot, on the Norfolk coast, in the summer of 1926. Grace and Stella both took a house there that year, as did their brother Jasper, with his wife and children. Priscilla, by then seventeen, did not consider herself a child any more. She spent most of the holiday sitting on the beach, sewing camisoles. The beaches were quite wild; and while the shells there were not so good as those at Hayling Island, one could find carnelians and amber, supposedly washed up from the shores of the Baltic. There were also shoals of jellyfish. Anne's brother Bob was badly stung, and had to spend the rest of the day in a bath full of bicarbonate of soda.

Anne had been given a small garage in which to do her 'botanizing', with help from Elizabeth and Katharine Ridley (Jasper's daughter). They would go to the beaches, gingerly collecting dead jellyfish in shrimping nets and bringing them back to the garage. Here the girls would press the jellyfish in between sheets of blotting paper, a technique developed by Anne: all the water came out, leaving just the skin. Many years later, Anne wrote to Elizabeth to congratulate her on being awarded the CBE. Elizabeth's reply included the remark that she had never been as happy as that summer, when she and Anne collected jellyfish together.

Life with a happy troop of cousins was very different from life with Aunt Violet, with whom they also stayed during the holidays.

Whereas Grace Wolmer's household was built around the children, Violet Gordon Woodhouse's household revolved exclusively around herself. Elizabeth was fascinated by this 'little creature with her autocratic kingfisher manners and her huge coal-black monkey eyes and her strange dark clothes which never looked sombre but somehow always sparkly and variegated. Her paste-buckled red-heeled Marie Antoinette shoes and the glass bubbles with tiny goldfish imprisoned in them which for years were her favourite earrings helped to make her look like a being from quite another species from our own.'[17]

Mrs Gordon Woodhouse was then in her fifties. She gave up playing professionally in 1927, at the height of her musical talent and her celebrity. She was financially secure, and preferred playing for small audiences of experts rather than for the general public. She was as extravagant as ever, and her every caprice was indulged: not only by her husband Gordon, but also by the other two men of her ménage – the Hon. Bill Barrington, and the Hon. Denis Tollemache. The four of them divided their time between London and Nether Lypiatt Manor in Gloucestershire.

On one occasion, Aunt Violet took Elizabeth and her sisters to see Douglas Fairbanks in the silent version of *The Thief of Baghdad*. 'I remember it still as a magical experience,' wrote Elizabeth, 'with that white horse gliding through the sky. Once was enough for me to remember it for a lifetime, but Aunt V. went to see it day after day, accompanied by Uncle Gordon, Uncle Bill and any other honorary uncles who happened to be around . . .'[18]

Elizabeth admired Violet: here after all was a woman of talent who had been clever enough to live her life exactly as she wished, regardless of the raised eyebrows and the whispers about what went on with all those 'honorary uncles'. She was also very generous, and kept her nieces amused with expensive toys, such as little musical boxes out of which a bird jumps up and sings. Yet with this undoubted generosity, there was a self-centredness of staggering proportions. Felicité stammered as a child, and found it very hard to get out any words at all – particularly when they were expected. One day Aunt Violet gave Felicité a teddy bear. Typically of Aunt Violet, it was a magnificent, fabulously expensive teddy bear, quite the most wonderful thing that anyone had ever given little Felicité. She clutched it, overcome with joy, unable to say a single word. 'Well!' said Aunt Violet. 'She can't even be bothered to say thank you.' With that she snatched the teddy from Felicité's arms, and Felicité never saw it again.

As time passed, however, Elizabeth did find the words, and the courage, to stand up to Aunt Violet. 'The time came when I – I can't speak for my sisters – got bored with Aunt V. saying she was looking after us because we were "Rupert's children", and Rupert . . . had been her favourite brother. One day I said, "Aunt Violet, don't you do anything for us because we're ourselves?" It was horrible of me, but she had asked for it. She was getting at my mother, I think. Children inevitably sense that kind of thing . . .'[19] Elizabeth had been told by a family friend that the feud between Violet and Stella had started during the First World War. Violet came to Eastbourne to give a benefit concert for one of the war charities; but all through her performance, she was driven nearly mad by the steady clicking of Stella's knitting needles. 'I'm afraid it all rings horribly true,' admitted Elizabeth.

Compared to the over-ornamented luxury of Aunt Violet's Nether Lypiatt, Wootton must have seemed a very comfortable and unpretentious place, and Elizabeth could recall some sights and smells of her first home with great affection. Her niece Sabrina, Priscilla's daughter, once gave her some parsley planted in a beautiful old red flowerpot. Elizabeth was delighted, saying that the pot could only have come from one of the old potting sheds at Wootton – which it had. And right at the end of her life, in a list of bequests, she left a picture of white violets to her niece with the words, 'When we were children we used to find white violets on the banks of the ditch or hedgerow along the Wootton back lane, and also somewhere on the way up to the church, also by the back way to Folkington and close to the little lodge.' It seems to have been the countryside rather than the house that she recalled in later life: the bluebell wood at the end of the garden, and the thyme-scented Sussex Downs.

* * * * * * * *

CHAPTER THREE

Paris and Munich

When Elizabeth was about sixteen, Stella made one of her rare and alarmingly sudden appearances at St Clare's boarding school. She was appalled to see her daughter Elizabeth wielding a lacrosse stick. Elizabeth pointed out that, in letter after letter, she had been begging her mother's permission to give up games. But at that moment, the prospect – however unlikely – of her daughter turning into a beefy team-sports girl made Stella decide that Elizabeth had had quite enough of boarding schools.

At that time Elizabeth nurtured an ambition, perhaps encouraged by the art mistress, to become a painter. Since no painting or drawing can be confidently attributed to Elizabeth, it is impossible to say whether or not she had any talent. If she did, it was inherited from her mother, who painted vibrant, precisely detailed flower paintings. Elizabeth scarcely mentions her teenage painting phase, and gives no idea of whether it was an all-absorbing passion or merely a congenial pastime. Yet Stella evidently thought Elizabeth's artistic promise was worth developing, and the natural place to start was Paris.

In Paris Elizabeth attended art lessons, and soon afterwards enrolled at the Sorbonne for a course in French civilization which covered history, literature and architecture. Then she chose to go one step further, and try for a diploma.

On 29 October 1930 Stella wrote, 'I am so glad you have found the Sorbonne what you wanted . . . As Paris suits you it's all to the good, and of course such a diploma would be one of the best things you can get . . . The only thing is be careful of your eyes . . . do see that the light is good as you read and write, as it is only in bad light and bad positions that you get bad eyes.' [1] Sensible advice, but Elizabeth's eyes were naturally weak and she wore spectacles for most of her life (though in youth, she always took them off before being photographed).

Elizabeth, and another girl called Marian Butterworth with whom she kept in touch for much of her life, were two of the three lodgers taken in by a certain Mme Barette. Mme Barette's house had no doubt been recommended to Stella by a friend, who must have told her that Madame was strict, respectable and charged reasonable rates. Stella would not have inquired about the food, beyond establishing that it was ample and wholesome. Yet as it turned out, it was with Mme Barette that Elizabeth was to have her first experience of excellent French cooking.

Mme Barette became 'Mme Robertot' in Elizabeth's later descriptions of her. (She almost always changed the names of people she poked fun at or disliked, while the good cooks she talked about were always accorded their real names.) Mme Barette lived with her grown-up children at 79 rue de la Tour, in the sixteenth arrondissement. Poor Léontine, their cook, worked like a slave for the Barettes, who were exceptionally greedy; but all the shopping was done by Madame. She got up at dawn twice a week to go to Les Halles and returned at about ten, puffing and panting, with four shopping bags bursting with meat and vegetables.

The Barettes did not spend huge amounts of money on food. 'What with the bargains from Les Halles, the wine . . . in casks from Bordeaux, and cream and butter from their Norman property, their food was lovely without being rich or grand . . . So what emerges from those days is not the memory of elaborate sauces or sensational puddings, but rather of beautifully prepared vegetables like *salsifis à la crème*, purées of sorrel and *pommes mousseline*. Many egg dishes, and soups delicately coloured like summer dresses, coral, ivory or pale green . . .'[2]

Yet even the food could not make up for the oppressive atmosphere of the house. The *pensionnaires* ate with the Barettes at lunch, and were closely questioned about the lectures they had attended that morning. They were expected to be present at Madame's gloomy tea parties on Thursdays, attended by half a dozen ladies in black. Then there was the ordeal of the boiled salt cod which appeared every Friday: 'Grey, slimy, in great hideous flakes, it lay plonked on the dish without benefit of sauce or garnish of any kind . . .'³ The fish was no doubt meant to be a penance, for the Barettes were very devout Catholics.

The atmosphere in the apartment was stifling, as was Madame Barette's preoccupation with food. She took a pride in eating well which had an almost moral dimension, as if her insistence on good food and clever marketing made her a better person. Elizabeth found the way the Barettes' lives revolved around their stomachs positively unappetizing, and she and her co-pensionnaires took every chance they could to escape the rue de la Tour and eat out. They enjoyed patronizing the noisy automatic restaurant in the Boulevard Saint-Michel, where a plate of ham and an orange came out of a slot machine. Madame had declared this place out of bounds, and the girls were interrogated on where they had eaten as soon as they returned home.

To escape Madame, they retired to their rooms to revise for their exams, which provided another excuse for avoiding meals. The result of this enforced studiousness was that Elizabeth gained her diploma. 'I was so very glad to get your news,' wrote her mother, 'and hasten to send my congratulations! Mme B. also wrote, wanting to know by wire, my wishes – it really makes very little difference to me, beyond the fact that I consider you've had enough of Paris, and ought to progress a bit . . .'⁴

A curious portrait of Elizabeth survives from this period, the product of the time one of her friends took her handwriting to be analysed by a graphologist. His report was written in February 1931, when Elizabeth was seventeen. 'She possesses an observant intelligence, served by an excellent memory. She is ambitious, needs to be a star – and is admirably equipped for it. Your young friend never gives herself any trouble unless she thinks it's worth it: she puts herself out only to those who will be useful to her. She is undoubtedly seductive, which many will find very engaging; but she takes a lot and gives little; she does not shine, she absorbs.'[5]

With her course over and her diploma achieved, Elizabeth might have returned to England; but Stella, on consulting her own travel arrangements, decided it was more convenient to keep her daughter in France for a little longer. Elizabeth accordingly went to stay with the Barettes at Biéville, a village near Caen in Normandy. Léontine was having a well-deserved holiday, and the cooking was done by Marie, a local girl only a few years older than Elizabeth. Her cooking was every bit as delicate and delicious as Léontine's; and one day, she came into the dining room with a large tureen of mussels. They were the first shellfish that Elizabeth had ever eaten.

'The appearance, the smell and the taste of those mussels were to me most fascinating and mysterious. The little black-shelled objects didn't seem like fish at all, they had the same kind of magical quality as mushrooms, the real field mushrooms which, as children, we had so often brought home for breakfast after a dawn search in the fields . . . So those Norman mussels, which reminded me, for whatever reason, of our secret childhood feasts, became forever endowed with the mystery of far-off and almost unobtainable things.'[6]

Elizabeth lived in France for no more than eighteen months, and in a few years she had forgotten much of what she had learned at the Sorbonne. She did, however, acquire a taste for good French couture, and the reckless joys of living on credit. By the time she left Paris Elizabeth had an outstanding bill at the dressmaker's for 643 francs. Stella, who was always lecturing her girls on the importance of economy, was furious – but she had to settle the account. It was not the first time, nor the last, that Stella was left to pick up Elizabeth's bills. Elizabeth was of course punished by having her allowance docked until she had paid her mother back, but her response was to run up even more bills. It was one of Elizabeth's ways of getting back at her mother, and a remarkably effective one.

Yet what remained above all was a taste for a kind of food quite unlike anything she had known before. She had taken little notice of it at the time, and had even tried to avoid it rather than eat with the Barettes. 'Ever since, I have been trying to catch up with those lost days when perhaps I should have been more profitably employed watching Léontine in her kitchen . . .'[7]

After the long summer of 1931, Stella sent Elizabeth to study German in Munich in October. She was placed under the wing of the Gräfin Mirbach-Geldern, and took German lessons three times a week. The family had an Austrian cook, who was particularly gifted with cakes and desserts. There was a chocolate and almond confection called *Mohr im Hemd*, tiny apricot and plum dumplings, and a delicious buttery bread which used to appear on Sundays at breakfast. Yet not all their dishes were so appetizing; one of their favourites was 'limp fried eel nauseatingly flavoured with sage'.[8]

In England, Stella was as usual worrying about her finances. In early 1932 she wrote to Elizabeth, 'I can't afford any more Germany after Diana returns in June . . . another year I want to do an *exchange*, possibly if a person came here for the summer holidays . . . Of course it must be understood that there can be no London and no parties . . . It's all I can do to live here [at Wootton] at all, and strict economy must be the order. Foreigners have an idea that English are millionaires. She would see a lot of country life of the best sort here . . .'

Although a German visitor would have to resign themselves to 'no London and no parties', Stella knew that she still had a duty to bring her daughters out into society. Elizabeth's coming-out was scheduled to take place that spring. 'Hope you are returning by April 1st – Countess of Midleton is presenting you, with her grand-daughter, Antonia Meade, some time in May . . .'

Yet if Elizabeth was to make the most of the opportunities that being a debutante provided, she would have to behave properly. 'Will you give me an undertaking, *if* I try and entertain a little for you, will you promise me to be punctual, and down in time to *receive* guests? This is a very important item – Priscilla always arrived after we had sat down to a meal, and gave a very bad impression. I heard a lot of complaints about it and it did her a *lot of harm*. Also she smoked too much. Mothers of Debs don't like it. You were very unpunctual all holidays here – I am not going to think of any entertaining, until I get your promise, as it's a waste of time and money – the whole point is to be asked back . . .'[9]

Coming-out between the wars was a rite of passage on the way to adulthood and independence, and the prospect of some new frocks and evening gowns (even if they were hand-me-downs) was not entirely unappealing. But Elizabeth dreaded the whole business. She also did not want to leave Munich, where she had been blissfully happy. She had developed an intense platonic relationship with an older man who was a friend of the Mirbach-Gelderns. He signed himself 'Lalt', and on the day she left for London he sent her this letter in English:

'Don't forget that sublime walk in Nymphenburg. All I can do today is to send you these few poor roses. Don't bother about them and simply push them into your trunk. I'd prefer that to finding them in the Habsburgstr. when next I go there. Say your English friend sent you them . . .'[10]

His next letter, dated 2 April and written in German, gives a touching picture of the young Elizabeth: 'Just think, the room which you filled with your dear being appears to get bigger and bigger every day. I miss you always more painfully. You were so enchantingly young and open and soft and devoted. In spite of the amusing makeup of your eyebrows, lips and cheeks, you were so natural, genuine, deep and melancholy. You had a certain seriousness which only children have. Your yellow and red flowers have got that from you . . . You and they have nothing of the greenhouse.'[11]

33

Elizabeth was now eighteen. She was very flattered by the attentions of an older man whom she admired, and she must have enjoyed seeing the effect her beauty had on him. Yet it is ironic that what most attracted Lalt to Elizabeth – her youth and innocence – were the very qualities that Elizabeth was keenest to lose.

* * * * * * *

CHAPTER FOUR

Acting it Out

Shocking news was waiting for Elizabeth on her return to England. Her cousin Edward Marjoribanks, who had been MP for Eastbourne since 1929, had committed suicide. He was only thirty-two, and seemed to have had everything to live for: he had been Captain of School at Eton, President of the Oxford Union, had published three books, and was considered one of the most promising young politicians in the House. He seems to have committed suicide in a moment of extreme nervous exhaustion: he had been overworking himself for some time, and the woman he loved had turned down his proposal of marriage. Stella was distraught: Edward had been her protégé, and had taken the place of the son she had never had.

Nearly forty years later, when her own sister Diana was contemplating suicide, Elizabeth was profoundly sympathetic. 'She knew of course how I felt – and feel – about this question. I thought it all out when my cousin Edward Marjoribanks, for whom I had great respect and whom I greatly loved, blew his brains out. I was seventeen [*sic*] at the time, and have not forgotten.'[1]

A few weeks later, on 11 May 1932, Miss Elizabeth Gwynne was presented at Court by the Countess of Midleton, as arranged by her mother. The dress code was elaborate: those to be presented had to wear a headdress with three small white ostrich feathers to which was attached a short tulle veil, a gown with a court train which trailed some eighteen inches behind the wearer, and long white kid gloves reaching well above the elbow. The debutantes were dressed by three in the afternoon, and had five hours of waiting before being presented to the King and Queen at about eight. Elizabeth endured it all in scowling silence, although Queen Mary thought the evening had gone well. In her diary she wrote that '. . . a good many pretty debutantes came. There were charming toilettes and it was a more interesting Court than usual.'[2] Elizabeth shared her coming-out dance with Karen Harris, who later married Osbert Lancaster.

No doubt coming-out had its pleasures, but by and large Elizabeth despised the gauche young men who could only talk of tennis and horses, the girls who thought only of men and clothes. She had nothing to add to their good-humoured banter, the shrieks and the braying laughs. In Munich, she discovered that she did have the power to charm men; but it was not the sort that could be turned on at will. Trying to make jolly conversation with Elizabeth must have been uphill work for the young men who tried: she hid behind an icy reserve, smoked incessantly and tried to look bored and sophisticated. Besides, the men she was attracted to were not the ones who made an effort. She liked the dangerous ones, the ones mothers disapproved of: but men of that sort were not interested in shy little girls from the Home Counties.

The debutante Elizabeth grew no closer to her mother. She told a friend that Stella's preferred means of communication with her daughters was by letter, which appeared on the breakfast tray brought into their bedrooms by the maid. These letters were basically orders for the day, with instructions of what they had to do and where they would be expected for lunch or dinner. Elizabeth was in London at last: but it was her mother's London, and she was still living on her mother's terms.

Although Elizabeth described painting as her first love, she had reached the conclusion that she was no good at it. She had to find some other way of occupying her time and earning some money. 'After my father's early death,' she wrote in 1985, 'we were very impoverished ... I knew I would have to earn my own living, although nobody, least of all my mother, provided me with the least idea of how that was to be achieved.'³ Elizabeth did find a way of earning a living, and did support herself for most of her life; but this letter implies that in 1933 her situation was much bleaker than it actually was. Elizabeth was presentable, very attractive and in her early twenties. Both she and her mother expected her to marry sooner or later. Until a man took on the responsibility of supporting her, she had an allowance. That allowance was not enough to survive on; but combined with a small but steady income, it could provide that modicum of good clothes, hats and books that Elizabeth would consider essential to life.

Quite what her job would be was not, at that time, very important. As to how it would be achieved, that was simple: in Stella's class, contacts were all you needed to get your daughter a safe if not particularly well-paid job. Her family were sufficiently rich and well-connected to get her out of any serious financial difficulties. After all, she banked at Coutts – where Uncle Jasper had been a director since 1921.

Thus Elizabeth could please herself in the matter of her occupation, and announced that she wanted to be an actress. Stella was appalled: not because she disapproved of the stage, far from it. But she knew her daughter well enough to know that in a carefree and bohemian world, Elizabeth would become dangerously headstrong. A tremendous tussle ensued between Elizabeth and her mother, in the course of which Elizabeth once again walked out of Wootton with her suitcase, vowing never to return. In the end Elizabeth's determination won. She joined the Oxford Repertory Theatre as assistant stage manager, which included sweeping the stage and making the tea.

For Stella, one redeeming feature of the Oxford Repertory Company was that she was an old friend of the manager, Stanford Holme. No doubt she told him and his wife Thea to keep a stern eye on Elizabeth and not let her get into trouble; but all too soon, the jovial and eccentric Stanford and Elizabeth were finding each other perilously attractive. For him, it was no more than a delicious flirtation; but for the young and passionately intense Elizabeth, it was love.

She was in love not only with Stanford Holme, but with a world in which she felt at ease. Here at last were people who lived entirely as they chose, who accepted her for herself, who didn't care about her family's connections: and to Elizabeth, it came as a tremendous release. Elizabeth was losing her innocence fast, and learning how to deal with the experience she was gaining. In the green room among the girls, she learnt about things her mother would have considered quite unmentionable. She also learnt about hard drinking, at post-performance parties and in long sessions at the pub, and discovered that she had a very strong head.

The actress Joan Hickson, who achieved fame in later life as Agatha Christie's Miss Marple, was also part of the company at the time. She wrote to Elizabeth many years later, saying she had an image of her cooking potatoes in a tin can over the prop-room fire. 'I don't actually remember doing so,' Elizabeth wrote back, 'but if you saw me doing it, I suppose it was for some stage meal. But I'm quite surprised to hear that I actually knew how to open a tin. I know somebody had to show me how to make tea for the cast.'[4] She took small parts occasionally, and these increased, but the training that proved most valuable in the long run was looking for props. She was sent out to find things like an eighteenth-century washstand, a hat-box suitable for putting a head in (as in *Night Must Fall*), plus the odd bed, grandfather clock or sofa. The company could not afford hire charges, so Elizabeth had to wheedle the shopkeepers into lending them – the only incentive she could offer being a credit in the programme. 'Well, one certainly learnt to be resourceful – and undaunted.'[5]

Elizabeth's Uncle Jasper, whose commitments took him to Oxford from time to time, was told to keep an eye on her. Meanwhile her childhood friend, her cousin Anne, was reading zoology at

Somerville. Anne remembers that after rehearsals, she sometimes joined Elizabeth for tea with other members of the cast. The meals were not memorable, but as far as Elizabeth was concerned, two years of 'landladies' food and fish teas at the Cadena Café did their part in sending me to the cooking pots'.[6]

Elizabeth was never afraid of saying or doing what she felt, which did not make her easy to work with – but she was thorough. She was particularly busy in the summer of 1933, since the stage manager was away on holiday for a month, leaving her in charge of *The Faithful Heart, The Sign on the Door* and *Almost a Honeymoon*. These were commercial plays, following each other in quick succession and aiming to please the widest possible audience. Stanford Holme kept his company on their toes, and the work was long and demanding.

Meanwhile, Stella's energy was spent on trying to keep Wootton away from her grasping brother-in-law Roland, but he was making her life there such a misery that she began to wonder whether the fight was worth it. It was a fight that she was bound to lose in the end, since although she had an interest in it, Wootton was no longer really her property. In the spring of 1933, Priscilla announced her engagement to a young officer in the Royal Engineers, called Richard Barnes Longland. She was twenty-four, and her life would take her wherever her future husband was posted. Elizabeth had not been back to Wootton for any length of time since she had left to become an actress, and had never shown any particular interest in the place. The two youngest sisters had not yet finished their education, but they were more likely to find employment – and suitors – in London than Sussex.

As for Stella herself, she had been a widow for eight years and was not quite fifty: a handsome woman with a growly aristocratic voice, and magnificent hair always elegantly arranged in a chignon. She wore dark, simple clothes with dramatic jewels. Stella had bought some excellent pieces of Victorian jewellery at a time when it was unfashionable and undervalued.

Stella did not want to waste the rest of her life on a battle for Wootton that she could never win, and her thoughts were turning away from England altogether. She had always gone travelling whenever she could, and had built up networks of friends in Washington, Egypt and Jamaica. It was in Jamaica that she had met Major John Hamilton: sometime ADC to the Governor, and owner of a plantation with a house and overgrown garden to go with it. Soon afterwards Major Hamilton came to England and stayed at Wootton. He seemed pleasant enough, and there was no doubt that Stella was happier than she had been since Rupert's death.

When Stella announced her intention to marry John Hamilton and make her home in Jamaica, her daughters – not unnaturally – took it with all the force of a double betrayal. Uncle Roland would evict them from Wootton, for Stella's life interest in it ceased the moment she remarried. In doing so, she was giving up not only their childhood home but everything that reminded them of their father. As if this were not enough, they were to be left in the care of relations while she swanned off to live with a man she scarcely knew on the other side of the world. Stella had packed up her belongings and left Wootton by the summer of 1933, and as soon as she was gone, Roland installed a tenant.

Stella's sister Grace and her husband Lord Wolmer, on whom much responsibility now fell, might have resented Stella's marriage too; but Grace declared that her elder sister had not been lucky in her first marriage and deserved this second chance to find happiness. In October 1933, Stella Gwynne became Mrs John Hamilton. She waited to see her eldest daughter married, and then sailed with her new husband to Jamaica. Her new house had neither water nor electricity, and the garden was a jungle; but Stella set to work on both with gusto. At the same time, she had not left England completely: she still had three daughters there, and usually returned for several weeks a year.

Priscilla was married from her aunt and uncle's house in Chester Gate in November, and then she too left England: Richard Barnes

Longland had been posted to Malta. Diana, now eighteen, was installed at Marlborough Hill with her Uncle Cony and Aunt Mania – that is, Count Constantine Benckendorff, DSO and his wife Maria Korchinska. (Here was another musical aunt: before escaping from Russia she had taught the harp at the Moscow Conservatoire, and had played at Lenin's funeral in 1924.) Felicité, aged sixteen, spent most of her time in Durham, where she stayed with a family friend and began taking courses in shorthand and typing.

Priscilla was badly missed, particularly by Diana and Felicité. They had lost not only their mother, but their childhood home and the life that went with it. To lose Priscilla as well made them both feel as if they had been cut adrift, though the turmoil was perhaps stronger in Diana, who had always been the most emotional of the four Gwynne sisters. She was also bitterly, hopelessly homesick for Wootton – which was not her home any longer.

In a fit of maternal solicitude, the just-married Stella wrote to Elizabeth from Jamaica: 'I do hope you will *try* at *least* to eat nourishing food even if not appetizing, as only good food will keep you fit and strong for good work – and if you want to get some Bovril and some plain chocolate please do so; that French Marmite, if you can get it is nice, and a change from Bovril, and a cup at night is a help.'[7] Whether her acting improved through drinking these fortifying beverages is doubtful, and when she did get the odd part, the other actors muttered that it was due to her relationship with Stanford Holme more than her talent. Elizabeth's cousin Anne described her acting as 'terrible', adding 'You either have it or you don't.' In any case, Elizabeth was wasting away with the emotional strain of being in love with Holme, who encouraged her one moment and rejected her the next.

Elizabeth's nerves were also being strained by her aunt Grace Wolmer, in whose house in Chester Gate she stayed when she was not in Oxford. Grace felt that Elizabeth's manners were not being improved by the louche company she was keeping. She made her feelings plain at breakfast one morning, and Elizabeth flounced out of the house. Back in Oxford, Holme was at first welcoming and even promised her some parts in his forthcoming productions; but all too soon he had lost interest in her.

In the late spring of 1934 Elizabeth left Oxford, and joined the Open Air Theatre in Regent's Park. This was a new company, founded in 1932 by Sydney Carroll. One of its members was Doreen Brownhill, a young actress who was to become one of Elizabeth's closest friends. Doreen never forgot the company's first sight of Elizabeth, as she stepped into the rehearsal room. 'She was wearing a black sponge-cloth dress with dramatic white organdie collar and cuffs, a black straw hat and gloves. We all stopped and stared at her – she looked stunningly attractive, and completely *wrong*. Everyone else was dressed in slacks and old sweaters.' Elizabeth realized her mistake, and soon she was dressed in slacks and old sweaters too; but she never really joined in the spirit of the company. 'She didn't talk much or give much of herself, just listened,' recalled Doreen. 'To me she seemed terribly grand and sophisticated, because she drank whisky almost non-stop – even first thing in the morning.'[8]

In May 1934, Sydney Carroll put on a production of *As You Like It*. The part of the wrestler, Charles, was taken by a dark, curly-haired actor in his late twenties called Leonard Gibson Cowan. He made the part of Charles so much his own that the name stuck, and that is how most of his friends addressed him. Elizabeth was an extra in this production, as was Doreen. Doreen did not much like Charles Gibson Cowan: she thought he looked dirty and ill-kempt. However, she noticed that many of the women in the company found him very attractive, including Elizabeth.

Leslie French, an actor who worked with Elizabeth in the Regent's Park days, remembers her as 'very serious, very reserved, very eager, and excited really, playing a waiting lady to Olivia; and you never saw a lady waiting so well, or so violently; she had tremendous poise – so much poise I feared she would topple over backwards . . . I remember her in *Twelfth Night* and in *Romeo and Juliet* always as a lady-in-waiting – I suppose she was waiting to be an actress.'⁹

For all the Open Air Theatre productions Elizabeth took part in, she never once had a speaking part. Her busiest season was the summer of 1934, when she was part of a throng of attendants in *As You Like It*, *Twelfth Night*, *The Comedy of Errors*, *A Midsummer Night's Dream*, *Androcles and the Lion*, *Joan* (by Michael Martin Harvey) and *Romeo and Juliet*. The end of the year saw her doing another spell as stage manager, in John Ford's *'Tis Pity She's a Whore* at the Arts Theatre. She enjoyed stage management more than acting, which she knew she was no good at. 'I didn't like it. That's the truth,' she admitted years later. 'I was hopeless. I don't know why I ever thought I wanted to be on the stage . . .'¹⁰

One summer afternoon she particularly remembered at the Open Air Theatre was when one of the leading ladies treated the whole cast of *A Midsummer Night's Dream* to ice cream ordered from Gunter's. The ices were passed around in huge pots, kept cold in pails of ice.

What an inspired treat. Rich, creamy, pale pink strawberry ice cream and slightly crunchy, grainy, bisque-coloured brown bread ice came out of those pots in a seemingly endless supply of voluptuous scoops . . . The becoming dresses, the magical singing of Leslie French as Puck, the presence on that day of, I think, the legendary stage idol Henry Ainsley, all combined with Gunter's ices to create an absurdly idealistic memory of just one early evening between the matinée and the evening shows in Regent's Park.¹¹

After a brief spell with her aunt in Chester Gate, Elizabeth took rooms in a big house in Regent's Park Road, Primrose Hill. She shared them with her old friend Marian Butterworth, with whom she had boarded with the Barettes in Paris. The sitting room was immense, with huge windows; but the kitchen, which was the first Elizabeth had ever had for herself, was really no more than a landing. However, it must have been fairly spacious; for here she installed a gas cooker, a meat-safe with perforated metal sides, and – thanks to a generous twenty-first-birthday cheque from her uncle Jasper – a refrigerator. Refrigerators had only made their appearance in Britain some ten years before, and at that stage they cost almost as much as a car. No wonder Elizabeth's friends thought it a very strange way to spend all that money.

Elizabeth's attitude to money veered from anxiety at how much she was spending, to that youthful disdain for money which often dulls anxiety – at least for a while. She opened an account at Selfridges, and was in the habit of saying 'Oh, just put it on my account' if Charles or Doreen or Marian expressed a desire for something. Elizabeth was also soothed by the knowledge that her mother was a Ridley, and the Ridleys were rich. On the other hand, extravagance was guaranteed to upset her mother. Sometimes Elizabeth didn't care, and on reckless days this might have encouraged her to spend more; but at the same time she did not want to alienate Stella completely. The urge to rebel was very strong; but with it went a healthy sense of self-preservation, and a taste for the good things in life.

The account at Selfridges opened up a new way of spending money. 'I had only to pick up the telephone for roast chickens, smoked salmon, butter, fruit, cheese, cream, eggs, coffee, to be delivered the next day. It wasn't until the monthly accounts seemed to be adding up to much more than I could afford that it began to dawn on me that having a roast chicken always handy in the fridge was a rather extravagant way of entertaining friends, and that anyway bought food . . . was not quite to be compared with the fine cooking I had been exposed to . . .'[12]

It was at Selfridges that she found the answer to the problem of her mounting food bills. When Elizabeth was in the store one day she came across a magnificent display of copies of a thick, enticing book called *Recipes of All Nations*, by a Countess Morphy. She bought it, and read it on the bus all the way home. It made her want to cook; though this impulse had already been activated by another book called *The Gentle Art of Cookery* by Hilda Leyel, a gift from her mother.

Both these books appealed strongly to her imagination, though they were very vague about things like quantities, timing and temperature. This could lead the beginner into serious pitfalls; but far from seeing their lack of technical guidance as a drawback for the beginner, Elizabeth saw it as a positive asset – especially in *The Gentle Art of Cookery*.

'I wonder if I would have ever learned to cook at all if I had been given a routine Mrs Beeton to learn from, instead of the romantic Mrs Leyel with her rather wild, imagination-catching recipes . . .'[13] As it was, Elizabeth felt there was greater merit in trying out Mrs Leyel's '*marrons glacés* in half an hour' than in learning that professional *marrons glacés* involve no less than sixteen separate and distinct processes.

Mrs Leyel spoke of hollowed-out lemons filled with salmon mousse to take on picnics, of pomegranate compotes, of melons steeped in maraschino-flavoured syrup and filled with white grapes, white currants and pistachio nuts. She was particularly fond of fruits, vegetables and salads, which was not surprising since she is principally remembered as the founder of the Society of Herbalists. There was also a chapter on 'Dishes from the Arabian Nights', redolent with honey, rosewater, mint and sweet spices. Here was food for the imagination, though the end result was often far from perfect. 'Had I known,' Elizabeth wrote later, 'how huge was the gap between the urge to cook and the instruction necessary in order to achieve satisfactory results perhaps I wouldn't have embarked on so perilous a course of action. As things were, I blundered on, not much daunted by mistakes.'[14]

An important addition to this fledgling cook's library was Ambrose Heath's *Good Food* which came out in 1932. His jocular style had a broad appeal at the time – 'The jolly lambkin, whose younger brothers leapt so artlessly on to our table in March, now gambols a hint more sedately'[15] – but the chief merit of the book was that it grouped recipes month by month, according to what was in season. It taught her the rudiments of planning a meal around whatever was best and freshest at the time, and what to look out for when she did the marketing.

The most subtle, imaginative and liberating food writer of his day was Marcel Boulestin. One of his most important ideas was that simple dishes like scrambled eggs and anchovy butter, which most people associated with high teas and bed-sits, were 'valuable resources which could be quite differently deployed',[16] as Elizabeth put it. She greatly admired the way he wrote about food, and the fresh, simple elegance of his dishes. But the fact that he was often writing for competent hostesses with cooks to instruct – women, in other words, like her mother – was less appealing, as was his enthusiastic anglophilia. (Boulestin is perhaps the only Frenchman on record who has admitted a liking for mint sauce.) Nevertheless, the profound influence of Boulestin was already permeating Elizabeth's own ideas and experiments.

After a spell in Regent's Park Road, Elizabeth and Marian moved into another flat overlooking the church in Camden Square. In 1934 or so, they were joined by Barbara Hunter, who had been at Godstowe at the same time as Elizabeth. She was having severe family problems at the time, and invited herself to stay in the spare bedroom. Barbara said that while she never remembered Elizabeth cooking a meal, their 'minute kitchen was heavily festooned by Liz with onions, peppers, eggplants and garlic'. (These vegetables, exotic as they were in the mid-thirties, were available in the Greek and Italian shops of Soho and Camden Town.)

One person who was much in evidence at the Camden Square flat was Charles Gibson Cowan, the dark, curly-headed actor whom Elizabeth had met at the Regent's Park Theatre. The double-barrelled name sounds rather middle class: yet in his first autobiographical novel, *Loud Report*, written when he was twenty-four, Gibson Cowan proclaims that his father was the only man he knew who called himself 'lower-class'. Cohen was the family name, but his father changed that to Cowan.

After a stint as a bootmaker, Charles's father had become a

chauffeur; and Charles (or Leonard, as he then was) was the only child of adoring parents. His uncle was a famous freethinker called Chapman Cohen, who encouraged the boy to read widely and question everything. At Leyton County High School for Boys he was the butt of anti-Semitic bullying – but perhaps the bullies also wanted to persecute someone who was clearly more intelligent, imaginative and articulate than they were. He left school at eighteen and, since there was no question of further education, went straight to work. Condemned to what looked like a perpetual grind of nine-to-five among people who saw no further than the next pay packet, he became profoundly depressed. Thanks to his Uncle Chapman, Charles knew there was more to life, though he had no idea how to find it. He gave up his work, stayed in his lodgings as long as he could, and then took to the road with his last half-crown in his pocket.

He spent the next few months scrounging and begging, always on the move, and *Loud Report* is principally an account of this period. While there is no doubt that Charles did live rough for a time, perhaps not all the experiences he recounts are his own: he heard a lot of stories on the road, and he was not a writer to let a good story go just because it hadn't happened to him. Charles later described *Loud Report* as a book of 'boasting confessions'.[17]

Loud Report tells how Charles made his way up from vagabond to fairground barker, and from there to writing his first play. By the time Elizabeth met him he had been making a living from acting, writing and producing since 1926. He knew about the professional theatre, having worked with Basil Dean, Miles Malleson and Robert Atkins; and though he was mainly interested in writing and production, his acting had that 'presence' that Elizabeth always felt she lacked. He was also married, with a young child; but he was already trying to disentangle himself from that commitment when Elizabeth came on the scene.

At that stage, Charles lived with several other people – including his wife – in a large house looking over the river at Wapping. There was a curious moment when Charles talked Elizabeth into delivering his baby daughter Lynn to her mother, who was some distance away by tube. Doreen accompanied Elizabeth, who tried to push the baby on to her but Doreen flatly refused. 'I wasn't going to take it, I didn't know anything about babies. Neither did Elizabeth. Seeing her holding that baby – I suppose it was about six months, perhaps a year old? – was one of the most incongruous sights I have ever seen.'[18] Elizabeth was remarkably free of maternal feelings. She always maintained that she would have made a terrible mother – and if her own mother was anything to go by, she was probably right.

Elizabeth was fascinated by Charles's courage, his sense of adventure, his devil-may-care attitude. She also admired the fact that he was a rebel, which was very much how she saw herself. There was also a gritty sexual attraction about Charles that Elizabeth found irresistible, and she did not seem to mind the fact that she was by no means the only woman in his life. At one point, Charles was having an affair with both her and her flatmate Marian. Marian Butterworth was very different from Elizabeth: she was very kind, and at first glance she seemed shy and rather innocent – yet this mousiness concealed a strong mischievous streak. Marian was, in her way, as naughty and unconventional as Elizabeth, even though she looked as though butter would not melt in her mouth.

As for Elizabeth, Charles was attracted by her elegance, her feline sexiness and her cavalier attitude to money (based on the certain knowledge that Mummy or Uncle Jasper would pick up the bill sooner or later). He was not so impressed by her family, who made no secret of their distaste for him. At one point, Stella summoned Doreen Brownhill to her house and said, 'Can't you get Elizabeth away from that *dreadful* man?' Doreen assured her that it was impossible. To Charles, The Hon. Mrs Gwynne must have looked like a character out of a play by Noël Coward – though it is doubtful that he ever spoke to her. Elizabeth was the kind of over-controlled character who liked to keep her life in rigidly separate compartments, and she was always profoundly uneasy if they overlapped.

What drew Charles and Elizabeth together was that they both

refused to accept the constrictions of their allotted place in the social system, and were reinventing themselves to achieve a new sort of social flexibility. Charles had come a long way from Leyton. Years in the theatrical world had changed his voice, though he never lost the twang of the East End. He was proud of his origins and never denied them. At the same time he evidently felt he could go further with a more resonant name: so he added his mother's maiden name of Gibson to the family one of Cowan.

Elizabeth too was trying to break free from the restrictions of her class. In her case, the problem was how to achieve independence and reject the conventions that irked her, while maintaining the security of an influential family, indulgent bankers and an account at Selfridges.

Elizabeth and Charles also shared a passion for books which are filled with social misfits and mavericks like themselves. It was a time of endless cigarettes, beer and whisky – but as they talked, they became the people they wanted to become. The following morning, when they woke up in grubby sheets with a terrible hangover, things were not so idyllic; but they were both still young and resilient. In 1935, Elizabeth was twenty-two, Charles thirty-one.

Diana was living a much more sheltered life with her Uncle Cony and Aunt Mania, her Benckendorff relations. Diana's gentle, dreamy charm had attracted a string of young men who longed to take her out to tea and the cinema, but Uncle Cony was very strict – at least inside the house. No young man was allowed to sit alone with Diana in the sitting room, for fear the servants might talk. However, she had formed an attachment to a young man called Roger Ellis, who came from a well-to-do family of mine owners in Nottinghamshire. He also knew Elizabeth, whom he remembered as very tall and dark, with a long sinuous neck, but with nothing soft about her sensuality, nor her heavily framed spectacles and her abrasive wit. Diana, in contrast, was a much gentler and less forbidding character.

Roger Ellis had rooms in Gloucester Place, and here he remembered Diana sitting on the floor by the fire while he read poetry to her. She had white skin, a soft voice and dreamy eyes, and none of Elizabeth's challenging sexiness. She was also very absent-minded, and hopelessly unpunctual. Ellis was too much in love to care, but worried about the impression she would make on his parents: they lived in a large house in Nottinghamshire, where everything ran like clockwork.

Diana did not make a very good impression. When the second gong went for dinner – it was a sacred rule of that house that everyone be in the sitting room by the time it was sounded – she was still in the bath. She panicked, rushed back to her room and dressed as fast as she could. The Ellises took a very dim view of her unpunctuality, but worse was to follow. In her hurry, Diana had thrown her sodden sponge on the bed, and by the time she came back to her room it had seeped all the way through to the mattress. 'I hope you never marry that girl,' said Roger's mother when Diana had left.[19]

Roger Ellis did propose to Diana, twice; but she wished he had not, because what she loved was the warmth and comfort of their friendship. She did not see him as a husband because, as he put it, 'she was waiting for someone to sweep her off her feet'. However, when Roger did become engaged, Diana was taken completely off guard: it was, for her, as painful as when Priscilla left for Malta: she had lost her surrogate parent.

Stella had not been settled long in Jamaica before she discovered that John Hamilton was a hopeless alcoholic. Their marriage was over in two years, and Stella moved back to England. She decided to set up an antiques business, and bought the Old School House in Dedham in which to live, do business and house her collection. At the same time, she was much preoccupied by Elizabeth. It was a time when a girl still had to consider her 'reputation'. Elizabeth was ruining her chances of making a good marriage by throwing herself away on a penniless bohemian, whom Stella suspected of being after her daughter's money.

Given Elizabeth's conventional upbringing, it is extraordinary how much independence she had acquired – even before the age of twenty-one. But Stella had no one to blame but herself for what had become of Elizabeth. Pris was a steadier character, Diana and Felicité still young enough to do as they were told. But Stella had abandoned Elizabeth for Jamaica at the very moment when she most needed firm guidance – just as she had joined the theatre and was entering adulthood. The headstrong Elizabeth made sure Stella never regained control. She was now impervious to any displays of authority or lectures on morals, because she knew her mother felt guilty.

In an effort to separate Elizabeth from Charles and her dissolute life, Stella decided that Elizabeth should be encouraged to travel. Elizabeth was delighted by the idea. Friends of Stella's in Cairo called the Goodwins invited Elizabeth to come out and stay with them, and the plan was that after spending several weeks in Egypt she should go to Malta to visit her sister Priscilla.

In February 1936 Elizabeth acquired a new passport. The photograph shows a young woman with wild black hair, and there is a hard look about her eyes and her narrow mouth. A few days later, she equipped herself with a visa for Egypt, but the Egyptian trip was postponed. It was decided that Elizabeth should go to Malta anyway, which she did that spring.

Priscilla had been in some ways more of a mother to Elizabeth than Stella herself, and Stella told Pris that this Maltese holiday was the ideal moment to bring Elizabeth to her senses. Elizabeth knew this, and being naturally secretive she didn't talk much about Charles to Priscilla. Besides, she did not know quite how she felt about him: with Elizabeth, feelings of love and sexual jealousy went hand in hand with a kind of irritation that she should be under somebody's spell.

Richard and Priscilla certainly took a great deal of trouble to give Elizabeth a lovely time. There were parties and sightseeing expeditions and picnics, and Elizabeth revelled in the comparative luxury of Priscilla's well-ordered house after her bohemian life in London.

Another bonus of the trip was that, for the first time in her life, Elizabeth had the opportunity to watch an excellent and enthusiastic cook at work. The cook was a Maltese woman called Angela, and Priscilla Longland – herself an excellent cook – allowed Angela a free hand with the meat allowance they were given by the army. Most English women of that time would have insisted that, whatever part of the carcass the meat had come from (and this was often hard to establish) it should be tied up into some sort of joint and served with two veg. Angela, however, was encouraged to make delicious meat stews in the Italian manner, making good use of the rough local wine which cost around ninepence a bottle. Angela could rise to the challenge of the most elaborate dishes; but the most important lesson she taught Elizabeth was that, in the hands of a good and careful cook, even an old bird and a stringy piece of meat can be made edible.

The Maltese trip was a success, but it failed to separate Elizabeth from Charles. As she had suspected, he had not been pining away in her absence – he had never made any secret of the fact that he believed in sexual freedom. So did Elizabeth and, according to her friend Doreen Brownhill, she did not seem to care much about Charles's constant infidelities.

Charles's enthusiasm for the stage was on the wane. He had been working in and around the theatre since the mid-1920s, and realized that he was never going to be a great actor or producer. But he still felt that he might make a good living as a writer, although his life did not inspire him with much to write about. He wanted to travel, and developed a passion for the sea. He bought a small boat, which in July 1936 he had sailed from Wapping to Lowestoft. Charles had plans to sail all the way round the British coast and, eventually, buy a bigger boat and sail the world.

Elizabeth and Charles compiled a book together in the second half of 1936, which they hoped – rather optimistically – would make them some money if they could find a publisher. The title-page reads, '*The King is Dead – Verses on the Passing of Royalty from the earliest printed copies to King George the Fifth, Written by Contemporary hands and collected from various sources. To which is added various notes for the interest of the reader by Gibson Cowan and Elizabeth Gwynne. 1936.*' Not surprisingly, it was never published.

In November, Elizabeth finally set off for Egypt to stay with her mother's friends, Dorothy and Teddy Goodwin. She was accompanied by her cousin Kit (Kathleen) Gwynne, the daughter of her uncle Nevile. Teddy Goodwin worked for Shell Oil. Like most of the bankers, businessmen and cotton brokers of the British community, the Goodwins lived far better in Egypt than they could have done in England. They had a huge house in Cairo, any number of servants and a villa in Alexandria. English social life revolved around racing, polo and cricket matches, all of which took place at the Gezira Club on the southern end of Zamelek Island. On Sundays, everyone assembled at St Mary's in Garden City, for a family service presided over by Bishop Gwynne of Cairo and Khartoum (possibly a distant cousin of Elizabeth's).

Elizabeth loved the expeditions into the desert, the days at the beach and trips to the bazaar; but as she sat around the Gezira Club lido waiting for yet another group of nice young people whom Dorothy Goodwin wanted her to meet, Elizabeth was keenly aware that she was in Egypt on her mother's terms, not her own.

One person who made a big impression on Elizabeth during her time in Egypt was the writer and traveller Robin Fedden, who was then working for the British Council in Greece. Fedden was tall, good-looking, immensely erudite and funny: ideal company for Elizabeth, and they took to each other instantly. Elizabeth could not remember for sure where she first met him, but thought it might have been in the house of Sir Walter Smart. Sir Walter Smart was Oriental Counsellor at the British Embassy in Cairo from 1929 to 1945. His Syro-Lebanese Christian wife Amy was a painter, and their house was filled with books and her brightly coloured paintings. At Walter and Amy Smart's one met not only English people, but Egyptians and Greeks; not only bankers and diplomats, but archaeologists, actors and poets. For Elizabeth, this was a glimpse of a side of Cairene life that she found much more appealing than the Gezira Club.

Before leaving Egypt Elizabeth went on a nine-day trip to the Levant in February 1937, visiting Palestine, Lebanon and Syria. Whether she went with the Goodwins or joined another party is unclear; but it must have felt very different from the comfortable expatriate life she had been enjoying in Cairo. It was closer to the sort of travelling she really wanted to do: rougher, less insulated, more adventurous. Elizabeth sailed from Alexandria in early March, and on her way home she stopped off to spend a month over Easter with Priscilla on Malta. There was a valedictory feeling about this visit, for Richard's posting to Malta was coming to an end.

Elizabeth had been away from home for about five months by the time she returned to England; and although she was now filled with new hopes and determination to get a job, they evaporated quickly. She could not find any work, either acting or stage-managing, and at the same time she was fed up with sharing a flat with Marian. She moved into a small apartment in John Street, Bloomsbury, where Charles too lived on and off. Elizabeth wished she could shake herself free of him. Not knowing quite what to do, she set off for Germany and the Austrian Tyrol, where she spent most of July. At some point that summer she went to stay in the south of France with Doreen, and when Priscilla and her husband came back to Britain on leave, she and her sister took a house in Wales.

Since 1935, Elizabeth and her sisters had got into the habit of spending at least a week together in Wales, usually when Priscilla and Richard were back. They would rent an old farmhouse or cottage, and at a time when their separate lives were inevitably drawing them apart, their holidays in Wales provided a period when they could reaffirm their closeness to each other. Elizabeth came to love the intimate river valleys with their isolated cottages and the wild hills beyond. It was a landscape that never failed to inspire and revive her; and she carried a memory of one particularly magical house, with a brook running through the garden, that she had seen at a place called Machynlleth.

Some of the time that hung heavy on Elizabeth's hands that year was spent on making a present for Marian Butterworth, whose friendship Elizabeth was more inclined to appreciate now they were no longer sharing a flat. She bought a stout exercise book with marbled endpapers, and in this she wrote out a collection of recipes. Among these are Cheese Loafers, Prunes à l'Indienne, Drop Scones, Nègre en Chemise (an attempt to re-create the *Mohr im Hemd* she had tasted in Munich), Hot Beetroot and Roast Rabbit. In a handwritten note attached to the book dated 1979, Elizabeth wrote that the recipes had several sources, among them Countess Morphy, Hilda Leyel and Priscilla's Maltese cook Angela. Some of the dishes sound more appetizing than others. One suggests combining cold chicken with the pulp of a grapefruit, and serving it in the shell; while Bengal Croûtes consist of crushed toasted almonds mixed with Sharwood's Green Label Chutney, spread on home-made cheese biscuits and baked for about ten minutes. Elizabeth took a lot of trouble over the book. The different sections on soup, fish, poultry and so on are marked by a page covered with a sheet of coloured paper, on to which she stuck little Victorian figures, perhaps from a Pollock's cut-out paper theatre.

At the end of that long, listless summer, Elizabeth took on a job as a 'showroom second' for the fashion house of Worth, at 50 Grosvenor Street. Every second was attached to a particular vend-euse, who was usually elderly, unmarried and bent on cultivating her own importance. The seconds were kept very busy dancing attendance on them, and helping clients and models in and out of dresses; but their main function was to order all the materials and accessories with which to make up the outfits which the client had ordered. These young women were theoretically entitled to earn commission, to make up for their miserable salaries (Elizabeth was paid ten shillings a week), but the vendeuses saw to it that they were kept as far as possible from the clients, who included Rose Kennedy and the Queen of Siam. The seconds also had to put up with constant admonitions. 'You are not here to think, but to do as you are told' – 'The seconds don't use the front staircase. Go up the back stairs.'[20]

Their only moments of rest occurred in the airless, windowless staff cloakroom in the basement, where they ate their lunchtime sandwiches. Cockroaches scuttled into cracks in the wall as soon as the light was switched on and, first thing in the morning, the girls often found the insects in their 'house shoes'.

'Still, there were good moments,' wrote Elizabeth many years later to Frances Harper, who had worked at Worth at the same time as Elizabeth. 'I remember the corset-fitter telling me, in a state of deep shock, that she had seen the shameless Lady Whoever stark naked in the fitting room. I never did discover how the lady was supposed to try on her corset without undressing. Then there were those extraordinary model girls. Once, as I was dressing one of them, she suddenly said, "Gwynne, I'd give a *pound* to sleep with Raymond Massey, wouldn't you?"'[21]

The way in which Elizabeth left Worth was perhaps predictable. 'One of the senior vendeuses overheard me telling a customer in the fitting room that the dress she was trying on didn't suit her and I thought it was hideous. There was an almighty rumpus. I'm not sure if they sacked me or if I did a Michael Heseltine, but I was certainly glad to be liberated . . .'[22]

Elizabeth left Worth in the spring of 1938 and spent the summer in the south of France with Doreen Brownhill. Doreen had a friend whose father owned a hotel called Les Roches Fleuris, near Le

Lavandou. As a friend of the family she was given very reasonable rates, which she often shared with friends – in this case, Elizabeth and a girl who was studying at Oxford, called Diana Anderson. They were not expecting to meet anyone else, but it emerged that four Oxford boyfriends of Diana's were staying near by. Their presence enlivened the party considerably. They spent their days in cafés or on the beach, and drank well into the small hours. One might think that this sort of life was only invented in the sixties, but for girls with independent minds and independent allowances, anything was possible in the late thirties – though Elizabeth does seem to have been considerably freer than her friends.

At the end of the holiday, Elizabeth decided to visit Corsica. The other girls very much wanted to join her, but their families would not allow it: the island was considered a dangerous place full of bandits. This did not deter Elizabeth. To the envy and admiration of her friends she set off for Corsica, and settled for a time in the little town of Piana on the west coast.

'I took a room in the house of a very humble family,' she wrote. 'There were a large number of children in their late teens. Their mother was a great big brawny woman with a robust sense of humour. Amid a tremendous clatter we would all sit down to meals at one big table. Madame's cooking was of the same nature as her own: rough, generous, full of character and colour. There were great dishes of ham and tomatoes, eggs and olives, plenty of salads and oil, huge hunks of bread and great bowls of bursting ripe figs. In all the years since then I have never forgotten the very special savour of that food.'[23]

At some point that year, Robin Fedden invited Elizabeth to Chantemesle, some fifty miles north-west of Paris, where his parents lived. On one side of the house was the River Seine, winding between little green islands alive with birds, and on the other, the abrupt ascent of a dry limestone escarpment. Cherry and apricot trees stood about the house. 'It was beautiful there. I have never forgotten it,' she wrote.[24] Perhaps it was then that Robin proposed to her: many years later, she admitted to Robin's daughter Frances that she and her father had been engaged. However, it must be admitted that Robin was very susceptible to women and did have a tendency to propose marriage. It may have been fun for both of them to try on an engagement like a suit of clothes, though it did not fit either of them in 1938.

Elizabeth came back to England and, inevitably, to Charles. They had now been living with each other, on and off, for three years. They were both rather fed up with their aimless lives, disenchanted with the theatre and sick of England. They would probably have drifted apart had they continued as before; but in the winter of 1938 they began to fantasize about buying a boat, and sailing away. It was a mad idea, with little behind it except a strong desire to escape; but it seized their imaginations, and both of them were ready for adventure.

In Charles's case, the urge to travel again may have been rekindled by the publication of *Loud Report*, the autobiographical novel he had written aged twenty-four about his time on the road. Its publication by Michael Joseph in 1938 was partly due to a current interest in accounts of proletarian life and social hardship: Orwell's *The Road to Wigan Pier* had appeared the year before. At any rate, seeing it in print must have given Charles a much-needed boost to morale. Perhaps he could make a living as a writer after all, and a voyage with Elizabeth might give him something to write about.

'We had to live somewhere,' he wrote later, 'and the Mediterranean was cheap. I should continue to write, only slightly more conscientiously. It was true that cruise books of the Mediterranean were ten a penny, and publishers positively curled up at the sound of voyages to the Greek archipelago, but something was certain to turn up to make this different.'[25]

They saved every penny they could, and Elizabeth went to her Uncle Jasper. Sir Jasper usually allowed her to overdraw, though he never failed to remind her gently that she really ought to curb her extravagance. He could not have guessed that, on this particular occasion, the overdraft was 'to enable me to pay for a boat in which to sail for Greece, no less . . .'[26]

* * * * * * *

CHAPTER FIVE

Norman Douglas

They found the *Evelyn Hope* early in 1938. Although she was basically a two-masted yawl with an engine and was described as a wooden pleasure yacht, Elizabeth thought she looked more like a black fishing boat. She needed a great deal of work, and cost almost twice what they could afford to pay. 'We stood in the mud, heedless of the rain, for the best part of an hour, and agreed it was a ship. We bought it, subject to a survey, and paid a small sum as an earnest of good faith. We went back to London full of enthusiasm for the first time in months.'*

The *Evelyn Hope* contained a cockpit, a saloon, a cabin containing one double and one single bunk and a washbasin, and a galley in the forecastle. The yacht was berthed on the River Hamble, which spills into Southampton Water. Here Charles and Elizabeth fitted her out for the long voyage. Elizabeth's contribution to the boat's library included works by Victorian travellers, seventeenth-century poets and playwrights, several history books, Homer, *Robinson Crusoe* and about a hundred paperback thrillers which she said could be thrown

---

* Charles Gibson Cowan wrote a novel about this voyage which he and Elizabeth made together. It was called *The Voyage of the Evelyn Hope*. Much of this book, written soon after the events it describes, is fairly faithful to what happened. The exception is its dramatic finale, which is purely fictional. Until that episode, the dates tally with those in Elizabeth's passport and other documents, and she herself read most of it in typescript in Alexandria. The only other significant change in the book was to Elizabeth's name. She is called 'Caroline'.

overboard after use. She had also installed cushions and covers and curtains, pots and pans, and tins of provisions. To spread the financial load, Elizabeth and Charles decided to take on a female paying passenger to Marseille. Her identity was never revealed.

As they were making last-minute preparations, Elizabeth was offered a bit part in a short film. She was irritated at the thought of having to postpone the voyage, but by early July she had done the job. Everything was ready. They hoped to be off on the 6th, but a gale sprang up from the south-west. By the 8th, the skies were clearer and the wind was now blowing from the west. 'I went below and started the engine,' wrote Charles. '[Elizabeth] let go forwards. We swung round with the current . . . It was as simple as that; we were under weigh.'[1]

It was warm and the sun was breaking through the clouds as they set out into the Channel, and by lunchtime the following day they had reached Le Havre. They stayed there until the 14th. 'The fête was dampened by a depressing drizzle,' wrote Charles, 'that started in the morning and continued all day . . . The French were either taking the political situation seriously or they were disheartened by the rain, for there was no dancing in the streets.'[2]

They took out the mast at Rouen, and sailed up the Seine in steady rain as far as Paris. After a day of sightseeing they found some friends in the Rotonde, who were much preoccupied with the possibility of war and were discussing it from every angle. Charles and Elizabeth took them for an evening on the river, which must have taken their minds off the Nazi threat for everyone got drunk.

Above Paris they had no charts for the river; but with help from some obliging bargemen, they reached the beginning of the Canal de Bourgogne, which has over two hundred locks. They locked themselves upwards in a leisurely way, shopping in the market of Marigny and drinking the wine of Pouilly, until they reached the two-mile tunnel which passes under the summit of the Côte d'Or. Three days later – the locks now descending – they were in Dijon, 'which possesses what must be the world's best restaurant, and worst museum'.[3] After a sumptuous meal at the Trois Faisans, they continued south: down the river Doubs, down the Saône to Lyon, which seems to have marked a low spot in the trip: 'the paying guest was more conspicuous than usual, Caroline was indisposed and a mechanic was on board most of the time we were there'.[4] They were obliged to take a pilot down the Rhône as far as Arles, sailed through the lagoons of the Camargue and finally dropped anchor in the old port of Marseille in the first days of September.

Elizabeth and the paying guest immediately went off to the Italian market, leaving Charles to enjoy the painted fishing boats, 'which came alongside to sell their loads of black mussels, purple sea urchins, blue crayfish and green and white oysters'.[5] Elizabeth and the paying guest did not come back until after dark, and had great trouble picking their way through the mooring lines back to the *Evelyn Hope*: the war scare had begun in Marseille, and the blackout was already in force. The following day, they found out that Germany had invaded Poland.

The paying guest immediately packed up and went home, but Elizabeth and Charles stayed on in Marseille. Fish, bread and Algerian wine were cheap. Sometimes they ate at a little Italian restaurant, 'where in an open brick oven the chef turned strange vegetable pies with an immense peel'.[6] (These vegetable pies, or pizzas, were not yet the ubiquitous fast food they were to become.) When the air-raid warnings began, they took shelter with the poor people of the Italian quarter in a railway tunnel at the back of the port, its walls dripping with water. 'We were all terribly afraid of gas,' wrote Charles. 'It was a word which crystallized our fear of the unknown chemical warfare we expected to drop from the skies.'[7] But the fear receded, and after a couple of nights in the tunnel, they decided to stay aboard the *Evelyn Hope*.

The boat needed repairs which took almost a week, while Charles and Elizabeth considered their options: whether to move on to a smaller and perhaps safer port, or even to give in and go home. At first, they were ordered to stay where they were; but after a few weeks, under the suspicious eyes of the maritime authorities, they moved to the harbour of Antibes, just south-west of Nice.

Here Elizabeth was delighted to find Mike and Nancy Cumberlege, whom she had met in Malta with Priscilla. Mike's father was an admiral and Mike had been brought up, as his friend Patrick Leigh Fermor put it, 'more or less amphibious. He was bookish, great fun, fantastically good-looking – and he had this small, close-fitting gold earring in one ear which made him look very dashing.'[8] He and Charles spent long sessions on board the *Evelyn Hope* discussing every aspect of seamanship and boats, for Mike at that time had little to do. He was a naval officer on the reserve and hoped to be used in some intelligence capacity, but so far he had not been called up. Unlike Charles, who described himself as a conscientious objector, Mike was very much a patriot and wanted to see action as soon as possible.

Mike and Nancy introduced them to their group of friends, and Charles and Elizabeth found that café life suited them both – even if conversation was dominated by the war and whether Italy would enter it. They also needed to get out. Life on the boat, cooped up in two small cabins within the high walls of the harbour, quickly became claustrophobic. Blackout regulations were strictly enforced, and they had to keep the portholes and skylights covered at night.

Elizabeth's relationship with Charles was based less on true friendship than on an attraction of opposites. The staleness that had begun to creep into their relationship in London became even more marked in Antibes, where there was nothing to do and only an uncertain future ahead. What made it worse was that they were dependent on each other. The boat belonged to Elizabeth more than to Charles, but she needed Charles to sail it if they were ever to leave Antibes.

The situation eased when Charles left in early December with Mike, to fetch a yacht back from Venice to Antibes. Charles, who had never been to Venice before, took the opportunity to do some sightseeing. Meanwhile Elizabeth had stayed with Nan in Antibes, though their friendship was becoming strained by the mood of enervated restlessness that the war had brought about. Elizabeth felt there was nothing to do but drink and write long letters to her sisters. Pris, Diana and Felicité were particularly important to her at this time, especially Pris, who sent her money whenever she could. Stella had more or less washed her hands of Elizabeth. Running off with Charles was bad enough, but the fact that he was a pacifist was intolerable.

Towards the end of 1939 another man came into Elizabeth's life, a man who was to inspire her more than any other. This was the author and traveller Norman Douglas. Norman had been based in the south of France since May 1937, having been forced to leave Florence in a hurry. The cause of his flight was a ten-year-old girl, who had been in the habit of coming to his flat. The very worst interpretation was put on these visits, but for once the old reprobate (whose tastes more often veered towards boys) was probably innocent. The girl's father certainly thought so: it was the puritanical, xenophobic Fascists who chased him out of Italy.[9]

Norman Douglas was then seventy-two, Elizabeth twenty-six, and the difference in their ages was if anything an attraction. They used to meet for drinks in the cafés of the old port, and go on to one of the restaurants where the management took a good-humoured view of the idiosyncrasies of 'Monsieur Doo-glass'. In the restaurant, he would bring a hunk of Parmesan out of his pocket.

'"Ask Pascal to be so good as to grate this at our table. Poor stuff, my dear, that Gruyère they give you in France. Useless for macaroni." And a bunch of basil for the sauce. "Tear the leaves, mind. Don't chop them. Spoils the flavour."'[10]

They also went for what Norman called 'little strolls' in the hills towards Vence – a little stroll, for him, being more like a day's hike for most people. Elizabeth looked forward eagerly to a day in his company, and felt flattered to be chosen as his companion; but she described herself as 'a feeble and unwilling walker', and found it hard work keeping up with him.

In the mid-thirties, she and her friend and fellow-actress Doreen

Brownhill had often walked through the night from Chelsea to Camden Town; while even in later life, she could stay on her feet for hours if she was hunting for books and antiques, or wandering around a market. But the rocky, uneven hills of Vence were another matter, and Norman was a vigorous walker. 'The way he went stumping up and down those steep and stony paths, myself shambling behind, reversed our ages. And well he knew it.'[11] However, at the end of the long haul there was always a café, more often than not what Elizabeth called 'One of those two-chair, one-table, one-woman-and-a-dog establishments.' Norman ordered a litre of wine, but Elizabeth was hungry as well as thirsty.

'Ha! You won't get much out of *her*. Nothing but bread and that beastly ham. Miserable insipid stuff.' From out of his pocket came a hunk of salami and a clasp knife.

'Do you always carry your own provisions in your pocket?'

'Ha! I should say so. I should advise you to adopt the same rule. Otherwise you may have to put up with what you get. No telling what that may be, nowadays.'[12]

In later life she often admitted, quite simply, that she had been in love with Norman Douglas. This was hardly surprising, for one of the strongest loves is that of a disciple for a teacher, and Norman was the best teacher Elizabeth ever had. She admired his rigorous scholarship and broad learning, and everything he said or did struck a chord in her. Much of what he taught her she already knew, on an instinctive level: what Norman did was to express, develop and refine the principles which she wanted to guide her life. Look for what is true and authentic; see things as they are; be constantly vigilant against the pretentious and the sham; above all, please yourself and take the consequences.

He was also, to the core of his being, a Darwinist and an atheist. He did not believe in loving one's neighbour, and loathed any system of thought that advocated either complete equality, or complete submission. Fascism and Communism both wanted to turn people into termites, and were therefore to be abhorred. Democracy was also dangerous because he believed it to be based on a fallacy – to him, people were anything but equal. Norman would not have tolerated Elizabeth's devotion if she had been one of the crowd, but in her he saw someone with the sort of fierce, self-contained individuality that he could admire. She was worth taking trouble over.

Norman was also exceptional – especially among Englishmen – because he talked about food at a time when educated people simply didn't, unless they were self-conscious epicures. He was not an epicure, in that the rarity or delicacy of a dish did not interest him. He talked of food because it mattered, because it was part of civilized life, to be enjoyed as profoundly as every other pleasure and accorded the interest and respect that, in Norman's opinion, too many pretentious people accorded to art. He once shocked the emaciated Nancy Cunard (who never gave a damn what she ate) by saying that 'a good dinner is worth all the Benozzo Gozzolis in the world'.

Norman was no cook himself, though he was acutely aware of the fact that everything worth eating had a family and a history. During the last summer of his life, on Capri in 1951, Elizabeth brought him some figs from the market. He asked her from which stall she had bought them.

'That one down nearest to the steps.'

'Not bad, my dear, not bad. Next time, you could try Graziella. I fancy you'll find her figs are sweeter; just wait a few days, if you can.'

He knew, who better, from which garden those figs came; he was familiar with the history of the trees, he knew their age and in what type of soil they grew . . . I may add that it was not Norman's way to give lectures. These pieces of information emerged gradually, in the course of walks, sessions at the tavern, apropos a chance remark. It was up to you to put two and two together if you were sufficiently interested.[13]

Elizabeth was not only interested: she hung on his every word. Where Mrs Leyel had filled her head with honey and spices, Norman taught her that with a little care and attention, one could eat good food every day. He also taught her how to search out the best, insist on it, and reject all that was bogus and second-rate.

In the course of her career Elizabeth wrote about a great many people including Eliza Acton, William Verral, Mrs Beeton and Marcel Boulestin. In each case she tried to describe their character as well as their work; but she approached them as historical figures. The two essays she wrote on Norman Douglas were completely different in tone, and quite unlike anything else she ever wrote. In those essays, she is not only trying to capture the essence of someone she loved: she is trying to remember, and record, the essence of every conversation she ever had with him.

Charles returned from Venice with Mike Cumberlege in time for a New Year's Eve party. Elizabeth did not turn up till ten that evening: she had been with Norman in Nice. In the days that followed, she showed no particular inclination to be with Charles. Her mornings were spent helping out in a soup kitchen, which had been set up by a wealthy philanthropist in a huge dining room panelled in oak with refectory tables and Jacobean chairs. The evenings she spent with Norman.

Charles liked and admired Norman Douglas. At the same time he resented the way that Elizabeth and the old writer had become friends so swiftly, and how they revelled in each other's company. Between them was a relaxed complicity, an understanding that he had no part of. Elizabeth made no effort to hide her feelings for Norman, and made it clear that he was not welcome to join their excursions. Rather than see them so constantly together, Charles spent more and more time on his own.

'I was too hard up to join in the social life of the Cap. When I could afford it I went alone by bus to Nice, where I spent the day wandering around the Italian quarter . . . and lunching at a restaurant with a small balcony . . . Many afternoons I sat there with the bottle of Armagnac left on the table, finding a companion to talk to, or merely watching the seagulls . . .'[14]

*

He and Elizabeth had now been in the south of France for over six months, and if they did not get out of Antibes that spring the opportunity might vanish altogether. Charles's sudden determination to set sail might also have been prompted by the thought that if he did not make a move soon, Elizabeth might refuse to go with him. He began to get the boat ready for the next leg of their journey, to Corsica.

Whatever she felt about Charles, and her feelings were very ambivalent, Elizabeth found that she was as keen to make a move as he was. Even Norman Douglas's company was not enough to relieve the boredom of life in Antibes. Elizabeth had never liked to mix her friends, and she had not encouraged Charles to develop a friendship with Norman. But she could not keep them completely apart, especially since Charles enjoyed talking to him. Norman urged Charles to travel while there was still time: he said he envied him the prospect of seeing Greece before it became completely spoilt by the twentieth century. Charles pointed out that they did not yet have a permit to leave the harbour.

'Bah! You'll be here for the rest of your life if you wait for permits. What is the use of a permit to a French official? Corsican savages, all of 'em . . . Don't take any notice of 'em. I'd come with you myself if I didn't hate boats. Uncomfortable things, smelly, never get any proper food, nowhere to put your feet.'[15]

Yet if Norman was encouraging Charles to leave Antibes, he rather hoped that Elizabeth might stay. He could see that she was tired of her lover, and that their relationship had been stretched thin by their monotonous and penny-pinching existence. This had not been quite so uncomfortable for Elizabeth as for Charles. Norman would have picked up the bill for most of her outings with him. She still had her allowance and, with the occasional handout from Priscilla, she could just about afford 'the social life of the Cap'.

Shortly before they were due to leave, Norman gave Elizabeth a copy of *Old Calabria*. 'Old-fashioned stuff, my dear,' he said as he presented it. 'Heavy going. I don't know whether you'll be able to get through it.' On the flyleaf he wrote 'Always do as you please, and send everybody to Hell, and take the consequences. Damned good Rule of Life. N.'[16]

Elizabeth understood that the inscription was a message, attempting to jolt her out of her entanglement with Charles. As she recalled the subsequent conversation, Norman said,

'You are leaving with him because you think it is your duty. Duty? Ha! Stay here with me. Let him make do without you.'

'I can't, Norman, I have to go.'

'Have it your way, my dear, have it your way.'[17]

Wise old bird that he was, Norman knew that there is only so much that can be learnt from another person.

* * * * * * *

CHAPTER SIX

The Loss of the Evelyn Hope

Charles and Elizabeth now realized that while the French authorities would not actually stop them from leaving Antibes in the *Evelyn Hope*, they would never grant them formal permission either. Fuel was already rationed, and what little they possessed had been begged from friends. However, they had managed to obtain visas for Italy and Greece, and decided to take their chances. On the afternoon of 20 May they gave a little cocktail party. 'Even Norman overcame his dislike of boats,' wrote Charles, 'and was on board. It was a brief leave-taking with time but for one drink, slightly sad.'[1] They set out for Corsica that evening, catching the icy mistral which blows from the north.

The exhilaration of the open sea brought back the zest to their relationship. To one of her closest friends, Elizabeth confided that Charles used to tie her up to the mast and whip her – which may have been no more than a joke, but it certainly implies that sex aboard the *Evelyn Hope* was exciting and inventive. They reached Corsica safely and spent some days in and around Bastia, visiting Erbalunga as Norman had suggested. Elizabeth wrote to tell him about it. He answered on 31 May.

Just got your lovely letter of Sunday [26th May] . . . I suppose you are on the briny once more and can only hope you don't have any trouble with Italian officials, who get more troublesome the further south you go.

Glad you found that restaurant at Bastia; not good, but better than most. And glad you went to Erbalunga, where I had some ultra-pleasant days (*very* rare in Corsica). As to that damned grotto – it is not worth looking at. But I suppose you went there all the same. I was there for the first time with Marion Crawford in 1898. Were you born? I don't think so . . .

My stomach was all right, but I ordered broad beans and bacon the other day and ate about 3 kilos of it, with the result that the business has started all over again, and when I visit the WC (about fifty-four times a day) the explosions are so formidable that – the walls being very thin – Mme Jeanne and her girls rush out of doors, thinking there is an air raid in progress. Heaps of love to Charles. N.

Just before Elizabeth and Charles left Corsica they heard that the Germans had crossed the Meuse. Within three days it had become clear that there was nothing the French army could do to stop a full-scale invasion.

They left Corsica on 28 May, sailing almost due east: past the Italian penal settlement of Pianosa, and past Monte Cristo, then a game preserve for the king of Italy. The weather was turning rough, but they managed to reach the tiny island of Giglio, which lies between Elba and the port of Santo Stefano. Here they were received with the greatest possible courtesy by the *capo doganiere*, and his interpreter, who was the island's schoolmaster. Full of enthusiasm for the new arrivals, the schoolmaster invited them to dinner at his house, promising that all the island would be there to meet them.

As it turned out, they were the only guests. The schoolmaster apologized profusely and was evidently very ill at ease, and the enormous dinner he had laid on was not a success. The following morning, one of the schoolmaster's friends came early, with an urgent warning.

'You must leave early, trouble begins. I cannot tell you more, but war is certain . . . Get your papers as soon as the office opens, but act as though you know nothing. The weather is still bad, but you must go. Everybody here wishes you luck, do you understand? . . . You should be able to reach Messina in five days.'[2]

They collected their papers from the *capo doganiere*, who begged them to come back to the island in happier times, and set off into a gale. It was the first week of June 1940.

The voyage down the west coast of Italy became tiring, for the uncertain and variable winds involved much changing of sail. They bought a lobster from a little fishing boat that drew alongside, near the island of Stromboli, and later they ate it with fresh mayonnaise. As they came closer and closer to Messina without being stopped or questioned, their spirits rose: it was doubtful if the Italians would stop them once they were through the straits and out into the open sea.

The straits came in sight on the evening of 10 June, but their hopes of getting through were dashed. Three Italian destroyers on patrol appeared. One of them approached the *Evelyn Hope*, and they were ordered to proceed to the Sicilian port of Messina. As soon as they had berthed an officer came on board. He was surprised to hear that they did not have a radio, and asked if they had heard the news. They replied that they had not. The officer told them that, as of 5.30 that afternoon, Italy and Great Britain were at war.

The men who came to search the boat were very courteous; but they removed every piece of paper on board – charts, notebooks, address books, photographs. They left an appalling mess, which Charles and Elizabeth had not the heart to clear up. 'Finally we roughly tidied the double bunk, and lay miserably in each other's arms. We tried to imagine what would happen in the morning. At last we slept.'[3]

Now began a period of utter misery for Elizabeth, which in later years she could scarcely bear to recall. The Sicilian authorities, suspicious of a British couple prowling round the straits of Messina just as war was breaking out, decided that they must be spies. Charles and Elizabeth were questioned at the *Questura* (police headquarters) for two hours, and then told to pack. The boat was impounded. Their statements were sent to Rome for verification, and while the Roman authorities decided what was to be done with them, they would be kept as internees in Messina. They were sent to the Pensione Vienna, a squalid little boarding house in the Via Industriale. Their luggage, including a trunk full of books, was delivered the following day.

June in southern Italy was relentlessly hot. Their room was 'fenced off from the kitchen by an unpainted wooden partition about eight feet high, and contained a [single] bed . . . The room opened directly into the main living room, but a certain amount of privacy was afforded by the position of the bed, which allowed the door to only half open.'[4]

From the kitchen ceiling hung a cage with a dead canary in it. When Charles pointed this out, the Austrian landlady merely said, 'Poor thing! He's been dead for fifteen days.'[5] She was a hard, grasping woman with broken teeth. The maid, who worked sixteen hours a day, received only her food in exchange and relied on tips from the guests to feed her illegitimate child. Charles and Elizabeth were kept on a diet of watery soup, a little pasta, dry rye bread and very salty olives – though they later discovered that the *Questura* had asked that they be well-fed, and paid extra so they could have wine with their meals. The small amounts of coffee and sugar that they had brought with them were whisked away and never seen again.

The boarding house consisted of six rooms, which contained various stateless, near-penniless and temporarily homeless people including two Egyptian families, a retired sailor and a pregnant girl who did not dare go back to her parents. Most of them were at liberty to come and go, and some had jobs. For the internees, there was nothing to do but read, and catch fleas on a bar of soap. The fleas were regularly displayed to the landlady, but she was not impressed. The four-year-old daughter of one of their fellow-guests used to stand at the door of their tiny room and stare at them with her mouth open. When Elizabeth and Charles could no longer stand her they would shoo her away, whereupon the child would dissolve into uncontrollable sobs.

Soon both Charles and Elizabeth were suffering badly from the lack of fruit and vegetables. The Austrian landlady made it plain that things might get better if Elizabeth or Charles offered her something to sell, preferably jewellery; but it was obvious that only she would benefit from the deal, so they declined. They had some French francs, but the landlady's husband was unwilling to give Charles more than fifty lire for a one-thousand-franc note. One day Charles took matters into his own hands: he forced his way into the kitchen, and seized two tomatoes and a hard-boiled egg, which he and Elizabeth ate while the landlady screamed at them. They then found out the food belonged to the mother of the four-year-old girl, who had bought them for her child: Charles's moment of defiance turned into one of abject apology. Things only improved when Charles began climbing over the partition that separated their room from the kitchen. He made a key to the pantry door from bent wire. 'We had a meal in our room every morning before [the maid] came down at six o'clock. Even so, by the evening we were usually feeling the want of food.'[6]

By the time they were into the third week of their internment there was still no news from Rome, and their repeated requests to see the American Consul were ignored. Elizabeth decided she could take it no longer. Poor food, claustrophobia and anxiety had already undermined her health, but now her acting talent was employed to make her appear seriously ill.

'Early next morning she awakened the household by a series of piercing shrieks, and as soon as enough witnesses arrived, rushed downstairs in her nightgown. I caught her in my arms at the door and called for help. Signor Pulfer helped me carry her to our room. I wrung my hands in despair . . . Caroline stayed in her bed, staring at any visitor with unseeing eyes, and repeating *The Golden Journey* in a tedious monotone.'[7] Charles told the landlady that he could not be responsible for her actions. She was in such a state that she might run out into the street or even smash up the hotel. Elizabeth's acting on this occasion seems to have been very convincing, for soon after they were told that they were to go to Rome. However, they were not allowed to reclaim any of the papers that had been confiscated, and the boat was to stay in Messina.

They were handed over to two young guards and put on a train, and by nine the following morning they were in Rome. Here they were handed over to another two guards, and told they were going to Venice – after which they would be free to go.

This sounded too good to be true, and it was. In Venice they were taken to the police station and questioned, and to Elizabeth's dismay, Charles was then taken away and locked up in an underground small cell with twenty-four other men while she had to wait in an office. They had had almost nothing to eat for two days. Elizabeth threw a scene in the middle of the afternoon, and was brought a plate of macaroni.

The train for Trieste did not leave until eleven that night, and Charles managed to persuade their Venetian guards that it would be very sad if Elizabeth were to leave their beautiful city without seeing anything of it. After some discussion, the guards agreed. There would be plenty of time to walk them through the Piazza San Marco. Charles had seen it for the first time the previous winter, with Mike Cumberlege, and now he wanted to show it to Elizabeth.

As they walked though the Piazza with their guards, Charles happened to see an acquaintance dining at Florian's, and managed to borrow some money. With it he was able to treat Elizabeth and the guards to dinner in a restaurant where, according to Charles, they drank a straw-covered flask of sweet white Chianti and Elizabeth ate her first *calamaretti*. They took a gondola to the railway station. One of the guards hoped they would come back when the war was over, and gave Charles his address.

Trieste had recently been bombed by the British, which was perhaps why Charles and Elizabeth were both locked up in the cells – but at least they were given a cup of coffee and some bread. The foul smell and scurrying vermin banished any thought of sleep, and Elizabeth was grateful for the company of a couple of prostitutes who were thrown in with her in the course of the night, and kept her supplied with cigarettes.

For the month they had been in custody in Italy they had continually tried to get in touch with a representative of the US Embassy. Finally in Trieste, with the help of the Yugoslav Consul, a meeting was arranged. The American Consul agreed to pay for their tickets as far as Zagreb; and after a few more hours in the cells, they were put on a train to Yugoslavia.

It was 29 June. They had spent nineteen days interned in Italy, and had lost almost everything. Charles was particularly upset about his typewriter, his notebooks and his manuscripts. Elizabeth mourned the loss of her collection of recipes, built up over the years till it was far fatter and more comprehensive than the book she had given her friend Marian as a wedding present. They were both run down and unwell, particularly Elizabeth: but at least they were out of Italy.

They crossed the Yugoslav border and, after several hours, the train stopped at a junction where Charles and Elizabeth were taken to a police station and questioned. The police roared with laughter at their adventures in Italy, and plied them with glass after glass of a fiery liquor made of plums. They were also given some sausage, and a great plate of sauerkraut. But their stomachs were weakened and quite unable to cope with such rough sustenance. They were both violently sick, and were still feeling very ill when they reached Zagreb. They spent three days in rainswept Zagreb, shivering in their thin clothes and drinking black beer, while the British Consul sorted out their visas and train tickets. When all was done they boarded the train, and on 2 July 1940, they reached Athens.

Elizabeth found several letters waiting for her, mostly from her family. There was also one from Norman Douglas.

3 June 1940. Dearest Liz . . . No particular news here. It is
barely 10 p.m., but this Glacier is already quite deserted, and
the streets are pitch dark . . . I wonder where you are now? I
do hope you passed through the straits of Messina by daylight
and had no trouble with the Italians. They can be very disagree-
able. Won't write any more, as I am being kicked out. All chairs
on the tables. To Hell with them . . . Heaps of love to Charles,
and tell me what the Hotel Mistra is like.

Elizabeth felt homesick and very far from her family, but England
seemed impossibly remote and vulnerable on the other side of
occupied Europe. The Italians and the British had begun fighting
in north Africa and the Mediterranean, Stalin had occupied the Baltic
States and Romania was under German protection by mid-July. The
Germans evidently thought that England could be brought rapidly
to its knees. Elizabeth worried about her sisters, and begged Pris to
send her a telegram to say they were all all right. There seemed little
chance of Elizabeth getting home now, unless she travelled to South
Africa or India first. She did not have the energy, or the money, to
contemplate such a journey.

The terrible precariousness of their situation sank in. She and
Charles were stuck in the honking, crowded, ramshackle squalor
of Athens, struggling with an unfamiliar language and the Greek
alphabet. They had almost no money, no means of having it sent
out from England and Charles had to find a job – though the fact
that he was 'living in open sin' with a woman swiftly got around the
gossiping expatriate cliques in Athens. The British Council were
extremely unhelpful, and no school was prepared to consider him
in the post of teacher. Elizabeth loathed the petty hypocrisy of the
British community in Athens and, sometime later, Norman Douglas
reminded her that it had always been like that.

I am much annoyed to hear about the gossip at Athens, but of
course you don't care a damn. Send them all to hell, and tell
them so. Athens British community has always been known as

the most scandal-mongering brood in Europe. As they are
nearly all sodomites or lesbians you should have no difficulty
in answering back.[8]

But neither Elizabeth nor Charles could afford to antagonize anyone
who might put them in the way of work. When not seeking a job,
Charles joined Elizabeth in wandering around the sights. On a good
day, one of the rich and generous Greeks who kept huge yachts in
the harbour at Piraeus might give them lunch. The evenings were
whiled away at a place called Ekali's, where they drank brandy and
soda into the small hours. In a letter to a friend, Elizabeth said she
could not take much more of this sort of life without going mad.

Charles went from one job refusal to the next. Even freelance
press-work proved a dead end, since there were many well-
established stringers and the Athenian telephones were so tempera-
mental. Eventually, through a Greek friend, he found a job teaching
four pupils English on the island of Syros. He set off in mid-August,
and Elizabeth followed soon after. She had little alternative.

They settled in the village of Vari: a cluster of cottages overlooking
a beach of white sand and a little bay. Their cottage was 'a white
cube of a house, two box-like rooms and a nice large bare kitchen'.[9]
There was no bath and no plumbing, but a well and a fig tree stood
outside the front door, and a few steps further on was the Aegean
sea. The village contained about three dozen houses, two churches,
a shop and a taverna where the men sat outside at wooden tables.
The owner of the taverna was called Josipi, and it was he who
furnished the newcomers with sheets and pillows, cushions and
crockery for their house. His brother-in-law Yannaki was a charming
wheeler-dealer, who assured Charles and Elizabeth that he could
provide them with anything from pins to cars, cigarettes and South
African sherry.

It was not until the asphodels came out that Elizabeth began to
enjoy life on Syros, and put the misery of the past few months

behind her. She learnt how to rely on the ancient, basic foods of the Mediterranean. The only stores she had to bother with were bread, olive oil, olives, salt fish, hard white cheese, dried figs, tomato paste, rice, dried beans, sugar, coffee and wine.

She bought fish from the fisher boys: usually small fry or squid, with the occasional red mullet or langouste. Josipi, who had taken a shine to Elizabeth, often gave her vegetables and fruit from his garden. Eggs were cheap and plentiful, but meat was only available on feast days and consisted of pieces of roughly hewn kid, lamb or pork. Elizabeth described her diet as 'limited, but at least [it] presented none of the meal-planning problems which . . . daily plague the better-off English housewife'.[10] It was also while living in Syros that she discovered rocket, which she used to flavour potato soup instead of parsley.

While Elizabeth and Charles were adapting to this primitive Mediterranean idyll, Spitfires, Hurricanes and Messerschmitts were fighting it out in the skies above the south coast of England. When Goering realized that the battle in the air had been lost, he ordered an all-out bombing campaign on British cities. On 6 September, troops in the south-east of England were told to prepare for invasion. The following day the whole of London's dockland was on fire, and a few days later much of the East End had been reduced to rubble.

On Syros the days passed easily. Three times a week Charles walked the five miles to the village to give English lessons to his four pupils; while Elizabeth swam, read, tried (not very successfully) to learn Greek, kept house, and did her best to provide the English delicacies that Yanniki craved for. It was important to keep Yanniki happy, for he lent Elizabeth his donkey when she needed to go into Ermopoulos, the main town, seven miles away. It was here that she stocked up on beans and oil, cheese and wine, and the boxes of *loukoumia* (Turkish delight) that were a speciality of the island.

What Yanniki really wanted was Heinz tomato soup in tins, and piccalilli pickles. She managed to find four tins of the soup, for which she paid 'a bundle of drachmas that would have kept me in wine and cheese for a month'. The gift was much appreciated: 'in return I was offered baskets of eggs, lemons, oranges, freshly dug vegetables and salads, glass after glass of wine in the tavern'.[11] But Yanniki was still longing to try the celebrated English pickles, and it soon became obvious that he was expecting Elizabeth to make some for him.

And so it came about that Elizabeth found herself on a Greek island, making English pickles. 'Long mornings I spent cutting up cauliflower and onions, carrots and cucumbers. Afternoons, I squatted in my kitchen fanning the charcoal fires into a blaze brisk enough to boil the brew.'[12] She packed them into the only vessels she could get hold of, unglazed earthenware jars holding about three pounds. She didn't like it much, but her Greek friends were delighted. What impressed Elizabeth was that, on the barter system, she might have lived for free had she been prepared to devote her entire life to pickle-making. Elizabeth found that she had made herself a niche in the village community, if not its economy. She was given an emaciated, flea-ridden white kitten, to which she became very attached.

On 28 October the Italians invaded north-west Greece. Josipi was one of many friends who set off to fight that gruelling winter war in the mountains. The Italian advance collapsed a few weeks later, and by 21 November the Greeks were pushing them back into Albania. The mood of the country was triumphant, and in the tavern people hoped Josipi would be home for Christmas.

References to 'Christmas pudding' began to crop up, and Elizabeth realized that this was the next English delicacy she was expected to provide. As one might imagine, she went about it with her usual thoroughness. The beef kidney suet came straight off the carcass and had to be cleaned, skinned, shredded and chopped. Then she had to stone bunch after bunch of raisins 'each one sticky as a piece of warm toffee'. Having made the puddings she then had to think of a way to keep them immersed in boiling water for nine or ten hours. This was quite impossible on the two charcoal fires let into the wall of her primitive kitchen; but she managed to get the villagers to make her a haybox, and when the puddings were finally done, she was pleased with the result.

The optimism that had sprung up with news of the Greek victories in November began to fade as more and more German divisions massed in southern Romania. 'In the church at Christmas,' wrote Charles, 'the peasants prayed before a tinsel crèche in which the infant Jesus was protected by two lead Grenadier Guards. Caroline and I spent the morning in Josipi's garden, where the fallen oranges lay unburied on the ground.'[13] Later that day, they gave a party for the villagers. The famous puddings were consumed, but people were less enthusiastic about them than Elizabeth had hoped. The local raisins, the delicious candied citron made by her neighbours and the Athenian brandy with which the puddings had been liberally doused made them taste disappointingly familiar.

The cottage became increasingly cold and uncomfortable, and fuel was hard to come by. Elizabeth had little to do but write letters. She wrote to Robin Fedden, the writer and traveller whom she had met on her visit to Egypt two years before. He was still working as a lecturer at the University of Cairo, and he urged her to come out to Egypt. 'What I wonder are you planning to do? Do come here! We shall give you what I believe is called "a great reception" – especially me.'[14] Elizabeth did not answer the letter until 16 April 1941, ten days after the simultaneous invasion of Greece and Yugoslavia by the Germans. Charles is not mentioned, as if she had already written him out of her life.

'My dear Robin, I eventually received your letter – in January I think it was – I should have answered it before, but letter-writing seems futile nowadays . . .' She went on to describe her life by the sea with the soothing sound of the waves, and how much she had detested Athens. 'I should like to get to Egypt but I really don't see how it is possible, particularly since the latest development here.

On the other hand don't be surprised if I should suddenly turn up, looking rather wild and probably dressed in rags (that's more or less the state in which I arrived in Athens) after some further ludicrous adventure. In that case I hope I shan't find that you have left Cairo the day before for some un-get-at-able country . . . With much love, Elizabeth.'

On 27 April the Germans marched into Athens, and the following day Syros was bombed. Elizabeth and Charles hastily gathered together as much as they could, and managed to pay their way on to a fishing boat bound for Crete. Elizabeth had to leave her white cat, and grieved for it like a child: its loss seemed to concentrate all the sadness and fear and uncertainty of being a refugee again.

The journey to Crete began on 29 April, and the following day they saw land. They thought it was the island of Sikinos, some eighty kilometres to the south and almost a third of the way to Crete; but unfortunately the pilot had lost his bearings, and the island ahead was actually Mikonos – thirty kilometres due east, in completely the wrong direction. A small mutiny ensued and Charles took the tiller.

They reached Heraklion, the main city of Crete, on 2 May. Here they found Mike Cumberlege, now working with Special Operations Executive (SOE). He was the skipper of a caique, one of those traditional fishing boats that plied their way among the islands of the eastern Mediterranean. This caique was called *Dolphin*. She looked innocent enough, but was armed with four anti-aircraft guns and had a two-pounder gun in the bows. Mike and Nick Hammond, a classical scholar, were reconnoitring possible landing places on the south coast of Crete: both for stores, and for smuggling agents and troops on to the island after the Germans had taken it. This could only be a matter of time.

Charles devoted the last section of *The Voyage of the Evelyn Hope* to a dramatic account of their escape from the island. It tells of how they saw Knossos before the great German parachute invasion began on 20 May, how they were caught on the edge of that terrible battle, how they made their way in an army lorry to Suda Bay on the north coast only to find that the evacuation of civilians was over, how they then had no choice but to turn south and stumble over the mountains – strewn with dead and wounded soldiers – to Sphakia, where at last they were able to scramble aboard one of the last of the Royal Navy warships evacuating the New Zealand, British and Australian troops. This makes out that they escaped on the night of 31 May. The structure of the book needs a dramatic climax, for it is in the course of this final section that Charles and 'Caroline' admit that their relationship is over; although the author implies that their shared experiences of internment, an idyllic Greek island and war have only deepened their friendship. After the book was completed Charles wrote, 'I did not see any shape for *The Voyage of the Evelyn Hope* until Crete suddenly provided me with a climax . . .'[15]

What actually happened was rather more prosaic. They spent a dozen days on Crete, by the end of which the island was undergoing fairly heavy nightly bombing, but they managed to leave on one of the many civilian convoys that were organized at the time. The embarkation permit for 'Mr and Mrs Gibson Cowan' is dated 14 May, and they arrived in Egypt on 16 May 1941. This was four days before the Germans began the massive parachute-born invasion which, after a week of bitter fighting, was to leave them in command of the island.

* * * * * * * *

CHAPTER SEVEN

Alexandria

Elizabeth's first glimpse of Egypt on 16 May 1941 was not encouraging. The great port of Alexandria was filled with warships and other vessels damaged in the evacuation of Crete. The quayside, where the refugees disembarked, was piled high with crates. Milling around them were dusty trucks, gangs of Egyptian dockworkers in their faded blue and white *gallabeias*, and everywhere, soldiers in khaki. The bright red caps of the military policemen blazed out of the mass. The smell of dust and petrol hung heavy, yet from almost anywhere in Alexandria, there was a glimpse of the sea.

From Alexandria Charles and Elizabeth travelled by train to Cairo, which was now the centre of operations for a theatre of war that included the Mediterranean, the Middle East as far as Baghdad, and the north African coast as far as Tunis. The city was ringed with garrisons, and every hospital, street and cinema was filled with Allied troops. The young King Farouk and his government chafed at the way they had been brushed aside to make way for the war, the way the British decreed and commandeered and expected them to fall loyally into line. Entrepreneurial Egyptians, however, welcomed the opportunity. They profited greatly from the situation, as did the naturalized Greeks and Levantines who made up much of the small-business community. Rents soared, new cafés and bars opened, the red-light district flourished, and everyone wanted to help the Allied soldiers spend their pay.

Charles and Elizabeth were lodged at one of the largest refugee hotels – the Luna Park. It boasted a certain amount of plush and gilding on the ground floor, but the rooms above were as small and bare as prison cells. Lawrence Durrell, who had arrived in Egypt from Crete two weeks before with his (first) wife Nancy and their baby daughter Penelope, predictably called it 'Lunatic Park' and spread the rumour that it had been a brothel.

Elizabeth had reached the end of the road with Charles, and yet she lacked the emotional energy to leave him when she felt so vulnerable. For days she was desolate and miserable, yearning for her little white house by the sea, unable to face the task of rebuilding her life in a cacophonous dusty city from which she might be hounded yet again. The authorities, who had a policy of getting civilian women out of the way unless they had secretarial qualifications, tried to put her on a ship to Bombay. This pushed Elizabeth into revolt. She was not afraid of making a scene, and no one in a khaki uniform was going to bully her into going to Bombay. When she started looking for a job and a place to live, she found that the city was filled with refugees like herself, all searching desperately for the same things. Yet Elizabeth did have friends in Cairo: the Goodwins, with whom she had stayed three years before, and Robin Fedden, who gave her the 'great reception' he had promised. Using her few contacts she soon found a job working in the naval cypher office in Alexandria. Her excellent French and good German no doubt proved an advantage.

The early summer of 1941 was a time of great anxiety. Rommel, who had arrived in north Africa in February, had forced the Allies all the way back into Egypt. In Britain, London was undergoing ferocious bombardment – three thousand people had died on the night of 10 May.

Elizabeth's first weeks in Alexandria were spent in a dismal little pension, and her job as a cypher clerk meant long hours and not much pay – but at least it was a job. She bought herself some clothes, having left Greece with little more than what she stood up in, and looked about for somewhere to live. She landed on her feet thanks to Mike Cumberlege, who had repeated his trick of turning up whenever Elizabeth arrived in a new place. 'I had run into him in the street in Alex,' wrote Elizabeth years later to her god-daughter Frances Fedden, 'and he had asked me to keep house for him in an absurdly grandiose apartment he had got hold of – there was even a bar made entirely of mirror glass.'[1]

Cumberlege's flat in the rue des Pharaons had one disadvantage. Its size and scale attracted almost everyone passing through Alex. Elizabeth never knew whether to expect five or twenty-five for dinner, and impromptu parties seemed to take place several times a week. All this did wonders for Elizabeth's social life, although in time it became very expensive – particularly since Mike was often away. He was a vital link, bringing stragglers off Crete under the noses of the Germans, and running in SOE officers and members of Cretan resistance groups.

The first cook Elizabeth and Mike employed was called Anastasia. She cooked very grand dishes like boned stuffed duck in aspic, dressed like a duchess and cheated her employers. She soon found herself in trouble with the military police for handling stolen goods from an Australian supply depot.

Anastasia was replaced by Kyriacou, of whom Elizabeth had far fonder memories. Kyriacou had once been a sponge diver, and suffered from the disease that affects many divers. It took the form of a sudden, agonizing pain in his right arm that forced him to drop anything he was carrying. Even this disability could not account for the amount of teapots he broke – Elizabeth eventually discovered that his way of making tea was to put the teapot directly on the gas burner.

She was working erratic hours based on naval watches, and often did not get back from work till early in the morning. This never prevented Kyriacou from waking her up to show her the contents of his shopping basket. '*Fresco*, Madame, *fresco*,' he would coo to her with pride, dumping his market haul of live fish, crabs and crayfish on to her bed.[2] Elizabeth did not complain about her working

86

hours; but the long periods she had to spend reading put a terrible strain on her eyes. 'I think perhaps it's the long hours working by electric light that make my eyes ache so bad – I have temporarily given up reading outside the office.'[3]

Since both she and Mike Cumberlege were at work all day, Kyriacou took it upon himself to organize much of their social life. He rang up those of their friends he liked best and would invite them to dinner, and not unnaturally, the people he liked were Greek-speaking or involved in the Greek cause. Then came the happy day when he heard that his wife and children had arrived safely in Palestine. Kyriacou invited all their friends and cooked a stupendous dinner to celebrate, the highlight of which was an octopus stew. 'With passionate concentration he prepared it, and I watched him build up in a deep pot a bed of thyme branches on which to lay a huge quantity of onions, tomatoes, garlic, bay leaves and olives, and then the octopus. Gently he poured red wine over his carefully constructed edifice, stirred in the ink from the fish, and left his covered pot to simmer for the rest of the afternoon.'[4] (A version of this recipe appears in Elizabeth's *Book of Mediterranean Food*.)

In July 1941, Elizabeth sent Charles a clipping she had cut out of the Egyptian *Gazette*, which advertised for a diesel engineer and sailors. Charles applied, and on 1 August 1941, he joined the *Samothrace* as bosun. Elizabeth came to say goodbye to him on the 4th, and brought him a present: the much-read copies of *Alice's Adventures in Wonderland* and *Through the Looking-Glass* that she had had as a child. They had accompanied her through all their adventures, and she described them as 'the most precious possessions of my childhood'. The following day, she wrote him a letter:

> We'll both think often of the things we have done together, of
> the canals and the wine and the red rocks of my beloved France,
> of the sea white with nautilus off the coast of Corsica, of dawn
> in the Bay of Naples, of a certain lobster mayonnaise we ate

87

between one life and another, of mountains of golden oranges in Joseph's garden and those purple islands lying all around us from the top of the hill behind our hovel. Thank you for the lovely experiences you have given me and remember that you made the Isles of Greece more than just a beautiful name for both of us and that these things can be done again.

Charles copied these words into his personal log, with no comment. But when the time came to prepare the dedication for *The Voyage of the Evelyn Hope*, he wrote TO E.G. WITH ALL MY LOVE, followed by the lines just quoted – though he changed the word 'hovel' to 'house'.

Charles had begun the war as a pacifist, but the 'burning convictions' he had held were wearing thin and he wanted to play an active part after all. There was no question of his joining any regular unit of the British Army in Egypt: at thirty-eight he was too old, and too much of a bohemian. One of the reasons he had joined the *Samothrace* was that it was eventually bound for England, where he hoped there might be something for him to do. That wish did not materialize. August 1942 found him in Kenya where he became Port Welfare Officer in Mombasa, and two years later, he was taken on in an official capacity as Chief Advisory and Instructional Pilot, Eastern Mediterranean. He and Elizabeth kept in touch, and Elizabeth's letters to him tell much about her life in Alexandria.

Many people passed through the flat and her life, but the closest friend from this period came through Robin Fedden. He had given Elizabeth a letter of introduction to a girl with whom he was very much in love called Renée Catsaflis. Her mother was Italian, her father an Alexandrian Greek of great charm. She was brought up a Catholic and went to school in France, and from a very early age displayed an iron integrity. In confession one day, the priest asked her to promise not to repeat the sin she had just confessed. Renée said that since she almost certainly would commit that sin again, there was no point promising. The priest warned her that in that case, she could not receive absolution and would therefore be unable to take communion. Renée walked out, and never took communion again.

She had a passion for mountain climbing and walking, which held no charms for Elizabeth; but they were both great readers, and Elizabeth recognized in Renée the same uncompromising honesty and strength of character she had herself. They became very close. On Elizabeth's day off they would make a picnic, and spend the day at the beach.

Renée introduced Elizabeth to Max Bally, a White Russian who had ended up in Egypt after the Revolution. He was an excellent tennis player and something of a playboy. Elizabeth was dazzled – although she took care not to show it, and spared him none of her forceful opinions. 'I do hope,' he wrote after one dinner, 'I will be allowed to reopen our spirited discussions on such grave war problems as the one which produced such eloquence the other evening! And please God, the duck will not have been killed by a landmine this time.'[5]

Elizabeth admitted that 'I was rather taken with Max myself, but he was only interested in Renée.'[6] In fact Renée, at this time, seems to have rather enjoyed the havoc she was causing. In September 1941, Robin Fedden came to Alexandria. 'His arrival was the signal for a series of parties and picnics,' wrote Elizabeth to Charles. 'Robin and Mike started by getting on very well but it didn't last and with Renée doing a butterfly dance between the two of them the situation was rather delicate . . .'[7] It was made worse for Elizabeth by the fact that Robin blamed her for not keeping a closer watch on Renée.

Reassuring news at last arrived from Norman Douglas. He had left Antibes for Portugal, where at her suggestion he had got in touch with her cousin Neil Hogg, who was working for the British Embassy. Neil was a cultivated man who enjoyed Norman's company: they shared a flat in Lisbon, and when Neil was posted back to London at the end of 1941, Norman went with him.

*

The flat on the rue des Pharaons eventually became impossible. So many people were dropping by or using it as a temporary base, and leaving their boxes and tin trunks behind, that it became like a hotel – and a bar, and a restaurant. At the same time, prices were rising every week, and Mike Cumberlege was spending more and more time away on secret operations in the Mediterranean. Towards the end of the year Elizabeth gave it up, and found a tiny flat on her own. When she moved in, the flat was filled with hideous heavy furniture and the walls were covered with dark brown wallpaper. All the furniture, except for bed, bookshelves and a divan, was relegated to the attic, and the whole flat was painted a light cream colour. 'It is thrilling to have my own flat again, and occasionally buy an ashtray or a cushion cover, which to my doting eyes make the place look different.'[8]

She was not lonely, for it was almost impossible to be lonely in Alexandria at that time. 'Hardly a day passes when I don't run into some old friend or relation from England – I am now so used to being clapped on the back and greeted with the words "Hello Liz, I thought you were in an Italian prison camp," that I have ceased to be surprised.'[9] Quite apart from her friends in Alex, there were friends in Cairo and people were constantly shuttling between the two. 'Romney [Summers] is in the Army and has a flat in Cairo . . . The Durrells have a flat also and Larry has a job at the Embassy but is quite unchanged and as amusing as ever . . .' She also enjoyed the company of Professor Robin Furness, who headed the English Department of Cairo University. Elizabeth found him wonderfully restful and refreshing: 'Spending the afternoon with him is like going for a row in a Mediterranean harbour at dawn, after having watched a particularly noisy circus for weeks on end without stopping.'[10]

Elizabeth had always kept in touch with her sisters, and sent home silk stockings, cigarettes and coffee when she could. From Priscilla came parcels of clothes – Elizabeth was particularly grateful for her favourite coat – and bundles of letters. News from home was good.

Priscilla was very happy with her two healthy babies, and Diana had married a young doctor called Christopher Grey on 7 August 1941. 'The wedding was a furore by all accounts,' wrote Elizabeth to Charles. 'Diana wore Mummie's wedding dress and looked gorgeous so Pris says, and Bulgie was bridesmaid, and the family turned up in force and there was a mob of Diana's disappointed boyfriends swooning around the buffet.'[11]

Her great friend Marian Butterworth also married that year, and moved into a house in Lincoln Street, Chelsea. Elizabeth did not much like her husband, whose name was Peter Thomas – which was almost inevitable, because Elizabeth usually disliked the people who married her close friends. 'I do hate all these things going on and me not there to see – and in a way I suppose I have always had the idea that I would like to share a flat or a house again with Marian. It no doubt sounds odd to say such a thing of one's girlfriends but I do feel that there was something between us that was very valuable in my life and hers too I think . . .'[12] But Marian was involved in her domestic life and longing for a baby, and not much good at writing letters. For quiet, intimate friendship with another woman, Elizabeth turned to Renée.

Elizabeth was now a part of that curious middle-class English-speaking society abroad that the war had spawned. She did her bit, worked in canteens set up for servicemen, and for a while she went to dance once a week with the sailors at the Under Twenty Club: 'It makes me feel like a grandmother, but wonderful exercise,' she wrote to Charles.[13] Among the women working as secretaries or cypher clerks for the British authorities, many had, like Elizabeth, fled from occupied Europe, and most were under thirty. So were the young officers in uniform, back for a few brief days of leave. These young men longed for female company: just to walk and talk with a woman was to remember a happier, less violent world, and the women – knowing the men might be dead the following week – were generous with their companionship. They had no children to worry about, no old aunts and neighbours to disapprove of how they spent their time. No wonder that in dimly lit restaurants and nightclubs, and in the rented rooms of once-sumptuous art-deco flats and crumbling *belle époque* palaces, buttons had a way of coming undone.

In that winter of 1941, Elizabeth met an officer in the 9th Lancers called Peter Laing. He had been educated in England, though his family had settled in Canada. When they met, Elizabeth was enjoying her independence too much to want an intense romance, and no doubt Laing felt the same. They had what they liked to think of as an uncomplicated friendship, but soon their feelings for each other began to run deeper than either wanted to admit. They corresponded during the spring and summer of 1942 while he was at the front, and saw each other when he came back on leave to Alexandria. 'I often look forward to getting back to Alex,' he wrote. 'Two hot baths in succession, a complete do at the barber's shop on the first floor of the Cecil, the luxury of the pâté at the Union Bar and many other things beside.'

The war was now entering a critical phase. Rommel had forced the British back into Egypt; but he was on the end of a supply line that went all the way back to Tunisia, and in July 1942 he was stopped at El Alamein. At this point the Germans were caught in a natural bottleneck between the sea to the north and, to the south, the Qattara Depression: an immense dip in the desert floor that was impassable to tanks.

Nevertheless, the unseemly haste with which the British withdrew eastwards in front of the Germans caused considerable unease in Alexandria. Most people did not really start to panic until late June, and the general hysteria came to a head on 1 July, a day which became known as 'The Flap'. Elizabeth came back to her flat to find it being dismantled by her dour Albanian cook, who was convinced that the Germans were already in town. It was a day of mass exodus, of frightened crowds of women and children surging into the railway stations, streets blocked with cars piled high with mattresses to protect them from air raids. The British authorities urged calm and restraint, while behind the scenes they were burning their confidential papers as fast as they could.

On 2 July, Elizabeth's office and all its employees – including herself – were transferred to Port Tewfik in the Canal Zone. Out in the desert, Rommel attacked the fortified positions of El Alamein again and again, but he failed to break through. For the rest of July he was on the defensive, while General Auchinleck (who had taken personal command of the battle from the end of June) kept up the pressure with repeated counter-attacks.

Elizabeth, meanwhile, was not well. She had developed an infection in her feet which flared up and died away again, but seemed to get no better. She was still in Port Tewfik, where her office was housed in a troopship, when she received a letter from Peter:

24 July [1942]. My dear Liz – I've gone and got myself in hospital, though with nothing at all serious . . . I contrived to get a pick head driven into my neck, but it has not really impaired my inefficiency in anyway. I got into Alex for one hour on the 29th but you must have left . . . Drop me a line when you have time, Liz, and look after yourself. Love, Peter.

Her reply was robust, to say the least.

PSTOE, Fleet Mail Office, Port Tewfik. I have never heard such a lot of nonsense in all my life – what with pickaxes stuck in your head and bits of shrapnel in your ear you must be in a pretty state . . . I am quite happily settled in a borrowed bungalow on the seashore a few miles out of Suez and living in surprising harmony with three other girls from the office. The whole thing is marred by the fact that we are obliged to keep trailing into the office to work, but otherwise the arrangement is excellent. We sleep outside and listen to the waves, and find heavenly release from the eternal flies and

hellish heat of Suez . . . The new Marx Bros. film has by some
sort of miracle arrived here and I'm going to see it tomorrow
and it's the most exciting thing that has happened almost since
I can remember.

In time Peter recovered from his wound and went back to his unit,
but the infection in Elizabeth's feet got steadily worse. She was in
bed for three weeks in Port Tewfik, but that remedy failed and her
walking was now seriously impaired. Nevertheless, she followed her
office on its next move, to Cairo. She took a room in the Continental
Hotel and hoped she would soon be mobile enough to look for a
flat. By now one of her feet was almost right again – but the other
was not improving, and she felt ill and exhausted.

She went to Alexandria on leave, and stayed with her friend
Georges de Menasce. The Menasces were one of the oldest and
wealthiest Jewish families in Alexandria, and Georges was a friend
of Stella's and the Goodwins, who had been Elizabeth's hosts in
Egypt before the war. Georges's passion was music. He was an
excellent pianist, and often gave concerts in his house – although
he always played from behind a screen. In his villa, Elizabeth was
ensconced in luxury; but her bad foot now became so inflamed that
she had to be taken to hospital, where it was operated on. Georges
de Menasce looked after her as though she were one of his family.
He kept Elizabeth in Alexandria for ten weeks, arranged for her to
be treated by his own doctor, and would not allow her to pay the
hospital bill. Elizabeth was grateful: not only for all her friend's
help, but also for giving her the rest she so desperately needed.

She returned to Cairo in the autumn of 1942, where the big event
among her friends was the wedding of Robin Fedden to Renée.
They were married on 3 October, but Elizabeth was still not mobile.
'I am quite unable to walk at all,' she wrote to Norman Douglas on
3 November, 'and I have had to give up my job [with the naval
cypher office].' Yet she could not afford to remain unemployed for
long, and it was Renée – then working with the publicity section

of the British Embassy – who provided the helping hand. 'I needed a job,' wrote Elizabeth, 'and she introduced me to a Canadian called Arnold Smith ... He needed a typist, but my typing was too rudimentary for him so he gave me a job in the newspaper section.'[14]

The newspaper section had started with an Arabic publication called *Akbar el Harb*, 'The Great War', and its purpose was to convince the Arabs that the Allies were going to win it. The office grew as other propaganda newspapers, in Greek, Amharic, Persian and even Serbo-Croat, were set up for distribution throughout the Middle East. Elizabeth had no time to describe what her job entailed in her letters to Charles, but she did say that the work was considerably more interesting and that she was no longer working the inhuman hours that the Navy cypher office had demanded.

That summer, General Bernard Montgomery replaced Auchinleck as commander-in-chief of the 8th Army. Since the winter of 1940, successive commanders had been obliged to spread their forces and equipment over three continents, with supplies and reinforcements constantly lagging behind requirements. By the time Montgomery arrived the war was focused in north Africa, and he could allow himself a period of planning, rearming and re-equipping the 8th Army such as Wavell and Auchinleck had only dreamed of.

On the night of 23 October, a thousand British guns opened fire on the Germans. The battle which was to drive Rommel out of north Africa had begun – but even the bullish Montgomery had never pretended it was going to be easy. Out of a total Allied strength of 220,000, losses numbered about a thousand a day.

One of the casualties was Peter Laing, whose jeep was blown up by a land mine at Mersa Matruh in November. His legs were very badly damaged. He was taken to Cairo and installed in the 63rd General Hospital, where first one leg and then the other had to be amputated. 'I have been a certain amount in the hospitals in Alex seeing friends at various times,' wrote Elizabeth to Charles in early

1943, 'but I haven't come in contact before with the badly wounded and have been completely shattered by the spectacle, and am helpless and hopeless in the face of such loathsome suffering and such fantastic courage.' Over Christmas with Robin and Renée, who had a house out by the pyramids, she visited Peter as often as she could. Elizabeth was in turmoil, for as soon as he was well enough Peter would be moved back to Canada. She knew that she was not the sort of woman who could nurse him through what was obviously going to be a long convalescence, and he did not press her: it was not within the terms of their resolutely 'unemotional' relationship.

They saw each other often in the weeks before he boarded the ship for Canada. He was back in Toronto in mid-April 1943. 'I have been more than a trifle busy,' he wrote on 10 May, 'with scores of relations that seem to infest this town. Most of them I have never seen before and two are clergymen, can you imagine . . . I miss your cooking very much, as everything served out here is very much men's food. You know, big clean vegetables, big clean steaks, big white clean potatoes washed down with a big white clean glass of milk. It lacks the savoury tang of the corrupt Orient . . .' Elizabeth also received a letter from his mother. 'He wrote to me at the time and told me how good you had been, bringing books, cakes and all manner of good things to amuse and divert . . . It was such a comfort to me to learn that he had even one visitor and especially a woman, for I had pictured him lying there with no friends to cheer and encourage him . . . so his news of your visits gladdened my heart greatly.'

Within two years both Peter and Elizabeth would be married to other people, but they kept in touch, and never forgot each other. When Peter came to England with his wife Kathleen McConnell, they sometimes visited Elizabeth in Halsey Street and she never failed to send them her latest book. Many years later, she gave her nephew Rupert Grey an introduction to Peter while he was travelling around Canada. Peter talked a great deal about Elizabeth. 'She gave me back the will to live,' he told Rupert. As for Elizabeth, in later life her regrets were reserved for another man; but in the list of bequests attached to her will she wrote, 'In a box on my dressing table . . . is a pair of heavy gold cuff links with the initials E.G. and P.M.L. These were made in Cairo for a man called Peter Laing who thought he was in love with me, and I with him . . .'

* * * * * * * *

CHAPTER EIGHT

Tony David

In the spring of 1943 the Germans were in full retreat back towards Tunis, and by mid-May the north African campaign was at an end. In Cairo, this meant that the enormous military bureaucracy had to be scaled down and restructured. One of the results was that responsibility for the propaganda office in which Elizabeth worked was removed from the Ministry of State and handed over to the Ministry of Information.

From its headquarters in Cairo, the Ministry of Information had to cover an enormous stretch of territory: from Tunisia to Persia and from Turkey to the Sudan. Officers and agents, experts and diplomats came and went in a constant stream, reporting to the Ministry on changes and conditions in countries all over the Middle East; and from this mass of data the Ministry dispensed information to its masters in Whitehall, to the military and, in varying degrees of fullness and accuracy, to the press.

It was decided that the time had come to start a reference library within the building, and Elizabeth was asked to set it up and run it. She leaped at the chance, and her bosses did not seem to mind that she had not the slightest qualification for the job. They no doubt saw a hard-working, intelligent young woman with an orderly mind and an eye for detail.

The office of the Ministry of Information continued to absorb new responsibilities as the military problems of the Middle East were replaced by political ones. A treasury official called Curteis

Ryan was appointed controller, and he came to Cairo with a small professional team. The office also changed premises: from an Edwardian villa in Garden City, to a soulless modern block facing the Anglican Cathedral. Elizabeth's reference library was housed on the ground floor, and was extremely well-run. A number of books were chosen by the Ministry of Information in London, 'who knew what was good for you'.[1] These included the usual works of reference and informative volumes on Egypt such as Sir Ronald Storrs's *Orientations* and the works of Lord Cromer. Elizabeth could also order books herself. There was a newspaper section too.

Thanks to her job, Elizabeth must have been one of the most well-informed people in Cairo. She had to keep abreast of all developments, both political and military, as reported in every newspaper, journal and magazine the Ministry could get hold of. She then had to index them: so that information on any topic, from production targets to Roosevelt's last speech, could be easily retrieved.

The library was open to anyone who needed information, but it was largely used by press attachés and war correspondents, who at various times included Alan Moorehead of the *Daily Express*; Alexander Clifford of the *Daily Mail*; Freya Stark, who had set up pro-Allied circles among the Arabs all over the Middle East called the Brotherhood of Freedom; Robin Fedden and others from the University of Cairo; and Lawrence Durrell, who ran the Information Office in Alexandria. At coffee time, the library also became a haven where colleagues gathered to laugh at and grumble about the bureaucratic pomposities of Mr Ryan, and Miss Glass, the tight-lipped registrar who sat just inside the entrance.

Roger Eland, who was in charge of *Akbar el Harb* and its satellite publications, remembers Elizabeth as very reserved, with rather severe and conventional clothes. These, combined with her heavy glasses, made her look like a quintessential librarian.

At the same time, there was another side to Elizabeth which those who saw only the librarian would scarcely have recognized. Her friend Christopher Kininmonth saw this naughtier, more rebellious side, and many years later he put a tiny vignette of her into his novel *Frontiers*: 'She laughed with her abrupt and vulgar cackle which contrasted with her speaking voice and her bloodstock kind of beauty. Her laugh brought her off any kind of pedestal one might have set her upon.'[2]

These two very different memories of Elizabeth give an indication of how she could compartmentalize her life; and in Cairo, a hotbed of rumour and gossip, people who were as reserved and secretive as Elizabeth took pains not to make themselves vulnerable. They changed, like chameleons, to blend in with whatever company they found themselves in. Yet whatever facet of herself she was projecting, Elizabeth was still grieving over Peter Laing – although she tried very hard not to think of him at all. All her energies went into her work and her friends, and somehow keeping herself on an even keel.

Cairo was a quieter place than it had been in the past two years, and sadder. So many friends had been wounded, killed or taken prisoner – yet life went on, as did the picnics and parties. Patrick Leigh Fermor remembers Elizabeth at one of them 'looking lovely in a sort of spangly *gallabeia*'. The journalist and seafood-lover George Lassalle, who was then working at GHQ Cairo, also remembered Elizabeth's 'brilliantly ornate ceremonial kaftans'. He never forgot an evening picnic with Elizabeth, Romney Summers and Robin Fedden, sailing lazily up the Nile. 'Romney, Elizabeth and I were reclining on cushions, sipping drinks, and Robin was prancing up and down like an elegant monkey in the rigging . . .'[3]

George Lassalle had ended up studying French at Oxford, after having tried and abandoned both forestry and law. He had been one of the six young patriots who had torn, from the minute book of the Oxford Union, the page which confirmed the motion that 'This House will not fight for King and Country'. He had joined the Sussex Regiment as a private, but was swiftly commissioned. In Cairo, he worked in GHQ for the intelligence service. Elizabeth was instantly attracted: he was light-hearted, charming, and like her he was pining for the life he had once known in the Greek islands. There was a raffish streak in George that Elizabeth found irresistible. He was already on his second marriage; but it did not stop either of them from launching into a companionable affair which, over the years, they were to leave off and pick up again whenever it suited them.

Elizabeth straddled many worlds in Cairo. Through Robin Fedden she had met Lawrence Durrell and Bernard Spencer, the poets who founded *Personal Landscape*, the most impressive poetry journal to come out of the war. They, like her, felt they were living in exile: not from England, but from Greece and the Graeco-Roman and Mediterranean world. Elizabeth was very fond of Durrell, with his verbal fireworks and his rumbustious company. They saw each other fairly often when she went to Alexandria. He had separated from his wife Penelope, but Durrell was not a man to stay single for long. In 1943, a year after he had moved to Alexandria as press attaché, Durrell had met Eve Cohen. She was to become his second wife, and much of her can be recognized in the character of Justine in the *Alexandria Quartet*.

Among Elizabeth's closest friends was the writer and traveller Patrick Kinross, who lived in the shadow of the Ibn Tulun mosque. He shared his flat with two other notable eccentrics: David Balfour, who had been a Greek Orthodox monk (known as Father Dimitri Balfour), and the scholarly diplomat Eddie Gathorne-Hardy. Through them and Robin Fedden, she would have been introduced to the world of British Council personnel and Cairo University lecturers. Unwilling to mix with the hearty polo- and cricket-players of the Gezira Club, the intellectuals and bohemians on the Cairo scene had colonized the Anglo-Egyptian Union. It was a far more democratic place than the Gezira Club, and in the tree-shaded garden they gathered to talk books, poetry and politics.

Among this set was the writer Olivia Manning, author of the Balkan and Levant Trilogies – six novels which, when completed in the 1970s, appeared under the title of *The Fortunes of War*. In these books Manning appears as Harriet Pringle, married to the irrepressible Guy Pringle. This character was closely based on her husband, Reggie Smith: an enthusiastic, bookish man who was intensely gregarious, and very promiscuous. It is possible that he was one of the many men with whom Elizabeth had casual affairs at this time.

Through her mother and the well-connected Goodwins, Elizabeth had friends among the grandest Egyptian families: wealthy British cotton brokers, businessmen and diplomats. Representatives from all these different circles could be seen at the parties given by Amy Smart, wife of the Oriental Counsellor Walter Smart. Amy Smart's parties combined everything that was most glamorous in wartime Cairo: dashing young SOE agents, visiting celebrities like Freya Stark or Cecil Beaton, travellers and intellectuals, as well as the most amusing and sophisticated of what Amy called '*la haute Juiverie, la haute Copterie, et la haute Mussulmanie du Caire*'. There was a cachet in being invited to Amy Smart's parties, and Elizabeth was invited every once in a while. This was an irritation to Olivia Manning, who resented the fact that she was not included on the Smarts' invitation list. She was a touchy, suspicious woman, who might have suspected Elizabeth of being one of her husband's innumerable girlfriends.

The pace of Cairo at that time was frenetic, particularly if one was a young working woman. Elizabeth was expected to be in her office by a quarter to nine, and she worked through till one. There was a long lunch break, with time for a siesta during the hottest part of the day, and people were back in their offices by four. They worked again until seven in the evening. There was just time to dash home for a shower and a change of clothes before going out again. There were not so many tanned young officers as there had been the year before, but there were still plenty of desk-bound ones with war-inflated ranks working in GHQ. A normal evening might well take in a bar, dinner on the rooftop of the Continental Hotel and afterwards a look in at Madame Badia's cabaret or the Auberge des Pyramides. Whisky and Indian gin were still plentiful. French wine had run out, but there was still plenty coming in from Palestine and Algeria.

Elizabeth found herself a tiny ground-floor flat, separated from the Nile by a busy road – part of what is now the Corniche. She always referred to this place as 'the cave', because it was so small and poky. The flat was reached by way of a car park, used by members of SOE and other clandestine organizations, whose nearby offices were known to all Cairene taxi-drivers as 'Secret House'.

Every foreigner with a flat, however humble, had a *suffragi*, an Egyptian or Sudanese servant who ran the household with varying degrees of efficiency. Elizabeth's first Cairene *suffragi* was called Abdul, who contrived to spill soup over her flatmate. After the departure of Abdul (and the flatmate) there was 'Hussein, who threw away the asparagus heads and served the stalks, alleging that that was the way the English liked them (and who was I to contradict him).' Hussein too went on his way. The next *suffragi* was called Suleiman, and Elizabeth soon realized that, as far as *suffragis* were concerned, she had struck gold.

He looked quite different from most people's cooks. His tarboosh was shorter and broader than that worn by other servants, and gave him a unique appearance; tiny eyes, a childlike expression and a rather tremulous smile combined to make him a most engaging figure. We conversed in French; he was very firm about the accounts and forced me to do them every day after lunch . . . For £5 a month he cooked, cleaned the flat, did the shopping, took my clothes to the cleaners, dealt with the *dhobi*, took shoes to be mended, brought a clean dress to the office if I had to go straight out to lunch, and in fact did everything for which in England one would employ a cook, a lady's maid, a butler and a housemaid.[4]

Helped by Suleiman, Elizabeth expanded her knowledge of Mediterranean food and entertained as often as she could. '[Elizabeth] was an enthusiastic and very skilful cook,' recalled Jim Richards, who had joined the Ministry of Information in Cairo in the spring of 1943 as Director of Publications. '[She] gave lunch parties every other Sunday after spending much of Saturday scouring the bazaars for the ingredients she wanted. Invitations to these lunch parties were eagerly hoped for.'[5]

The lunches, as Elizabeth was the first to acknowledge, were a joint effort between her and Suleiman, on fairly primitive equipment. They had a portable charcoal grill and two primus stoves, while a square tin box perched on one of the stoves served as an oven. Since there was no ventilation in the kitchen, every time kebabs had to be cooked Suleiman had to run through the sitting room in a cloud of smoke and set the charcoal grill out on the river bank. 'The charcoal, the open air, Suleiman's rather lavish hand with the herbs and seasonings, his devoted watch over the meat all combined to produce a marvellous flavour, even if occasionally the quality of the meat left something to be desired.'[6]

Suleiman also made ice creams, 'with the help of an ancient ice bucket, which made the most fearful clatter as he whirled the handle round. However, everyone was used to it since the old ice pail, like a lot of other equipment, did the rounds in wartime Cairo and everybody was used to talking above it.'[7] As for everyday food, Elizabeth lived on 'highly flavoured, colourful shining vegetable dishes, lentil or fresh tomato soups, delicious spiced pilafs, lamb kebabs grilled over charcoal, salads with cool mint-flavoured yogurt dressings, the Egyptian fellahin dish of black beans with olive oil and lemon and hard-boiled eggs – these things were not only attractive but also cheap'.[8]

Another who remembers her well from those days is Josette d'Amade, a young girl from a middle-class Egyptian-Jewish family who also worked at the Ministry of Information. Josette used to walk home from work with Elizabeth, who often talked of her days in Paris and of the Barettes. Josette was sometimes invited to her lunches, which were very unlike what she was used to at home. 'The other guests were usually men – one was an illegitimate cousin of King Farouk – and most were in uniform. I couldn't join in much of the conversation, which seemed very sophisticated, and I knew it was rude to stare; so I spent most of the time quiet as a mouse, with my eyes lowered . . ."[9] Josette, who had been brought up in a conventionally bourgeois family, had never met anyone like Elizabeth and found her an inspiration. Josette remembered Elizabeth saying that everyone should cultivate a measure of independence, in however small a way. On the other hand, her liberated attitudes were rather shocking to one who had been so strictly brought up.

Quite fortuitously, Josette had met Charles Gibson Cowan in Alexandria. She was staying with an aunt and uncle, and they had invited the skipper of a yacht in the harbour to dinner. Since he did not know the way, they walked the skipper back to the harbour at the end of the evening. They came on board, where Josette detected a delicious, lingering smell of something like coq au vin, which she immediately associated with Elizabeth. The cook turned out to be Charles. She told Elizabeth about the incident on her return to Cairo, and was amazed to hear that Elizabeth knew him well and that they had been together for the first two years of the war. Josette assumed they had been engaged. 'Good heavens, no!' laughed Elizabeth. 'I would never have *married* him.'[10]

Elizabeth and Charles had stayed constantly in touch since she had said goodbye to him in the summer of 1941. He had sent her the early chapters of *The Voyage of the Evelyn Hope* as he had written them, though there were certain passages she would not read. 'After Corsica you remember everything as well as I do,' she told him, 'and I don't want to think about it, talk about it or read about it ever again. From the minute we entered the straits of Messina until about the time the asphodels came out in Syros was just sheer torture.'[11]

Elizabeth was uneasy and confused about Charles. She wanted to think of him as a friend, but he was also part of an experience she was trying very hard to forget. She wished he would go away, without her having to spell it out – but instead he sent her long, entertaining letters, and presents from his travels around Africa: old coins, a silver bracelet (perhaps the one she is wearing in the photograph of her at her desk in Cairo), books, an African carving – even, on one occasion, two bottles of good French wine. Elizabeth thanked him warmly for these gifts, her gratitude tinged with guilt.

Her real feelings emerged rapidly in August 1943, when Charles announced he was back in Alexandria and would like to come and see her in Cairo. She immediately sent him a telegram[12] begging him to leave her alone, and followed it up with two letters.

> Please forgive me for what follows. Really and truly Charles I should prefer not to see you ... Two years ago I would not have had the courage to so wound somebody, but I have been so inexpressibly hurt and unhappy that I feel I cannot bear any more. I have changed very much and I never want to have anything more to do with my life of before the war. To see you would rake up hellish memories of Athens. Be kind and don't make it happen.
>
> After so many efforts I have met a man with whom I think I could be happy in a very unemotional way. I never want to feel a scrap of emotion for the rest of my life. He has been badly wounded and has gone away.

Her next letter was written along much the same lines, and she added

> It's not that I don't feel a great gratitude for the time we spent together, but I rather thought you had understood that it was over really before we ever came to Egypt. I have had two rather painful years since you left, but I think I have found the answer now, and I do absolutely dread any emotion or the reminder of the unspeakable miseries of Italy and Athens and the first weeks in Cairo ... I will never never return to the kind of existence I led before the war. I am a thousand times happier doing a job I love, living among my friends, than I was bashing

around the place never knowing where I should be next week. I have learnt to make up my mind for myself, and not be influenced by emotions.[13]

Charles respected her wishes and, later that month, joined a secret mission organized by the naval section of the American Office of Strategic Services (OSS). This operation took him, mostly by night, to a number of Greek islands – including Syros. 'I passed near enough to Josipi's to see that the lemons were already ripe,' he wrote in his log on 15 September. He also plucked a branch of the dry thorn they had used for kindling, and sent it to Elizabeth when he got back.

This memento, touching as it was, failed to rekindle Elizabeth. She resolutely turned her mind once again to her work, her friends and her lunch parties. Occasionally she went up to Alexandria, staying either with Georges de Menasce or with Eve Cohen and Larry Durrell at the Villa Ambron. They sometimes had Charles to stay too; though Elizabeth made sure they did not coincide.

In February 1944, Elizabeth met an Indian Army officer, Lt Col. Anthony David. Tony David was a small, fastidiously dressed man with kind eyes and a quick, diffident smile. Elizabeth found him attractive and she enjoyed watching the effect she had on him: this young Lieutenant Colonel from the Royal Deccan Horse had obviously never come across anyone like her before.

Tony David was the youngest son of Ivor David, who had been Inspector General of Police in Ceylon. He was born in 1911: ten years after his sister Yvonne, and nine years after his brother Richard. With such an age gap, Tony felt almost like an only child. His father had died in 1913, and his mother Beatrice moved back to Llandaff, where his father's family came from.

He was sent to Bradfield College in Berkshire, where he made friends with a boy called Owen Llewellyn. Owen was a few months older than Tony, who happily tagged along. Owen asked him home for the holidays, and Tony was delighted. For the first time in his life, he found himself in a noisy household full of children and dogs, and – best of all – the Welsh ponies bred by Mrs Griffith Llewellyn, Owen's mother.

This arrangement suited his own mother rather well. A young boy needed the company of other boys and men, and with the Llewellyns Tony would have it – leaving her with more time for her older children, and her own interests. Beatrice David was by all accounts a glamorous, cosmopolitan woman. She had no particular desire to be stuck in Wales with her husband's family, and escaped to Paris or Vienna whenever she could.

With the Llewellyns Tony learned to ride, taking to it naturally, and his happiest childhood holidays were spent with them. But while he was always willing to join in, he did not shine in a crowd. He was always on the edge of the circle.

After Bradfield Tony went to Pembroke College, Cambridge, in 1930. He had already decided on a career in the Army and so did not take an honours degree but an ordinary BA, specializing in history and military subjects. After taking his degree he applied to join the Indian Army, and went out to India in 1934 as an officer cadet attached to the First Battalion The Cameronians (Scottish Rifles). After this spell of service with a British regiment, each young officer spent a probationary period with the Indian regiment of his choice – in his case, the Royal Deccan Horse.

The fact that Tony had gone to Cambridge rather than Sandhurst automatically made him something of an outsider in the tight community of young officers. He soon developed a reputation as a chap more comfortable with women than with men, and his success with the opposite sex did little to endear him to his brother officers. There was also his dark wavy hair, and his name – in other words, the hint of an unspoken suspicion that he might be Jewish. Indian cavalry regiments were not renowned for their liberalism.

'We all tried to be nice to him, but he didn't fit in at all,' said one of his contemporaries. 'He just wasn't one of us.' No doubt Tony

1. Stella Gwynne, Elizabeth's mother, soon after her marriage in 1905
2. Rupert Gwynne MP, Elizabeth's father, c.1910
3. Wootton Manor, showing the main Jacobean part of the house with later additions by Detmar Blow

4. Elizabeth, aged ten, by Ambrose McEvoy (1878–1927)

5. Family group at Wootton, taken not long before Rupert's death in 1924: *clockwise starting with Rupert*:
Rupert, Elizabeth, Felicité, Stella, Diana and Priscilla
6. Stella and her daughters, late 1920s:
Felicité, Priscilla, Diana, Stella, Elizabeth

7. Elizabeth as an actress. On the reverse of this publicity photograph
she jotted down her details: '5' 6½"; Dark, fluent French and German.
Leeds, Oxford, Bournemouth, Seafield; Open Air Theatre 2 seasons.'
8. Charles Gibson Cowan. In his book *The Voyage of the Evelyn Hope*,
Caroline (Elizabeth) says: 'Never wear anything but a blue jersey and an old
pair of flannel trousers. Never wash the salt out of your hair . . .
Then perhaps I shall stay in love with you.'
9. Peter Laing, in the uniform of the 9th Lancers, *c*.1942
10. Norman Douglas. 'Always do as you please, and send everybody to Hell,
and take the consequences. Damned good Rule of Life. N.'

11 and 12. Elizabeth and Tony David:

twin portraits taken at the time of their marriage, Cairo, 1944

13. Elizabeth at her desk in the Ministry of Information, Cairo, *c.*1943.
The silver bracelet she is wearing may be one given to her by
Charles Gibson Cowan
14. Tony David at his desk in Cairo, 1943
15. Cairo group, 1944: Patrick Leigh Fermor, Denise de Menasce,
Patrick O'Malley (who married Lesley Pares) and Major Scott
16. Renée Fedden

felt it too. When he left in 1938, to be ADC to Sir Henry Craik, Governor of the Punjab, his brother officers were relieved. 'We knew he would never come back.'

In 1941, he transferred to the Indian Army Ordnance Corps: which, from a cavalry point of view, was a considerable step down, even if it meant accelerated promotion. He arrived in Egypt in July 1942, at the time of Alamein. A year later, in October, he was posted to GHQ Cairo. Here he met up again with Hermione – by now Lady Ranfurly – and Daphne Llewellyn, his friend Owen's younger sisters. Daphne was then working with SOE. Every morning Tony would pick her up from the Continental Hotel, where she lived, and gave her a lift to work in his car. He treated her with a sort of cosy protectiveness, as though she were a younger sister.

Despite his change of regiment, Tony never lost his passion for horses. He raced and played polo at the Gezira Sporting Club, exercised horses in the desert, and was a regular in a number of Cairene cocktail bars. He was often with a girl, the larger the better. He was particularly smitten by Miranda Lampson, the wild niece of Sir Miles Lampson, the British Ambassador in Cairo.

That this kind, rather uninteresting young man should have fallen head over heels in love with Elizabeth Gwynne is not surprising. He admired her fearlessness, her wit, her sensual beauty, the line of her long neck as she smoked or drank. She gave a sharp edge to life; and in her he saw the colour and the sparkle that he himself lacked. As for Elizabeth, her restless and abrasive character probably found his uncomplicated devotion rather restful. In one of his letters he recalled the first time she had rung him up. When he asked why, she had replied, ' "Just to talk." I think that's the first time I thought you considered me as more than just someone to pass away the time with, and I was so pleased.'[14]

Soon after that, Elizabeth came down with influenza. Tony came round to see her in the little ground-floor flat and asked if he could join her there. 'Thank God you were ill and didn't have the energy to say No,' he wrote later. So Tony moved in. She must have been quite fond of him because he came with a dog: a large, panting Alsatian called Bruce.

Her illness proved worse than influenza: it was a form of smallpox (fortunately too mild to leave scars) which was going around Cairo. Elizabeth was whisked away to a quarantine hospital in Kantara. Tony came to fetch her when she was eventually allowed out, and one of his happiest memories of her was as she ran down the path towards him.

In the spring of 1944, Elizabeth and Tony became a recognized couple on the Cairene social scene. Elizabeth's friend and lover, George Lassalle, sometimes used to borrow his Royal Deccan Horse mess-dress uniform because he liked it so much. But while George was swaggering about impressing the girls in Tony's dark green jacket and gold waistcoat, Tony and Elizabeth led a quieter social life. It would begin when he came to pick Elizabeth up in the evenings. 'When I came to fetch you,' he remembered, 'you used to look up and say in a very quiet voice, "Hello Tony." '[15] From there they would go for drinks at the Eugène or the Pickwick, where there was a gramophone, then on for shrimps at Hedjaki's, and from there to one of the little restaurants by the Nile. Daphne Llewellyn remembers seeing them in a crowd of people. Tony had eyes only for Elizabeth, but she paid very little attention to him. Back in the privacy of 'the cave', however, things were different. Tony's letters imply that their lovemaking was intensely satisfying for them both.

As the weeks wore on, it became increasingly likely that Tony would have to leave for Italy. They were in bed and asleep when the summons came, in the early hours of one morning in mid–May.

Elizabeth found herself alone with Bruce the dog, who was not perhaps the best memento of her lover. She had no alternative but to take Bruce to the office every day and, if invited out to lunch, she had to take the dog with her. Tony often found himself having to soothe Elizabeth's irritation, and excuse Bruce's bad behaviour. 'Sweetheart Bruce has *never* done that previously and I can only think his tummy must have been upset.'[16] Or, 'I know that hysterical yap of Bruce's well. It's slightly nerve-racking but shows he is devoted to you . . ."[17]

In Italy, Lt Col. David found that he was either worked to the point of exhaustion or – once the crisis had passed – left with almost nothing to do. Either way he missed Elizabeth cruelly and wrote to her once a day, if not more. One of the most poignant things he wrote to Elizabeth was 'You made me love coming home, a thing I have never done in my life. Everything was such fun. Do you remember cooking supper about two nights before I went, we had fried bananas, eggs, tomatoes, fried bread and bacon. I've seldom enjoyed a supper like it.'[18]

She made life utterly delightful, and he was startled by the intensity of his feelings for her – and his sexual jealousy. Elizabeth had made no secret of her previous affairs and had made no promises to Tony. She was not the sort of girl to sit at home and wait, and there were plenty of men waiting to take her out. Every letter from her, however affectionate, reminded him of these facts.

'I think it nothing short of rude, the three boys renewing their attentions the morning after I left,' he wrote. 'Don't lose your head over Jim Scott-Ellis and if you can hold out for longer than three months this time, for the first time in my life I should mind terribly – Is that an awful thing to say darling?'[19]

Tony became convinced that the only way to hold on to Elizabeth was to marry her. On 21 June, a month after they parted, Tony found out that he would be entitled to return to Cairo on leave in some six weeks' time. He plucked up his courage, and proposed:

'Elizabeth, please marry me darling and if you will, marry me when I come on leave. I want it more than anything else in the world . . . Your letter today was so sweet that I've just said to myself, "I'll try."'

He was in agonies the following day. 'I'm going to spend the most unpleasant fortnight of my life now until I get your letter in answer to mine of yesterday . . . You once said, "It doesn't matter what we do, I'm sure we'll do it well and enjoy it madly." We always did, didn't we and there was never a dull moment, even when you threw the work-basket at me.' (This was what happened on the one occasion Tony asked her to sew on a button.)

Tony's letter threw Elizabeth into turmoil. She knew that she did not really love him, and that he was not her intellectual equal. She did not even like the institution of marriage, which seemed deadening and claustrophobic. Yet she yearned for stability, and was also a pragmatist. It was a fact of her world that until a woman married, she had very little status; and once married, she could command a respect that was seldom granted to a spinster. If she did not accept Tony, who was at least kind and devoted, might she ever be asked again? All the women she felt closest to were married – her sisters Priscilla and Diana, her friends Marian, Doreen and Renée. If she did not join the clan soon, it might be too late. At the end of the year she was going to turn thirty-one. It was a sobering thought.

Her letter back to Tony was anguished, fretful and still undecided. 'Darling I can just imagine the state my letter put you into,' wrote Tony, 'because I do know quite well how madly you've always thought and fought against marriage . . . I know it was an awful thing to . . . spring it on you like that . . . but when I heard I really could come [to Cairo on leave] I just prayed and hoped you wouldn't mind . . . No darling I promise I won't refer to you in your presence as my wife.'[20] In another letter he also promised her that, if they ever went to India together, 'you won't have to flog the natives or watch polo – ever'.[21]

Elizabeth eventually accepted Tony, but everything was to be done in the greatest secrecy, 'with no squawking'. He wrote back at once, assuring her that they would be married in the very greatest seclusion. He begged her to ask Robin Fedden to arrange the calling of the banns: that was what took time, and he wanted that over by the time he came back so that they could be married at once.

In the days that followed, Elizabeth evidently grew more accustomed to the idea, to Tony's intense relief. 'I'm glad that you are happy about marrying me darling, and that you like my name and won't mind being Elizabeth David.'[22]

A few days later, Tony collapsed and was taken to hospital. He had gone to the doctor for sleeping pills, and had mistakenly been given a drug which produced a high fever and dysentery. He was in hospital for a good two weeks, during which time Elizabeth sent him a letter full of misgivings. She pointed out her faults and all her previous affairs, said she did not like the idea of India (apart from the fact that she could wear slacks there more often than in Cairo) and perhaps they should call the whole thing off. Tony lost his temper.

> Now listen, enough of this, whether you get a sensation out of informing me you are going to go to bed with someone or what I don't know, but I was stupid enough to tell you how much I minded once and I can't have these long-drawn dissertations on the reasons for your frailties in the past. I dislike them more than I can say even in the lightest vein, and it's no good saying, 'I thought you would much rather I was frank about it,' because I wouldn't . . . And what's more it is going to be a good idea if we get married. If we can live together in the cave for even the short time we did and not kill each other I think it's a good enough test . . . And you can quite well come to India for a short time and like it. It will be a novelty, and I certainly shouldn't dream of allowing you to wear slacks even if you want to . . . I can't think where you got the idea that the whole of India goes about in them . . .[23]

In Elizabeth's pocket diary for 1944 (a document she used only sporadically) there are no entries at all from 18 August, which was probably the time Tony came back. Perhaps she joined him when he took a few days' leave to visit his mother, who had now settled in Kenya; but they were back in Cairo at the end of August. On the 30th, which was a Wednesday, Elizabeth wrote '*Married*'. The civil service was about as quiet and simple as it could be, since none of Elizabeth or Tony's family were present. It is significant that no photograph of their wedding exists, or has survived.

They spent their honeymoon in Cyprus with relations of Tony's called the Grisewoods, and they were happy – or at least Tony was. After the honeymoon they moved back to Cairo, where Elizabeth resumed her job. In November, Tony was posted back to Italy.

He wrote every day: mostly the stuff of love letters, but one letter gives a vivid picture of their early married life. 'I'm longing to do things with you again,' he wrote on 18 November, 'to dance with you like we did at the Carlton, to go to parties and hear people say how nice you look, to stay at home and mix the drinks while you are giving some unfortunate hell in the kitchen for boiling the artichokes too long. And then to have you erupt from the kitchen and demand your drink as though you hadn't had one for a week, actually . . . having just returned five minutes ago from an hour and a half's solid drinking in our various bars.'

Elizabeth was resigned to domestic life with Tony. After all, many marriages had started with less and fared well, and the advantage of not being wildly in love was that she had fewer expectations. She could never have married Peter, of that she was convinced; and whatever Tony's shortcomings, he loved her wholeheartedly and exclusively. She had never had so much love before, and for the moment, her misgivings melted in its warmth.

Her family wished her well, though her sister Diana recognized that Elizabeth's marriage would never be as fulfilling as her own. 'I'm a little sad for her,' she wrote to her husband Christopher on 2 September. 'It's not a wild love affair on her part – but he sounds very nice, and she wrote to Mummie and said that they would be very happy – he adores her.'

Diana had never met Tony and so was prepared to give him the benefit of the doubt; but Elizabeth's friends in Cairo could not understand why she had married him. Renée Fedden made no secret of the fact that she thought the match a mistake, and Georges de Menasce remarked that Elizabeth marrying Tony was 'like a horse marrying a fish'. Hermione Ranfurly admitted that she knew Tony far better than Elizabeth; but she assumed the only reason for Elizabeth's decision to marry was that 'she needed a good ADC'. Tony was always only too happy to make himself useful, especially as her chauffeur: Elizabeth never did learn to drive.

Elizabeth was too perceptive not to be aware that many of the people she most respected were not impressed by Tony. Perhaps this was why she always seemed rather reluctant to talk about him, and certainly her letter to Peter Laing announcing her marriage was reticent in the extreme. 'Many thanks for your letter telling me of your marriage,' wrote Peter from Montreal on 10 December. 'I hasten to wish you every happiness and I am sure you will be happy too. Your brief note, however, does not disclose in any manner the identity of the fortunate man. In fact, it is written in such a way that all that appears to have occurred is that you have changed your name.'

As for Norman Douglas, the man whom Elizabeth admired most in the world, she could not bring herself to tell him. He found out, of course; but being acutely aware of people's privacy, and perhaps guessing that he would not think much of her choice, he waited for her to mention it first. On 31 July 1945, he wrote, 'Yes! I knew about your marriage ages ago through Neil. But he could not remember your name, and perhaps I haven't got it right either. Anyhow, I hope all goes well?'

Many years later, when Olivia Manning's *Fortunes of War* had been dramatized for television and the books were being read by a new generation, Elizabeth told a friend that she had been 'very much in that world'.[24] There is no character in the novels who is remotely recognizable as Elizabeth, least of all Edwina, a beautiful but empty-headed good-time girl. Yet the point at which Edwina announces that she is going to marry a dull army major called Tony, while still in love with a far more exciting man called Peter, must have given Elizabeth a stab of recognition:

'Good heavens,' said Dobson, 'not Tony Brody!'

'Why not? He's a major and a nice man.'

'I should have thought you could do better than Brody.'

Edwina, sniffing behind her curtain of hair, said dismally: 'There's not much choice these days. The most exciting men have all gone to Tunisia and I don't think they're coming back.'

'Even so. Be sensible and wait . . . You're still as beautiful as a dream and you don't want to marry Brody.'

'Oh, I might as well. If you can't marry the man you want, does it matter who you marry?'[25]

* * * * * * *

CHAPTER NINE

Indian Interlude

The war was over, but the grief over dead friends and family was still painfully raw. Elizabeth had lost her cousin Jasper Ridley (son of her Uncle Jasper and Aunt Nathalie) in 1943, and Mike Cumberlege had been taken prisoner while trying to plant mines in the Corinth Canal. Elizabeth knew he had been captured; but it was only later that she heard what happened to him. From Greece Cumberlege was eventually taken to Sachsenhausen. There he was interrogated, tortured and kept for many months in solitary confinement. He might have survived; but in 1945, a few days before the arrival of the advancing Allies, he was taken out and shot.

In June 1945, Tony David was posted back to India, as one of the great swarm of staff officers surrounding General Auchinleck in New Delhi. Elizabeth stayed on in Cairo, bound by her job with the Ministry of Information. Towards the end of the year she managed to wangle a trip on Ministry of Information business to Athens. This city, which she had once loathed and where she had been so miserable, now seemed intoxicating and was full of friends. Elizabeth was delighted to be in Greece again, a feeling heightened by the fact that she had already decided she was not going to like India.

She saw in the New Year at the hospitable house at Bulaq Dacrour, where she had spent the miserable Christmas of 1942 with the Feddens while Peter Laing was in hospital. This time, the party consisted of Patrick Leigh Fermor, Patrick Kinross, Eddie Gathorne-

Hardy and Elizabeth. Paddy Leigh Fermor described it as a memorable evening: 'There were a lot of jokes, a lot of loose and reckless talk, and I suppose we all got pretty tight.'

Tony had been allocated a flat in a series of modern blocks on Kingsway in New Delhi. It was bare and cheerless; but Tony had done his best to make it more comfortable before Elizabeth arrived, and while waiting he spent most of his free time at the Gymkhana Club, around which the lives of horse-loving British officers revolved. Among the friends he met at the Gymkhana Club were two people who became so important to Elizabeth that she dedicated two of her future books to them: Veronica Meagher and Peter Higgins.

Peter Higgins was a stockbroker by profession, who was then in the uniform of the King's Royal Rifle Corps. To his regret he did not join his battalion when they went to fight in north Africa in 1941. He was given a staff appointment instead, which took him first to Algeria and then to Italy, before being sent to India, where he became involved in the enormous task of repatriating the British side of the Indian Army before independence (for which he was awarded the OBE in 1945). He appeared in New Delhi some time after Tony: they became friends through a mutual interest in horses and racing. Peter was a man of great charm and entertaining conversation. He was good-looking in a fair, Anglo-Saxon way, though his tendency to put on weight led his less charitable friends to call him Piggins.

Veronica Meagher had come out from England as a junior civil assistant, a post created for young women so that they could take over army desk jobs, thus releasing young officers for more important duties. She, Tony and Peter often found themselves together, and Veronica became more and more intrigued by the idea of Tony's wife. Elizabeth was due to come out and join her husband that winter, and Tony could think of little else. He became increasingly nervous as the time for her arrival drew close.

In January 1946, Elizabeth finally arrived in India. Veronica remembers seeing her for the first time. 'She was wearing a fly-fronted, square-shouldered jacket, and looked terribly chic and sophisticated.'[1] Tony danced attendance on her, eager for her slightest smile; but while she seemed perfectly agreeable to him, she was not demonstrably affectionate. Elizabeth probaby met Tony's friend Peter Higgins at about the same time. It became obvious very soon that Elizabeth did not find India as congenial as Cairo; but with Tony, Veronica and Peter Higgins for company, life was bearable.

Elizabeth was touched by the pains that Tony had taken to make their flat habitable; but she was appalled by the kitchen, a stuffy room which made the one she had had in Cairo look positively well-equipped. One of Elizabeth's favourite writers, Col. Kenney-Herbert, had in the 1870s written in thundering tones about the squalor of the average Indian kitchen: it was usually the dirtiest and foulest room in the compound, with no running water and sited next to the cesspit. Seventy years later, Elizabeth found the state of kitchens was still very primitive – but when she tried to improve matters, even she found that the pace of change could not be forced.

The cook (who more or less came with the flat) was very indignant when he realized that Elizabeth thought of his kitchen as her territory. Memsahibs were there to give orders. They didn't cook, and they certainly weren't supposed to introduce diabolical foreign contraptions (a Primus stove) that might well have burnt the flat down. Two cooks were fired in quick succession, and Elizabeth developed a reputation for upsetting servants.

Veronica was at that time living with the Earl and Countess of Carlisle. Biddy Carlisle was Director of the Women's Auxiliary Corps in India, and cultivated a wide circle of cosmopolitan friends. Through Veronica, the young Davids were invited. Tony, who enjoyed rubbing shoulders with the smart set, was delighted; and one might have expected that Elizabeth would have found Biddy Carlisle's guests more interesting than the usual round of officers and memsahibs. However, Elizabeth refused to be drawn in. She adopted an air of studied nonchalance which infuriated her hostess. 'Where does she come from? What sort of a name is David anyway?' demanded Lady Carlisle. She had no time for young women who did not pull their weight at a dinner table.

Right from the start, Elizabeth loathed British India. She hated the colossal scale of Lutyens's and Baker's ceremonial centre, and the monotony of the residential districts that radiated from it. And in Connaught Circle, the much-vaunted shopping centre that claimed to be the most exciting spot in New Delhi, there was not a single café or bar in which to while away the hours. Part of her frustration with India was that after having held down a responsible job, she had no work and nothing to occupy her time. She did not attempt to get any work, probably because she knew that she could not work with people she found so complacently dull. Even England would look exciting after a few months in New Delhi, surrounded as she was by people whose lives revolved around racing and polo, and who could not see further than the next vice-regal garden party. And however much she hated being a wifely appendage to Tony, she had no excuse for missing the races or polo matches he took part in.

The food too was very frustrating. On the British side, it consisted of boarding-school fare, in which a meal began with a nondescript bowl of Brown Windsor soup, went on to boiled beef and carrots and ended with chocolate shape. Then there were supposedly French dishes spiced with hot green chillies and, 'oddest of all, Edwardian fantasies of the school which liked to present food in any form but its own (mashed potatoes got up to resemble a roast chicken, mushrooms made out of meringue and the like)'.[2] On the Indian side, she was at first rather encouraged: meals were served like Middle Eastern food, with lots of inviting little dishes full of different things; but when she tasted them, Elizabeth found the ubiquitous taste of hot chilli peppers so overwhelming that it killed everything else. However, she did love the pilafs and hot Indian breads.

*

The only thing that made life pleasant was the little clique of herself and Tony, Peter and Veronica, who became her closest friend. Veronica admits that she was nothing like as well-read as Elizabeth, who spent much of her time in India rereading Proust and Henry James. But she was lively and fun, and Elizabeth was grateful for her company. As for Veronica, she found Elizabeth fascinating. One minute she could be so difficult and prickly that everything seemed to rub her up the wrong way; and the next she was being wonderfully funny and light-hearted, and it was with Elizabeth that Veronica most enjoyed 'the giggly side of it all'.

Having nothing better to do, she and Veronica often went to the cinema, or to have their hair done. Veronica remembered that Elizabeth's thick, already greying hair was arranged in short, tight curls which suited her very well. Together they explored the markets of Old Delhi – something Elizabeth also enjoyed doing with her young maid, a beautiful girl scarcely older than a child. At first she was terribly shy, and very reluctant to go to Old Delhi; but Elizabeth befriended and reassured her, and the girl did her best to satisfy Elizabeth's persistent curiosity about everything they saw.

On another occasion Elizabeth, Tony, Veronica and some other friends went for a moonlit picnic in the grounds of the Qtub Minar. They had only just arrived and were pulling the cork out of a bottle of Australian wine when they suddenly found themselves surrounded by a pack of dogs. The dogs did not seem to be interested in the food: 'they simply formed a circle round us at a respectful distance and stared and howled.'[3] They were chased away, but came back in even greater numbers, howling as loudly as ever, and since they made conversation impossible, the party was obliged to pack up and go home. This little glimpse of her Indian life is from *Summer Cooking*, and is one of the very few times when she recalled her time in India in writing.

With the coming of summer, Delhi began to get stiflingly hot. The climate brought Elizabeth a severe attack of sinusitis, and to get away from the cauldron she and Tony went on a trip to Darjeeling.

They took the night train to Calcutta, and then took the astonishing mountain railway to Darjeeling itself. They went to their hotel and, still feeling dazed from the altitude and the ride, repaired to the bar where Tony ordered a couple of martinis. The barman gave the usual virtuoso display with the cocktail shaker, though he confided to Tony that there was no ice: the hotel's refrigerator had broken down. Elizabeth never forgot that warm martini, which they drank while looking on to a landscape of eternal ice: the freezing summits of the Himalayas. Their hotel had other interesting features. Orchids grew out of the mud floor of the bathroom, and just below their bedroom was an open-air cinema where they were showing *Salome* with Yvonne de Carlo – in continuous performances, for most of the night. She and Tony were warned to watch out for cat burglars. These highly skilled thieves, they were told, always tickled the toes of their victims to make sure they were properly asleep before rifling through their possessions. To Veronica, who had just gone to Rome, Elizabeth wrote that all was well, and that so far their toes had not been tickled.

They returned to Delhi on 6 July, but Elizabeth was no better: she was finally taken to hospital on the 12th. The doctors told her she stood no chance of recovery if she spent the rest of the summer in the heat of the plain: she must go home. She hoped to stop off in Cairo on the way back. Eddie Gathorne-Hardy was delighted at the idea, and in a long letter gave her the latest news of the Feddens, and Norman Douglas, whom he had seen in England. 'He had rather been taken under the wing of Viva and Willie King who are old friends of mine. He spoke very affectionately of you. He was just off to Naples. A little gaga he was, and boozing fairly hard, but awfully sweet, amusing and cynical, not to say dirty-minded. I love him.'[4]

Elizabeth left India in early August, and did not stop off in Cairo. Soon after her return, she went to lunch with her Aunt Grace and cousin Anne in London. Anne recalled that Elizabeth was really vehement in describing how much she had loathed India. She and her mother were both left with the impression that something had gone terribly wrong there.

* * * * * * * *

CHAPTER TEN

Back in Blighty

Elizabeth arrived home with even less than when she had set out. Her luggage consisted of a few light clothes, some books and a haphazard collection of recipes. Little remained of the life she had once had: her own possessions, put into storage in 1938, had been destroyed by bombs. She had been away from England for six years, and in that time she, and England, had changed beyond recognition.

In those six years, she had found a mentor in Norman Douglas, spent a winter in Antibes, sailed into the war on the *Evelyn Hope*, been interned, lived in Athens, Syros, Alexandria, Cairo and India. Norman Douglas had laid the foundations of the way she thought not only about food, but about history, the Mediterranean world and the way life should be lived. In Syros she had had to cope with enforced loneliness and idleness; but she had also learnt how to cook the everyday food of the Mediterranean, a process continued in Egypt. She was a long way beyond the 'marrons glacés in half an hour' school of cookery. In Cairo, the experience of setting up and running a reference library had given her a far clearer idea of what she could achieve as a professional working woman, and developed her taste for scholarship as well.

Emotionally too she had grown up, and discovered just how much of herself she could give to a relationship. While she had been prepared to devote herself to Peter Laing in hospital and give him back the will to live, she would not follow him to Canada and share the burden of his disability. She was still brooding and grieving over that decision when Tony appeared. He was perhaps the only man in her life to love her so completely, but she was well aware that while he had married for love, she had made a marriage of convenience.

Seeing her mother and sisters again amply made up for the greyness of London, at least at first. Priscilla had two little girls, Sabrina and Julia, while Diana was expecting her first child. Among all the other family news, Elizabeth also heard the details of the terrible rift that now divided Diana from their Aunt Violet.

Diana had once been Violet's favourite niece, and it was confidently expected that Violet would leave Diana her magnificent collection of jewellery. However, Violet had disapproved strongly of Diana's engagement to Christopher Grey, because she had a pathological hatred of doctors. The final break between aunt and niece had taken place some time after Diana's marriage. Diana had been at lunch with Violet, who had launched into a tirade against the man she held personally responsible for the continuation of the war – Winston Churchill. Diana, whose husband was serving in Burma in the Royal Army Medical Corps, understandably lost her temper. Fierce words were exchanged, after which Diana walked out and never entered her aunt's house again.

Dr Grey had returned home safely, and he and Diana settled into 9 Abingdon Road, Kensington, where he had his practice on the ground floor. The house was set back a little from the road. Two trees had been planted either side of the path, and these had grown towards each other at such an angle that a tall man, like Dr Grey, had to duck under their branches to reach the front door.

Elizabeth moved in with them and, as Diana's first pregnancy wore on, she took over the shopping and cooking. 'One day,' wrote Elizabeth,

I took back to her, among the broken biscuits and the tins of snoek . . . one pound of fresh tomatoes. As I took them out of my basket to show her I saw that tears were tumbling down my sister's beautiful and normally serene face.

'For God's sake, what's the matter?'

'Sorry. It's just that I've been trying to buy fresh tomatoes for five years. And now it's you who've found them first.'[1]

Elizabeth's first flat in London was within walking distance of Diana at 29 Cheniston Gardens, just off Kensington High Street. The kitchen table was also the cover for the bath; but she did have a gas cooker and a small fridge.

She was not without friends, many of them from Cairo: David and Mary Abercrombie, Lesley O'Malley, who had worked with Elizabeth in the Ministry of Information in Cairo, the art historian Cecil Gould, Denis Freeman and Neville Phillips, and Renée and Robin Fedden – he had just started his long career in the National Trust as curator of Polesden Lacey. Elizabeth also ran into Olivia Manning's husband, Reggie Smith, whom she had not seen since Cairo. She was rather startled when he greeted her with the words, 'Elizabeth, how lovely to see you! Let's fuck.'

While descriptions of wartime London are familiar, it always takes an effort of imagination to remember just how bleak it was – particularly to someone who had been living in warm climates without bombs and rationing. For Doris Lessing, fresh from South Africa, London was an assault on the senses. 'It was unpainted, buildings were stained and cracked and dull and grey; it was war-damaged, some areas all ruins, and under them holes full of dirty water, once cellars, and it was subject to sudden dark fogs . . . No cafés. No good restaurants. Clothes were dismal and ugly . . . Everyone was indoors by ten, and the streets empty . . . Any conversation tended to drift towards the war, like an animal licking a sore place.'[2]

As far as rationing was concerned, 1946 had been a very disappointing year. Fears of a world famine meant that bread was rationed for the first time in Britain. Rice was no longer imported, and increases in the allowances of meat, bacon and eggs failed to materialize. Nevertheless, Elizabeth saw rationing as a challenge. 'Everyone else had hoards of things like powdered soups and packets of dehydrated egg to which they were conditioned. I started off untrammelled; an empty cupboard was an advantage. With whatever I could get I cooked like one possessed.'

Elizabeth's satisfaction at her empty cupboard also indicates that while she had to cope with current shortages like everyone else, she had not experienced the solidarity that rationing had given people while the war was being fought. The fact that *everyone* was eating vegetable mince and steamed bread pudding while the lads were at the front had made women feel involved in the war effort. As Marguerite Patten wrote in *The Victory Cookbook*, 'We people at home could not let the forces down, we had to play our part too.'[3] And, as the same author points out, there was much to be celebrated. The population as a whole had a healthier diet than before the war and had become skilful at making the most of what little they had.

Elizabeth, on the other hand, could only compare English food with what she had become accustomed to. 'What I found out when I returned to England . . . was that while my own standard of living in Egypt had perhaps not been very high, my food had always had some sort of life, colour, guts, stimulus; there had always been bite, flavour and inviting smells. These elements were totally absent from English meals.'[4] Entertaining was still possible, with a little imagination. Everyone contributed, and every gift – no matter how odd – was celebrated as a change from the monotony of everyday wartime food: a wild goose, mock liver pâté from Fortnum's, British-Government-bought Algerian wine. 'One of my sisters,' wrote Elizabeth, 'turned up from Vienna with a hare which she claimed had been caught by hand outside the State Opera House.'[5] It was Felicité. She had worked for the Admiralty during the war, which had brought her typing and secretarial skills up to a high level. She had then joined the British administration of occupied Vienna.

'Game was plentiful that year. Even if one didn't actually catch pheasants in Kensington High Street, one could buy them very cheaply in the shops. Wild duck, although distinctly fishy some of them, were not more than a shilling apiece. My landlady, living in the flat below mine, was saintly. Not once did she complain about the cooking smells, the garlic, the onions, those eternal bacon bones simmering in the stock . . .'[6]

No doubt the landlady recognized that whatever was cooking in Elizabeth's pots smelled rather good; but not everyone was convinced by the sort of cooking Elizabeth practised.

'About a year after the end of the war,' she wrote, 'I spent a couple of months in a large, bleak, isolated country house trying to help out a woman friend with the cooking and domestic chores.' This friend of hers, whom Elizabeth calls 'Janet', had two children and no domestic help of any kind; and with grim determination, she cooked what she thought was sensible English food.

What struck Elizabeth was the sheer amount of hard labour that producing such food entailed. Potatoes, sprouts and cabbage all had to be peeled and prepared for the Sunday lunch, and each boiled up separately on top of the stove and cooked till flabby – which was not a very economical use of fuel. Elizabeth suggested that the weekly hunk of ration meat be stewed with the vegetables, which would have meant less work and less fuel. ' "The children," said Janet in a chilly voice, "look forward to their Sunday roast. We can't deprive them of it." It wasn't for me to try and deflect Janet from what she conceived to be her duty.'

One day however, 'I got fed up with the loathsome job of making the traditional-style gravy to which Janet had been taught to add the cabbage water as well as some sort of thickening. Deceitfully, I chucked the cabbage water into the garden . . . and added to the meat juices instead a glass of cheap red wine. Janet had no objection to this at first, but suddenly became alarmed at the way the children' (then aged six and four) 'spooned the wine-flavoured sauce into their mouths with such evident relish.' Elizabeth assured her friend that her children would not turn into juvenile alcoholics, since all the alcohol had evaporated in the cooking; but Janet was not convinced. 'Back we had to go to that barbarous gravy routine. And so it went on. Back-breaking cleaning of vegetables, boiling of stodgy puddings, painful waste of fuel. I had always thought it impossible not to enjoy cooking, but now it had indeed become that drudgery of which so many English women complain all their lives.'[7]

Looking back, the woman who refused to let Elizabeth David cook for her attracts the same sort of incredulous pity as the publisher who turned down *Pride and Prejudice* – yet her reaction is understandable. Elizabeth was probably none too tactful in presenting her ideas, and Janet no doubt felt she was being steamrollered into a way of cooking that was, to her, totally alien.

The winter of 1946–7 was the coldest in living memory, and the cold set in in November. Elizabeth, who had spent the last six years in hot climates, had no store of old coats and darned cardigans. 'At this moment somebody put into my head the idea of going to stay, at reduced all-in rates, in a hotel in Ross-on-Wye. You may well ask . . . I didn't. I just went.'[8]

The 'somebody' was George Lassalle, that raffish, funny, fish-loving friend of Elizabeth's who used to borrow Tony's uniform in Cairo. The son of a doctor, George had strayed from his strict Catholic upbringing and, at this stage in his life, was following his inclinations wherever they led him. Unlike many men he was not daunted by Elizabeth.

They had been lovers off and on in Cairo, and now their affair blossomed again with a new intensity. They were both disenchanted with their own marriages, admitted to each other that they had made a mistake. George felt that at one moment 'marriage was in the air'[9] between them, yet Elizabeth would never have taken the idea seriously. She was very fond of George and loved his company, but he lived life for the moment, and did not have the sort of steadiness that Elizabeth looked for in a potential husband. She was also dubious about the combination of her own dark looks and his: 'We might have black babies,' she laughed. (Curiously, Elizabeth's sister Diana worried about having 'black babies' too, and mentioned it more than once to her friend Roger Ellis. Perhaps the Gwynne girls feared that the Indonesian genes of the Purvises might suddenly re-emerge in force.)

Having babies was not, however, something that Elizabeth ever seriously considered. She was remarkably free of all maternal feelings, rather as her mother was; babies stirred nothing in her but a faint distaste. Elizabeth had seen how motherhood, especially on a budget, destroys all independence, and she had no intention of letting it happen to her.

As for George, the idea of marrying Elizabeth was considerably discouraged by the blatantly snobbish attitude of her mother and sisters. One might read their chilliness towards him as dismay: here was another of those ebullient, bohemian, 'not-quite-our-class' buccaneers who, like Charles Gibson Cowan, Elizabeth seemed to find so irresistibly attractive.

They left London with a lot of books and all their warmest clothes and snuggled down in a hotel at Ross-on-Wye. It was one of three hotels belonging to a well-known chain (Trust Houses Ltd), and Elizabeth's room was deliciously warm after London: there was a coal fire in the public sitting room, and a maid to bring hot-water bottles and breakfast in bed.

Ross-on-Wye provided little entertainment, beyond the pubs which were such a feature of the town. She and George went on pub crawls sampling innumerable different varieties of cider, but they also found considerable amusement in Miss Deakin's antique shop. It was piled from floor to ceiling with a jumble of antiques and bric-a-brac, and Miss Deakin had no hesitation in pulling out anything her customers might wish to see from any part of the pile. Elizabeth bought a Leeds dish, the pair to which was (like so much of Miss Deakin's stock) already broken. It was George Lassalle who rescued, and gave to Elizabeth, a white jug with black transfers of John Wesley's head and a building called the Centenary Hall, dated 1839.

As Miss D. took my cheque her elbow jogged the tap of a copper tea-urn perched on top of a model four-masted barque in a heavy box frame. It knocked over a solid silver clock representing General Gordon sitting on a horse, which fell against a scrap screen, a japanned tray and a tortoiseshell and silver-inlaid musical box. The guts of the little musical-box cracked out on to the floor. Miss D. was unshaken. 'Take care how you go out,' she said.[10]

But even the warmth of the hotel and the thrills and spills of Miss Deakin's antique shop could not make up for the misery of the food. 'Conditions *were* awful, shortages *did* make catering a nightmare. And *still* there was no excuse, none, for such unspeakably dismal meals as in that dining room were put in front of me. To my agonized homesickness for the sun and southern food was added an embattled rage that we should be asked – and should accept – the endurance of such cooking.'[11] She thought of going back to London, but by that time the ice and snow had given way to heavy rain and severe flooding. Stuck in Ross-on-Wye, there was nothing to ease the 'embattled rage' but pen and paper.

Elizabeth had been collecting, refining and developing recipes for at least ten years. She lost one collection when she and Charles were forced to abandon the *Evelyn Hope*, and had amassed another during her time in Greece, Egypt and India. Yet all her previous writing had been geared to recipes: what ingredients to use, what one might add, the best way to cook a dish. In Ross-on-Wye, she was not writing lists and instructions; for the first time, she was writing *about food*: a food that was not only unavailable, but that could not even be approached without a completely different set of priorities than those that governed kitchens in wartime England.

She began 'to work out an agonized craving for the sun and a furious revolt against that terrible, cheerless, heartless food by writing down descriptions of Mediterranean and Middle Eastern cooking. Even to write words like apricot, olives and butter, rice and lemons, oil and almonds, produced assuagement. Later I came to realize that in the England of 1947, those were dirty words that I was putting down.'[12]

As soon as travel was possible again Elizabeth escaped the hotel and rejoined George Lassalle, who had moved into a bungalow some friends had lent him near Gloucester. 'I read Julia Strachey's review of Elias Canetti's *Auto da Fé* in *Horizon*, and thought it the most dazzling piece of book-reviewing I had ever seen. By some fantastic chance I found a copy of the book itself in Smiths in the town which was a bus ride away . . .'[13] One evening, however, she and George found a book in the bungalow that was even more riveting.

They had eaten a cassoulet of bacon bones, beans and herbs, accompanied by generous quantities of Algerian wine before finding it, hidden in the shadows of a bookshelf. It was very large, and on the cover was printed CONFIDENTIAL: TO BE KEPT IN THE SAFE. . . It was a pre-1939 Trust House hotel cookery book, catering and food-costing manual.

'I did not steal it,' wrote Elizabeth. 'The temptation to do so was truly appalling: I wish now that I had looked in the neighbourhood for someone with a typewriter to copy out for me some of its most instructive pages. I . . . would have been in possession now of the secrets of Trust House hotel soups; I could have told you how to turn *Potage parmentier* into *Potage cultivateur* with a flick of a ladle . . . How to make lobster patties for twenty-five with one lobster and I forget how many pounds of cod.'[14]

This book of trade secrets also made a profound impression on George, who was struck by two particularly sinister items. 'One was a detailed instruction on how to make imitation French sauces . . . The other was an advisory paragraph on how to meet the need of a sudden influx of casual customers when there was insufficient food in the kitchen to feed them. On no account should such customers be turned away. There followed detailed instructions on how to perform a miracle of the loaves and fishes and turn food already prepared to feed twenty hotel residents into a banquet for forty.'[15] From then on, in their separate lives, George and Elizabeth lived in the hope of tracking down another copy of this book. Both were resourceful bibliophiles, keen trawlers of street markets and second-hand bookshops. They never found one.

Elizabeth's experiences of hotel cookery, combined with the discovery of the caterers' manual, unleashed the source of the creative rage that drove what she wrote. In that miserably cold winter of 1947, she found the heart of her own blazing fire. Of course, she did not always write in the white heat of passion: there is no point wasting emotional energy on custard powder and gravy mix. But whenever she tweaked the noses of pompous restaurateurs, laughed at a factory-made pie or poked fun at the sacred cows of British cookery, she was tapping into the same incandescent exasperation that drove her to put pen to paper in Ross-on-Wye.

Elizabeth felt she owed something to Trust Houses Ltd, because her first book might never have come into being without them. 'I should have dedicated [*Mediterranean Food*] to Trust Houses Ltd. It was ungrateful of me not to have done so. For better or for worse the book brought me a new job and a new life.'[16] In a much later letter to Elizabeth, George wrote, 'Yes, 1947 was a very bad winter indeed but I seem to remember there were compensations for all that snow.'[17]

Tony David came home in the spring of 1947, and her family were profoundly relieved by what they saw. He was well-mannered, eager to please and had a good seat on a horse. The only worry was that he had no job, having left the Indian Army, (his decision to go being more influenced by Elizabeth than by the prospect of Indian independence.)

That summer, Elizabeth and Tony travelled round France with Doreen Brownhill, who had made an unsuccessful marriage during the war and was now separated from her husband. They did not go by barge, as they had once dreamed of doing in Cairo, but in a second-hand Rolls-Royce which they bought for £550. It was a dashing thing to do, and reality caught up all too soon. It ate and drank petrol, the exchange-rate was appalling, the tyres were old, the roads were war-scarred, and they had their first puncture just outside Calais. But despite all obstacles, and the irrevocable puncture of the spare tyre at Lyon, they went as far as the Italian border before heading for home. The way home was even more nerve-racking; but the fact that they got the car home at all was 'a triumph, and like all triumphs it left us in a state of nervous exhaustion'.[18]

That autumn, the Davids were told that the owners of their flat wanted it back. They had by now bought quite a lot of furniture, mostly through Elizabeth's mother Stella. Antique shops were springing up all over the south of England, but Stella Hamilton knew what she was selling.

Rather than rent another flat, Tony and Elizabeth decided to buy: and the house they settled on was No. 24 Halsey Street. Halsey Street is a residential street of white terraced houses, linking Cadogan Street at the south end with Milner Street to the north. That particular area of Chelsea had been one of the first to benefit from the magnificent water closets designed and made by Thomas Crapper, and the lavatory in the basement of the Davids' house boasted an early model from the great man's workshop. The house, though small, was on several floors. The Davids decided to convert it so that the top two floors could be let, to augment their income. They had moved in by early November, and continued to use Stella Hamilton as their main supplier for everything from curtains to sconces, pine tables to soup plates.

Elizabeth had asked for Stella's help in buying the house; but while Stella was willing to underwrite the mortgage, she was also convinced that Elizabeth was financially irresponsible. When Elizabeth was in her twenties, she had indeed been extravagant: not only Stella, but Priscilla had often helped her out, more generously than Elizabeth deserved – although she was always profoundly grateful for their generosity. Elizabeth was by now in her mid-thirties, and had put her reckless youth behind her. Stella, however, still felt it wiser to put the house in Tony's name.

However, the spender in the David ménage was Tony, not Elizabeth. When they went shopping together, he was the one who spent, she the one who held back. The conversion of the house required a certain amount of building work; but that was not the only reason for Tony's spending.

He had gone into partnership with Douglas Grey, the youngest brother of Diana's husband Christopher Grey, who had inherited some money from his mother. Together they bought the lease on No. 12 Herbert Crescent, with the idea of turning it into a relaxed, informal club. Once again, Stella was asked to provide the furniture.

'I have a pine stool which is too low for the bar, but am going to ask my Mr Knott if he can make six bar stools similar – as it is very pretty and will let you know. Should they slant or be quite level and what is the exact height? I suppose you will glamorize the bar – green and gold or somehow embellish it . . .'[19]

This letter shows that Stella, at least, was interested and involved with the project; but Elizabeth was becoming anxious. 'I began to feel uneasy about the amount of money that was being spent on the club scheme. My husband, however, was confident of its ultimate success.'[20] In mid-January 1948, Tony became seriously ill. 'I am more than désolé [sic] to hear about Tony and all,' wrote Stella on the 23rd (of January, presumably). 'Awful strain for you, too, nursing, etc. I am so sorry, and wish I could do something useful. I have found some Jamaican Turtle, but no receipte [sic]. It has to be soaked and boiled . . .' The rest of the three-page letter deals with a Victorian buttoned sofa, a low pine table, a pair of pelmets, a clock, a 'hideous' oak cupboard, and the costs and frustrations of shipping in midwinter. Stella's business was never far from her thoughts.

Quite what Tony was suffering from is difficult to guess, at this distance; but it took him several weeks to recover. In February, he asked for an estimate for work that still had to be done on the club's main room and bar; but it is doubtful that the work was ever done. This was because Tony David and Douglas Grey had gone ahead with their plans without doing much paperwork in advance. They had failed to secure the permission of the local authorities for their scheme, and the club was shut down even before it opened. Elizabeth wrote that 'most of [Tony's] available capital had been spent on it, and little was salvaged'.[21]

Tony managed to find employment for the second half of 1948, managing a firm called Piccadilly Parcels which exploited a clever way of getting around rationing. A great many things, such as orange marmalade and biscuits made with white flour, were available in Britain but only for export. People living abroad wrote to Piccadilly Parcels and ordered export-only goods, for which they paid in foreign currency; the parcels were sent either to them or to their ration-starved relatives in England. For a while the Davids' financial situation improved, while Tony David's nephew Patrick Lewin had the pleasure of receiving real Huntley & Palmer biscuits at Eton – which considerably impressed his schoolfellows and made him very popular.

In the early part of 1949, the sixteen-year-old Patrick Lewin became very ill with bronchitis. His parents lived in Kenya, so Elizabeth and Tony took him away from Eton so as to nurse him back to health in Halsey Street. Patrick felt that they looked after him extremely well, and he never heard a cross word between them. 'Elizabeth and Tony were both good cooks,' said Lewin, 'united in their hatred of the latest gadget on the market – the pressure cooker.'

Veronica Meagher, whom they had last seen in India, got in touch with them, and for a while she lived in the large back room that was then being used as a dining room, and was to become Elizabeth's kitchen. The Davids had hoped that Veronica would take the flat they had made at the top of the house, and at first she had agreed; but friends thought it was a bad idea. The Davids' marriage was under strain. Veronica also felt that while she was very fond of Elizabeth, she was too strong a character to live with.

Instead, the upstairs flat was let to Denis Freeman and Neville

Phillips, whom Elizabeth had met in Cairo. They too were aware of the tension between Elizabeth and Tony, which was not helped by the fact that he was a fish out of water among Elizabeth's friends.

Neville Phillips remembered taking Elizabeth to a matinée performance given by Roland Petit's ballet company, which was then causing a sensation in London. They reached their seats and there, sitting in a box above them, they recognized the great Vaslav Nijinsky. Later that evening, Neville and Elizabeth met up with Denis and Tony for dinner, and Neville mentioned that they had seen Nijinsky. 'Who's he?' asked Tony. Elizabeth explained that he had been a great dancer, star of the Ballets Russes, and celebrated for his breathtaking leaps. 'Oh yes,' said Tony enthusiastically. 'I had a horse just like that in India.'[22] Elizabeth shot Neville a look which implied she had given up on Tony's cultural education.

She was also rapidly losing confidence in her husband, who seemed incapable of finding a 'proper' job. He spent more and more time at home, getting up late and drifting around the house. He was still useful for grinding the coffee, mixing the drinks and driving the car; but it became painfully obvious that Elizabeth's feelings for him had been reduced to irritation and contempt.

Her faith in him was finally shattered in the new year. Tony had always been evasive about their debts; when pressed, he would answer with vague and reassuring noises. But in early 1949, Elizabeth insisted on knowing the details of their financial position: at which point, Tony admitted that nothing whatever had been paid either on the mortgage, or to the builders. He seemed quite relaxed about the situation, and suggested they sell the house. Elizabeth, still in a state of shock, pointed out that this was hardly the best solution since they would be obliged to sell at a very considerable loss. Tony, however, did not see this as a disadvantage, and suggested they go and live abroad. He had no idea of what they might live on. As for the bills, he could not understand why Elizabeth found them such an obstacle: 'He could not understand my attitude. He thought it was very priggish of me to insist that bills and debts must be paid.'[23]

Elizabeth made no secret of her disappointment in Tony. His failure had humiliated her in front of her family, and she was mortified at being so deep in debt.

* * * * * * *

CHAPTER ELEVEN

Mediterranean Food

The 'agonized craving for the sun' which Elizabeth had begun to work out of herself in Ross-on-Wye had grown into a collection of recipes which she already thought of as *A Book of Mediterranean Food*. They were based on the food she had cooked for the past twelve years, though at this stage she was soliciting contributions from her friends as well. At the same time, prompted by their financial situation, Elizabeth started to write some articles on cookery. If published they might bring in a little money, and it was a good way of turning her back on Tony as she sat at her desk in silent concentration.

It was Veronica Meagher who had, in Elizabeth's words, 'talked, not to say nagged' her into assembling the book; and Veronica now did what she could to find sympathetic readers who might give good advice about publication. One who sprang to mind was John Carter, the European agent for the American firm of Scribner's. His wife Ernestine was then fashion editor at *Harper's*.

'Would you consider showing the MS to [John] Carter?' wrote Veronica. 'A pretty desperate step . . . but Mr Carter works for Scribners . . . They [he and his wife Ernestine] are also best friends with the Hamish Hamiltons, Messrs Chatto & Windus and the rest . . . PS: Alternatively if I could borrow the book I might make Anne abandon Robin Adair.'[1]

Anne was Anne Scott-James, editor of *Harper's Bazaar*, while Robin Adair was the magazine's cookery correspondent. He was a close friend of Marcel Boulestin, but this did not alter the fact that he never filed his copy on time. Veronica knew that Anne, though not particularly interested in cookery herself, might look favourably on any possible replacement. Veronica told Anne that she knew of someone very good, who was just starting; and Anne agreed to look at Mrs David's work.

Elizabeth was very keen for her articles to be accepted, and asked Veronica to help her achieve the right journalistic tone. Veronica did not take her seriously at first; but Elizabeth was so insistent she obliged, and drew the article into line with the bright, cheerful, occasionally girlish 'Harper-ese'. Elizabeth was not impressed. She submitted her work, for better or worse, in its original form.

Anne Scott-James recognized that the articles were written by someone with an independent mind, who had travelled widely: in fact, she liked the way they read more like travel pieces than cookery. From the spring of 1949, Elizabeth's articles appeared regularly in *Harper's Bazaar*.

She was very professional: the copy was always delivered on time, and was never unreasonably overlength. Yet she was not easy to work with. The sub-editors were never allowed to get their hands on Elizabeth's text – if any alterations had to be done, words cut or a line filled in, it was Anne who did it, and then telephoned Elizabeth. 'I would explain what had to be done and there would be a long silence at the other end, before she would say, "I would like it to go in as I have written it." "Yes of course," I would reply, "but the fact remains that either you must cut three words or I must because I cannot make the page any bigger." Difficult as she was, Anne Scott-James could not help admiring her stubbornness. 'Her work was holy and she was the priestess of it . . . She was a perfectionist, and great perfectionists are also great egotists.'[2]

Straightforward as ever, Elizabeth had told the editor of *Harper's* that she was hoping to publish some of her recipes, including those which had made an appearance in the magazine. Anne accepted this with equanimity. 'We were not so worried about copyright as we are now.'

John Carter looked at her manuscript and said that it was no more than a collection of unconnected recipes. It needed more text to bring it together but at this stage Elizabeth had very little confidence in herself as a writer. She did not want to copy Veronica's slick, upbeat journalese, nor the cheerful practicalities of most cookbooks of the time; but she was still unsure of her own voice. She kept her prose as spare as she could, but sometimes it sounded almost terse – on the other hand, she was determined to avoid sentimentality. It was for this reason that she relied heavily on other authors to describe Mediterranean life: Henry James, Marcel Boulestin, Robert Byron, Lawrence Durrell and D. H. Lawrence were among those she pressed into service – and, of course, Norman Douglas. Many of the passages are, not unnaturally, chosen for their seductiveness; but Elizabeth quoted from travel books, not travel brochures, and Mediterranean food was not all olives and sun-warmed figs. Théophile Gautier thought the gaspacho he found in Spain in 1840 was quite revolting, and no one would seriously contemplate starting the day with the gargantuan breakfast Lt-Col. Newnham-Davis recommends in Venice. The descriptions she uses are there primarily to evoke a specific time and place, and to illuminate the Mediterranean approach to food, which was then so alien to the British.

On the other hand, the whole book is infused with that love of the Mediterranean that was so characteristic of the time. She had first found it through the eyes of Norman Douglas, and later, she had made friends with writers who celebrated the Mediterranean for an entire generation: Lawrence Durrell, Patrick Leigh Fermor, Patrick Kinross, Robin Fedden. After the war everyone who had ever been abroad was longing to go again; they were sick of the grey drabness of England and its shattered cities. It was not only warmth and colour they wanted: those little white villages clustering in front of the sea, with olive groves beyond, represented a world that had not yet lost its innocence

The recipes she had put together were made with good but not extravagant ingredients. They had been used year-in, year-out, as the seasons changed, by people who did their own cooking and marketing; and while olive oil and wine and aubergines may have sounded expensive and exotic in the England of 1949, they were not so in the Mediterranean. Elizabeth brought the recipes to life with little details that gave them a history and a personality. The stuffed mussels had been prepared for her on a boat, by a fisherman from Marseille. On late Sunday afternoons in Spanish courtyards, you could see serried ranks of metal paella pans left drying in the sun. (At this stage, she herself had never seen them: she first visited Spain in 1964.) The Greeks sent their lamb to be cooked in the village oven, and it was incomparably more delicious than anything that might emerge from a domestic oven; though in case this pronouncement discouraged her readers, she added that in England one could at least enjoy the dish hot: everything in Greece – even fried fish – was served tepid.

Denis Freeman and Neville Phillips had a friend called Robin Chancellor, who worked for the Museum Press. He had blithely said that he was sure his firm would publish it, but when it was submitted, his superiors turned it down. But he had contacts in other firms as well, and the typescript went the rounds of several publishers. The firm of Herbert Joseph wrote to say that her book was 'a very interesting work but I am sorry to say that we do not feel ourselves able to make an offer . . . Firstly, a part of the contents of your book is already covered by our existing publication *Recipes of All Nations* by Countess Morphy . . . Finally the bookshops are at present flooded with cookery books.'[3] Publisher after publisher turned it down, until the book finally arrived in the office of John Lehmann Ltd.

John Lehmann was best known for being the editor of *New*

Writing, the most influential literary magazine to appear during the war. Its pages featured work by W. H. Auden, Louis Aragon, Stephen Spender, Federico Garcia Lorca, Louis MacNeice, Robert Graves and Laurie Lee, to name but a few; but this gives an idea of how open and attuned Lehmann was to new voices. He had no particular interest in food or cookery, and the 'unprepossessing bundle of grubby typescript', as he called it, was given to Julia Strachey (whose review of *Auto da Fé* had so impressed Elizabeth two years before). She was a niece of Lytton Strachey, and was then working as a reader for Lehmann.

Julia was impressed. Here was a book which was beautifully written, with the quiet authority of someone who knows what they are talking about. The author made no concession to austerity, talked of eggs and cream and butter as if they were freely available, and had the temerity to propose a Turkish Stuffing for a Whole Roast Sheep at a time when meat was still rationed. (Meat did not come off the ration until June 1954.) The book was even extravagant with time: anyone wishing to attempt Senator Couteaux's Lièvre à la Royale must be willing to set aside seven hours for its preparation, and the recipe takes up five pages. Elizabeth did not seriously expect that many of her readers would try stuffing a sheep, or even cooking a hare for seven hours: those recipes are included for sheer pleasure, and for the glimpse they give into a world where it was not considered pretentious, or bad form, to care about food.

Lehmann had never imagined himself publishing a cookbook; but he was delighted by the idea of stuffing a whole roast sheep and trusted Julia's judgement. He wrote to Elizabeth on 27 October 1949.

'Dear Mrs David, I tried to telephone you today, but you were evidently out. Do you think you could ring me here tomorrow (Friday) morning between 11 a.m. and 12.30, so that we can arrange a meeting? I like your book on Mediterranean Food very much, and hope we shall be able to agree about publication.'

*

Elizabeth had no idea what to expect as she walked into the office in Henrietta Street and shook hands with a tall, brisk man with thin hair, and eyes of a startlingly pale blue. Lehmann offered her £100 advance, with half on signature of the contract and half on publication. He said that he wanted to give the book a feeling of cheerfulness and abundance, and suggested that it should be illustrated by John Minton.

John Minton was an immensely talented neo-romantic painter, to whom Lehmann gave a lot of work; but people said there was more to their relationship than that. Minton's charming, gangly figure was often seen at Lehmann's celebrated parties in Egerton Crescent, and he was also a welcome guest at the publisher's cottage near Three Bridges in Sussex. Since both men were homosexual, people naturally assumed they were having an affair. Minton's biographer, Frances Spalding, thinks this is unlikely; but Lehmann was, like many people, fascinated by Minton, in whom he found 'a compelling charm'.[4] Lehmann showed Elizabeth a recent jacket design by his protégé, for a book about Corsica by Alan Ross called *Time was Away*. It showed a man sleeping in a boat under a hot sun in a Mediterranean landscape, and Elizabeth agreed that it was very effective.

All that was lacking was an Introduction, which Elizabeth was to write, and the only problem was the title. For some reason Lehmann did not like *A Book of Mediterranean Food*, and wanted to call it *The Blue Train Cookery Book*. Elizabeth pointed out that the Blue Train, which had epitomized the excitement and romance of foreign travel for the pre-war generation, had never gone as far as Alexandria and Cairo. She felt very strongly that the word Mediterranean was vital, but Lehmann still clung to the Blue Train idea. They both agreed to give the matter some thought.

Elizabeth left John Lehmann's office in a daze of delight and misgivings. Would he really insist on changing the title, and what on earth was supposed to go into the Introduction? She was still puzzling over these things a few days later, when Lehmann rang her up to say that perhaps she was right, and the title could stand. Elizabeth was profoundly relieved, and felt she had won an important victory. She would often say that if Lehmann had had his way, her first book would never have enjoyed the success it did.

That still left the Introduction. Having no idea how to go about it, Elizabeth once again turned to Veronica. Veronica wrote a short piece 'in the buoyant, jokey style I was trained in', but Elizabeth didn't like it. What she wrote instead was short and rather formal. Her aim, she said, was 'to give some idea of the lovely cookery of those regions to people who do not already know them, and to stir the memories of those who have eaten this food on its native shores, and who would like sometimes to bring a flavour of those blessed lands of sun and sea and olive trees into their English kitchens'.[5]

At one point during the preparation of the book, Elizabeth went to visit Lady Sibell Rowley. Before the war, Sibell was one of the three Lygon sisters whose house, Madresfield, had been a constant refuge for the young Evelyn Waugh. In 1939 she had married a fighter plot, Michael Rowley, and they lived in a large house, with its own farm, called Payne's Place near Tewkesbury. Sibell was a countrywoman through and through, who hunted and kept a pack of hounds. Elizabeth had no interest in either, but she was fascinated by the farm on which Sibell did almost everything, from looking after the chickens to killing the pig. She was also a good cook, and a good friend.

'To put up with me for three weeks,' wrote Elizabeth, 'either clamped to the Aga or spreading mountains of papers and books all over the sitting room was really an act of nobility . . . You have given me such a gorgeous opportunity to do proper cooking with not only delicious cream and bacon, geese eggs and the rest – I am eternally grateful to you. I am now of course complaining of the difficulties of cooking on a gas stove . . .'[6]

Elizabeth had returned to London, and the rapidly cooling ashes of her marriage. As far as she was concerned, it was over – but Tony still loved her, and was deeply hurt when she began a flirtation with one of their friends, Peter Higgins. As a couple, Tony and Elizabeth had kept in touch with Peter, whom they both found entertaining: he could talk horses to Tony, and food to Elizabeth. It was he who introduced her to a book by Lt-Col. Newnham-Davis and Algernon Bastard called *The Gourmet's Guide to Europe*. Peter wrote out for her the colonel's magnificent breakfast in Venice, which she included in *Mediterranean Food*. 'Incidentally,' he added, 'I ate the "steaming risotto with scampi" in June 1946 at the Quadri, but not for breakfast, and very good it was.'[7]

He also very much appreciated the food Elizabeth cooked for him. 'Delicious though the food is in your house always,' he wrote in April, 'that ham which I ate on Thursday night called for appreciation in writing. Don't tell the public how to do it, because it's far too good for them.' This particular letter ends, 'love to you both': Tony was still on the scene, though he had no doubt guessed that something was brewing between Elizabeth and Peter. A friend remembers him at this time as a rather sad, reproachful figure.

In the summer of 1949, Tony was offered a job running a club in Walton-on-Thames. He accepted, and moved down there. When she came to write out the circumstances of their separation some years later, Elizabeth was at pains to make out that this was the moment they moved apart, and that they never again shared a roof. However, the situation seems to have been far less cut and dried, and as far as most of their friends were concerned they were still together – even if they were living apart for the present. When he came up to London Tony stayed at Halsey Street, and they still attended parties and the odd family occasion as a couple.

Elizabeth also emphasized that they were still on cordial, if not intimate terms. They appeared together at the wedding of her cousin Robert Palmer in 1952; and a friend, who happened to be in the sitting room at Halsey Street having coffee, witnessed a moment of affection from Elizabeth as Tony was about to leave. She saw him to the door, put her hand on his arm, and asked him with a smile to stay a little longer; but Tony said he really had to go.

It was during this time of separation from Tony that Elizabeth made herself a new kitchen, in what had been the dining room, which was a few steps down from the tiny hall. With three exterior walls, it had always been the coldest room in the house; but that made it a good larder temperature, and it was rendered slightly warmer by the addition of a wooden parquet floor. Elizabeth relied on an electric heater and the heat generated by cooking to keep the place habitable; but when it became very cold, she lit the gas oven and opened the door.

The kitchen was lit by a window looking out on to the tiny area, where Elizabeth kept a few pots of herbs and, in later years, the overflow from her collection of pots and storage jars. She had no garden, nor did she seem to miss one. For someone who so appreciated the fruits of the soil in their proper seasons, it is curious that she was such an urban animal: in general, Elizabeth preferred markets to gardens.

In front of the window was a chaise longue, where Elizabeth used to rest and read. To the right of the window was the butler's sink, built into a cabinet with a teak draining board. Immediately below was a space for chopping boards and other things that needed to be instantly accessible. To the other side of the draining board stood the New World gas cooker, and above them was a Victorian wrought-iron lamp on a hinged arm. To the other side of the cooker was a white-painted dresser, the shelves of which contained stoneware storage jars and pots overflowing with small implements, with decorative plates propped up behind them. At this stage, the plates were coloured and patterned: Elizabeth's passion for plain white plates did not develop until later. At the end of the room, facing the window, was a heavy French armoire in which she kept glasses, crockery and herbs. (In later years it contained pans and earthenware.)

Elizabeth never liked the idea of having her fridge in the main part of the kitchen. Fridges in those days were a great deal noisier than modern ones, and since her kitchen was both the place where she studied and the room in which she entertained, it is not surprising that she wanted it out of the way. Her fridge was kept cooler and therefore quieter by being on the landing outside: which was easier on the motor and involved less defrosting.

Two more pale wooden dressers occupied the wall facing the cooker, their shelves crammed with madeleine moulds, saucepans, preserved fruits and more plates. On the first dresser stood whatever needed to go in a bowl: eggs, apricots, walnuts, lemons or shallots, depending on the time of year. On the second stood more equipment, plus a collection of liqueur and wine bottles and a large alarm clock. Elizabeth always complained of the clutter in her kitchen, but her curiosity and interest in all culinary objects was insatiable and she was an instinctive collector. As her nephew Johnny remarked, 'She loved the cooking utensils as much as the china and thought them equally worthy of display.'[8] She could never have lived in a minimalist kitchen.

There was nothing that could be described as a work surface, except for the scrubbed pine table that dominated the room. Everything focused on this table, which was lit by a large nineteenth-century oil lamp with a glass shade. This was where Elizabeth read, made notes, and wrote the books and articles that were to make her name over the next decade. Here too she prepared food, checked recipes, measured quantities, checked timings, chopped, diced, whisked and folded.

Then, at lunchtime, all the books and papers were moved down to one end to make room for her friends. It is not unusual for someone to work and entertain in the same room, particularly if space is limited – but the room is usually divided in such a way that work and play take place in different areas. Elizabeth had the use of a sitting room as well as a kitchen. She was also the sort of person who liked to keep her life in separate compartments. Yet the fact remains that she chose to write, cook, entertain her friends, eat, drink, relax and talk, not only in the same room, but at the same table.

As her guests came in, they would be led downstairs and sat at the end nearest the window. Here they would find perhaps a bowl of olives, some radishes, a fresh loaf of bread (she did not yet make her own, since her local baker made what she called 'a passable French loaf') and a slab of butter. There was also, invariably, a bottle of wine.

'When guests were invited to lunch,' wrote Johnny Grey, 'she would only have one dish ready; the ones to follow would be prepared over a lengthy pre-lunch conversation and guests were usually asked to assist . . . If you were lucky and some experiment had taken place the previous day, she would offer it to you in a matter-of-fact way and ask you to try it . . . She never boasted about her cooking skills – her whole attitude to cooking was one of interest, inquiry and very occasionally genuine pleasure when a dish turned out well.'⁹ The lunches went on until well into the afternoon, over the kitchen table.

Elizabeth took a great deal of care over her kitchen. Everything was considered to make it comfortable and practical, but it went directly against the mainstream of kitchen design in 1949. Most housewives at that time aspired to spotless acres of laminated surfaces, plastic-covered chairs, linoleum floors and chrome handles to fitted units.

With Tony now drifting into the distance, Elizabeth's emotional life was filled by the elusive, charming Peter Higgins. He used to say that his mother had been a Gibson Girl, 'though not one of the grand ones who dressed up like a cracker',¹⁰ and he claimed to have been born in a hotel in Dorchester. His father Rupert Higgins was a man about town, an Edwardian charmer who enjoyed living close to the rich and grand; and because he was entertaining and amenable, the rich and grand enjoyed his company. Peter was brought up a Catholic and went to the Oratory School near Reading. He did not go to university, the most likely reason being that there was no money to pay for any further education. Instead, he went into the City and became a stockbroker.

He had no particular fondness for his chosen profession; but it provided him with a good living, and enough extra to hunt and ride and go to the races whenever he could get away from London. From his father Peter had inherited a taste for the high life: on the horsy side, he was friends with Harry Stavordale (later 7th Lord Ilchester), and the hunting and racing sets of Dorset and Gloucestershire; while on a more raffish, sophisticated side, he was taken up by Hamish St-Clair Erskine, the son of the 5th Earl of Rosslyn. Erskine, now best-known for being an early love of Nancy Mitford's, used to claim that he had 'discovered' Peter and often referred to him as 'my débutante daughter'.[11] Considering Erskine's homosexual tendencies, and the fact that he and Peter had once shared a house, some people whispered that they were lovers. Peter was in fact firmly heterosexual, and since he was also very attractive to women, he soon had a string of love affairs to prove it.

By the time Peter met Elizabeth in India he already had one marriage behind him, to Kathleen (Kit), daughter of the Canadian lawyer and banker Sir James Dunn. The marriage was over by the end of the war, and she later married Col. Robert Adeane. As for Peter, he seemed quite happy to stick to the principles of his Catholic faith, and said he would not marry again. He settled in Devon, where he became a farmer: an occupation which, he hoped, would enable him to ride more often than if he were still in the City. Yet it soon became obvious that, farmer or not, Peter Higgins could not quite tear himself away from the racing season and the social life of London.

Elizabeth had always liked easy, confident men, the kind who brightened up a room just by walking into it, whom people were always pleased to see. She also noticed that although she herself cared nothing for horses, in later years she had become rather attracted to these hard-riding types: perhaps they reflected something of the intense, childish memories she still cherished of her dead father.

During the early years of their affair, Elizabeth often accompanied

Peter and his friends to the races, to which he was addicted although he never gambled. Elizabeth, on the other hand, hated racing; and her opinion of the racing fraternity was expressed with a distinctly caustic wit over the magnificent picnics she prepared for these occasions. But the highlights of the racing calendar gave her an opportunity to be with Peter, and these were too precious to waste. Peter and Elizabeth sometimes came to spend the weekend with Michael and Sibell Rowley. Sibell remembered them as being very happy. On one occasion, Elizabeth brought Sibell a present of avocados, which (for want of anything better) they ate with Worcestershire sauce.

Priscilla's marriage to Richard Longland was over in 1949, leaving her profoundly depressed. Elizabeth's own marriage was crumbling as well; yet she continually urged her friend Veronica to settle down and choose one of her many suitors. 'It's absurd, of course,' she would say, 'but a woman must marry.' On 21 October 1949, Veronica married Major John Nicholson, who had been courting her for many years and whom she always thought she would settle down with. They went to France for their honeymoon, leaving Elizabeth with the key to their flat; and when they got back, they were very touched to find that Elizabeth and Tony had gone in and made up the bed.

'Then began,' wrote Veronica, 'the era of long luncheons between Elizabeth and me. We would meet at her house or at my flat at about one, and break up just in time to go home for dinner.'[12] Veronica did her best with Elizabeth's recipes when she came to lunch, while Elizabeth's lunches were usually trial runs of the recipes in her next article – though they did not always turn out right. On one occasion clouds of smoke, produced by a batch of choux pastry that Elizabeth had forgotten about, obliged them to abandon the kitchen altogether.

A Book of Mediterranean Food was published in June 1950 and reviewed with great enthusiasm. No one got the point of it better than Elizabeth Nicholas, a travel writer and reviewer, whose piece in the *Sunday Times* gave Elizabeth particular satisfaction. Nicholas called Elizabeth 'a gastronome of rare integrity. She appreciates the present deficiencies of the English larder, but at the same time if she wants to say "take a large piece of rump steak", she says it. She refuses, in fact, to make any ignoble compromises with expediency.'[13] Nicholas also noted with approval that the book contained 'not one reference to Brillat-Savarin'. Even those with reservations about the book could not fail to succumb to its enchantment. John Chandos, in the *Observer*, wrote rather severely that

The book claims that it evokes 'all the colour and sun of the Mediterranean', yet it is precisely those native physical and climactic elements which the recipes require for their proper consummation. Let no one eating in London – with whatever abandon – imagine that he is eating Mediterranean food in the absence of Mediterranean earth and air. With that reservation it may be admitted that Miss [*sic*] Elizabeth David has assembled as potent a bundle of spells as ever made a culinary Witches' Sabbath.[14]

The only real complaint came from the RSPCA, which rightly considered her recipe for Roast Lobster needlessly cruel – it was to be tied to a skewer and roasted alive, basted with champagne, butter, pepper and salt. The recipe came from *Spon's Household Manual*, a book dating from the 1880s. In later editions Elizabeth pointed out that this recipe was not to be taken seriously, but was only given as an example of the 'lavish and somewhat barbaric' recipes of the time.

Elizabeth felt that much of the success of *Mediterranean Food* was due to the authors she was able to quote and John Minton's jacket design. She was not very enthusiastic about his pen and ink illustrations, but the jacket she described as stunning. 'In the shop windows his brilliant blue Mediterranean bay, his tables spread with white cloths and bright fruit, bowls of pasta and rice, a lobster, pitchers and jugs and bottles of wine, could be seen far down the street.'

She was aware that, as a cookbook, it was not unflawed: prevailing conditions dictated that the recipes were more evocative than accurate. And yet for those who knew what they were doing, it was profoundly stimulating.

'I consider it easily the best cookery book that I have read dealing with . . . south European and Arab cookery,' wrote one of her readers. 'Although I really have read an enormous number of books which have purported to touch on this kind of cuisine, they have *all* failed to give me a clear picture of the more exotic recipes. The writers . . . have tasted and seen, but probably not having lived there nor speaking the language, they have failed to understand the fundamentals. You have definitely filled in this gap, and I am very grateful.'[15]

Another grateful recipient was Lawrence Durrell, who wrote to her in June 1950 from Ischia. He was revisiting the Mediterranean for the first time in many months, and he felt back in his natural element at last. Durrell describes his house and his friend Zarian (who appears briefly in the passage Elizabeth had quoted from Durrell's book *Prospero's Cell*), and added, 'All this is to tell you that not only was your book deeply appreciated but we were lucky to be able to take it with us and read it in a proper setting and in good company.'[16]

Elizabeth later described her first book as 'a very primitive effort', but she was fond of it none the less. 'It is a love letter to the Mediterranean.'[17] Although she was 'not the sort to dance a jig',[18] as Veronica put it, Elizabeth was tremendously pleased by the success of *Mediterranean Food*. Of course she saw the limitations of the book; but it showed her that out there were people who were eager and willing to hear what she wanted to say.

Journalistic commissions followed. Lord Kemsley, the owner of the *Sunday Times*, had recently bought up a travel magazine called *Go* in order to satisfy the public's increasing demand for everything foreign. Kemsley put Leonard Russell, the *Sunday Times*'s literary editor, and Elizabeth Nicholas, who had written the most perceptive review of *Mediterranean Food*, in charge of the new venture.

Elizabeth David was one of the first people they contacted; and over the coming months she not only wrote for *Go*, but also contributed a long piece for the *Sunday Times Travel Guide to France* on the area between Marseille and Menton. At the same time, John Lehmann was keen to publish another book by Elizabeth David, and he and Elizabeth agreed that the new book should present the simple, but beautifully prepared dishes of rural France. This was a logical successor to *Mediterranean Food*, for it grew out of the same collection of recipes that Elizabeth had been amassing for years.

The sixty-guinea advance from the *Sunday Times*, plus an advance from John Lehmann, made Elizabeth decide it was time to take a trip to France. In August 1950, two months after the publication of *Mediterranean Food*, she and Tony set off for their last holiday together. They joined another couple in what was supposed to be a comfortable and leisurely trip. The car, however, turned out to be extremely unreliable, and a lot of time was spent walking long distances for help and waiting around for mechanics.

Elizabeth was still writing for *Harper's* on subjects which included pasta, spring vegetables, hors d'oeuvres and alfresco lunches. She even wrote an article in praise of the freshness and convenience of airline food (possibly for *Go*). Two of the pieces she wrote at this time were, however, particularly important. 'Cooking with Wine' (February 1950) began with the words, 'Nobody has ever been able to find out why the English regard a glass of wine added to a soup or stew as a reckless foreign extravagance, and at the same time spend pounds on bottled sauces, gravy powders, soup cubes, ketchups and artificial flavourings.' Many people think of Elizabeth David as a cook for those prepared to take infinite pains. It is worth remembering how liberating and refreshing her work was too, and how she never missed an opportunity to point out when things could be done better, more cheaply and without cluttering up the cupboard.

'Batterie de Cuisine', on the other hand, which appeared in January 1950, shows Elizabeth at her most briskly didactic. Any young bride-to-be must have felt her heart sink as she read that the ideal kitchen should contain at least nine saucepans, four frying pans, earthenware casseroles, egg dishes, soufflé dishes and gratin dishes, plus a large selection of knives, mixing bowls and muslin squares. Too much information was packed into this article, with not enough room to say why all these objects were so vital. However, in its final, more developed form, this piece became one of the most useful and delightful of all her essays.

With one book out, the next commissioned and a fine collection of articles already under her belt, one might assume that Elizabeth had by now mastered the art of typing; yet Elizabeth never got beyond the hunt-and-thump stage. For her, the feel of a pen or pencil in her hand and the paper under it was part of the process of writing and thinking, and, as in her cooking, she did not like to be separated from the creative act by a machine.

For most of her work, the typist was Elizabeth's youngest sister Felicité. Rightly or wrongly, Felicité always saw herself as the runt of the litter. Her low opinion of herself was summed up in the nickname that she had put up with since childhood – Bulgie. It was an affectionate name, and a part of Felicité always answered to it, but another part of her rather wished she could shake it off. She was not quite seven when her father died, and from then until adulthood she lived in an almost exclusively female world. The feeling that she was always trying to catch up with her sisters remained, for she never had enough emotional support from her mother and sisters. As soon as she was old enough, she sought it from her boyfriends instead.

For Felicité, as for many people, the war was one of the happiest and most independent times in her life. She felt at ease in the company of people who had nothing to do with the world she had grown up in, and was more relaxed with her Austrian and Polish friends than she had ever been with the awkward young Englishmen she had come across. But once she was back in England, the past and her family re-exerted its power. She still needed her family's approval, and they teased her about her foreign boyfriends. So she kept them in the background, and once again started to live according to her family's expectations rather than making her own.

She found a job in a bookshop called J. A. Allen. It specializes in horse books, though Felicité ran its small general section on the ground floor. Work in bookshops is not usually very remunerative, and J. A. Allen's was no exception; but Felicité came to a mutually beneficial arrangement with her sister Elizabeth. The top flat had been rented out to Denis Freeman, the actor friend from Cairo, and he had become very short of cash towards the end of his tenancy. Elizabeth asked him to leave; and as soon as he had done so, in 1950, Felicité moved in. Elizabeth kept the rent for the top flat very low, and in return Felicité did Elizabeth's typing.

Elizabeth finished the manuscript of *French Country Cooking* in October 1950, delivering it early in the new year. In her covering letter to John Lehmann, she asked, 'Can I reprint three or four basic recipes from *Mediterranean Food*, or is this cheating?'[19] Lehmann evidently thought it was: 'I can imagine a reviewer making a song and dance about this that would spoil everything.'[20] She had considered another artist to do the illustrations, but Lehmann felt he was 'sophisticated in the wrong way for our public', so once again the drawings were by John Minton. Elizabeth had by now become quite fond of Minton, so she did not complain. The one thing she insisted on was that in this book, there should be drawings of various pots and pans and kitchen implements – not just because they were evocative, but to convey information: the tools that people used to cook with were an integral part of the cooking process. Minton did a number of drawings of these objects, and they have dated better than his impressions of sultry French peasants and the jovial bourgeois family at lunch.

With *French Country Cooking* safely delivered, Elizabeth decided to go and live for a while in France. Not only would she increase her knowledge of the country, but, away from Paris, one could live far more cheaply than one could in England. By renting Halsey Street, she might support herself, and put more distance between herself and Tony – who was by now, in most people's eyes, a sad figure more sinned against than sinning. 'Sympathy with Tony is general,' wrote her mother, 'and I think rightly so ... People like Tony, and think you are treating him rough, though they don't actually say so.'[21] Elizabeth found a house to rent in the village of Ménerbes in Provence, and let her house. Felicité was still in the upstairs flat, on hand to call in the plumber or the electrician in case of emergencies.

Elizabeth travelled to Provence by train in March 1951, and found Ménerbes magnificently isolated like a stone ship on the top of one of the rocky hills of the Lubéron. The house, belonging to Tony and Thérèse Mayer, was called La Carméjane, after the sixteenth-century Baron de Carméjane who began but never finished it. From the front, La Carméjane presents a massive wall with shuttered windows; but the effect is alleviated by the addition of an ornate little bartizan tacked on to one corner. The main part of the house consisted of three vast rooms, one above the other, which looked on to the hills of the Lubéron. Part of the ground floor room had been partitioned to make a tiny kitchen. There was only a small garden behind the house, but it led to a large terrace looking on to a cherry orchard, with the countryside rolling away beneath it. To one side of the terrace was a little two-bedroom house known as le cabanon. All this sounded delightful; but the weather was freezing cold, and everything was in a dreadful state of repair. Elizabeth had to deal with broken windows, a broken lavatory seat, a cantankerous cooker and only a trickle of hot water.

One of the first people to join her there was Romney Summers, the painter whom she had met in Cairo. A friend described Summers as 'Round, kind and the sort of person who did everything no one else wanted to do.'[22] They were soon joined by Hamish Erskine. Hamish went through a period of profound depression for the first few weeks when the weather was so miserable. Elizabeth's friend Doreen arrived at this time too. 'We sat for hour after hour at this huge table, on hard chairs, trying to keep warm and drinking foul wine – I think it was half-French, half-Algerian – out of a huge barrel, while the wind and rain lashed the windows.'[23] The wine was very rough. Elizabeth described it as the sort of wine that should be drunk in tumblers, heavily diluted.

Even on a tight budget (Summers kept detailed accounts of their spending) there was never any lack of what Elizabeth would have regarded as the necessities of life: bread, olives and wine. At first, their staples were chickpeas, lentils, old carrots and tomato paste. Elizabeth did not mind the food so much as the cold, and the constant buffeting of the mistral, the enervating wind that tears its way through the Rhône valley and is at its most violent in the spring.

Eventually the weather cheered up, and so did Hamish. He and Doreen would go for long walks, collecting wild flowers which they pressed. Elizabeth did not join them, since she 'hated walking more than an inch'.[24] Hamish stayed for most of the summer, and when he finally moved on he left his collection of French berets behind. 'You were so very sweet and kind to me,' wrote Hamish to Elizabeth when he finally got around to his thank-you letter in September, 'that except for hangovers and cold my spring and early summer were bliss.'[25]

With the warm weather the wind died, and then came glorious abundance. Eggs were so cheap they were almost given away, and 'we were able to buy a kilo of tomatoes, broad beans, haricots verts, peas, fennel, artichokes or courgettes for a few francs. Asparagus and strawberries were so cheap we could afford them almost every day, and not just for a few days but for weeks on end . . .'[26]

For a real treat she had the truffles of the Vaucluse, which are not considered as fine as those of the Perigord and are therefore cheaper. The centre was Carpentras, where the truffle hunter told her that the best way to enjoy the truffles was to scrub them well and slice them raw into a bowl of eggs, cover the bowl and then leave it to stand for two or three hours before cooking them. Twice a week they went to Avignon to do the shopping, and after the excitement of the market Elizabeth and whoever had come with her would repair, exhausted and laden with shopping, to the Café

Molière, a modest establishment which served a particularly delicious omelette. Parmesan is added to the eggs before cooking, and it is filled with thick cream and gruyère cut into tiny cubes. The secret of this dish is that not more than one tablespoon of each ingredient should be added to three eggs.

The summer brought more friends. Everyone helped with the bills, and many were paying guests. A woman from the village came to cook once or twice a week and clean the house, and Elizabeth did the rest. Some were more appreciative of Elizabeth's cooking than others: Felix Hope-Nicholson, a friend of Hamish Erskine's, was evidently not impressed and claimed to have been poisoned by something he called 'Liza's Balkan stew'. George Lassalle saw Felix a few weeks later in London and wrote, 'Felix H-N you must have bruised a little. He did not give me that instantaneous reaction of praise I expect from people who have lunched and dined with you.'[27]

Stews and casseroles featuring the cheaper cuts of meat seem to have appeared on the menu with considerable regularity, perhaps because they did not require much attention. She was researching at this time – in small hotels, kitchens behind little hardware shops and railway stations – following local recommendations, relying on the bus service to get from place to place. She was also learning the tact, the diplomacy, the patience that is required to persuade the French to give up their recipes. At the same time, she was still producing regular articles for *Harper's*, and in May she sent them a choice of two – one on Catalan cookery, and another on holiday cookery. They decided to go for the Catalan option: as the assistant editor explained, 'The holiday piece we felt entailed rather a lot of effort for women less devoted than yourself, who are generally lazy during their summer holidays.'[28] Elizabeth was also correcting the proofs of *French Country Cooking*, which she dedicated to her mother. 'I shall be greatly honoured should you really dedicate your new masterpiece to me,' wrote Stella. 'I am no cook, in fact, can hardly boil an egg, so it's really too unsuitable . . .'[29] But she was deeply touched.

Elizabeth was so happy in Provence that she even considered buying a house in Ménerbes called the Castellet, which stands beyond the graveyard at the most commanding end of the village and was for many years inhabited by the painter Nicholas de Staël. She never did; but she made a habit of returning to Ménerbes and La Carméjane, and something of those summers is in a soup of courgettes, tomatoes, broad beans and basil which appears, in *Summer Cooking*, as Soupe ménerboise.

It is possible that Peter Higgins came out to join Elizabeth for a week or two that summer, but he would have known the place anyway, since Elizabeth took the house again and again for several seasons. Her happiest memories of Peter were set in the landscape of Provence, which they travelled extensively together, and for many years Elizabeth thought of Ménerbes as a second home. In 1966, when those days were over, a friend sent her a postcard of La Carméjane. 'I arrived home at Halsey Street . . . this evening to find your postcard lying face upwards on the door mat. It gave me a terrible pang.'

* * * * * * *

CHAPTER TWELVE

Italian Food

Elizabeth left Ménerbes at the end of June 1951, leaving Romney Summers in charge of La Carméjane, and moved on to Italy with Hamish Erskine to see Norman Douglas in Capri. She was detained in Naples by water on her ankle. Resting it helped, but it would swell up again as soon as she put her foot to the floor.

Since 1947 Norman had been living on the ground floor of the Villa Tuoro, owned by his friend Kenneth McPherson. But his health had been deteriorating, and the heat of summer made things no better. His taste in food was getting very idiosyncratic: he had a passion for hard-boiled eggs, of which he ate only the whites, and Elizabeth, hating to see them go to waste, ate the yolks. She left the island on 25 August, and Norman's parting present to her was a copy of Lindsay Drummond's *Late Harvest*, in which he wrote, 'For Liz. Farewell to Capri.' From there she made a journey round the Italian Riviera, to research an article commissioned by *Go*.

Back in England, she went to stay for a few weeks with Doreen in Cornwall, and then returned to London. Since her own house was still let, she moved into a flat adjoining that currently inhabited by George Lassalle and his third wife Judith Richardson (the sister of Picasso's biographer, the art critic John Richardson.)

French Country Cooking was published in mid-September. It was not, as she said in her introduction, haute cuisine: it was the everyday food made by wives and housekeepers for doctors, curés, gendarmes and post-office officials – the petite bourgeoisie of France, who might not have had much money, but who loved their food and took it seriously. Elizabeth had learned a great deal since writing her last book; not only about food, but about her readership. She knew that the average post-war English kitchen lacked the necessary equipment to cook the sort of food offered by the recipes, so it opened with a section called 'Batterie de Cuisine'. This was basically the same list that had appeared in *Harper's* the previous year, but now she had larger print and more space at her disposal. Thus the piece became amusing as well as informative, and she was able to develop the reasons why the items she deems essential are so important. In the original article, for example, she only had room to say that earthenware dishes should be in every household. In *French Country Cooking* she can make the point that these dishes are far more than mere containers: they retain heat, add flavour and resonance to the food, and make it more beautiful to look at. In its extended form this piece remains one of the most useful that Elizabeth was ever to write, and holds as good today as it did in 1951. It also contains, in one sentence, a perfect little still life of kitchen gadgetry which sums up the relationship Elizabeth had with the tools of her trade.

As time goes on, you accumulate your own personal gadgets, things which graft themselves on to your life; an ancient thin fork for the testing of meat, a broken knife for scraping mussels, a battered little copper saucepan in which your sauces have always turned out well, an oyster knife which you can no longer afford to use for its intended purpose but which turns out to be just the thing for breaking off hunks of Parmesan cheese, a pre-war sixpenny tin-opener which has outlived all other and superior forms of tin-opening life, an earthenware bean-pot of such charm that nothing cooked in it could possibly go wrong.

This was followed by her (essentially unchanged) piece for *Harper's* on 'Wine in the Kitchen', and another on 'The Menu'. This was a subject she was to develop again in later books, but one part of the message remained unchanged and liberating: there is no commandment which says that meat must be served with two veg and potatoes. One vegetable may be served with advantage as a separate course, dressed with nothing more than butter and parsley; and as for potatoes, they can be omitted altogether. Serving vegetables before the roast was an old French custom, to which Marcel Boulestin had drawn attention in 1937 if not earlier; but the idea still sounded new in 1951.

The book was enthusiastically received, though it did contain one majestic howler. At one point, where Elizabeth had meant to say 'take 2 to 3 eggs', the instruction in print read 'take 23 eggs'. Elizabeth was appalled, but the letter she received from Lehmann's office laid the blame squarely on her. 'The printers could have only taken your mark to mean that the quantity should be 23. I have the proof here and if you care to come and inspect it, please do.'[1]

With another success on her hands, Elizabeth told John Lehmann that her next book would be about Italian food. Very little was known about Italian food in the early 1950s. Elizabeth did not know very much about it either; but her journey through Italy to Capri had given her a glimpse into what was obviously a very rich tradition, in a country that had been unified for less than a hundred years – so the regional differences promised to be every bit as varied as they were in France. Elizabeth had also done enough reading to know that Italian cooking not only had variety, it had history, contained in a bibliography which went back to ancient Rome. Scholars had written endless books on the history and techniques developed by French cuisine; but Italian food had been completely neglected.

John Lehmann was easily persuaded, and not simply because Elizabeth had already produced two excellent and successful books: the time was ripe. In the same way that people were rediscovering the Mediterranean, John Lehmann wrote that one of the most exciting things for his generation, after the war, was the rediscovery of Italy. 'When fascism had at last been brought to its absurd and bloody end, I think that most of us were only too eager to resume a relationship that had brought so much happiness, and had been so fruitful in the past.'[2]

He commissioned Elizabeth to write a book on Italian food, with an advance of £300. It was generous for the times, but Elizabeth was only given £100 of it and had a great deal of travelling to do. She planned to let the house again, and start her sojourn in Italy in the spring of 1952. Elizabeth had promised herself, in what was going to be a period of very hard work, the treat of a visit to Norman Douglas in Capri; but on a dark, rainy day in February, she heard that he was dead. He was old, ill and uncomfortable, and had swallowed two bottles of pills to release himself from the burden of living. Elizabeth missed him painfully. One of his most important messages to her was to say what she thought and damn everybody else; but she had written with him in mind, and without him part of her felt cut adrift.

Elizabeth set off for Italy by train in early March, with an entire trunkful of books. Among the volumes were Osbert Sitwell's *Winters of Content* (1932), Charles Edwards's *Sardinia and the Sardes*, Tobias Smollett's *Travels through France and Italy* (1776) and – of course – Norman Douglas's *Old Calabria*. After a day or two in Paris, she reached Rome on the 9th. It was in the period leading up to Easter (which fell on the 25th that year) and Elizabeth was astounded by the riot of rainbow-coloured sugar work so proudly displayed by the Roman confectioners. In a country in which the food was normally presented with a beautiful simplicity, she mused, it seemed odd that they should dress up their cakes and sweets in such exuberantly bad taste.

Her base in Rome was two rooms in the Palazzo Doria, where loneliness increased her grief over the death of Norman Douglas. But there were friends: Archie Lyall, an enormous gentle elephant of a man who had been in SOE during the war and whom she had known in Cairo, and Arthur and Viola Johnson. Arthur was an international lawyer and art collector who also had a passion for books. His wife Viola was half English, half Italian, and just the sort of woman Elizabeth liked: a generous and highly individual character, whose intelligence was spiked with an irreverent wit. They were also very interested in food, and their knowledge of where to buy the best of everything impressed Elizabeth. 'The Johnsons' Parma ham is better than anything I ever tasted in its way. Sweet, tender, not too fat.' They also had a vineyard outside Rome, at Grottaferrata; and she always associated the taste of its red, heady wine with her months in Rome.

The Johnsons were also regular visitors to Capri, and from Rome the three of them spent Easter at their house there, the Molino a Vento. Elizabeth brought a pot of basil to Norman Douglas's grave, but admitted she never shared his 'melancholy taste for graveyards'. She preferred to remember him in one of his sanctuaries: a little taverna, sheltering in the ruins of the old archbishop's palace now overgrown by a lemon grove. 'Capri wine at the lemon grove . . . white, earthy taste, unmistakably genuine. Country sausage. The scent of lemon skins exquisite. Nobody will get the name of that place out of me.'[3]

At the Café Caprile in Anacapri, Elizabeth found the taste of true southern Italy. The cook was a woman called Mafalda, who gave Elizabeth many of her recipes. Mafalda used to make particularly good bottled pimentos, and Elizabeth badly wanted this recipe; but it was the wrong time of year for bottling them. 'Come back in the summer,' said Mafalda.

Elizabeth took notes all the time, and although only a few of her notebooks survive, they throw interesting lights on the things which struck her, whether meals at specific restaurants or observations people made. The Richietti girls thought that cooking with pork or bacon fat was *vulgare* and heavy; one authority, called Carluccio Civitella, informed her that anything cooked with aubergines was far better with zucchini, and that the celebrated *ragù* (Bolognese sauce) was a *plat de concierge*, stewed until black. She also noticed the way that Roman shopkeepers sold their chickpeas ready soaked.

With little money or experience of Italy, Elizabeth had taken the trouble to get advice from the best possible sources: the High Commissioner for Italian Tourism and the Ente Nazionale Industrie Turistiche. They were very helpful, and smoothed her way into the most celebrated restaurants in Italy. Yet even she was surprised by the extraordinary richness and variety of Italian food, both in its regional specialities and its traditional cookery. She wrote to John Lehmann to tell him, saying she would need more time to research the book. She also complained of the amount she was having to eat, though on this point Lehmann was not very sympathetic: 'You poor suffering martyr to the gastronomical future of the benighted Anglo-Saxons. I have been weeping at the thought of your liver, as I crumble up a little slice of cold luncheon meat.'[4]

Her first series of journeys took her north: first to Siena and Florence, and then to Venice. In Siena she found *panforte* ('like cold plum pudding, with whole almonds and pieces of peel') and little *pecorino* cheeses covered with a red rind. She also noticed that Siena was the only town in Italy where tarragon was much used, and available in all the shops.

Her first call in Florence was to the painter Derek Hill, who occupied the Villino Corbignano in the garden of Bernard Berenson's I Tatti. They ate a memorable meal prepared by his cook, Giulia Piccini: *ravioli verdi*, followed by chicken with anchovy butter, and Mocha pudding, which consisted of a sponge cake soaked in black coffee, smothered in cream and sprinkled with roasted almonds. She later gave Elizabeth some recipes, including one for *riso ricco* which, for all its simplicity, even Elizabeth calls 'a tricky dish'. Derek Hill passed them on, with a note about the wines which had impressed her: 'Osbert Sitwell's white Montegufoni, a light semi-sparkling summer wine, and as red the Contini Bonacossi's Capezzano. The French Consul, who's possibly even greedier than you or I, came to luncheon and said they were the best wines he had drunk here. Rare praise indeed – so after butterpatting myself I had better close as museums always say.'[5]

In the market place in Florence were rolled fillets of pork adorned,

'almost embroidered', with rosemary. Elizabeth thought the Floren-
tines were rather too fond of this herb; but their *finocchina*, a salami
flavoured with fennel seeds, was one of her favourites of all Italian
salami. She noticed that there were no pizzerias in Florence, and
the restaurants seemed more crowded than those in Rome. In the
Sabatini restaurant she spent many hours in the kitchens, and found
'the best coffee in Italy so far'.

On her first visit to Venice she was welcomed by Signor Zoppi
of the Taverna La Fenice. 'Alfredo Zoppi is a man to clamp to your
heart with hoops of steel,' she wrote in her notebook. 'A man who
knows his own mind, and furthermore knows the exact anatomy,
habits and cooking quality of every beast in the Adriatic sea.' Like
Elizabeth he had a particular sensitivity to the appearance of food:
in *Italian Food*, a description of his restaurant accompanies one of
her favourite desserts: *aranci caramellizzati*.

Elizabeth was keen to do some sightseeing as well. On the way to
Verona, she was 'appalled'[6] to find that she was the only person who
would get out of the bus to see Palladio's theatre in Vicenza when it
was raining; she also thought that the presentation of the Montecchio
castle was 'as bogus as Anne Hathaway's cottage'.[7] In Verona she
was taken to the Trattoria Molinara, where she ate a very plain
risotto, adorned only with a few tiny squares of ham: 'one of the
best I have ever had'.[8] It is in Lombardy and Piedmont that the best
risottos are made, with the rice of the Piedmont which makes them
unique. 'The fact that this rice can be cooked contrary to all the
rules, slowly, in a small amount of liquid, and emerge in a perfect
state of creaminess with a very slightly resistant core in each grain
gives the risotto its particular character.'[9]

She made the journey from Verona to Milan in pouring rain, on a
road that passes along the southern shore of Lake Garda. 'Shall never
learn to love lake scenery, even in sunshine,' she grumbled, 'and if
anyone says Gabriele D'Annunzio again I shall go off my head.'[10]

In Milan she saw mascarpone cheeses wrapped up in white muslin,
ate slices of sturgeon in oil, and a particularly good salad of raw

artichokes. She also discovered *mostarda di Cremona*: a traditional accompaniment to boiled meat, it consists of figs, apricots, melon, citron, orange peel and pumpkin, in a delicate syrup flavoured with mustard. Now the confection is a shadow of what it was and is sold in small jars; but in Milan, in the early fifties, it was sold in wooden pails. It was also in Milan, on 5 May, that she saw the first of that season's green almonds.

She spent a day in Como, where she ate a risotto made with dried mushrooms, and then moved down to Genoa, 'the noisiest city in the world'. Among its dishes is the *cappon magro*: a combination of vegetables and fish, served on a ship's biscuit rubbed with garlic, and accompanied by a sauce which includes parsley, hard-boiled eggs, garlic and anchovies. Yet the most famous Genoese speciality was, and still is, pesto, which in its place of origin enlivens everything from soup to pasta or red mullet: 'They say the basil in Genoa has quite a different flavour from anywhere else. Also they have it all the year round.'[11] Elizabeth maintained that the Genoese trenette (thin, match-like pasta) with pesto was the best pasta dish in all Italy. She could never resist a fish market, and found the one at Santa Margherita (just to the east of Genoa) particularly beguiling. The shellfish called *moscadini*, brown and pale green, were set out in baskets 'like newly washed pebbles'; and one can imagine her going from one stall to the other, peering closely into everything with a fastidious, inquisitive expression, asking the names of every-thing. The thin, rose-coloured, slippery little fish for *fritture* were called *signorini*; she also came across a fish called *gallina di mare* – 'sea chicken' – with a huge head and a little body; and tall baskets of *tonnetto*, long fish packed in head first 'like loaves of French bread, shining with phosphorescence'.

From Genoa she went to San Remo, where she was impressed by the wine of Dolcecagna – and amused by 'the candid young man who said he would not invite me to dance, "*parce qu'on fait ça seulement pour des raisons érotiques, n'est ce pas, Madame*"'.[12] She visited Florence again and then Perugia, where the pork was roasted with fennel rather than the ubiquitous Florentine rosemary. She was back in Rome on 15 May, in time to meet Peter Laing, the wounded officer whom she had loved in Egypt. He was on holiday in Italy with his wife Kit.

Elizabeth spent the rest of the month in Rome, and then went back to Venice for ten days. Like many people, she could not have enough of the city. The cooking, with its delicate rice dishes, its fresh anchovies and crabs and scampi, was very much the sort of food she best liked to eat. She also had the company of a delightful friend, Archie Colquhoun, an Italian scholar who had translated, among other works, Giuseppe di Lampedusa's novel *The Leopard*. On 15 June, they decided to visit the Rialto fish market, which has to be seen at dawn. Rather than face the chore of getting up at that hour, Elizabeth and Archie stayed up all night, reaching the market at sunrise. As they wandered around, watching the traders and boatmen hailing each other as they swung the dripping baskets and boxes of fish off the boats and thumping them down on to the stone floor, they came across the Sicilian painter Renato Guttuso who was on his way to the railway station.

Guttuso was considered one of the most important painters working in Italy at the time, and Elizabeth had seen his work at the Venice Biennale. She was overwhelmed by the power of his still-life paintings, in which even artichokes and lemons were embued with a blazing vitality: and there and then, she decided that she wanted Guttuso to illustrate *Italian Food*.

In that particular Venetian dawn everything went Elizabeth's way. Archie Colquhoun was a friend of Guttuso, and they began talking. Colquhoun introduced Elizabeth as a great fan of his work, explained that she was writing a book on Italian food, and – to her astonishment – Guttuso immediately agreed to do the illustrations for it. Whether it was the joy of meeting Guttuso or the magic of the moment, that morning at the Rialto market was to inspire one of the most intensely visual and lyrical descriptions of a market that Elizabeth was ever to write:

The light of a Venetian dawn in early summer – you must be up at about four o'clock in the morning to see the market coming to life – is so limpid and so still that it makes every separate vegetable and fruit and fish luminous with a light of its own, with unnaturally heightened colours and clear stencilled outlines . . . In Venice, ordinary sole and ugly great skate are striped with delicate lilac lights, the sardines shine like newly minted silver coins . . .[13]

John Lehmann was in Venice too that summer, and Elizabeth had urged him to see the Guttusos: she wanted his opinion, for as her publisher he was the one who would commission and pay for the art work. Lehmann was not impressed. He was put off by the fact that when he was not doing still-life paintings, Guttuso was an ardent Communist, who embraced social realism and all the ideals that went with it.

'If you want your next book to be illustrated in a social-realist manner, with . . . a picture of Stalin tasting the macaroni on the frontispiece, then Guttuso is your man. Otherwise heaven forbid. Anyway you might as well ask Picasso to do it.' However, he soon realized that Elizabeth had made up her mind about Guttuso. 'If you are really keen and confident about his capacity, I would not object,' he wrote.[14] But he made it plain that he could not offer much more than £60, and that Elizabeth would have to handle all the negotiations herself.

From Venice she moved on to the airy district of Parma, where she saw the curing of Parmesan cheese or *grana* (the cheese is tested with a skewer, by men who have spent a lifetime learning its secrets) and hams (part of the pigs' diet is the whey from the cheeses).

She returned to Rome to meet up once again with the Johnsons, with whom she took a trip to Sorrento, Salerno and Paestum. Compared to the north of Italy, Elizabeth found the food and wine of the south disappointing; but in the hill town of Ravello, they discovered an unusual red wine called Gran Caruso. The family that made it also owned the local hotel, where the food was as good as their wine.

Elizabeth spent the rest of the summer with the Johnsons in Anacapri. She found plenty of time on her hands, for she was waiting for Mafalda of the Caffe Caprile to announce that the red and orange peppers were finally ripe enough to bottle. For this particular recipe, Elizabeth had to learn the patience of a wildlife photographer waiting to film a particularly elusive specimen.

By the end of August the pimentos, piled in great heaps in the market, looked ready to burst with ripeness; but they were not yet good enough for Mafalda. Elizabeth had to wait nearly a month before the great day came, 'while my host and hostess on the island must have been wondering if I was ever going to leave'.

She was back in Rome by early September, from where she wrote to Renato Guttuso with some trepidation. Guttuso was a serious artist with a world-wide reputation who could command substantial sums of money for his work, and she feared that John Lehmann's £60 might appear insulting.

'I have heard from my publisher John Lehmann. He tells me that unfortunately the most he can offer is £60 (about 100,000 lire) . . . If by any possible chance you would still consent to do the work, I need hardly tell you that I should be overjoyed . . .'[15] To her enormous relief, Guttuso did not go back on his word. 'He said the fee was pretty absurd, but he would do the work all the same.'[16]

Towards the end of September, she took the boat to Sardinia, which was then scarcely visited by tourists. The island was not only wild and beautiful, it had developed a highly individual cookery. Myrtle was much used, for flavouring everything from fish to thrushes to baby pig. The Sardes hunted wild boar and even made hams from it, though by 1950 this was becoming rare; yet perhaps best of all was the multitude of brightly coloured fish so abundantly displayed in the market in Cagliari. She was also struck by the elegance of the Sardinian national dress, on which she took detailed notes: the men wore white linen shirts with black jackets and white breeches, while the women wore finely pleated red or black skirts and medieval-looking headdresses.

Her next destination was Bologna. 'Gastronomically speaking,' she wrote in her notebook, 'Bologna is to Italy rather what Strasbourg is to France.' The food was richer, more heavily laden with cream, truffles, cheese and ham than in most Italian provinces; yet it was also exceptionally good. Like Strasbourg, Bologna's unique culinary tradition was much appreciated all over the country. In almost every Italian town, noted Elizabeth, there was at least one Bolognese restaurant.

In Bologna, the Bolognese restaurant – considered the best in Italy – was the Papagallo, and here Elizabeth tasted *filetti di tacchino in pasta sfoglia*: a turkey breast covered in a sauce of mushrooms, ham and cheese, and served in a puff pastry case. This famous dish was almost too rich and cloying for Elizabeth, and she much preferred the delicacy of their chicken mousse served in broth. Altogether, she felt more at home in the trattoria of Zia Nerina. It was Nerina who gave Elizabeth her recipe for *ragù*: only in Bologna do they add cream to it.

Throughout her Italian journey, Elizabeth had made a point of learning as much as she could about Italian wines. In the early 1950s there were very few of them on the English market, and they were little known because the best ones could not compete in price with their French equivalents. Over the years, more and more Italian wines appeared in England, and more and more people travelled to Italy, so inevitably the chapter on wine is one of those that changed most throughout successive editions of *Italian Food*. Perhaps the wines changed too. In early editions she describes Soave as 'perhaps the most delicious white wine of Italy', whereas in the revised 1987 Penguin edition, she recommends her readers to 'try something other than the Soave, so often flabby and insipid . . .'

She had by now been away for about seven months, and was looking forward to going home; but she felt she could not leave Italy without visiting Turin at the height of the truffle season. She did not regret it. 'Truffles large as tennis balls,' she wrote in her notebook. 'Shops packed with food – game, little birds, cheeses, truffles, huge funghi.' She also visited the Turin market on Saturday, when the piazza was filled with baskets of autumn-coloured mushrooms and truffles, as well as game, sausages and creamy cheeses.

Her engagement book for 1952 charts the journey from town to town. She had contacts in many places, and yet she was touched by the time and trouble people took to show her around their native city, provide guides and introduce her to the *padroni* of the best and most interesting restaurants. The friends she had met in Rome would have passed her on to friends of theirs in other places, but one has the feeling that much of it was a solitary journey. She travelled from one hotel to the next, reading on trains, taking notes in the markets and trattorias and restaurants. She also noted a few of her impressions of Italy. 'They all seem to regard it as the most normal thing in the world that they started the war on one side and finished it on the other . . . they are bitter about Trieste, and clearly see no reason why they should pay for losing the war. Well, why should they?' Yet while Elizabeth developed a tremendous admiration for the abundant creativity and generosity of the Italians, for their rollicking good humour, she could not cope with the noise. Quite apart from the honking horns and roaring traffic, every restaurant was dominated by the sound of cooks pounding veal and turkey breasts; while at night she had to endure the 'excruciating cacophony' of assorted guitarists, violinists and singers.

Italians are not known for their punctuality, so she wasted many hours in waiting for people to turn up, days waiting for the *festa* at which a certain dish was to be made. When the cooks were ready she could not afford to blink or lose the thread for a second, for they talked and cooked with more speed and energy than she felt she could keep up with. Her Italian was, as she described it, 'the wrong side of adequate'.

It was hard work; yet she was utterly absorbed, and exhilarated by a sense of discovery that she had never experienced before. 'As recipe after recipe came out and I realized how much I was learning, and how much these dishes were enlarging my own scope and enjoyment, the fever to communicate them grew every day more urgent.'[17] People at home had told her that she would find Italian cuisine so limited that she would be obliged to invent recipes. Invent! Elizabeth was itching to get home, to tell everyone that Italian cooking consisted of a good deal more than spaghetti, veal and tomato sauce.

She was back in London in late October, and took a room at the Grosvenor Hotel since Halsey Street was still let. From here she got in touch with Peter Higgins, who had given up farming in Devon and had returned to stockbroking, with the Guinness Peat Group in the City. They went out to dinner, stayed out late, and on their return Peter made a fuss because the hotel manager, mindful of his licence, refused to serve them any drinks after hours.

Elizabeth was at the height of her beauty, elated by the success of her trip, and more in love with Peter than ever before. Emotionally, she was about to embark on the happiest years of her life. In her work, she was about to begin a book that (as she already knew) would prove extremely difficult to write, but into which she always felt she had put the very best of herself.

In October 1952, tea came off the ration; and as Christmas approached, Marguerite Patten was able to demonstrate a 'fairly basic Christmas pudding and cake' on BBC television. There were better supplies of fish, vegetables, fruit and poultry, but butter, cooking fat and meat were still firmly controlled by the Ministry of Food. It was not until the following spring that egg distribution was freed of government restrictions.

Ingredients were not the only problem. Generous and obliging as they were, Italian cooks took very little interest in quantities or measurements. Elizabeth had armed herself with a measuring jug, marked out in both imperial and metric measurements, and on occasions 'I stood over the cooks and simply forced them to show me what they meant by a handful.' However, this was not always possible. A handful of flour, a bunch of spinach, a few spoonfuls of sugar, a lot of oil – all too often, these were the instructions she found when the time came to test the recipes.

That too posed a difficulty, for with the house let she did not have a kitchen. She spent the next three months with Doreen and her second husband, Colin Thornton, who had just moved into a house some thirty miles outside London, near Gravesend. Meopham Court was a huge house that had been divided into three. The Thorntons' end was Victorian Gothic and while the rooms were generous enough, the kitchen was minute. In no time at all Elizabeth had taken it over, and there was fresh pasta draped over every chair. The food she cooked was wonderful, but she was so engrossed in her work that she had lost all sense of time. She always offered to make dinner, and when Colin came back from work he was tired and hungry. But Elizabeth had barely begun to cook supper by nine, and often they did not sit down to eat until eleven.

A fast train service to London meant Elizabeth could make the occasional visit to the Italian shops of Soho to buy olive oil, parmesan cheeses and Italian rice. She was also lucky in that there was a farm near by where she could buy cheese and cream, but these were still rationed. So was meat, which came in hunks 'designated as suitable for roasting, frying, grilling, or stewing. To ask your butcher for special cuts (and foreign ones at that) was to ask for a sardonic laugh . . .'[18]

Difficult as it was, the writing of *Italian Food* liberated a lyrical, evocative streak in Elizabeth's writing. In previous books, she had been always inclined to quote from writers she admired, rather than attempt set-piece descriptions herself. In *Italian Food*, she allows herself to be carried away by the extraordinary delicacy of a plain risotto, the market in Venice and the kitchen of Signor Zoppi.

*

In the winter of 1952, when she was still lost in the long and arduous task of writing the book, she received some very bad news. The publishing firm of John Lehmann Ltd was being closed down. Financial control of the company had for many years been in the hands of Purnell, a West Country printing firm. In 1952, Purnell's chairman Wilfred Harvey made it known that he was not satisfied with the profits of John Lehmann Ltd, and planned to wind up the company. With the backing of a young publisher called Robert Maxwell, Lehmann tried to buy the list from Purnell – he was desperate to save it, for the company bore the biggest asset he had in publishing: his own name. But rather than sell John Lehmann Ltd for less than the monstrously large sum he had demanded, Harvey preferred to let the company fold. Journalists, writers and academics sprang to Lehmann's defence with innumerable articles and letters, deploring the fact that such a magnificent and pioneering house should have come to such a miserable end.

John sent Elizabeth a copy of a short statement in which he divorced himself from the company, with a letter dated 2 December: 'I fear the little announcement I enclose will startle and shock you. There is a very nasty story behind it, and I think I should tell it you as soon as possible.'

Elizabeth was deeply shaken by the news; her relationship with Lehmann had been 'friendly, fruitful, civilized';[19] and after hearing the 'nasty story', she was even more alarmed to hear that Purnell wanted to hold on to only two of Lehmann's authors: herself and the American writer Paul Bowles. They were to be handed over to Purnell's satellite company, Macdonald, who published school textbooks and *Jane's Fighting Ships*.

In January 1954, Elizabeth delivered the typescript personally to Wilfred Harvey's son, Captain Eric Harvey, MC, who was the managing director of Macdonald. As she sat in his office in Maddox Street, Elizabeth noticed how Harvey looked at the thick pile of paper on his desk with some distaste. He said it looked very long. It did not conform to the set pattern of cookery books. (The pioneering spirit, that had been such a feature of John Lehmann's company, evidently had no place at Macdonald.) Elizabeth admitted that that was the case, but she had found a great deal of material, and it had anyway been her intention to break new ground. Captain Harvey then looked up the contract in his filing cabinet.

'Good gracious. I see Mr Lehmann contracted to pay you an advance of three hundred pounds. Is that right?'

'Yes.'

'Three hundred pounds. THREE HUNDRED POUNDS? For a *cookery* book? . . . No wonder Mr Lehmann's business wasn't making a profit.' The brave captain sighed a surly sigh. 'Well, all I can say is that I hope we get our money back.'[20]

The delivery of a typescript that represents two or three years of work is always a shaky moment for an author, and to have it received in such a churlishly unsympathetic manner was a shock. 'The surrender into hostile hands of the book with which I had lived for two years and which had caused me much anguish but which I felt did all the same represent some advance over my previous work was traumatic.'[21] Yet that was only the beginning. 'Had I known what I was presently to discover about Macdonald I would certainly have preferred to abandon two years' hard work, return the hundred pounds which was all I had received of that famous advance, and cancel the contract.'[22]

Instead, she began writing pieces for the *Daily Express*, pieces largely written with an eye to value. They had titles like 'Some Leading Questions to Put to Your Butcher This Morning', and 'A Good Dinner Need not be Expensive'. Elizabeth had never had much money, so her concerns in these fields were the same as the editor's and her readership. But Elizabeth could also be rather dogmatic, and the *Daily Express*'s food editor sometimes felt the need to keep her in her place.

In a collective article called 'Is Butter Better?' Elizabeth wrote out why she gave butter an unequivocal 'yes'. However, the cookery editor felt that margarine did have its place for use in cakes, white sauces and strong fish like kippers and bloaters, and ended with 'Perhaps the last word on the question is that the better cook you are the more margarine you can use.'[23]

At the same time, Elizabeth began work on one of her most light-hearted books, *Summer Cooking*. It was a far less demanding project than her previous one, included all the kinds of food that she herself most liked to eat, and she wrote it just as those foods came into season.

By March or April 1954, with the publication of *Italian Food* scheduled for November, Elizabeth had received nothing from Guttuso. He would not answer her letters, while Macdonald were getting restive: time was pressing. Elizabeth turned for help to her friend Derek Hill, who knew Guttuso well. Hill managed to persuade him that Elizabeth needed the illustrations urgently and, in ones and twos, they began to arrive: seven pen and ink drawings, and one magnificent watercolour of artichokes, a bundle of chard and a straw-covered flask. Elizabeth was completely delighted. These intense and vibrant images did not merely illustrate her book: they confirmed everything that she thought and felt about Italy, and that she had tried to convey in *Italian Food*. 'Long before the pictures were out of my hands and delivered into those of the publishers, they had become for me an integral part of my book. Once again, the whole idea made sense.'[24]

Italian Food came out in November 1954, dedicated to Arthur and Viola Johnson, in appreciation for all the help and hospitality they had given her in Italy, and for Viola's work in checking and correcting all the Italian words and phrases. The book received an enthusiastic reception. Freya Stark, writing in the *Observer* on 14 November, observed that in times of 'culinary stress', a good cookery book 'has the same effect on one's morale as the thought of the evening's dinner, gently simmering in an Alpine hotel, has on the tired legs of the returning mountaineer ... Mrs David may be counted among the benefactors of humanity.'

Her book was also reviewed by Olivia Manning, in her 'London Letter' in the *Jerusalem Post*. She identified *Italian Food* as one of a new breed of cookbooks written for 'the New Poor' – those who would have had cooks and housekeepers before the war, but who now had to do their own shopping and cooking. These books 'do not dictate ... they inform with all the knowledge and charm their authors can bring to their art'.[25]

The book was undoubtedly a success, but it had very little impact outside the home counties, and none further afield. Even several years after the publication of *Italian Food*, when Ann and Franco Taruschio set up their restaurant at the Walnut Tree Inn near Abergavenny in 1963, their earliest customers had no idea what cannelloni and lasagne were.

However, the first print run of *Italian Food* sold out in three weeks, and Macdonald – despite their direct connection with the printers – reprinted too late, thus missing the Christmas market. In the New Year, Evelyn Waugh wrote in the *Sunday Times* that *Italian Food* was one of the two books he had most enjoyed that year. 'I was, and still am, stunned by the compliment and by Mr Waugh's tolerance at my amateur's efforts at writing,' wrote Elizabeth in her introduction to the Penguin edition. Here was no false modesty. If Elizabeth thought of herself as proficient in anything, it was in food and cookery – she never saw herself as a professional writer, certainly not in the same league as Waugh, and her opinion of her own writing never rose very high. Ten years later she could still write, 'I'm *not* a writer really you know, only a self-made one ...'[26] Yet whatever she thought of her writing, it was exasperating to have the book out of print when this testimonial was arousing people's interest.

Macdonald held the rights not only to *Italian Food*, but to her two previously published books as well. It seemed to Elizabeth monstrously unjust that they should have such contractual power over work that, if Eric Harvey's reaction to *Italian Food* was anything to go by, they would never have had the imagination to publish themselves. John Lehmann had put Elizabeth in touch with the literary agents Pearn, Pollinger and Higham (later David Higham Associates). She was represented by Paul Scott, later to achieve fame as the author of the *Raj Quartet*. But although he was unable to extricate her first two books and *Italian Food* from their grasp, he did get them to waive their right to a first option on *Summer Cooking*, which in the course of time was published by the Museum Press.

Elizabeth asked her friend Adrian Daintrey to illustrate *Summer Cooking*. Summer had long passed when he took up the commission, and neither he nor Elizabeth liked the idea of setting up fake summer scenes of strawberries and peaches. Instead, Daintrey would come round to Halsey Street, and do sketches of compositions set up mainly by Elizabeth. Daintrey was a curious character, rather threadbare and lugubrious in appearance; yet he had a great many friends and was a fund of stories and gossip, delivered in a very amusing, deadpan manner. His work at Halsey Street was congenial for both of them, and often turned into a long lunch. One of the most evocative of his sketches shows Elizabeth's trusty old gas cooker, on which a stout earthenware pot is cooking something warm and comforting. 'Some people liked Adrian's illustrations,' she wrote, 'others thought them old-fashioned, which they are. I still think they have a good atmosphere, and for those who chose to look there was useful information in them.'[27]

Despite her success, Elizabeth was not yet the household name that she would become. Her first three books had reached an enthusiastic, but still fairly narrow section of the population: mostly those middle-class, educated people who had experienced good food, and were keen – now that they no longer had staff – to train themselves in cooking French and Italian dishes. But she was about to be given an important break, which would open up her work to the paperback market. Penguin Books were interested in publishing an edition of *Mediterranean Food*; and Elizabeth discovered that the person responsible for bringing her book to the attention of Penguin's chairman, Allen Lane, was his only woman director, Eunice Frost.

Eunice Frost had first spotted the book in the Lehmann catalogue, and was intrigued by the new offering – not because it was a cookbook, but because it looked so interesting. 'I am not a cook', she said, 'then no more than now. I read it as an artist, and I felt ravished. It was so visually exciting, so illuminating, with such a sense of purpose and place – it was like finding yourself in an oasis filled with beautiful and delicious things, and it made one realize what one had missed all through the war.'[28]

In the 1988 introduction to *Mediterranean Food* Elizabeth David recorded her debt to Eunice Frost, thanks to whom 'My book had been given a dazzling opportunity.' Elizabeth goes on to say that Miss Frost had supported her book against considerable opposition, though Miss Frost could not recall that *Mediterranean Food* met with many reservations within the firm.

Macdonald passed on the Penguin offer, with a covering letter suggesting that Elizabeth might find it rather 'infra dig' to see her work in paperback. 'Silly asses,' wrote Elizabeth in the margin of the letter. Her reaction was quite the opposite. She wanted her book to reach as many people as possible, and the paperback price of two shillings and sixpence (as opposed to ten and six in hardback) put it within reach of almost everybody.

Macdonald insisted on taking 50 per cent of all the royalties from Penguin. It was quite normal at the time* but Elizabeth thought it scandalous. Her opinion of them sank even lower when, for the second year running, they allowed *Italian Food* to fall out of print just before Christmas.

Most galling of all was Macdonald's reaction to the revisions she

---

* Even now a 50 per cent cut is not unreasonable – though in this country, 60 per cent of paperback royalties is more likely to be the author's cut. The main difference in publishing contracts today is that authors' hardback advances are far higher than they were in the mid-1950s, largely because they take future paperback rights into account.

had made to the Penguin edition of *Mediterranean Food*. These revisions were essential in view of the fact that the book had been written in 1949, and conditions had changed dramatically since then. But Macdonald refused to budge: not only did they forbid Penguin to call their edition 'revised', but they also refused to reset the hardback edition in line with the much-needed changes.

At the most important and productive period in her life, Elizabeth was in the hands of publishers who were, at best, remarkably unsympathetic. This did not, in the long run, damage either her reputation or her books; but in that part of Elizabeth's mind that was always fuming, always enraged, a dangerous resentment was building up.

* * * * * * *

CHAPTER THIRTEEN

Friends, Editors and
Other Enemies

Whatever he still felt for Elizabeth, Tony David had tired of England. In 1953 he decided he could do better by moving to Spain. With Tony gone, Halsey Street underwent another transformation. The original kitchen, which had been in the basement, was transformed into a tiny bed-sitter into which moved Lesley O'Malley. She made a very dashing entry to Halsey Street, perched on a small sofa which was lashed to the top of a friend's Land Rover.

The arrival of Lesley O'Malley was very welcome. They shared many friends in common, such as the painter Derek Hill, the writer Roald Dahl and his wife Pat, and the rest of the Cairo set; while their own friendship had a delightful complicity that meant they were never bored in each other's company, never wearied of each other's jokes. Lesley was also very close to Felicité; but whereas Felicité and Elizabeth ate together only on birthdays and feast-days, Elizabeth and Lesley ate and drank together several times a week, and often went out to the theatre or the cinema. They had more than friendship in common. Both had been married in Cairo, both were now separated; but while Elizabeth's marriage was over primarily because she had grown bored with Tony, Lesley had had to endure life with a violent and abusive man.

Lesley had found a good job in advertising after the war; but her confidence had been undermined by the dreadful years with her ex-husband, and she was now deeply involved with a married man. She had met Patrick de Morny in Cairo. He had married after

Lesley, and was now as unhappy in his marriage as she had been in hers. But although he was very much in love with Lesley, he felt unable to leave his emotionally fragile wife.

Elizabeth seemed to be drawn to women whose love life had gone wrong, to have a sort of tacit empathy with them. Another of her closest friends was Joyce Murchie, a New Zealand heiress who had come into her fortune at the age of twenty-one and was spending it fast. Small, with ginger hair and freckles, Joyce had married a dentist and tried to become a normal housewife – but the effort was too much for her. She was too much of a hedonist, and was the sort of generous, ebullient person who paid for every round of drinks she and her friends could order. She did not live anywhere in particular, preferring to stay in hotels or the guest bedrooms of her friends. She travelled a good deal, and – when she had run through her fortune – went to live cheaply in a little flat in Asolo. She had been truly in love only once, with a young soldier she had met in Cairo. After the war they had travelled across north Africa; but one day, when her lover was in the car on his own, he drove into a sandstorm and perished.

Lesley and Elizabeth gave a joint cocktail party on one occasion. They had made a magnificent spread of *mezze* (one of Lesley's specialities) and the party went on till four in the morning; but when Elizabeth attempted another cocktail party, it was not a success. She invited far too many people, had no time to heat up the food she had planned under the grill, and one of her dearest neighbours – Walter Baxter, who later became the owner of the Chanterelle restaurant – was insulted by a fellow guest. When it was over, Elizabeth swore that never again would she invite so many people 'who couldn't even get on over drinks'.

Felicité was still living in the top flat, and she and Elizabeth maintained a scrupulous respect for each other's privacy. If Elizabeth was entertaining one of their mutual friends, Felicité came downstairs for a drink but always vanished before dinner. And when Felicité was entertaining, Elizabeth did the same – except that she sometimes brought a terrine or a pâté, and left it as a parting gift with the words 'I thought so-and-so ought to have something decent to eat.'

The underlying reason for this arrangement was that their attitudes to food were so different that they constituted a mutual irritation. In contrast to Elizabeth, Felicité was completely uninterested in food. But sometimes, if Felicité was going to have someone special round for supper, she would ask Elizabeth to cook something for her. Elizabeth always obliged, leaving the dish discreetly in Felicité's tiny kitchen while she was still at work.

One cannot help thinking that Felicité's life might have been more fulfilling if she had left at some point, and branched out on her own. She was very much her own person and knew her own mind, and Elizabeth valued her judgement and her companionship; yet as the years went on, Felicité felt rather oppressed by Elizabeth's fame. She had always wanted to write poetry, but she was much too diffident to show it to Elizabeth, who probably never gave Felicité's writing talents a thought. Felicité was left with the feeling that fate had given all the literary gifts to her elder sister.

At the same time, Felicité had the Gwynne strength of character, and she had that confidence which comes from a certain family pride. She was also a good talker, and a great gossip. She knew everyone in the street, always had time for a chat, and was intensely curious about everything that was going on among the neighbours: 'She was the sort of person who couldn't talk to you for two minutes without trying to ferret something out of you.' She dressed soberly, and bicycled everywhere. Her main extravagance seems to have been her expensive Knightsbridge hairdresser, whom she went to at least once a week – as much for the gossip as for her hair.

Another major element in Elizabeth's life was her sister Diana, who lived in the house with the leaning trees in Abingdon Road. Her first child, Rupert, had been followed by another son, Jonathan (always known as Johnny), in 1951; and two years later she gave birth to her only daughter, Christabel. She was to have two more children: Steven, and Christopher, known as Christo. Diana and her husband were devoted to each other and, although money was always tight, their marriage was happy. Elizabeth used to grumble that Diana's life was one of non-stop drudgery, and that it was Christopher's fault for giving her too many children; but at the same time she was very fond of her attractive brother-in-law, and was one of his patients.

Dr Christopher Grey was doing well. He combined great charm with exceptional skill as a doctor, and he travelled between his patients, and the various academic institutions to which he acted as physician, in the old Rolls-Royce he had bought from Elizabeth and Tony.

It soon became the custom for Elizabeth and Felicité to spend Christmas with Diana and her family. Christopher would come to Halsey Street with the Rolls, and get them – plus all the presents, and baskets of food, wine, preserves and provisions cooked by Elizabeth – into the car. All three sisters were close, and Diana and Felicité were quite capable of standing up to the famous Liza.

Johnny Grey, Diana's second son, was terrified of Elizabeth as a child. But he was also intrigued, and a trip to Aunt Liza's in Halsey Street was always looked forward to. She had an alarmingly brisk manner with children. Yet in her rather aloof and distant way she could respond, because like them she understood the magic of things. He remembers being taken to her house to learn how to cook a chicken, and on another occasion, she noticed that he was fascinated by two or three Japanese paper fans with landscapes printed on them. 'You can have those,' she said – and made a friend for life. Little Johnny was stunned by the generosity of her gift, and lost in admiration that Aunt Liza could give away such precious and beautiful objects.

Her god-daughter Frances Fedden also remembers the nervousness and interest that Elizabeth excited. When she and her sister Kate came to Halsey Street – the Fedden family would always visit Elizabeth on Boxing Day, her birthday – Elizabeth fussed about, trying to keep the children from touching anything. But if either of them expressed an interest in something, she would take the object in caressing hands, talk about it and invite them to hold it. Frances also remembered how good she was at giving just the right present to excite a child's imagination. She did not necessarily wrap it up; but she would stroke and handle the object before bestowing it, giving her gift a significance that no amount of tissue paper and ribbon could have achieved. She remembers in particular a little painted tin box that Elizabeth gave her, cunningly disguised as a pile of books bound with a strap.

Elizabeth's mother Stella had moved from Dedham to a smaller house, in Brighton. She still carried on dealing in furniture and antiques, and used Priscilla's house in Kensington as her London base. Priscilla's younger sisters used to come and visit their mother there; but Pris herself was no longer the centre of their world, as she had been in the thirties and forties. She was wrapped up in her daughters and her own circle of friends, and grew further apart from her sisters – especially Elizabeth, who was rather contemptuous of what she saw as Priscilla's social pretensions.

Within her immediate neighbourhood, Elizabeth had a number of friends: Joyce Murchie, when she was around; Walter Baxter; and Kate O'Malley, who was Lesley's sister-in-law. In 1948 Kate married Paul Willert, who had served with the French Resistance during the war before becoming an oil dealer. Friends from Cairo, such as the Feddens, Burnet Pavitt, Patrick Kinross and Eddie Gathorne-Hardy were still much in evidence, and when George Lassalle married Judith Richardson in 1951, Elizabeth prepared the wedding breakfast. Some friends felt that Elizabeth had been weeping into the salmon she so lovingly cooked, mourning the loss of George; but Elizabeth was probably sadder about losing a friend than a lover. She sometimes resented the women who took away her male friends, and it took time for her to come round to them.

Elizabeth had also kept in touch with one of her mother's most prickly and amusing friends, Arthur Lett Haines. Haines was a painter, now best known for being the partner of the painter and horticulturalist Cedric Morris. Together they had started the East Anglian School of Painting and Drawing, at Benton End, Hadleigh. Their establishment could put up about fifteen students at a time, its most distinguished alumnus being Lucian Freud.

It seems to have been a wonderfully disorganized and stimulating place, not so much a school as a way of life devoted to gardening and painting. Cedric was usually up at dawn to tend his irises, while Lett woke at noon for a cocktail. Lett was an inspired cook, and did the cooking for the whole establishment. He was more interested in food than most, and his strong views usually (though not always) coincided with Elizabeth's.

Elizabeth bought a painting from Cedric Morris called *The Eggs*, which had been painted in 1944. 'Cedric told me he painted the picture during one of the rationing years of the last war and that . . . Arthur Lett Haines repeatedly demanded that the eggs be released because they were actually needed in the kitchen – which was run by Lett, since Cedric never in his whole long life put saucepan to stove . . . I forget just when I bought *The Eggs* from Cedric but I think it was in 1953 because I remember the City bedecked with flags as we drove up to Suffolk in the early morning so it must have been coronation year.'[1] Elizabeth bought the painting for £100, and eventually left it to the Tate Gallery.

Elizabeth never had enough money to collect paintings as well as books; but over the course of her life she bought some beautiful things. She had three pen-and-ink drawings by Henry Moore, and three still lifes by an artist called Eliot Hodgkin, who was a friend of Felicité's. She also had a portrait of herself by John Ward, and a portrait of Norman Douglas by Adrian Daintrey, who illustrated *Summer Cooking*. In her hall hung a set of strange, primitive flower paintings that her mother had found in a junk shop. The painter John Nash, who had taught patients in a mental institution, said they were almost certainly the work of someone very disturbed. 'It's obvious when you look at them,' wrote Elizabeth. 'They are curious and interesting, and very obsessive.'[2] Cedric Morris's *Eggs*, however, remained the most important piece in her collection.

She would sometimes go and spend the weekend with him and Lett Haines at Benton End, and sometimes, when Lett came up to London with one or two of the students, they would all go out together. The painter Antony Daniels remembers one occasion when, after an evening's drinking, they all came back to Halsey Street for supper. While someone opened a bottle, Elizabeth, who had a cigarette in her hand, got a chicken out of the fridge. She dropped it on the floor before it reached the table where – the cigarette now transferred to her lips – she proceeded to hack it up with a cleaver. There were sarcastic comments and much laughter about how uneatable supper was going to be. 'Just you wait,' said Elizabeth. After a little oil, salt and herbs had been thrown on to the chicken pieces, they went under the grill – and emerged, of course, succulent.

The pattern of her life developed its own routine. She woke at four or five in the morning, in her four-poster bed hung with its white crochet-work curtains, and started reading and writing with a thermos of black Nescafé beside her. Work resumed at the kitchen table where she wrote and cooked for most of the morning, and by eleven or twelve, she had done six or seven hours' work and was ready to relax. Elizabeth entertained a great deal at this time, and it was seldom that she had lunch alone: apart from anything else, she was constantly evolving and trying out recipes; and neither she, nor her friends, could bear the idea of those delicious meals going to waste. Often, the food had been cooked – or at least prepared – in advance; although those who did see her in the act of cooking said that she had a marvellous dexterity, an economy of effort. This made everything look easy, though of course such ease can only be achieved with long practice.

She did have a sitting room, and in the fifties and early sixties it had not yet been choked under drifts of books, catalogues and pieces of pottery. But the sitting room was not really where she felt at home, and more often, she took her guests straight down to sit at the kitchen table. The wine was already open – Elizabeth had probably started it while she was cooking – but before handing her guests a glass, Patrick Leigh Fermor remembered how she used to polish it carefully with a clean tea towel. A heap of books and papers had been pushed up at one end to make way for lunch, set with white starched napkins and satisfyingly heavy cutlery. On the table, as always, were a few olives, bread and butter.

Elizabeth was in no hurry. She liked to sit talking, with her back to the stove, and occasionally she would swivel round and adjust a knob or peer into the oven. When the food arrived, it was presented in the earthenware pots it had been cooked in, without fuss or comment, as was the perfect cheese and beautiful fruit that usually followed. If she served a salad, it was dressed at the table and tossed with her hands. This sometimes caused an involuntary gasp from one or two of her guests, but Elizabeth insisted that this was the only way to ensure that every leaf was properly coated with oil.

The conviviality was more important than the food, and Elizabeth liked to sit for hours talking and drinking wine after the meal was over. Yet she was not good at the early stage of a conversation: she seemed preoccupied, not fully engaged, as if her thoughts were still with the work she had been doing that morning. 'She talked obliquely,' said Veronica Nicholson, 'and it was up to you to get the conversational ball rolling; and sure enough it would start to unravel, and soon the whole ball would be coming undone – and late in the afternoon I would go home, thinking what a wonderful talk it had been.'[3]

She went out in the afternoons, or cooked and wrote in the kitchen, and more friends appeared in the evenings (though she did not usually cook more than once a day). She retired to bed, and her books. The light seldom went out until the early hours.

Elizabeth's journalism had appeared mainly in *Harper's Bazaar*. She almost signed a contract with *House and Garden*, owned by Condé Nast, in late 1953; but she was not aware of the intense rivalry between the publications. When it emerged that an agreement with them would prohibit her writing for *Harper's*, owned by the National Magazine Company, she backed down. 'I must say I was absolutely amazed to receive your letter this morning,' wrote *House and Garden*'s editor Anthony Hunt. 'When you left, I believed that we had made an agreement which only needed written confirmation . . . It appears, however, that in the meantime, without letting us know, you reopened negotiations with *Harper's.*' Despite Elizabeth's unprofessional behaviour, Hunt did not close the door in her face: 'I only hope that at some future time we may be able to come to a better arrangement,' he wrote.[4]

Harper's did not object to her writing for newspapers. She had written for the *Daily Express*, which had not made the best of her, and she also worked as cookery reader and editor for the publishing firm of André Deutsch. Then, in 1955, she was taken on by the *Sunday Times*. Leonard Russell had published an extract from *Summer Cooking* in 1955 when the book came out, and Elizabeth wrote for the paper regularly for the next five years.

Elizabeth had great respect for Leonard Russell. He was nominally the literary editor, but he had enormous influence on the whole tone and direction of the paper. He came across as brusque and rather unwelcoming; but this was partly an affectation, and people would find, to their surprise, that he was much more approachable than he appeared at first. Elizabeth described him as the sort of editor who could 'sometimes persuade or cajole me into writing what I had thought I couldn't, although never what *I* knew I wouldn't'.[5] Her pieces for the *Sunday Times* were short, lively and eminently practical: there was one on 'Bedsitter Tips' (eggs can be cooked, covered, on a plate over a steaming saucepan of vegetables) and another on 'Cooking on Your Own'. Elizabeth knew that she was writing for people who did not want to spend a lot of time at the stove, and in her articles she gave them the best she could, without wasting their time or their money. 'The first thing I want to know about a recipe, whatever its cost, is whether it's going to produce real food as opposed to a piece of frippery nonsense.'[6]

However, the nonsense put out by the food industry was always good copy, and Elizabeth could never resist taking a well-aimed shot at food fairs – usually the plumpest of sitting ducks. It is interesting to see what was on offer at the Olympia Food Fair in 1956. Frozen meals had now evolved into the TV dinner with everything all ready on a plastic tray, 'so that the awful fag of transferring the frozen chop and two frozen veg from shopping basket to dish is eliminated'; while the Gas Board was trying to tempt the housewife back to the stove with dishes called Huffkins, Fidget Pies and Bedfordshire Clangers. From Eastern Europe were huge sacks of dried mushrooms, juicy little plums and a bewildering selection of sausages; from the US, hot-dogs and donuts. Two Spanish senoritas were doing a flamenco in honour of Spanish olive oil, while the English cheeses stood by in 'rugged dignity'.[7]

For the first three or four months, all went smoothly at the *Sunday Times*; until Ernestine Carter was appointed to edit the Women's Pages. Mrs Carter, originally from Savannah, Georgia, was a formidable woman and had been a curator of the Museum of Modern Art in New York before going into journalism. She was, by all accounts, very effective and good at her job; but her high opinion of her own talents produced a correspondingly low opinion of her contributors. She had no qualms about chopping and changing their copy to suit herself.

Elizabeth always took care to hand her copy in on time, so that she could make any alterations or cuts necessary on the proof that she always insisted on seeing herself. To her editors, she always gave the same reason for this: cookery writing, if it had any claim to honesty, depended on precise instructions, and a line that might seem extraneous to an editor could contain the vital point on which depended the success or failure of a dish; only an experienced cook could recognize what was essential and what could be cut. Most editors were happy to bow to Elizabeth's authority.

Mrs Carter, however, thought she was quite capable of cutting the work of this tiresome woman who took herself so seriously; and as to being a cook, why, Mrs Carter had written a cookbook herself. She describes the book, and her attitude to cooking, in a volume of memoirs entitled *With Tongue in Chic*: 'I had become seethingly resentful of the prepare-lovingly-marinate-for-twenty-four-hours-school of cookery . . . A maximum effect with a minimum of effort was my aim; the recipes were brief and to the point.'[8] (Her book was called *Flash in the Pan*, published in 1953.)

Elizabeth became exasperated by the frequency with which her pieces, already cut to the required length by herself, were being hacked into yet again by Mrs Carter. Every week there was yet another squabble between them, yet another exchange of icy, outraged letters. Elizabeth developed a hatred for Mrs Carter that, to her friends at least, bordered on the obsessive.

* * * * * * *

CHAPTER FOURTEEN

On the Road
in Provincial France

During the time Elizabeth was locked in battle with Mrs Carter, she also met one of the best editors she was ever to have in her life. In 1956, she was lured away from *Harper's* by Audrey Withers of *Vogue*, an editor of great imagination and energy, who was constantly on the lookout for fresh talent. She not only recognized Elizabeth as a superb writer: she also saw that *Harper's* was not making the best of her. Anne Scott-James, who had been Elizabeth's first editor on *Harper's*, had left the magazine in 1951. Elizabeth stayed on; but by 1956 she had been doing the same sort of piece for years, with very little change in the way of presentation. What Audrey Withers proposed was far more exciting. Elizabeth would be paid more money and have her own page, which would be in the centre rather than the back of the magazine; her work would be illustrated by a full-page photograph, and she would be given star treatment. Elizabeth was delighted by Audrey Withers's proposal, and *Harper's* made very little effort to stop her going.

Vogue announced the forthcoming appearance of 'ELIZABETH DAVID, world-famous cookery expert and author' in their April issue. She would start with a series of monthly articles on 'food in season, and how to make the most delicious use of it'. Since she was now firmly in the Condé Nast stable, Elizabeth also began to contribute regularly to *House and Garden*.

The twelve articles were illustrated with full-page colour photographs by Anthony Denney, another of Audrey Withers's discoveries. She had first seen his photographs in a book, during the war. She was very struck by his work, and keen that he should come into the Condé Nast fold; and with considerable difficulty she tracked him down to India, where he was working for British Intelligence.

After the war, he did come and work for *Vogue* and *House and Garden*; but Denney was much more than a photographer – he was also a very gifted decorator. At the time, it was still uncommon for decorators to juxtapose antiques and objets d'art with the latest Italian and Scandinavian furniture. Denney could do so because he had a profound knowledge of furniture, art, sculpture and design – both ancient and modern – and was a compulsive collector. Over the years, he had developed a sureness of taste and style which was reflected in everything he did.

At first, Elizabeth had been dubious about the idea of food photography. She doubted, too, that she could get herself and a dish of cooked food to the Condé Nast studio without both looking flat and harassed on arrival. It was Denney who suggested he might take the photographs in her house. 'The photographs he took of my food,' wrote Elizabeth many years later, 'were, I think, the first of their kind, in that, as always, I sought to make the subjects of the pictures useful as well as attractive, and atmospheric, but also realistic.'[1] Considering that both she and Denney were perfectionists used to having their own way, these sessions might have become extremely tense. However, in each other they both recognized a true artist, and someone they could learn from. Elizabeth, especially, acknowledged Denney as a formative influence: not only on her taste, but on her powers of observation:

Anthony showed me what a quantity of small and important details I was missing, and how many inaccuracies and blunders I was allowing to get by. He is the person who sees and notes the difference between the way the French put a knife and fork on the table, and the way the English do it; how the lemons are cut in Spain and how exactly a loaf is cut or broken and asks why – and detects anything arty quicker than you can say knife. It was the demonstration of this painter's eye, the visual memory he has plus his feeling for authenticity which is a bit like Norman [Douglas]'s that I found such a pleasure, and the stimulus all this produced that made our working relationship so fruitful – it was a slow explosion for me, like a marvellous love affair . . .[2]

It was an immense satisfaction to Audrey Withers to see such a successful collaboration; and with a whole page at her disposal, plus all the run-offs she wanted, Elizabeth could afford to enrich her pieces with many more comments, subtleties and details than those she had written for *Harper's*. At the same time, Miss Withers felt – as good editors do – that she could coax more out of Elizabeth.

During the 'Food at Its Best' series, Audrey and Elizabeth had often talked about her work, over lunch near the *Vogue* offices. Audrey was impressed by the intensely personal way Elizabeth talked of her experiences of eating in specific houses and restaurants in France, and felt that the dishes and foods that Elizabeth wrote about would be even more vivid if accompanied by the stories of how something was displayed in the market, how a certain dish was only made in one place, who had cooked it for her, where she was sitting when she ate it and what wine she drank with it. Hitherto, Elizabeth had reserved her more personal voice for her books rather than her articles.

Audrey Withers's plan to ask Elizabeth for more of herself was bolder than it might appear, because she was so intensely private. She was one of those people whose reserve is like an invisible wall: you know it's there, but you only know you've crossed it when it's too late and offence has been taken. Would she be offended if asked to put more of herself into her pieces? Audrey put her request so tactfully that Elizabeth was not offended; but she pointed out that she only had a certain number of those vivid personal anecdotes and descriptions that Miss Withers required, and new ones could not be conjured up from books and evocative recipes alone. She had to keep her knowledge of France fresh; and while on £20 a month she could afford ingredients, she could not afford trips abroad. Miss Withers agreed, and took the unusual step of allowing Elizabeth the occasional research trip to France, armed with £100 or so of Condé Nast money.

For Elizabeth, this presented a tremendous opportunity. She had already made herself an expert on French food, and had amassed a large collection of French cookery books – as well as an impressive array of traditional French pots, pans and cooking utensils. She had decided that her next book was going to be a definitive work on the everyday cooking of provincial France; but the problem was that this sort of food changed not only from one region to another, but across the seasons as well. There was an enormous amount of research that could only be done on the spot. She would have completed the research by herself, eventually; but the help and encouragement she received from Condé Nast and Audrey Withers now meant that she could go to France more often than before, and be paid for it.

The Condé Nast allowances were not extravagant; but like the clever French housewives she admired, Elizabeth spent the money well. When on the road in France, with whatever friend she had taken along to act as chauffeur, she would usually have a picnic lunch. This gave her the opportunity to see what was in the shops, sample the local cheeses and sausages, and see what vegetables were at their freshest and best in the market. Later on in the day she tried to arrive at her destination in good time for dinner, so as to have time for a chat with the *patron*. She would make friends with Monsieur or Madame, talk to them about what she had seen in the markets and sampled during the day, give them an idea of the sort of things she would like to eat, and listen to their suggestions. The *patrons* were usually flattered to find someone who took such an intelligent interest in the local produce and dishes of the region, and did their best to please her.

'Under such circumstances,' she wrote in *French Provincial Cooking*, 'I have eaten some of the most enjoyable of French country meals; unexacting ones, ordered and served with the minimum of fuss.' And by describing her simple technique for ordering a good dinner, she must have saved many of her readers from ordering an expensive and over-elaborate one.

Elizabeth's diaries are sketchy, and it is difficult to reconstruct the order of her trips to France, who she went with and where she stayed. She often went with Doreen Thornton, who drove her all over France in her Morris Traveller. Elizabeth was good company, and good at map-reading – though because she only looked at the map and not at the signposts, they often got lost in towns. 'Just take the first left and we'll be in the main square,' she would say, unable to appreciate that they were locked into a labyrinthine one-way system. One thing that struck Doreen was how few notes Elizabeth took during these trips. 'We shared a room so often, on so many journeys, but I never saw her writing anything down. She relied on her extraordinary visual memory.'[3]

The presence of Elizabeth's companion – usually Doreen, sometimes Peter – is only referred to in the most indirect way: 'our coffee, when it arrived' – 'I knew where we would go to look for the dish.' What is in these articles, however, is exactly what Audrey wanted. How she chased two hundred miles across France for a dish of pork and prunes, how her memory of the beauty of the Place Stanislas in Nancy is inextricably linked with the little orange and gilt boxes of the Bergamottes de Nancy, how an old lady in a shop in Provence kept everyone waiting while Mademoiselle cut just the right slice of ham for a dish of petits pois.

The series opened with the food of Paris, which was the most personal piece in the series. It is not only a wonderfully funny and penetrating evocation of Mme Barette and her family, their cook Léontine and their lovely food; it also gives the reader a unique insight into how an ordinary (though admittedly very greedy) Parisian family shopped and ate.

In 1956, in Provence, she was appalled to see the damage done by the previous winter. 'The whole landscape was gashed with ugly black wounds. Hundreds of olive trees, withered and blighted by the frosts and the all-blasting mistral winds which followed them, had been cut down or were standing like ancient skeletons . . .'[4] Only one place had escaped, surrounding a little village in the Ventoux called Beaumes de Venise. On that occasion, she did not taste the golden muscat wine that she later helped to make so famous – for the simple reason that no one in the hotel where she ate lunch thought it worth mentioning.

The following year she made a long research trip that was to prove particularly important, for on it she discovered a lodestar: one of those restaurants which epitomized, to her, everything that was most admirable in the French attitude to food, from its cooking to its presentation. The journey had begun in Alsace, then continued into Lorraine and down through Burgundy, and so to Lyon. Lyon is reputedly the Olympus of French provincial cooking, and here she ate some of the best fish dishes she had ever tasted; but for the most part the food of the Lyonnais, rather like that of Bologna, was rather too rich and heavy for her taste. From Lyon they went south, and then, at Valence, due west into the hills to Lamastre.

The Hotel du Midi already had two Michelin stars and a fine reputation when Elizabeth first visited the establishment in the summer of 1957. At that time there were fifty-nine two-star restaurants in the whole of France, and they were not cheap. They usually boasted about half a dozen *specialités de la maison*, most of which could be sampled at one gargantuan sitting by choosing the *menu gastronomique*. However, it was possible to arrange demi-pension terms. Elizabeth and her companion were so delighted with the hotel and the welcome they received from Mme Barattero that they immediately decided to stay a week – and for her companion, who had driven all the way, it must have been a well-earned rest. The food on offer at demi-pension terms was simple, not extravagant; but the kitchens were run by a master chef, M. Perrier, who put the same care and experience into his vegetable soups as he did into his *pains d'écrevisses sauce cardinal*. Thus they enjoyed, over the course of seven days, some of the simplest and best-prepared food in France – as well as the *pains d'écrevisses*, the *galantine de caneton* and the *poularde en vessie* which were the specialities of the house.

Elizabeth was so impressed by the Hotel du Midi, that every evening's menu was described in her article. This was to make two essential points about French restaurant cooking: first, its variety, and second, how worthwhile it is to eat simple dishes cooked in a first-class manner. When the article was eventually published (in September 1958) it was unique for a *Vogue* cookery article in that it contained not a single recipe.

Yet Elizabeth was not stuck on the perfected principles of French cookery – far from it. The late 1950s were a time when many new food products were coming on to the market, and Elizabeth was naturally bombarded with samples and invitations. She did not always enjoy her experiences. A trip round the Walls sausage factory made a lasting and painful impression. She was, however, willing to try out new things and could make some surprising comments. When sent a sample of Uncle Ben's 'converted' rice, she noted in her diary that it looked rather like Patna rice and she tried it out in a risotto: 'to one (US) cup full of rice, 4 scant cups of liquid, including half a cup of wine. Cooked about twenty minutes. Very good.'[5]

While Elizabeth was working at *Vogue*, her sister Felicité embarked on a new business venture. A young man called John Sandoe, who had worked with her at J. A. Allen, suggested that they go into business together. Felicité had no money of her own to put into it; but she found the premises, in Blacklands Terrace, that the shop still occupies to this day. Felicité was a voracious reader, of everything from novels to histories. She had very strong enthusiasms, which she frequently imposed on her customers. One unwary passer-by, who dropped into the shop for a new book and was unprepared for Felicité's hard-sell techniques, emerged with a full set of the Mapp and Lucia novels by E. F. Benson. Felicité was at John Sandoe's for the rest of her working life, and kept Elizabeth supplied with books and catalogues.

The summer of 1957 marked the high point of Elizabeth's relationship with her publishers, Macdonald. They not only agreed to incorporate her revisions for *Mediterranean Food* and *French Country Cooking* (this last title was also due to be published by Penguin), but they also agreed to lend her two of the Guttuso drawings that had illustrated *Italian Food*.

It was Roald Dahl who suggested to Elizabeth that she should break into the American market, though as he acknowledged, 'everything in this life depends on fucking timing'.[6] He had sent *Italian Food* and a selection of her journalism to his American agents Ann Watkins Inc., and they approached Dahl's publisher Alfred Knopf. Knopf did not offer much because, as they told her frankly, they did not expect to sell many. They did not want the Guttuso illustrations, and they told Elizabeth that the book needed substantial alteration for the American market.

To the astonishment of Alfred Knopf, Elizabeth refused the offer. She heard that Knopf was so furious that her name was never again to be mentioned in his presence – although he was still interested in the book. Elizabeth was only prepared to negotiate on two conditions: they could not publish the book without the Guttuso illustrations, and her book was not to be Americanized. 'I am prepared,' she wrote to her agent Paul Scott, 'to barter financial gain for the minimum of interference with my work. Knopf must surely see that if he wants to preserve the character of the book there is no point in turning it into just another American-Italian cookery book, of which there are already scores.'

Knopf grudgingly agreed, and the work of Americanizing the book without losing its character was given to someone who translated *Fritto misto* as 'Mixed Fry' and *Melanzane e funghetti* as 'Fried Eggplant'. This editor did not last long, and Knopf's next choice of editor was far more suitable. Avis de Voto admired Elizabeth's writing and understood Elizabeth's point of view, but she was equally determined to make the book easier for the American cook. So great were the difficulties of translation that at one point Elizabeth had to send Avis a food parcel, containing things like sultanas, ground rice, haricot beans and a yeast sample. 'None of us have seen anything like it,' she wrote back.[7] After months of work the book came out, and Elizabeth was pleased with the result. Yet it made very little impact in the States, and after all the time and effort put in by herself and Avis de Voto, Elizabeth wondered whether the exercise had been worthwhile.

The articles on French regional cooking were published between May 1957 and April 1958, after which Elizabeth did a series on Italian cooking – this was far less arduous, being based on research already done. It was also very popular, because everything Italian was now fashionable – especially the coffee bar.

The coffee bar is one of the most interesting social phenomena in London in the late fifties, though Elizabeth seldom mentions them. She was never particularly interested in coffee: she had acquired a taste for Nescafé during the war, and never wished for anything better. Another reason was that the coffee bar, and coffee bar culture, was above all a manifestation of youth. One of the most famous coffee bars, The Two I's, had a tiny basement in which people squeezed to hear Adam Faith, Little Richard or Tommy Steele. 'For the first time, the young had somewhere to hang out. The counter was dominated by that hissing, spluttering machine which kept the room (and its windows) reassuringly steamy – and, with the cigarette fug (everybody smoked then) the coffee bar became a teenage sanctuary.'[8] Elizabeth, however, was writing for their mothers. After the series on Italian food Elizabeth went on to 'Cooking Hazards'. This was in direct response to the letters of her readers, who wanted her reassurance on supposedly tricky problems, such as cooking rice and how to roast meat.

Elizabeth's main preoccupation at this time was how to get Tony to agree to a divorce. He had been very much against the idea, but in 1957 he made a blunder which gave Elizabeth the opportunity she needed. While living in Spain, Tony had been cited as co-respondent in a farcical divorce case complete with jealous husband and private detectives. It was gleefully reported in the *Daily Express* by Nancy Spain, one of the most aggressive gossip columnists of her day. Tony was quoted in her article, and made the mistake of referring to Elizabeth as 'my ex-wife'. In July 1958, she filed for divorce, and as far as she was concerned it was not a moment too soon, for Tony was becoming an embarrassment. To avoid the scandal in Spain he had moved to Tangier, where she heard he was running a club-cum-restaurant called the Mille et Une Nuits.

Her main reasons for initiating proceedings were that their marriage had been at an end for the past five years, and that it was based on a misunderstanding: 'He did not realize that my wish was to settle down and lead a reasonably ordered life not more than normally harassed by bills and debts. His broken promises, evasions and deceit in these matters eventually caused me to lose all respect for him.'[9]

Elizabeth had never forgiven Tony for his fecklessness; but perhaps her anger was also partly tinged with guilt – as a wise man once said, it is hard to forgive those one has injured. As for Tony, he was much more forgiving. He never ceased to love her, and followed her career with pride.

Elizabeth spent part of the summer in France with Peter Higgins, and in August she went to stay with Derek Hill on Tory Island, off the north-west coast of Donegal. While Elizabeth was not one for long walks, she loved the wild landscape and the changing light of Tory Island. She also loved sitting at the kitchen table, talking to Derek and his cook, Gracie McDermott. Elizabeth said that Gracie was one of the best natural cooks she had ever met. On one occasion when they were talking about salmon, Elizabeth remarked that it was impossible to make a good soup from this fish. Gracie said nothing: but a day or two later, she served up a most delicious, perfectly flavoured salmon soup. From the mid-fifties to the mid-sixties, Elizabeth often spent Christmas with Derek on Tory Island. It was a haven of peace and tranquillity, compared to the frenetic, over-commercialized atmosphere of Christmas in London.

She also kept in touch with Doreen and Colin Thornton, with whom she would sometimes spend the weekend. Doreen had been given a copy of Charles Gibson Cowan's book *The Voyage of the Evelyn Hope*, which had been published soon after the war. Doreen had not read it, but on one weekend in 1958 or 1959 when Elizabeth was coming to stay Doreen thought she might be amused to see the book, and put it in her room. It was evidently the first time that Elizabeth had ever seen a finished copy. She had read the early chapters in Alexandria, but she had never read the ending, which is a completely fictionalized account of them escaping from Crete with the German airborne invasion in full swing. Elizabeth was so enraged that she pulled the book to pieces in front of Doreen, hissing, 'Never, *ever*, let me hear that man's name again!'[10]

Elizabeth's journalistic life at this time was sharply divided. She was very happy at *Vogue*, where Audrey Withers had given her work a new dimension. At the *Sunday Times*, on the other hand, her relationship with Ernestine Carter had reached breaking point.

The idea of grouping a series of articles together by theme had been extremely effective and successful, and towards the end of 1958, Audrey Withers and Elizabeth decided that she should do a series on the markets of France; the trip was scheduled for mid-June 1959. A month before that, Elizabeth's battle with Ernestine Carter reached its climax. As she wrote to Jean LeRoy, who was on the editorial staff of the *Sunday Times*,

two of my recent articles have been hacked about in such a reckless way that I can no longer afford to keep silent. Mrs

Carter's interference is resulting in serious damage to my reputation . . .

Indeed I go further and accuse her either of deliberate sabotage of my work or of selfishness over her own space amounting to egomania. For I cannot believe that anyone in her position is brutishly stupid to the point of not being aware of what she is doing.[11]

With that, she resigned. Harry Hodson, the editor, politely expressed his regret but did not offer to make any changes to existing arrangements. Mrs Carter, for all her abrasiveness, was too valuable to lose.

Glad to be free of the *Sunday Times* but still shaking with rage, Elizabeth set off with Doreen Thornton and Anthony Denney on what proved to be a gruelling trip. The schedule was very tight, and they were badly let down by the weather; but Doreen Thornton had succeeded in getting a very smart car for the journey. In return for an article in the *Standard-Triumph Review*, Doreen was to test-drive the new Triumph Herald Coupé. The trip began badly, with an accident in Kensington High Street. But they had an uneventful crossing to Boulogne on one of the very latest ferries, which boasted *two* car decks.

They arrived in Normandy in a hurricane, hoping to catch the market at Rouen; but despite having gone to enormous lengths to get a list of market days, the information was wrong. However, they were able to see the wholesale butter market at Yvetot, where the butter was sold in huge cones weighing seventy or eighty kilos.

As they went on they discovered that it was the small towns rather than the big ones that were the most photogenic, because many of the large ones had covered markets lit with fluorescent tubes, making photography almost impossible.

Since they had failed to do as much as they had hoped in the first half of their ten-day trip, the second half became manic, with the drivers making dashes of 250 miles in all directions to catch the best markets; but they needed more than just a time and a place, if Elizabeth's written account of the markets was to have any depth; and Audrey Withers wanted her readers informed on a great many details.

Yet as Elizabeth discovered, the French are not inclined to reveal the fruits of their culinary knowledge and experience without 'extensive, cautious and tactful preparation of the ground beforehand. You just cannot blind [*sic*] into a place at eight o'clock, hurl the luggage out of the car, and then expect the cook and the *patron* to jump to attention and produce recipes and local colour before you get up next morning at 4 a.m.'[12]

Some fairly desperate driving enabled them to spend one night with Mme Barattero at Lamastre. 'Although we arrived fairly late she rolled out mink carpets for us in every direction, gave us an absolutely fantastically beautiful dinner, and was in tears at dawn when we went to inspect the market at Valence.'[13]

Dull and stormy weather washed out any hopes of Valence, and there was nothing for it but to head south as fast as possible. The market at Cavaillion was every bit as 'beautiful and abundant' as Elizabeth had remembered it, so there things went smoothly; but the fish markets of the coast presented formidable difficulties since all depended on when the catch came in. At Martigues, there was not a moment to be lost. She and Anthony were sprinting from boat to boat like maniacs looking for the best shots, with their drivers puffing to keep up under the weight of Anthony's equipment, followed by hordes of inquisitive boys and hungry cats. Then they had to try and persuade the anxious fishermen and their wives to stand still for a moment with their loads of fish before they whisked them off to auction.

By the end of this whirlwind tour of French markets, Elizabeth felt that they had got a pretty good cross-section of market life. Wholesale markets, big- and small-town markets, specialized markets like those selling butter in Yvetot, melons at Cavaillion and fish at Martigues. Not only that, but they had managed to find evocative corners of big markets showing such details of French household requirements as the stalls specializing in herbs and salad materials, in vegetables ready tied up for soup, in olives and oil and cheeses.

Anthony went back to Spain after a night at Carré le Rouet ('real postcard Mediterranean'), while Doreen and Elizabeth turned the car north-east. Elizabeth had hoped to move on to Annecy and Chambéry, 'a place where the cooking is famous but which I don't know at all'; but they had to abandon the project: it would have been too expensive a detour, and the bad weather was closing in again.

Doreen's article made the trip sound positively leisurely, compared with Elizabeth's letter to Audrey Withers on which the above description is based. However, there was no doubt that the Triumph made the trip considerably more pleasant than it might have been otherwise. 'My passenger, who had been on many similar journeys with me in other small cars, said that she had never had such a comfortable ride.'[14]

* * * * * * *

CHAPTER FIFTEEN

The Year of Betrayal

In some ways, *French Provincial Cooking* could be described as a book that only needed assembling. It is prefaced by some of the most evocative articles Elizabeth had written for *Vogue*, and the bulk of the recipes had been in the process of refinement and rewriting for many years. This makes it sound, to use the cookery presenter's cliché, like a 'here's one I made earlier' sort of book. In fact, it was the culmination and synthesis of a decade of work and thought.

During her research trips, the food she sampled was that cooked in good, unpretentious restaurants rather than in private houses; but ultimately, the recipes in *French Provincial Cooking* were presented in such a way that they could be reproduced in Britain, by untrained British cooks in British kitchens. To perfect her recipes, she relied heavily on her collection of French cookery books: not only historical ones of the eighteenth and nineteenth centuries, but also more recent ones with comfortable titles like *Les Secrets de la bonne table* (Benjamin Renaudet), and *L'Art du bien manger* (Edmond Richardin). The recipe for any given dish might vary considerably among the different volumes she consulted and the different restaurants she had eaten it in. Elizabeth's skill was that she knew how to reduce a recipe to its bare essentials, and then reconstruct it – an exercise she recommends to her readers: 'You may well find that the dish is more pleasing in its primitive form, and then you will know that your recipe was too fanciful. If, on the other hand, the dish seems to lack savour, to be a little bleak and insipid, start building it up again. By the end of this process, you will have discovered what is essential to that dish, what are the extras which enhance it, and at what point it is spoilt by over-elaboration.'[1]

Not every reader perhaps feels up to deconstructing their *Râble de lièvre à la crème*, but the point was that Elizabeth had. This is why every recipe is given with such authority: she has tried it and presents it in print at its most authentic, and any departure from the traditional is clearly signposted. In the recipe mentioned above, for example, she calls for two tablespoons of wine vinegar – 'half a claret glass as specified by Tendret being too much for my taste'. This *Râble de lièvre* is a tricky dish, requiring a good deal of blind faith – for much of the cooking the sauce looks as if it is on the brink of separating. But it does sort itself out in the end, and as Elizabeth points out, 'if you don't look at the sauce you won't see any sinister happenings'.

These were the most strenuous years of Elizabeth's life. She was deeply involved in her work, and because she wrote so regularly and so well for a number of different magazines and newspapers, she made herself a fine reputation and acquired the social standing that goes with it. 'I see your name everywhere now!' wrote Lawrence Durrell. 'You have become a sort of Lord Chesterfield of food. How splendid and how deserved.'[2] She had always been independent; but she had developed a taste for scholarship and knowledge that meant that she needed a lot of time to herself. Being no longer married, she had the space she needed; and since she had no one to look after but herself, she could afford the dark tailored suits, white silk shirts and Parisian hats that she loved.

Elizabeth always behaved like a married woman. It was, after all, a part of the job: she had to present herself as, and sound like, a busy woman with people to feed – and it was, for her, the most congenial role. The quality of her hats and shoes, her practicality, and the way she turned the first rather rackety years of her adult life into the authoritative statement 'Mrs David has kept house in France, Italy,

Greece, Egypt', etc., all conveyed the desired impression – and no one had any reason to challenge it.

As a career woman ahead of her time, Elizabeth was to some extent lucky that the professional and personal sides of her life were relatively easy to reconcile. All she wanted from her private life were her family, her friends and Peter – all of whom were easily accommodated around her various commitments. She did not regret being childless and, on one or two occasions, had deliberately chosen to remain so. On the subject of pregnancy she once remarked, 'I always managed to get rid of mine.'

Nothing remotely like marriage existed in her life, least of all with Peter Higgins. Peter loved her wit, her quickness in spotting humbug, the sheer exhilarating fun of being with her – though the speed with which her mood could suddenly change, the way she could take offence over the faintest slight or the most casual remark was rather tiring. As their relationship went on, he also began to resent her jealousy. She wanted to know where he was every minute of the day, and he was irritated by her uncontrollable desire to cross-question him about everyone he saw and everywhere he went.

He probably did not realize the extent to which her emotional well-being depended on him. She still loved and needed him with an intensity that she had never felt for anyone else; but as the 1950s drew on Elizabeth was dismayed to find that Peter's feelings for her were changing. He still enjoyed her company, but he was beginning to get bored, and her reliance on him was beginning to chafe. As he pulled away from her, she became more desperate, and angry. Her jealousy provoked terrible rows between them, which she inevitably regretted. In an undated letter she wrote,

> If I was rude to you as your savage and public rebuke seemed to indicate I apologize my love. It must have been due to some childish desire to pay you out because you have made me suffer so hideously. Whereas my only feelings should be of gratitude to you for the years of love and content you gave me. And anyone

who has had the magical good fortune to have experienced happiness such as I had with you in Provence has no right to complain of what happens afterwards.

In the summer of 1958, with *French Provincial Cooking* well under way, Elizabeth's agent Paul Scott had negotiated a contract with the publishers Michael Joseph. Elizabeth knew no one in the firm, and very little about it: but the things she did know were reassuring. Michael Joseph himself, who had died two years before, had built up an excellent reputation as a mainstream publisher who could count C. S. Forester, H. E. Bates and Monica Dickens among his authors. He had also been President of the Siamese Cat Society of the British Empire. This last fact struck a deep chord with Elizabeth, who felt that no firm with such an engaging founder could go far wrong. At that time, she was sharing her house with a black cat called Squeaker. (Elizabeth had adopted Squeaker on impulse, having spent a weekend with Doreen, whose cat had just had a litter of kittens.) Another very good reason for choosing Michael Joseph came from Felicité. As a bookseller of many years' experience, Felicité was of the opinion that Ian Keik – Michael Joseph's London sales representative – was the best in the business.

It was to Anthea Joseph, the editorial director and widow of the publisher, that Elizabeth presented the typescript of *French Provincial Cooking*. She was by all accounts a remarkable woman of great charm, who fought hard for the authors she believed in (she insisted on publishing James Baldwin's *Another Country* against the advice of the firm's lawyers). Yet she and Elizabeth got off on the wrong foot. The typescript was partly to blame: in their earliest stages, Elizabeth's books were a daunting pile of pages, with many handwritten notes, references, corrections and insertions held in place with pins and paper clips. When Elizabeth came in to discuss it, Mrs Joseph looked rather alarmed. 'It isn't quite what we were expecting,' she ventured. 'It seems to be quite different from your other books . . .'[3] She also felt it was in need of serious cutting.

With the high hopes she had built up of the firm, Elizabeth was disappointed, to say the least. It seemed to her that publishers always wanted to see the book she had last published, rather than the one she had just written. Yet in the end she came round to Anthea Joseph, who admitted that she might have been wrong about demanding all those cuts.

Elizabeth got on far better with Peter Hebdon, the firm's managing director. He had always been more involved with the sales and marketing side of the business, but in the early 1960s the division between sales and editing was nothing like as rigid as it is now. Hebdon was a man of unselfconscious integrity, who never hesitated to say what he thought: the sort of person Elizabeth always admired. She saw Hebdon as her best friend and ally within the firm, and felt that the continued success of *French Provincial Cooking* owed much to him. Peter Hebdon promoted it well, was generous with reprints and revisions, and seemed genuinely concerned for the book's welfare. 'Peter cherished his authors,' wrote Elizabeth. 'He was proud of publishing their work. In return his authors, or at least this one, loved and looked up to him.'4 When the book came out, many people assumed that the dedication *To P.H. with love* referred to Peter Hebdon. Elizabeth made little effort to correct the rumour, which provided an effective smokescreen for the real P.H.'s identity. No one beyond her closest circle of friends knew that P.H. stood for Peter Higgins.

For the illustrations, Elizabeth chose an artist called Juliet Renny. For six months this very shy and retiring artist came to Halsey Street, working more slowly than Elizabeth could have wished; but the fact that she took endless pains to get every rivet, lid and handle exactly right made up for it. 'I was anxious that such details should be put on record,' wrote Elizabeth, 'because some of these regional cooking pots are already becoming very hard to find in France, so that in some sense Juliet Renny's drawings constitute a little historical record in their own right.'5

*

The book was published in November 1960, and was received as warmly as her previous books; but hers was not the only cookery book jostling for attention. Two books in particular could be seen as direct competitors: *The Classic French Cuisine* by Joseph Donon, a professional chef's presentation of five hundred recipes from the very summits of haute cuisine; and *The Art of Simple French Cooking* by Alexander Watt, which brought quick bistro cooking into the English kitchen. Books of a kind tend to be reviewed in large batches, the reviewer's job being merely to give a taste of each, but it is interesting to note the little flash of colour and depth coming into the descriptions of *French Provincial Cooking*. Where it was reviewed at greater length, there was a general recognition that the book was beautifully written, profoundly researched, entertaining, informative and more than the sum of its parts: it makes you want to cook. 'If I had my way I would have a copy purchased by public funds and presented to every young wife on her wedding day,' wrote Vivian Rowe in *The Traveller in France*. Even the *Daily Worker*'s reviewer enjoyed it, which should go some way to redressing the absurd contention that Elizabeth David was élitist and only addressed the upwardly aspiring middle classes: 'a textbook not just on French food, but on good cooking and intelligent eating'.[6] She received an enormous number of letters from readers, and the reaction of her friends too was very gratifying. In thanking her cousin Neil Hogg for his letter Elizabeth wrote, 'Of course the book is full of idiosyn-crasies and faults of style, and omissions, and repetitions, and it isn't intended to be read right through at one go, although to my dismay that's just what people are doing. They must be getting awful indigestion by about page 150.'[7]

Two other publications from the autumn of 1960 are worth mentioning. One was a pioneer of its kind, and opened up a promising future for a new sort of cookery book. It was called *Cookery in Colour*, edited by Marguerite Patten. The recipes were printed on coloured paper, alternating with double-page spreads of full-colour photo-graphs – which would have been prohibitively expensive to produce in England. Paul Hamlyn could afford to sell it for twenty-five shillings (ten shillings less than *French Provincial Cooking*) because he had invested in a massive print run, and had had the book printed in Czechoslovakia: it sold two million copies.

The past was represented by Ward Lock's centenary edition of Mrs Beeton's famous *Book of Household Management*, now renamed *Cookery and Household Management*. Fifty-five experts were credited for their work on the new edition, and apart from one or two useful chapters, Elizabeth thought the result was a mess: uneven, contradictory and confused. 'We feel that Mrs Beeton promises us the godlike wisdom of a revered professor combined with nanny's protective comfort. We don't get it.'

The article was published in the *Spectator* in October, just as her own book was being launched. 'I know I was asking for trouble writing in those rather thundering tones so soon after the appearance of my own book,' she wrote to Neil Hogg. 'I suppose it would have been more dignified to keep silent on the matter – but . . . I was, and am, really outraged when I think what Ward Locke have perpetrated in Mrs Beeton's name.' She was also rather surprised by the enthusiasm with which the new Mrs Beeton was received: 'it emerges that I seem to be the only person who has said it's pretty mediocre . . . or else I'm utterly wrong'.[8]

The article on Mrs Beeton was one of the first she wrote for the *Spectator*, for which Elizabeth produced some of the best articles she was ever to write. She had first been approached, almost off the cuff, by Katharine Whitehorn, who at that time combined the job of arts editor on the *Spectator* with being fashion editor of the *Observer*. She wrote to Elizabeth on 25 May 1960: 'I do think it would be splendid to have an article on casseroles and other sorts of kitchen equipment; but – this is the first thing that I must admit occurs to me – oughtn't it to be you that writes it and not me? . . . I can think of nothing the *Spectator* would like better than to have you write an article or a series for us. But perhaps, considering our rates, it is an impertinence to suggest it.'

The *Spectator* in those days was owned by Ian Gilmour and edited by Brian Inglis; and although the pay was less than what she was used to, she liked the fact that what the *Spectator* wanted was her writing, her unmistakable voice. What she wrote about was up to her, and no one cared whether she included recipes in her articles or not.

The tone of the magazine was set by what Whitehorn called 'a close-knit gang of disillusioned radicals' which included herself, Cyril Ray, Bernard Levin and Alan Brien. They were all young left-wing liberals, all had jobs on other papers as well; but at the *Spectator*, they felt they were in their element. Work at 99 Gower Street was punctuated by long drinking sessions at the Mortimer Arms, and one afternoon a week was devoted to the *Spectator* lunch. Supplies for this occasion were organized by Cyril Ray, who in the course of his career had been war correspondent for the *Guardian*, Moscow correspondent for the *Sunday Times* and editor of an annual called *The Compleat Imbiber*. He shared a dusty cubby-hole of an office with Katharine Whitehorn, who described his position on the *Spectator* as 'foreign, diplomatic, food, espionage, drink and military correspondent with a spot of labour relations and law reform thrown in'.[9] He was known to many as the Bollinger Bolshevik; and his arrival on lunch days, in a taxi laden with food and unbelievable quantities of wine, rather shocked the younger and more junior members of the *Spectator*'s staff.

It was Cyril who edited Elizabeth's copy; though he often had to bully her for it. She was used to editors who were chiefly interested in recipes or, like Audrey Withers, who had established themes for a series of articles. It was hard to think up ideas when the guidelines were so loose.

She joined the *Spectator* just in time; for she was coming to the conclusion that she no longer wanted to work for *Vogue*. Anthony Denney had left the magazine, and in the second half of 1960, Audrey Withers was succeeded as editor of *Vogue* by Ailsa Garland.

Elizabeth struggled on for a bit, but in October she wrote to the new editor asking to be released from her contract. She felt she was an anachronism in the bright, hard-edged, teasing tones of the new magazine: 'I have a feeling that you may be glad of the opportunity to look for a cookery contributor who takes the whole business a bit more lightly than I do, and I wouldn't blame you.'[10]

Elizabeth also admitted that she was desperately tired. Being as conscientious as she was about her work, it demanded a lot from her both physically and mentally; she had not taken a non-working holiday for years.

Freed from the *Sunday Times* and Condé Nast, her work did ease up a bit: but Elizabeth needed to be busy. She took on a column for the *Sunday Dispatch* in 1960, and another for the *Daily Telegraph* in 1961. It was a particularly interesting time to be writing about food, at a time of such rapid social change. Advances, in everything from technology to ease of transport, were fuelling the huge and fashionable debate about food that raged in every newspaper and magazine.

Elizabeth's line was predictable. She hated the proliferation of supermarkets, the advances in freezing and preserving that were touted at every food fair and the free samples of bottled sauce and packet soup that clogged up her mail and her dustbins. She hated the way fresh vegetables and fruits of the season were being elbowed out by freezer cabinets full of strawberries and 'garden-fresh' peas; yet at the same time, there was much to welcome.

More and more people were going abroad, and they came home wanting to cook some of the dishes they had eaten in France or Italy. This was good for British cooking in general, and the sales of her own books in particular. At Harrods the meat manager, Mr Ducat, was opening a *boucherie* which offered French cuts of meat, and he also began doing Elizabeth's recipe for spiced beef at Christmas. Even if one could not afford to shop at Harrods, one no longer had to go as far as Soho to find good coffee, olive oil and wine vinegar. Elizabeth was delighted when her local Sainsbury's brought out little packets of freshly-grated parmesan, and said so in the *Spectator* – to the rage of one of her correspondents who wrote from Lahore: 'I enjoy your column, although I am occasionally badly shaken when you suggest the purchase and employment of pre-ground Parmesan and such. That kind of thing just *won't do*, and I am sure you know it.'[11]

In wine, too, things were improving. An enterprising wine-merchant called Gerald Asher, one of the founders of Asher, Storey & Co., was exploring French vineyards for unusual, little-known wines that had not been available in England before. 'He used to go looking for . . . wines he had read about, but which no one imported,' said his friend and fellow wine-expert Anthony Hanson. 'Jasnières, to the north of the Loire, the name kept alive by three people growing vines at the back of a vegetable patch, or Jurançon, or Frontignan, or a Costières du Gard . . .'[12] These were just the sort of wines that Elizabeth liked. They were not classed growths or prestige bottles, but they were made by small wine-growers who took trouble, and each wine was an expression of a time and a place.

Despite a rapidly developing food and wine market and a consuming interest in abroad, some English people still insisted on maintaining heavily entrenched positions. At the beginning of 1961, Elizabeth wrote a piece in the *Daily Telegraph* entitled 'Crisp Salads to Cheer Gloomy Days', which provoked a furious response from one reader. Who did that Mrs David think she was? To throw oil and vinegar over pears (the pear Elizabeth had referred to was an avocado) was nothing short of barbarous. She was fed up with hearing about 'those queer messes which foreigners called food', and claimed that a diet of roast beef, Yorkshire and two veg followed by fruit tart with custard was good enough for most people and could not be improved upon.

The insularity of this attitude was eccentric even in 1961 and a host of other readers sprang to Elizabeth's defence; but Elizabeth did not like the way the whole thing had been handled by the

Telegraph. She had been given no warning of the outraged letter, which had been deliberately exaggerated in print by clever editing; and when she was allowed to reply, it was some time later and on the back page.

Elizabeth's articles upset the food industry more often than her readers. In an article she wrote for the *Spectator* called 'Lucky Dip' (29 June 1962), Elizabeth mentioned that she had given the filling for a commercial veal and ham pie to her cat, who had turned it down. A complaint was made to the editor, now Brian Inglis's successor Iain Hamilton. He passed on the indignant letter, with the remark that 'if their pies are anything like their ice cream I'd shoot the lot of them'.[13] Elizabeth had great fun composing her reply to the offended manufacturers.

> The Editor of the *Spectator* tells me that your board takes serious exception to my cat's reported attitude to a . . . pie. Of course, my cat was serious too, but in recording her lack of enthusiasm I did not intend to imply, nor do I think would any intelligent *Spectator* reader infer, that the pie in question would have necessarily been rejected by a human being – or indeed, by all other cats. Standards differ . . .
>
> The Editor also tells me that you have been so kind as to invite me to see over the factory. I have already had this pleasure. I found the experience most instructive and impressions are still vivid in my mind, so I will not put your directors to all the trouble again.[14]

As a cookery writer, Elizabeth was constantly invited to visit commercial premises producing food in one form or another – both in England and on the continent. Like most of her European contemporaries, her work was not much known outside her own country: but people in the food business knew that she wielded enormous influence in Britain. Elizabeth's professional life was punctuated by jaunts organized by cheesemakers, grape growers or houses of commerce. Such trips are not in themselves worth recording; but they often provided

Elizabeth with the raw material for her articles, and it is worth looking at one to see the lengths to which people were prepared to go to impress her.

This particular trip centred on the town of Nantes, where Elizabeth was interested in the sardine canneries. It took place in September 1962, and was organized by the Centre National du Commerce in Paris, treating her as a VIP. In the course of her visit Elizabeth was not only shown over the celebrated canning factory of Philippe Cannaud; she also saw the Biscuiterie Nantaise and several vineyards (Gerald Asher had advised her on which to visit, and given her letters of introduction), and was treated to meals in what were considered the finest restaurants in the area. Elizabeth was touched by the efforts everyone went to on her behalf. She was an appreciative guest, but not an easy one; for once she had become interested in something, she would not let go of it until she had learnt everything she wanted to know. One of her letters was to Mme Audas, who ran the estate of Les Perrières with her husband, producing Muscadet.

'I'm afraid I took up too much of your time, but it was such a beautiful day and everything you showed me was so interesting and such fun, that I quite failed to notice the time. When I realized that you were going to set to work cooking your ducks that evening I was really horrified to think that I had stayed so late . . .'[15]

It was soon after her return that Elizabeth was contacted by a very young, enthusiastic man who, at the age of twenty-four, had just been appointed by André Simon to edit the magazine of the Wine and Food Society. His name was Hugh Johnson. On a copy of the magazine immediately preceding his appointment, Johnson wrote the names of the people he hoped would contribute to 'his' magazine. Top of the list was Elizabeth David. 'I remember saying, "Unless we can get her, there's no point going on."'[16]

Elizabeth always enjoyed the adulation of good-looking young men; but Johnson's enthusiasm, not only for her work but for the whole business of good food and wine, reflected her own inclinations. He wanted to make the magazine more visually exciting, more literary, and hoped eventually to launch it commercially. In all these areas, he eagerly sought her guidance. This was an approach that always brought out the best in Elizabeth, who, whatever her faults, was a great teacher. Before long Johnson was a regular visitor to Halsey Street, sitting at the kitchen table, scribbling notes, while Elizabeth ferreted through her books to find exactly the illustration she was looking for. He also started taking her out to lunch, usually to new restaurants.

Hugh Johnson was editor of *Wine and Food* for two years. During that time, Elizabeth contributed articles which had arisen from research she had followed up for her own interest and enlightenment. Hugh Johnson admitted that he 'never dared to change a comma'.

One of these *Wine and Food* articles was on the eighteenth-century cook, William Verral – her second on the subject, the first having been published the year before in the *Spectator*. This one is particularly interesting, however, since it gives a glimpse of her particular taste for scholarship: a kind of scholarship that looked through the historical text to the people who had written it.

The presence of ingredients which might strike one as outlandish or redundant, recipes which appear preposterously lavish even for large numbers of people are often quite easily explained if one takes the trouble to inquire a little into the personality of the author (it is curious how seldom cookery writers are regarded as people, or even as authors) . . . Was he or she a practising cook, and if so, in what kind of household or catering establishment? Urban or rural? Housekeeper to a great landowning family? A noblewoman more than normally preoccupied with the domestic arts? (You can always tell those. They give a lot of ghoulish recipes for feeding the poor.) Simply a copyist perpetuating a medieval superstition? . . . A physician? (they are the bossiest cookery authors of all.)[17]

Shortly after her trip to Nantes, Gerald Asher invited her to a lunch he was organizing at the premises of Asher Storey. When he had first had the idea of entertaining his friends and clients to regular lunches, Elizabeth had helped him find a cook; and now Asher and the cook went into serious discussions about what to give her. Since she had recently written a piece in the *Spectator* about sardines, they decided to give her a delicacy called Mature Sardines. These were tins which had been ageing for anything from five to twenty years, and according to one aficionado, 'the oldest made foie gras seem maigre. I almost slobber when I recall them'.[18] The tins were duly bought, one for each guest, and the day had arrived before a hideous problem presented itself: how does one serve Mature Sardines? Asher had never eaten them and neither had his cook. In the end, they decided to serve them in their tins, the lid rolled back. With good bread to mop up in every last corner, it was the perfect solution. Elizabeth was very appreciative, and Gerald Asher breathed a sigh of relief.

This lunch with Asher was probably one of the more convivial events in a diary that was filled with appointments: sometimes, even making a date with Higgins was a problem:

Friday p.m. I never seem to be at home these days. I long to see you, and to cook some civilized food. Next week is hideous. Port on Monday in Belgrave Square, wine on Tuesday at lunchtime at the Aldwych, the French on Wednesday evening, Lyon on Thursday oh God perhaps we could have dinner here on Monday or Tuesday – or lunch on Wednesday. I want so much to see you – I miss you horribly when I don't.

I think it is ten years since I came home from Italy and stayed in that ludicrous Grosvenor Hotel, and you made a scene because they wouldn't give us a drink after hours . . . Darling, for a great deal of perfectly extraordinary happiness in those ten years I have to thank you.[19]

At the end of 1962 Elizabeth turned forty-nine, and was entitled to think that after ten years of extremely hard work she could relax a little and enjoy the fruits of her labours. Yet as it turned out, 1963 was to prove the most turbulent and painful year of her life. It got off to a bad start.

Penguin had decided to drop the John Minton illustration from the cover of their edition of *Mediterranean Food*, and replace it with a food photograph which would bring the book in line with the rest of their cookery list. Elizabeth was appalled by the draft cover she was sent, and wrote a 'cry for help', as she put it, to Eunice Frost, the most senior person she knew in Penguin. 'I don't remember ever writing anything about cooking onions in a Turkish coffee pot with a roll of paper and three slices of slimy tomato; nor about inserting a hard-boiled egg into the belly of a shrivelled aubergine . . . Now what has all that to do with the Mediterranean? Or with cooking?'[20] She had not been that attached to the Minton illustration: what annoyed her was that Penguin had not given her the opportunity to set up the shot herself, and have it taken by Anthony Denney. There was also a principle, which was much on her mind at the time. This was that a book's text could not be divorced from its cover or its index, without substantially changing its impact. 'I am not saying that they are perfect. I am saying that they are all of a piece. John Lehmann made me see the importance of this point . . .'[21]

It was especially true of the illustrations that Renato Guttuso had done for *Italian Food*. To Elizabeth, they were as indispensable to the book as the references to Parmesan cheese – without them, a whole range of colour and taste was lost. They had never belonged to her yet Elizabeth felt intensely proprietorial about the Guttusos: after all it was she who had found him, and she who had conducted the negotiations for his pictures.

Then in March 1963, she was told by the Penguin production department that, in their forthcoming edition of *Italian Food*, they would have to work from the old blocks because Macdonald had mislaid the originals. Elizabeth said that there had been some mistake, and contacted Macdonald herself. It seemed that the Guttusos had been lent to others in the office, or mislaid in the move that the firm had recently made from Maddox Street to Portman Street. No one was really sure.

Elizabeth was very anxious about the illustrations and exasperated at Macdonald's incompetence, particularly since they were again baulking at the idea of a full revision of *Italian Food*. However, she was reassured that the Guttusos would probably turn up, and three days later, she set off on a trip to Tangier.

Her hosts (Mr and Mrs Rex Henry) were old friends of Lett Haines, and they had been looking for someone to teach their Moroccan-born, Italian-trained cook some of the refinements of European cuisine. Elizabeth agreed to help, and in exchange they agreed to pay her air fare and have her to stay as their guest, in a house which was by all accounts luxuriously comfortable. She needed a holiday, and thought it might be fun.

It was a nightmare, from start to finish. 'I don't know when I've ever come across a more odious pair, boring, pretentious, sterile, utterly without sense of humour, not enough to drink except Moorish wine at meals and black looks at my cigarettes.'[22] Her host fancied himself as an epicure, though all he really wanted were basins full of ice cream and chocolate. Her hostess hated anything with alcohol in it and fussed over her husband's health. 'There is a fearful lot of *"Chéri, tu n'as pas froid?"* and *"Mon amour, tu n'est pas fatiguée?"* and I fancy they simply hate each other . . .' They had an annoying habit of saying they did not want any dinner, and then looking incredulous when there was nothing to eat at dinner time. They also constantly countermanded each other's orders – and Elizabeth's. All her frustrations were vented in a long letter to Lesley O'Malley:

Friday, there was a big lunch for eight which ended, as I thought it would, in tears. I prevented them from having *filets de sole à la crème* as well as an ice cream, with saddle of lamb and three vegetables in between. There were delicious little *loups de mer* in the market for grilling. I told the cook to buy one per person, and Monsieur sent him back for eight more . . . Madame countermanded the second lot, and Monsieur insisted. My ice didn't freeze, the lamb was overcooked and hacked to pieces. A shambles. Over a dinner of bread and water there was a fearful post-mortem. I waited until they were both exhausted and then said, now you will listen to me – and delivered my well-known lecture on pretentious food and second-rate grand cooking, and vulgar display and trying to impress people, and giving the cook new dishes to try out for a party, and asking far too much of him and bringing me out here to make a monkey of me, etc., etc., etc. And swept up to bed sobbing . . .[23]

The only person she liked in the household was the cook, who was 'handsome and gay and charming, with beautiful manners . . . and really no end of a dish'. He was also a 'damned good cook, and I hope they lose him. I'm doing my best to undermine his loyalty . . .'

Just when Elizabeth thought she had had enough, Veronica and John Nicholson appeared: they were on holiday, with a car – and for a few glorious days she joined them on a little trip into the desert and the Atlas mountains. With them, Elizabeth was able to vent her frustrations; but at the same time, she seemed to need an emotional whipping boy: Veronica was the butt of all her jokes, and was teased mercilessly from morning till night. John Nicholson had never really liked Elizabeth, and this particular jaunt – during which she was so poisonous to his wife – did nothing to improve his instinctive dislike of her.

Back in Tangier, Elizabeth decided she could take no more. She returned to England at the end of April, feeling ill and run-down. Then Penguin rang with some bad news: Macdonald said the Guttusos were irretrievably lost. When Elizabeth rang Macdonald herself, no one wanted to talk to her; and when she finally buttonholed Walter Parrish, the art director, he told her bluntly that they were 'gone for good'. Elizabeth was still brooding over all the accumulated grievances Macdonald had caused her when she was contacted by a friend of hers and Peter's, who had known them both for years: Lady Sibell Rowley. What she had to say gave Elizabeth a shock from which she claimed she never really recovered.

*

Being the rigidly self-controlled person she was, Elizabeth had learned to live with the sadness of her lopsided relationship with Peter, so passionate on her side, so light-hearted on his; but what she had never imagined was that there could be another woman in his life who might matter more to him than she did. Yet there was, and Peter was in love with her. Her maiden name was Anne Fane, and she was at that time still married to her second husband, Thurston Holland-Martin. Elizabeth had no idea about Anne – although everyone in her circle knew, including Felicité and Veronica Nicholson. Felicité had told Peter that he must tell Elizabeth himself – he was still seeing her once or twice a week; but he always found a good excuse not to.

When Felicité and Veronica realized that Peter would never get around to it, they persuaded Sibell Rowley that only she, as a close friend of both parties, could tell Elizabeth the truth. When she did, Elizabeth turned on her in a fury. She became extremely unpleasant, more or less accusing Sibell of inventing the story out of jealousy; but when Sibell had gone the truth sank in. Felicité came downstairs, in an attempt to calm and comfort her sister – but Elizabeth was beside herself with grief and rage, flinging herself about and hurling things across the room.

Soon after, Elizabeth collapsed. She was found one morning by Lesley O'Malley, who was horrified to see Elizabeth trying, but unable, to talk. She was taken by ambulance to the National Hospital for Nervous Diseases in Queen Square and treated for a cerebral haemorrhage. Often triggered by stress, a cerebral haemorrhage is something like a stroke, and this is how Elizabeth's friends referred to it: they said it was astonishing that she should sustain such a thing, at her comparatively young age. Yet Elizabeth had been working too hard for years, and took very little exercise. Doreen Thornton, who used to come to Halsey Street at this time to help Elizabeth with typing and filing, also noticed that she was taking sleeping pills and drinking a great deal of brandy.

On 4 May, Elizabeth received a telegram from Peter: 'HOPE YOU ARE COMFORTABLE WILL COME AND SEE YOU SAT.' When he came, she thrust a letter into his hand and turned away.

* * * * * * *

CHAPTER SIXTEEN

Farewell to P. H.

Elizabeth remained in hospital for a few weeks. Her speech returned. The doctors advised complete rest, but Elizabeth was back at work even before she left hospital, finishing an article she had begun for the *Spectator* called 'Points de Venise'. Her description of the fish market was, if anything, even more intensely visual than that which she had written in *Italian Food* all those years ago. 'In the dawn light of the Rialto markets . . . a sole isn't made of old white cricket flannels but of pale lilac silk, and . . . if you are looking you may see a pyramid of apricots radiating rose and gilt reflections from a catch of red mullet . . .'[1] This piece elicited a particularly warm fan letter, from the journalist and novelist Sybille Bedford.

> Dear Mrs David,
>   Your article in June 14th *Spectator* has given me such intense pleasure that I feel I ought to write to thank you. I read 'Points de Venise' about six times, and aloud to friends, it is so beautifully written.

On first reading it, she had been on the point of leaving Asolo; but on the strength of Elizabeth's article:

> I drove off to Venice, walked the streets till after midnight, slept at the Albergo Fave (ten steps from the Rialto and built inside a live printing press and very cheap), and up again – alarm clock – at 4.40 a.m. for the Adriatic dawn. There's the power of the pen for you.[2]

This generous letter could not have arrived at a better time. It not only gave her a much-needed boost to the morale, but from her reply there's a sense that Elizabeth felt she had found a true friend.

Dear Mrs Bedford,

You wrote me such a beautiful letter about my Venice article. I have written you at least three replies. None of them has reached the letter box (one actually got lost on the way to the typist – it was too lengthy to send to you in longhand. At least you were spared that one) . . . I think I may have told you on a previous occasion how great is my admiration and love for your own beautiful books. Two copies of *The Legacy* are always near me – one in my bedroom, one near my work table. The passage about Melanie and the *loup de mer* I know by heart like I know Durrell's piece about black olives from *Prospero's Cell* – all the same I still want to get the sensation of actually reading them on the printed page . . .

Incidentally, about that Venice article, I have been told since (*a*) that Alfredo Zoppi of the Fenice has died . . . (*b*) that Proust did go to Venice (*c*) that there is no early morning market near the Rialto. What has happened? . . . I wrote part of the Venice article in hospital, with the doctors telling me that I had better not – perhaps they were right . . . I only hope I didn't make you get up for nothing.[3]

21 Sept., Les Bastides
Dear Mrs David,

Such a very delightful letter. I am overcome. To be told that one's books are actually *used* . . . that seems to me the only real reward of writing. But then I don't write with ease. Do you? You read as if you did, but I know that is no indication. To me, it is all anguish and stone-heaving work . . .

As to the rest, Mrs Bedford was reassuring: Proust had dithered so much about whether to go to Venice that no one knows for sure whether he did or not; and when she reached the Rialto at dawn, there was the fish market, just as Elizabeth had described it.

They had already met, at publishing parties and the like; but after their exchange of letters, Elizabeth invited Sybille to dinner. Sybille passed through the narrow hall, made so much narrower by the piles of books on either side – 'you could only just pass through'.[4] Elizabeth gave her a white Beaujolais, which Sybille had never tried before; and the meal consisted of *mezzes*, a few grains of perfectly cooked rice, a salad, and a bottle of red wine – 'good, but not great'.[5] They were neither of them at ease in a crowd; both preferred books, wine, simple dinners and intimate conversation that went on till 'birdsong', as they called the early hours of the morning. Sybille would drag herself away and then, as was her habit, walk around the quiet streets for a while before returning to her London base, which was a small flat in Chesham Place. They were both nocturnal: walking back through Halsey Street, Sybille often noticed that Elizabeth's bedroom light was still on, at two or three in the morning.

Sybille knew a great deal about food, and even more about wine: she could appreciate fine vintages in a way that Elizabeth always claimed she never could. Whenever Elizabeth was given a really fine bottle of wine she would give it to Sybille: 'It was true generosity, because she knew I would take it away and drink it by myself.'[6] Sybille's idea of a perfect evening was to drink a great wine, with just the right piece of music to go with it. That was another taste that Elizabeth did not share. She was untouched by music in any form – whereas Sybille positively needed it.

Over the next decade, Sybille and Elizabeth had endless lunches and dinners together, usually in restaurants. 'I was an innocent in those days, I thought we were equals,' said Sybille. However, she did not fail to notice Elizabeth's somewhat prima-donna-ish style in restaurants, and she soon found out that their friendship was on Elizabeth's terms, not hers. The invisible wall she had erected around herself could not be crossed with impunity. One evening Sybille happened to mention, because she was so full of it, that she was in love –

'and I knew it was the wrong thing to say the moment I had said it'.[7] Elizabeth froze and glanced away. The conversation moved on.

Another friend Elizabeth made at this time was the American cookery writer Julia Child. With her co-authors Simone Beck and Louisette Bertholle, she had written a classic of American cookery writing *Mastering the Art of French Cookery*, the English edition of which had just been published by Cassell. Elizabeth had given it a very favourable review, and Mrs Child was deeply grateful.

> We are simply overwhelmed with your review of our book. It's the first time we've had a serious comment from a pro, and you have brought out the gist of what we tried to do in writing it. That we have succeeded, in your eyes, to make cooking a bit easier and more understandable is of the deepest satisfaction . . . The important thing is that you quietly and firmly get back your health . . . Thank heaven you can be quiet and work on the *Spectator* articles, and have nothing else pushing at you.[8]

As soon as she was well enough, Elizabeth went to France and from then on down to Italy, to stay with Viola Johnson. She and Viola visited the truffle town of Alba near Turin, which led to another of her best-known *Spectator* pieces, 'Trufflesville Regis'.[9]

Another particularly effective piece she wrote for the *Spectator* at this time was called 'Golden Delicious' celebrating a wine called Beaumes de Venise. Elizabeth was introduced to this golden muscat dessert wine by Gerald Asher, who had begun importing it and gave her a bottle shortly before Christmas. Elizabeth was entranced; and the aura of mystery which seemed to hang about the wine added another dimension to its haunting, flowery taste. Elizabeth told her readers that 'Nobody, it seems, quite knows when the muscat grapes of Beaumes de Venise were first planted nor how the sweet wine from the vineyards of this tiny area protected by a fold in the hills from the savage north winds acquired its reputation. Certainly that reputation has always been a local one only.'[10]

All that was about to change. In the mid-sixties there were only two growers of Beaumes de Venise, producing about 200 hectolitres a year. But thanks to Elizabeth's enthusiasm the wine caught on to such an extent that, thirty years later, Gerald Asher wrote '200 hectolitres would now scarcely keep the market going for half a week'.[11] During her weeks in hospital and the brief convalescence she allowed herself, Elizabeth had found herself doing a lot of re-reading: of writers who had been formative influences, and also of earlier English cookery writers. The previous year, she had written about Eliza Acton and William Verral. In the later half of 1963, the *Spectator* published pieces by Elizabeth David on Hilda Leyel, Florence White and Countess Morphy; on Mrs Beeton; and (an honorary Englishman) Marcel Boulestin. As far as any casual reader of her work could see, all was well.

Elizabeth had not given herself the time to recover fully from her stroke. She did not want anyone outside her immediate circle to know how ill she had been, particularly among those who commissioned her work; and besides, she hated the idea that her friends might be discussing her health behind her back. The result was that that winter, she succumbed to a bout of severe depression. It was not just that she still felt physically and emotionally drained; the cerebral haemorrhage had also impaired her sense of taste and, unlike her speech, it was not coming back. Friends noticed that she was doing much less cooking than she used to, and when she did, she often asked them to taste whether the food was properly salted. Friends might arrive at Halsey Street to find four or five little white dishes, each containing a differently salted sample of whatever she was cooking. The guest had to try each one and say which was the best. At the same time, she could not bear the smell of fried onions, which seemed ten times more pungent and pervasive than it had been before.

Elizabeth had always had a strong head for alcohol, and had been drinking a good deal of spirits before her stroke. The doctors had warned her off the hard stuff, and she seldom drank spirits again; but she still drank a great deal of wine to dull the pain of what seemed like an emotionally empty life. A friend recalled that she was profoundly unhappy at this time; and when she came round of an evening, she used to drink till she became 'quite sodden. Not violent, not unpleasant, just sodden.' She stopped writing for the *Spectator*, though this was mostly because she could not think up enough subjects to be able to fill a page twice a month; and while Cyril Ray and Katharine Whitehorn were full of ideas, none of them seemed to appeal to her.

Instead she brooded over the Guttusos, fretting and fuming over their loss in a way that was clearly obsessive for she had never owned them: they had been paid for by her publisher. She hired a solicitor, Michael Rubinstein, to prepare a case against Macdonald. Rubinstein told her that she stood very little chance of proving that she would lose either royalties, or the prospect of a future edition of *Italian Food*, due to the loss of the illustrations. But when she set out the list of incompetence, obstructions and aggravations she had had to endure from Macdonald since she had had the misfortune to fall into their hands, Rubinstein thought that they might be persuaded to release the rights they held over her first three books. This case took up an enormous amount of her time and energy, and she talked about it to anyone who would listen. It was a way of channelling the anger that burned inside her, the real cause of which could never be mentioned: the loss of Peter Higgins.

Peter's new love, Anne Holland-Martin, was young, rich and much more in tune with Peter's hunting and racing set than Elizabeth could ever be. Their affair had been going on for about a year, during which time they shared the top flat of a house in Chapel Street. At some point soon after they started living together, perhaps in the autumn of 1963, Peter had had a serious riding accident in Rotten Row which had badly damaged his pelvis. He was in hospital for months in traction, during which time Elizabeth had come to see him. Anne and Peter planned to be married as soon as her divorce came through. But Peter did not want Elizabeth to think that he had merely discarded her, no longer cared for her; and in the spring of 1964, a year after her haemorrhage, he rang her up. They agreed to meet for lunch on 6 May. Elizabeth wrote 'Beau Higgins lunch' in her diary, and drew a little heart beside his name.

If she had any hopes, they were soon dashed. Peter told her that their affair was over, but he was still very fond of her and wanted to stay friends. He assumed she had another lover by now, but Elizabeth told him there was no one else – no one who mattered. Painful as it was, all this was bearable; but when he began to apologize and make excuses for not telling her sooner about Anne, Elizabeth lost all patience. She felt bitterly disappointed and humiliated, and as always, these feelings turned to anger. Over the next few days she wrote Peter a letter, which she worked over and over. Even in its fullest form it is not complete, and some paragraphs stand by themselves without being incorporated into the main text. It seems less of a letter than an attempt to make sense of her emotional turmoil.

20 May 1964

I think it must be just exactly a year ago to the day that I started writing you the letter which, as things turned out, I shoved into your hands the night you came round to see me after I had had that brain haemorrhage. If you ever read the letter you will have thought it was the product of an already disordered brain boiling up for an explosion. Certainly I was already ill and in a state of shock following the disastrous trip to Morocco and the revelation by my publishers of the loss of the Guttusos. But as far as you were concerned my head was perfectly clear. There were things which had never been said, and could be said only when I knew for certain and sure that a long period of emotional misery was forever over.

The little tiny malign blow which wrecked my sense of taste has also put an end (some might think high time too) to any interest I might still have had in sex. After you got bored with me I didn't think much of the whole idea anyway. But now it wouldn't be any use even if I did. I am half-numbed physically, and can't feel anything. Relinquishing something I cannot have is therefore of no account, since I do not want or need it. I am lucky. Most people have to learn this the hard way. You, with all your endearing lack of the possessive instinct, have never wanted to renounce entirely any woman you have ever fancied.

Your emotional confidence suited me, (all other serious attachments I ever had came to grief because I could not stand being suffocated with love) and your gaiety was, and still is, adorable. For a long time, during all those years of excruciating pain after you got bored of me and I wasn't bored with you I fought to get rid of you. Once or twice I nearly succeeded but in the end you always defeated me and betrayed me into making a spectacle of myself. Of course you made me work too. The book I dedicated to you was the product of those hateful years.

I dedicated my book to you because it was you who provided the conflict and the stress which, for such as I, alone make writing possible. For that matter, for better or worse, it was you who were responsible for all my books, right from the beginning. It was childish, but I had to show you, while you were busy down in Devon pretending to be a farm labourer, that I could do something with my time . . . It is not, you know, my illness which has stopped me writing. It is the ending of a necessity, and of a prolonged torment . . .

This letter is unique in that it makes a connection between Elizabeth's work and her private life. It is hard to believe that Peter was 'responsible' for all her books. He might have inspired and encouraged the writing of them; but to make him 'responsible' for them was a way of telling Peter what she felt at the time – that he had ruined her life, and that she would probably never write another book again.

* * * * * * *

CHAPTER SEVENTEEN

The Shop

Anthony Denney came to the rescue. He was one of the few people who could not only stand up to Elizabeth, but bully her as well. Her doctors had told her she needed a rest and a complete change of scene, and he was going to see that she got it. He persuaded her to come to stay with him in Spain, on a little estate he had in the almond- and lemon-growing country near Valencia. It was called La Alfarella.

Elizabeth had never been to Spain before; but as soon as she felt the sun and the pull of the Mediterranean again, she began to feel better. The isolated, whitewashed farmhouse built around a stone courtyard had been a ruin when Denney bought it in the late fifties. Now it had water and electricity, but the cooking arrangements were still rudimentary. The food was usually prepared in earthenware dishes, heated directly over the Butagaz or on the hearth. It was served on the veranda whenever possible, and eaten overlooking a magnificent view of the mountains.

The pieces that Elizabeth wrote from La Alfarella have an extraordinary freshness, as if she is seeing a new-born world for the first time: discovering that, after all the pain and illness of the past year, she can write again – even eat onions again.

'The enormous ridged tomatoes were cored with a little sharp knife, cut round roughly into sections, thrown into a shallow bowl, mixed with thickly sliced raw onions, mild and very sweet. Salt, a sprinkling of olive oil and wine vinegar were the only seasonings

. . . It has no regional or picturesque name. It is just *ensalada*.'[1] Among the lemon and almond trees of La Alfarella, and in that very simple dish, 'so rich in flavour, so sweet, so cool, fresh', Elizabeth found that life was still worth living.

A muddle over dates with the travel agent meant that Elizabeth was forced to stay in Spain a few days longer than she intended, and had to miss a signing session that she had committed herself to in the book department of Harrods. She was very unhappy at having to drop this professional commitment, and as soon as she was back in England she went to apologize. The management were very understanding, and from the sales staff she learnt that the paperback of *French Provincial Cooking* had been one of the top six best-sellers for the last three weeks – 'after the latest James Bond and before the Kama Sutra, which gives one a certain amount of pleasure'.[2]

In her letter of thanks to Anthony, she described her three weeks in Spain as 'a door to new and marvellous things . . . which only you could have shown me, and I feel my life is quite changed, and none too soon, either. Except for the small inevitable leftovers of that annoying illness of last year, the ones which will always remain, all the rest is forgotten, as if it had never been. A lot more unhappi-nesses and anxieties [are] gone too. In their place a tremendous whirl and surge of new vistas and a different outlook on everything.'[3]

She visited Anthony again in October of 1964; and the feeling of renewal that La Alfarella bestowed shines through one of the most beautiful of her *Spectator* articles, 'Para Navidad'. The title refers to the way everyone in that part of Spain was making delicious things and storing them up for Christmas: the piece is imbued with the excitement of something to work towards and look forward to.

La Alfarella was the perfect rest cure, and in Denney's stimulating company she found the strength to face the future. No one since Norman Douglas had taught her so much or been on her wavelength to such an extraordinary degree. They shared not only a highly developed artistic taste, but also the same mischievous sense of

17. Elizabeth and George Lassalle on the steps of Halsey Street,
early 1950s

18. Lesley O'Malley in the basement flat at Halsey Street, early 1950s

19. Elizabeth, taken by Doreen Thornton, early 1950s.
This was one of her favourite photographs
20. Elizabeth's sister Diana's wedding to Christopher Grey, 1941
21. Elizabeth with her publisher John Lehmann, early 1950s

22. Elizabeth in her kitchen in Halsey Street, mid 1950s

23. Elizabeth, mid 1950s: 'She laughed with an abrupt and vulgar cackle which contrasted with her speaking voice and her bloodstock kind of beauty.'
Christopher Kininmonth, *Frontiers* (1971)

24. Elizabeth, 1956 or 1957. She noted on the reverse:
'Had forgotten I once had a white streak in my hair. Oh dear, that raggedy finger bandage would never get past today's salmonella vigilantes.'

25. Elizabeth by Anthony Denney, 1964

26. Peter Higgins

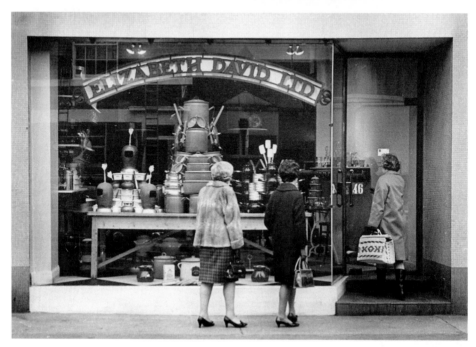

27. Elizabeth in the shop, mid 1960s
28. Anthony Denney arranging the stock, mid 1960s
29. Elizabeth David Ltd, 46 Bourne Street, Pimlico

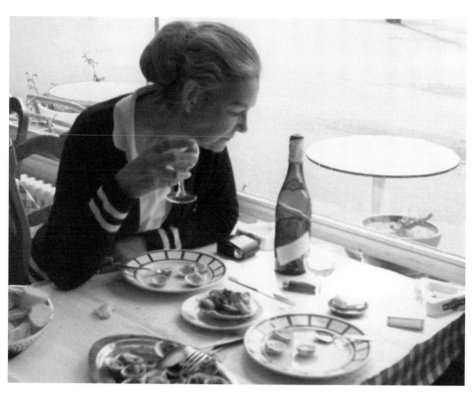

30. Elizabeth, taken by Renée Fedden on one of their last buying
trips to France, *c*.1971
31. Elizabeth's sister Felicité, early 1980s

32. Elizabeth in old age, late 1980s

humour, the same sharp nose for humbug. Denney had once had a school report which described him as 'naughty and defiant', and part of him still was. As with Douglas, sex did not come into it. Denney had three children from a previous marriage but that had long been over, and the only other guest at La Alfarella was his Australian partner Alex Collins, who ran the financial side of Denney's decorating business. They were just the people with whom to discuss the project that she had been thinking about for some time: a shop for cooks.

In the late 1950s, most people in England bought their cookware, dishes and utensils from hardware shops, where they were displayed alongside dusters and shoe polish, fly swatters and clothes-pegs. What there was was serviceable, and some of it was excellent: Union-Brand enamelware, Kenrick cast-ironware, fine stainless steel knives from Sheffield, beechwood rolling pins and spatulas, Pearson's stoneware, and bakery tools from Errington's of Portsmouth.

For the sort of cooking Elizabeth wrote about, however, the local hardware shop was not so well stocked. Earthenware was scarcely used for cooking any more, having been replaced by paler, less porous dishes from the big china manufactories since the mid-eighteenth century. Sheffield knives were good and easy to look after; but they were no substitute for the carbon-steel knives used in France, thin as paper and sharp as razors. The other problem was that even in the better-stocked shops, very few of the sales assistants knew anything about what they were selling.

There was only one shop in England where real French utensils could be bought, things like mandolines, carbon-steel knives and snail tongs: Madame Cadec's in Soho. Madame Cadec, a sprightly figure with dark hair and almond-shaped glasses, had run the shop single-handed for the past fifteen years since her husband's death. She had become an institution, and a password: those who mentioned her name in a knowledgeable way were assumed to be serious cooks. Her shop was small and dark, filled to bursting with equipment which was piled, higgledy-piggledy, from floor to ceiling.

Elizabeth wanted a shop where the staff would know about what was on sale, and where all the beautiful cooking tools that she herself would use could be found. Unlike Mme Cadec's, which looked like an old tool shop cum ironmonger's, she wanted hers to look stunning. Only one man could design such a place, and that was Anthony Denney. Denney agreed in principle, which must have been a relief to Elizabeth. She trusted his eye completely, and she would have felt far less confident about the project had he not been a part of it. She went back to London full of hope for the future, and feeling stronger than she had for many months.

The idea for a shop was not hers alone. In the late 1950s she had made a new friend called Peter Trier. He owned a company which made copper pans and also re-tinned them, and in 1960 he began importing Le Creuset's enamelled cast-iron ware. Elizabeth had long been complaining of the paucity of good cooking utensils in England, and kept urging Peter to make more things himself. Over long sessions at Halsey Street, they talked about what might be done to rectify this hole in the market. Others became involved. Peter Trier brought in his wife Jenny, and Elizabeth pressed Renée Fedden into joining them; at the time Renée was deeply troubled and unhappy, and Elizabeth felt she needed something to occupy her time and fill a part of her life. On several occasions, this small group had got together to think about whether they could raise the money to get the idea off the ground.

One of the factors that inspired them to go ahead was the appearance in May 1964 of a new shop, on the corner of the Fulham Road and Sloane Avenue, owned by an enterprising young designer called Terence Conran. It was called Habitat, and among many other things it sold bright textiles, china, glass and furniture for urban nomads. Conran had found inspiration for his ideas across the world, from Scandinavia to Japan; but he was always particularly fascinated by the solid, unpretentious work of French ironmongers. Their knives, their beautiful black pots and pans, ladles and tongs were on display alongside carafes, pepper mills and butchers' aprons, and Japanese-inspired paper lampshades. The shop was a sensation: Habitat not only offered a world that everyone under thirty wanted to be a part of – it was on sale at an affordable price. In later years, Elizabeth was rather scathing of 'Tattycat' as she used to call it; but there was no denying that it filled a gap. To a reader she wrote, 'They have the French [Le Creuset] vitreous-enamelled cast-iron cooking pots and quite a lot of good sensible things.'[4] Another factor that encouraged Elizabeth and her friends to clinch their decision was the announcement that Madame Cadec was about to retire. Elizabeth got in touch with her, offering to buy her leftover stock.

Towards the end of 1964, Elizabeth was persuaded to join the team of writers that was being gathered together for a new magazine called *Nova* – probably because they had promised that Anthony Denney would illustrate her pieces. Every magazine claims to be new, but *Nova*'s claim was justified. There was an immediacy in the way big black headings jumped out at the reader, the way a single photograph of a bowl of lemons filled an entire page right to the edges. It was not only more topical than most women's magazines: it also had a mind of its own. Magazines had discussed divorce before, but *Nova* was among the first to question the usual conclusion that it was the woman's duty to stick by a marriage come what may. Elizabeth contributed eight articles for *Nova*, from February to November 1965; and her appearance in the newest and most radical women's magazine gave her just the right 'profile' when the time came to launch the shop.

Another factor keeping Elizabeth firmly in the public consciousness was that all her books save *Summer Cooking* were now published by Penguin. Elizabeth had never ceased to bless Eunice Frost for bringing *Mediterranean Food* to the attention of Allen Lane, and putting her books within reach of a far wider readership. However, given the public interest in cooking, Penguin's cookery list was relatively small and in the mid-sixties the management felt the time had come to build it up. They had only one woman editor at the time, Jill Norman, so she was automatically given the cookery list –

though she was also handling contemporary poetry, the Penguin Classics and foreign literature.

Soon after taking over as cookery editor, Jill had to prepare Penguin's first edition of *Summer Cooking*, which Elizabeth had revised and enlarged. She used to go round to Halsey Street, and together they worked at the kitchen table. Elizabeth got on very well with Jill: she was not only sympathetic (all Elizabeth's best editors had a good desk-side manner), she paid rigorous attention to detail, and had a determination to get things right.

In the early spring of 1965, shop premises were found at 46 Bourne Street, just behind Sloane Square. Jenny Trier, who had inherited some money, bought the lease. They planned to open in the autumn, but before then the stock had to be ordered and the shop set up, and Elizabeth was still writing her articles. There were times when the immensity of what she had undertaken and the stress of ever getting it all ready in time got the better of her.

'Sorry about the outburst yesterday,' she wrote to Denney. 'I'm harassed and tired beyond endurance, and feel trapped like an escaping prisoner, back to bashing out another of those god-awful articles just when I thought I was free . . . [The shop] *has* to go right. I've involved three people in it, and you're involved too, I can't help it.'[5]

At this point two more people joined the venture: Bryan Llewellyn, who had experience in marketing and was then the Controller of Regional Marketing for Thomson Newspapers, and his wife Pam Pugh. Bryan Llewellyn had been approached by the Triers, who felt that the venture needed someone who had experience of marketing. He and Pam Pugh formed two of the five partners in the shop, the others being Jenny Trier (not Peter), Renée Fedden and Elizabeth.

Madame Cadec had told Elizabeth that she would be delighted to sell what was left of her stock – though perhaps the partners expected rather more than there was. Elizabeth wrote that she, Bryan and Pam 'spent an exhausting but entertaining afternoon with Mme Cadec in her warehouse, going through crates of rusty knives and ancient ironware, which I suppose we have to buy from her in return for information and her blessing plus a few bottles of her tarragon vinegar'.[6] Throughout 1965, Peter and Elizabeth made a number of trips to France in his van. They would park it in the courtyard of one of Peter's friends, who was a sculptor, and then do the rounds of all the old wholesale firms dotted about in the Parisian suburbs. Elizabeth had been collecting the names of good firms for many years, long before she started thinking of a shop. Once inside a warehouse she would not rest until she had explored every corner of the premises, and once she found something right her excitement was palpable. During these trips, they ate in a wide variety of restaurants – some not bad, some very rough indeed; but Elizabeth never seemed to mind, and Peter found himself learning a lot in her company. 'She was so funny, so cynical – her language was pretty rich too . . . and no one could bullshit her when it came to food. She was a great debunker.'[7] At the same time, the shop was being made ready. Elizabeth told Anthony that Bryan Llewellyn had bought a letter box and got the glass-cutters in to make an aperture in the plate-glass window, but 'they said it was much too dangerous to tamper with it. It's armour-plate glass. The wall took nearly a week to knock down. The place must have been built as a gangster's refuge.'

Elizabeth's excitement and enthusiasm, so long dormant, bubbled into a sort of skittish quality that was quite uncharacteristic. Her letter to Denney hopes that he is already planning the next shop, which will have '(*a*) a place for a letter box and (*b*) a staircase so we don't have to put a net at the bottom to catch the customers as they fall down . . .'[8]

She also has plans for books, lavishly illustrated by Anthony. 'I'm fed up with working for nothing. It's very nice having a lot of compliments and grateful readers and knowing that one has done some not bad work which everyone has tried to copy . . . and

E. David Ltd is going to make money too. You'll see. You've only known me as a writer, so it seems wrong to you that I should try and be anything else."[9]

There was no doubt in anyone's mind, least of all Elizabeth's, what the shop would be called. By now even people who did not cook had heard of Elizabeth David, and those who had never read a word she had written had probably absorbed the idea that her name was synonymous with good food and a certain integrity. As for her loyal and ever-growing band of followers, they would travel from all over England to visit what they saw as her shop. To her partners, the words ELIZABETH DAVID LTD that hung over the shop in massive, hand-forged, gold-painted iron letters were a lucky amulet. They were essential to publicize and launch their venture, and they would remain a symbol of the quality of the shop. To Elizabeth, however, the name meant far more. Only she knew how much work it had taken to make that name what it was, and in the window of the shop it was a promise to her customers. They would know that everything on display was there because she had chosen it, and it carried the stamp of her approval. At the same time, there was a risk in giving one's name to a business venture, as her first publisher, John Lehmann, had discovered to his cost.

Renée and Jenny were rather worried by the fact that although Anthony Denney had agreed to design the shop, he produced no plans or sketches at all. Elizabeth told them to have faith: she had complete confidence in him, and she was right – for when all was ready, the shop looked spectacular. Immediately behind the great wall of armour-plated glass was a massive wooden table, on which Anthony Denney erected dizzying, acrobatic pyramids of wire whisks, brioche tins, sugar casters, soufflé dishes, wire egg baskets and ramekins. These displays were lit from above, and stood out dramatically. Inside, a series of plain white shelves stood against the pale grey-blue walls, each supported by a deep iron frieze (designed by Denney) which hid the lighting of the shelf below. On these stood piles of the largest and heaviest items of stock: casseroles, bean-pots, storage jars, cheese stands and fish platters. On the black-and-white tiled floor were more piles of bowls and casseroles, and a round marble table at the back of the shop provided further room for displays. On the back wall, painted a deep blue, a white arrow invited the customer into the basement, which was reached by a narrow flight of stairs. Here the only decoration was bare brick and whitewash, with wooden warehouse shelves supported on perforated steel units; but the piles of fish kettles and sugar boilers, the drifts of omelette pans and terrines, and the warm russet colours of earthenware cocottes and gratin dishes, the bags of *gros sel* and the baskets of wooden and horn spoons gave the place all the exoticism of a Middle Eastern bazaar. Under the stairs was a little office.

The shop opened on 1 November 1965, on which occasion Elizabeth received good-luck telegrams from several of Britain's most cele-brated gastronomes: Philip Harben, Len Deighton, Fanny and John-nie Cradock, Robert Carrier and Robin McDouall. Terence Conran sent a huge bouquet of flowers, and she also received telegrams from Peter Higgins, and Tony David, who had now settled in St-Juan-les-Pins. Elizabeth had granted the *Sunday Times* an exclu-sive interview to be published the day before, on Sunday 31 October; but word got out before the paper went to press, and so many papers took up the story that by nine o'clock on Monday morning there was a queue outside the door. The day passed in a flurry of tissue paper and the ringing of the till, and at the end of the afternoon it appeared as if they had made over a million pounds – but this was primarily due to Renée's daughter Frances, who had obviously not quite mastered the cash register.

For the past fifteen years, Elizabeth had spent her working days by herself. The writer's life is one of solitary concentration, immense effort in an empty room. Now she was with other people, and rather enjoying it. She was, after all, the star of the show; and she was also a natural teacher, to pupils of any level. Jill Norman, who had known

Elizabeth only as a very reserved and retiring person, was astonished at the transformation that came over Elizabeth in the first few years of the shop. 'Suddenly she was available to everyone. She tried to establish exactly what people wanted, what they needed; she'd give them advice on presents, on cooking – and she loved it. There was an enthusiasm, a desire to share all her knowledge and experience, and the reclusiveness was just . . . *gone*.'[10] One observer remembered Elizabeth taking endless pains to find just the right sort of pan for an American lady with three children, who needed a skillet large enough to fry three pancakes at the same time. Sometimes, no trouble was too much. On one occasion, someone came in looking for a specific implement in just the right size, and was very crestfallen when told it was not in stock: 'But if you come back tomorrow,' said Elizabeth, 'I *think* I've got one at home . . .'

There were some things she refused to sell, such as wall-mounted knife sharpeners and – one of her pet hates – garlic crushers: 'Squeezing the juice out of garlic doesn't reduce its potency, it concentrates and increases it. I have often wondered how it is that people who have once used one of these diabolical instruments don't notice this and throw the thing into the dustbin.'[11] Elizabeth urged people to use the flat blade of a knife and a scrap of salt instead, but not all customers were happy to accept this particular tablet from the mountain. One was heard to say, 'And who are *you* to tell me I can't buy a garlic crusher?' To which Elizabeth tartly replied that the lady was at liberty to buy one wherever she pleased, but not in *her* shop.

When not upstairs with her customers, Elizabeth spent most of the day in the basement in her little office. Much of her time was spent working on mail-order catalogues, to which she devoted the same fanatical attention to detail as she did to her books. She also, in the early days, checked orders and dealt with suppliers. While working, she smoked untipped Gauloises by the packet; but while she never minded working with the bustle of the shop going on around her, she could not bear the noise of the air-conditioning and always switched it off as soon as she came in. Sooner or later, someone unable to breathe through the cigarette smoke any longer surreptitiously turned it on, and it would clatter away until Elizabeth turned it off again.

Elizabeth shared her office with a huge collection of reference books on food and cookery. These were tools she could not have lived without, and they were also used to answer the customers' questions. Customers were encouraged to use the shop as what one would now call a help-line, whenever their soufflé fell or their sauce curdled, and they availed themselves freely of this extremely useful service. Behind the desk were Elizabeth's treasures: pots and pans and tins, specimens of white china rimmed with shades of blue, different bowls and moulds all crowded together on a series of deep shelves. These were her personal things, not for sale; but each was a benchmark of its kind, and Elizabeth used them for reference and comparison with the orders.

To Drusilla Beyfus, who interviewed her for the *Telegraph* Magazine, she confided that 'this life is a million million times easier than writing a book';[12] but it was not plain sailing either. Many years later, she told Jane Grigson that dealing with suppliers was exhausting. 'Visits entailed endless argufying. And in spite of it all the sizes ordered were seldom sent, lids rarely tallied with the pots (but of course duty still had to be paid, no matter how long you had to sit on both waiting for them all to be matched up before you could sell them . . .)'[13]

Elizabeth was also responsible for generating certain discrete little crazes. Once it was coeur-à-la-crème dishes, and once – having got in a consignment of vinegar jars – Elizabeth started a vinegar 'mother'. This slightly opaque, gelatinous mass is required for the proper fermentation of good vinegar. A piece of it can be removed and, like a yeast, it can be used to form a new vinegar mother. People were constantly coming in to ask for a bit, till there was such a demand (it was like having the relic of a culinary saint) that Elizabeth wished she had never introduced it.

One thing she never regretted introducing was the olive oil of Poggio Lamentano. She had always loved real, unfiltered olive oil; but she did not know about this particular one until, one day in the late 1960s, she received a parcel. It was very badly wrapped, very greasy, and inside were the smashed remains of a bottle of olive oil. She wrote back to inform the senders, and they sent her another bottle – this time more carefully packaged. It was dark, murky green, intensely aromatic, and the best she had ever tasted. The people who made it were Lesley and Aleksander Zyw, and their son Michael. Aleksander was a Polish artist, Lesley came from Edinburgh. They had known nothing about olive oil when they bought the property with its eight hundred abandoned olive trees in 1961. Elizabeth described the oil as 'one of the supreme pleasures of my life', and the shop soon stocked it in five-litre cans, driven back from Tuscany in the Zyws' Land Rover. Michael Zyw was particularly grateful that she allowed them to use her name for publicity, and on the bottle labels: 'Not many people understood about good olive oil and having E.D.'s seal of approval convinced them to try it out,' wrote Michael Zyw. 'She most definitely did make a practical contribution both to the sale of our olive oil, and our perseverance in producing and marketing it.'[14]

The shop also generated a certain amount of publicity, which Elizabeth tried to keep strictly on her own terms. Whenever anyone wanted to interview her, the first reaction was, 'Why should anyone want to know about me?' In 1966, when the *Sunday Times* said they would like to do a profile of her, Elizabeth agreed only on condition that Sybille Bedford do the interview and that no personal questions should be asked. The interview was conducted over a series of dinners; and to reassure Elizabeth, Sybille showed her the finished piece. On handing in the copy to the features editor, however, Sybille was appalled to hear her say, 'Well, now that Elizabeth's checked it, let's put in some personal bits.'[15] Sybille indignantly refused to add a word.

Sybille told Elizabeth what had happened, but was unprepared for the force of her reaction. Not only was she outraged that the editor could have dared to suggest such a thing: she never forgot it, and never forgave the editor concerned. Fifteen years later, at a party to celebrate Sybille's OBE, the editor came to say hello to Elizabeth, who was enthroned in a chair with many people dancing attendance about her. Elizabeth cut her dead.

The shop became the focus of Elizabeth's life and she more or less settled into it. It was her club. In Bourne Street family and friends knew they could always find her, and here country readers breathless to meet the great Mrs David were granted an audience. An order was made for a case of wine per week, from Asher Storey: six bottles of Soave, and six of an inexpensive red wine Elizabeth called 'Flaming Carthage'. She often brought lunch for the staff: delicious terrines and egg dishes, olives and radishes, that were beautifully laid out on a little marble table downstairs.

Over the years, there was quite a turnover of staff in Elizabeth David Ltd. Some were very young, like Renée's daughter Frances Fedden and Celia Royde-Smith, who had been introduced to Elizabeth by her godmother, the cookery writer Margaret Costa. It was a first job too for Antonia Graham, who went on to found her own shop, Graham & Greene, some years later. Some were old friends of Elizabeth's – like Joyce Murchie, who came in once or twice to help out.

Rosalind Jenkinson, a bohemian and strikingly beautiful ex-model who became manageress of the shop in 1970, felt that it had a particularly intimate and relaxed atmosphere. It was generated by a collection of people who had nothing in common except that Elizabeth had seen, in each of them, something that she herself responded to. There was April Boyes, who became Elizabeth's most trusted right hand and who eventually undertook the cataloguing of Elizabeth's library; Rosi Hanson, who had learnt to cook in France and only read Elizabeth's books after returning to England with her husband Anthony, who was writing a book about wine. There was also

Ellen-Ann Ragsdale from Little Rock, Arkansas, and Elizabeth Savage, who succeeded to April's role when April decided to devote more time to her husband and daughter. Each felt particularly grateful to Elizabeth: to work with her was an education in itself. But to some she had also given new confidence, and a new lease of life.

When Anthony Denney and Celia Royde-Smith announced their engagement in 1969, almost everyone in the shop was taken by surprise – except Elizabeth. She had engineered their coming together from the first. Frances Fedden remembered seeing her mother Renée and Elizabeth together one evening with their backs to the fire, giggling delightedly, while Elizabeth tacitly congratulated herself on this fine bit of matchmaking. 'Some marriages are made in Heaven,' said Celia; 'ours was made in Halsey Street.'[16]

She was a thoughtful friend. Birthdays were marked by the little presents she was so good at giving, or a dedicated recipe. Yet she expected a lot from her staff, and anyone who slipped from her exacting standards was immediately corrected. April remembered that while everyone was expected to know what things were for and encouraged to ask if they did not, their ignorance was not always met with understanding. 'Sometimes she would be happy to tell you but at other times she would say rather severely, "Haven't you read my books?" We were all expected to be familiar with the sacred texts.'[17]

On window nights, everyone was expected to work late. Elizabeth would bring a picnic supper, and several bottles of Flaming Carthage helped to make it a convivial evening – but it was hard work. The girls went up and down the stairs with armloads of things for Anthony Denney, who constructed new ziggurats and miniature Chrysler Buildings with madeleine tins and asparagus kettles on the display table. When Anthony moved to Spain, the window was entrusted to a young artist; but it was Elizabeth who decided the theme, what would be displayed, and until she was satisfied the work went on – sometimes until nine or ten at night.

The mood among the staff was very cheerful, although there was a general feeling that it was more fun to be downstairs in the basement where Elizabeth held court. Most customers went downstairs too, for that was where the less bulky items of stock were. Someone was always supposed to be on duty upstairs, where there was a till, but the rule was not always obeyed. The result of this negligence was that on one occasion, not just the money in it but the upstairs cash register was stolen – and it was some time before the loss was noticed. The loss of the money was not as bad as the loss of the till, which was a brand-new one purchased to cope with the decimal coinage introduced in 1971. 'Now that's what I call cash and carry,' remarked Ellen-Ann in her Southern drawl.

Behind the scenes, however, cracks were opening up between the directors. The Triers, Bryan Llewellyn and Pam Pugh felt that the business should lead the enterprise: new suppliers should be found, new stock lines considered; Elizabeth should be compiling kitchen starter-packs, presentations for brides, arrangements for wedding lists. Elizabeth was impatient of such things, seeing it as her role to concentrate on publicity and aesthetics. Items ordered by another partner, or even items she had chosen herself but changed her mind about when they arrived, would be pronounced '*Hideous!*' and banished from sight. The fact that money had been paid for them and that they were there to be sold seemed no longer relevant. Renée was caught between the two. Helped by a friend called Rosemary Peto, she had put about £5,000 into the shop – more than twice Elizabeth's financial stake; but out of loyalty, she usually backed Elizabeth.

The shop failed to make as much money as they had hoped in the first year, and in 1966 they branched into mail-order and wholesale. Elizabeth was in charge of compiling the catalogues, and with her scholarly mind and eye for detail, they were very good. The company took a lease on a warehouse under the railway arches at Vauxhall (which Elizabeth used as a dump for the 'hideous' things that she could no longer bear to see in the shop). The office here was big enough to house Renée, Pam – who worked on the orders and accounts – and Mrs Goldsworthy, the book-keeper. Mrs Goldsworthy was in close contact with the spirit world, and kept a crystal ball and tarot cards in a drawer beside the petty cash.

In Bourne Street, at least outwardly, things went smoothly enough. Princess Margaret paid it a visit, and everyone was rather shocked that she walked around smoking a cigarette through a long holder – though there were usually at least two or three overflowing ashtrays downstairs in Elizabeth's office. The *gros sel* was joined by herbs, grainy French mustard and green peppercorns – though this only provoked more questions from the customers on how to use them. Since this was not a question that could be answered in one go, in 1967 Elizabeth wrote what was to be the first of a series of little booklets – *Dried Herbs, Aromatics and Condiments*. This was followed in 1968 by *English Potted Meats and Fish Pastes*, and in 1969 she brought out *Syllabubs and Fruit Fools* and *The Baking of an English Loaf*. The little books were not only for immediate sale: they were stepping stones towards a future series of books. Since she had so little time for cooking and writing, she saw the booklets as a way of getting the ideas and main headings together one by one.

Apart from these little books and the odd article, Elizabeth was working too hard in the shop to write; but the resonance of her name, and the impact of her work had never been stronger. Her books to date had made food as much a subject for discussion as the latest novel, foreign travel or French cinema, and there were more cookery books on the market than ever before. She had proved that people liked their cookbooks well-seasoned with history and travel writing, and that they were not afraid of sound scholarship either. Three writers emerged at this time whose work was influenced by Elizabeth and who benefited from the fact that she had blazed the trail.

In 1966 Elizabeth had been sent the typescript of a book called

Charcuterie and French Pork Cookery, by Jane Grigson. She was impressed. Here was someone who researched her work with as much thoroughness as she would have done herself, while at the same time writing with an enthusiasm that brought the subject to life with a wealth of historical detail and anecdotes. A year later, the *Observer* contacted Elizabeth and asked her to write a food column. Being too busy with the shop, Elizabeth declined – but suggested they ask Jane Grigson, who wrote for the *Observer* from then on until her death in 1990.

Jane Grigson was profoundly grateful to Elizabeth, and they became close friends. They were very different in character: Jane was much more open and accommodating than Elizabeth, who expected everyone to come up to the standards she set for herself. Yet they shared a boundless curiosity about everything to do with food, corresponded on subjects such as medieval English bread laws and eighteenth-century French ice creams, talked on the telephone every Sunday, and often had lunch or dinner together when Jane came up to London. Jane once said that she had only met two people in the world with perfect taste – her husband, the poet and critic Geoffrey Grigson, and Elizabeth David.

Another writer to emerge was Claudia Roden, who came from a close-knit Jewish family in Cairo. In 1956 her family, like many others, was banished from Nasser's new Egypt. As they spread all over Europe and the Americas the traditional food they had eaten in Egypt, which had always been important, began to take on a far greater significance. People preserved their cultural identity by giving feasts to entertain visiting cousins, by talking about what they had lost, by recalling the food from the past and preserving the stories and recipes that went with it. There is a parallel in the way that Claudia Roden and Elizabeth were impelled to write about food: both wrote from a place of exile, in an attempt to re-create the tastes they had known. Roden also acknowledges her debt to one specific sentence in Elizabeth's *Mediterranean Food*, which describes her few Middle Eastern recipes as 'the tip of the iceberg' and urges someone to explore further. 'Why not me?' thought Roden; and the stories and recipes she had been collecting for many years took form as *A Book of Middle Eastern Food*.

Elizabeth was not as impressed by Roden's work as she had been by Grigson's. She felt that, like her own first book, the recipes were inconsistent, and the whole not sufficiently scholarly. She was much happier to encourage Alan Davidson, a career diplomat who had produced what he called a 'primitive booklet' called *Seafish of Tunisia*. He had been attached to the British Embassy in Tunis at the time, and his booklet had been cyclostyled in the office of the information officer, Roger Eland – who had known Elizabeth in Cairo. Eland sent a copy of the booklet to Elizabeth, who was very appreciative. She had long been puzzling over the difficulties of correctly identifying Mediterranean fish, each of which might be known by a handful of different names in different countries; and in April 1963, in the pages of the *Spectator*, she had saluted Davidson's little book for tackling the problem head on. This had created a considerable demand: on 10 June 1963 she wrote to inform him, 'A lot of maddened *Spectator* readers and friends are still shrieking for your book.'

Elizabeth felt he could find a publisher; but Davidson was still a diplomat, and it was not until 1969 that he approached Elizabeth again. If he had his book – now much enlarged and called *Seafish of Tunisia and the Central Mediterranean* – privately reprinted, would she be willing to sell it in the shop? Elizabeth wrote back at once, with a decisiveness that Davidson found very encouraging. On no account was he to contemplate a reprint. His work must be presented as a proper book. He should immediately approach Jill Norman at Penguin and mention her name. Davidson followed her orders: the consequence was that Penguin did publish his *Mediterranean Seafood*, and it has been in print ever since. Soon after, he gave up diplomacy to become a full-time writer and editor.

Elizabeth never failed to notice food writers whose work she found good, and she was generous in her praise – even of one, like Jane

Grigson, who might have been seen as a direct competitor. Unfortunately, she was less quick to see how her attitude in the shop was beginning to arouse resentment. Minor differences between the partners were turning into fault-lines and getting deeper. Elizabeth, who was on a retainer of £1,000 a year as 'consultant' for the firm, felt that she should be paid more for her work on the catalogues. The other directors, already irritated by her high-handedness, pointed out that they too were working long hours with little to show for it, but this was something that Elizabeth seemed unwilling to acknowledge. In 1969 she nearly walked out of the shop because she felt Pam Pugh hated her. This was an exaggeration: what Pam objected to was the way that Elizabeth, thwarted of any rise in salary, tried to make up for it with perks and privileges that Pam did not think were valid. She also disliked Elizabeth's cavalier attitude to bills: some were incomplete, some badly calculated, and she had a tendency to give away small items of stock (admittedly these were usually slightly imperfect 'seconds') to people she liked. In the end it was Pamela who resigned.

Elizabeth and Renée made several buying trips to France during these years. Renée would plan the journey and do all the driving, while Elizabeth saved her energies for the suppliers and the warehouses. It was probably on one of these trips with Renée that Elizabeth had her last meeting with her ex-husband, Tony David. He had left Tangier after the zone lost its international status in the late 1950s, and moved to Ibiza. Here he ran a guest house with his French girlfriend Lélie, and when Tony's divorce came through in 1960 they married and moved to France. Eventually they settled in St-Juan-les-Pins where – quite fortuitously – they had a shop selling kitchen equipment. Quite what Elizabeth and Tony made of each other on the occasion of their meeting is not known, but Elizabeth was glad that she had made her peace with him because Tony died in 1967, at the age of fifty-six. One of Elizabeth's friends remembered the tears coming into her eyes, as she said that Tony David was dead. She mourned the only man who had ever loved her unconditionally, and whom she had been incapable of loving back.

Elizabeth needed Renée very much at this time, for she was becoming increasingly disenchanted with her other partners. Everyone who knew Renée Fedden agrees that she was very supportive when her friends were in trouble, and no doubt she listened to Elizabeth with a great deal of sympathy – particularly about Pamela, with whom Renée had her own differences.

Yet the shop was not Renée's only concern. Robin had left her for another woman, and Renée had found solace with an old friend – the painter Rosemary Peto, with whom she was to spend the rest of her life. Rosie Peto told Elizabeth that she had never loved anyone as much as she loved Renée, who inspired her paintings – although Renée was not very complimentary about them. She often told people that Rosie's paintings were no good, which obviously hurt the artist. When people urged her to be kinder Renée would say 'I can't help it, it's true.' Despite this forthright honesty, Rosie felt intensely protective towards her. For Renée's sake Rosie invested in the shop, although she soon began to resent the way the business seemed to devour all of Renée's time and energy. Rosie wrote impulsive letters to Elizabeth on the subject, complaining that Renée was being exploited by Elizabeth and the other partners.

It has been suggested that Elizabeth herself was lesbian, and that she and Renée were lovers. It has even been rumoured that Elizabeth felt betrayed when Rosie and Renée began living together, though this is highly unlikely. The loves of Elizabeth's life were all men. As for Renée, Elizabeth wrote that Rosie was 'in love with Renée, and I am not, and never have been – we were friends'.[18]

On one of their buying trips, Elizabeth and Renée visited the medieval town of Conques in south-western France, and stood in silence in front of the golden, jewelled figure of Sainte Foi – Holy Faith – whose hands are ever open and forgiving. Both Elizabeth and Renée were pagan, if not atheist; but they were both going through a period of change and upheaval, and they found themselves strangely moved by this tenth-century figure and its ancient benediction.

* * * * * * *

CHAPTER EIGHTEEN

Salt and Spice

Elizabeth's failure to notice the storm gathering at the shop came partly from a growing tragedy within her own family. Her favourite sister, Diana, was being inexorably destroyed. For some months, she had been suffering from tinnitus, ringing in the ears. Many people have to endure this condition in varying degrees; but Diana's case was particularly severe, and the fact that nothing – even electric shock therapy – could be done to alleviate the incessant torture had brought on a profound depression.

Her condition cannot have been helped by the fact that still having three teenage children and one under ten to look after, Diana was often tired and run-down. Dr Christopher Grey made a good living, but with seven to support, money had always been tight. When Diana came into a little inheritance she bought a small cottage in Hampshire, where they spent their holidays; but there was no let-up in the work Diana had to do, to keep her household washed and fed.

Elizabeth and her brother-in-law Christopher agreed that a rest and a change of scene would do Diana a great deal of good; so Elizabeth decided to take Diana and her husband on holiday to Venice, a place that Diana had always wanted to visit. It was the first foreign holiday the couple had had without their children. The tickets were arranged through Christopher's brother Douglas (once Tony David's partner in the ill-fated club in Herbert Crescent), who was then deputy traffic and sales director of BEA. Douglas did a lot to smooth their way. They were met at the airport, and taken by water-taxi to the Hotel Monaco, a few steps from St Mark's Square and next door to the best restaurant in Venice, Harry's Bar.

It was early May 1969, and Venice was every bit as magical as Diana had hoped it would be. Elizabeth took them to see the Byzantine cathedral on the island of Torcello, and they had lunch a short walk away at Cipriani's Locanda. They had ordered and settled down to the jug of wine when Elizabeth noticed an elegant couple near by, in raptures over their risotto. 'They in turn noticed my curiosity. With beautiful Italian manners they passed some across to me, explaining that it was a risotto unique to Venice and unique to this particular season. It was made with a green vegetable called *bruscandoli* . . .'[1] Elizabeth thought it so good that she called the waiter and changed her order. The manager told her that *bruscandoli* was a sort of wild asparagus, which can only be found in the flat marshy country of the Veneto during the first ten days of May.

They ate it the following day on the island of Burano, and returned to Torcello again to eat it once more; it was the last of the season. Elizabeth was told that if she hurried, she might still find some in the Rialto market. She was up at dawn the following day, and found one old lady with a few bunches for sale. She took the *bruscandoli* back to the hotel and put it in a glass of water, planning to draw it later; but when she returned to her room, the over-zealous chamber-maid had thrown it away – and the following day at the Rialto, the old lady was no longer there. This was just the sort of mysterious encounter with something delicious that Elizabeth relished, and back in England she was even more intrigued when she could find no reference to *bruscandoli* in all her books. It took her months to unearth a reference, which described them as wild hop-shoots.

Diana had been enchanted with the vegetable market, and especially the astonishing variety of salad greens that could be bought there. She came back to England with a passion for rocket, several limp samples and packets of seeds, and planted her garden in Hampshire with every variety of salad she could find. Yet while Diana and Christopher had returned feeling a great deal better for their holiday, the effects were only temporary. The tinnitus, which had never completely gone away, came back with a vengeance.

Elizabeth returned to the bustle of the shop; but she had felt for some time that she ought to be writing another book, and a lunch with Jill Norman sparked off a new trail of ideas. They were in an Indian restaurant, somewhere near the Post Office Tower; perhaps chosen because Elizabeth had recently been reading around the subject of Anglo–Indian food.

She had no particular interest in learning more about the food she herself had eaten in India: that was a part of her life she had no wish to relive. But she was very intrigued by the use of spices, and one of her favourite cookery writers was Colonel Kenney-Herbert, who in the great days of the Raj had thundered against the filth of Indian kitchens and the memsahib's reliance on tins and bottled sauces. At the same time she was contemplating, without much enthusiasm, the prospect of writing a book about Christmas food. The family festival of Christmas held no particular attraction for Elizabeth. As a child she must have suffered from the fact that her birthday on Boxing Day was invariably an anticlimax, and resented those relatives who gave her one present for both occasions. (It must have been just as bad for Priscilla, who was born on 27 December.) Yet the food associated with Christmas did hark back to an earlier tradition of cooking in Britain, when spices were used far more liberally than they are now.

As Elizabeth and Jill talked and talked over lunch that afternoon, they became fascinated by the English taste for hot spicy food. The conversation grew into a discussion of English food in general, and Elizabeth talked of other books that could be developed from the little booklets she had written: on spices and condiments, the baking of an English loaf, potted meats and syllabubs. Jill felt that they should become a series, which Elizabeth decided to call 'English Cooking Ancient and Modern'.

The following year, 1970, Elizabeth published the first book she had written for a decade. It was called *Spices, Salt and Aromatics in the English Kitchen*, and it heralded a new departure in her work. One glance at it shows that it is not a recipe book. Elizabeth had had enough of that particularly laborious and painstaking process, and most of the recipes she includes in this book are either her own tried and trusted ones, or quoted straight out of old cookery books, some dating back to the seventeenth century.

The point of this remarkably elegant book is not just how to use salt (to which she devotes five pages) and spices. It also explores the particularly English attitude to them. Contrary to many claims that the English like their food plain, the history of the subject tends to prove the opposite. The English went to great lengths and prodigious expense to acquire spices. They used them in their food not just as status symbols, nor to disguise the taste of bad meat – but because they liked the taste of spicy food. This taste was rediscovered by the soldiers and civil servants of British India who came back with their kedgerees and curries and was subsequently developed and refined by the Indian immigrations of the 1960s. She also points out that the English fondness for spices is enhanced by their appeal to our sense of romance and our longing for the exotic, so powerfully evoked by writers like Mrs Leyel.

This theme weaves through a book that is as full of stories and quotations as Elizabeth's previous works, but there is also a new note of rather intimate, relaxed reflection – perhaps the result of there being more text and fewer recipes. She recalls making pickles and Christmas pudding in Greece, and the curries and Edwardian nursery food of New Delhi. The book does, however, still bear traces of the Christmas book that was still in the back of her mind: in it are recipes for spiced beef, plum pudding and mincemeat.

There were one or two enthusiastic reviews, but because *Spices, Salt and Aromatics* was not what people had come to expect from Elizabeth David it was not given the rapturous welcome accorded to her earlier books. In the public mind, Elizabeth was firmly associated with France, Italy and the Mediterranean. The switch to

English food was seen as rather abrupt; but in the shape of Elizabeth's life and work it was a development that had been coming for some time.

Arabella Boxer, a writer who has been particularly interested in the subject of English food, began writing when Elizabeth was at the height of her fame. She has always acknowledged Elizabeth's achievement; but in the introduction to her book on English food, published in 1991, she expresses reservations about the nature of her influence. By introducing cheerless post-war England to the delights of olive oil, parmesan and garlic, Elizabeth diverted our attention from the 'brief flowering' of English food that had taken place between the wars.

In the 1920s and 30s, the pomposity and heaviness of Edwardian repasts had given way to informal meals, of three courses rather than eight. Egg and vegetable dishes were given greater prominence, simple grills and roasts were followed by fruit fools, summer puddings or Bakewell tarts, while cold meats and salads became more interesting. This type of cooking had absorbed a lot of French and American ideas; but it was still based on traditional, home-produced ingredients. It had begun in the sophisticated houses of London and the home counties, and might have spread its beneficial influence throughout society had it not been cut short by the Second World War.

When the war and its aftermath of austerity was over, Arabella Boxer feels that we should have picked up this promising thread where it left off; but thanks to Elizabeth David, whose vision of the Mediterranean was so intoxicating, we threw ourselves happily into coq au vin and daubes, vitello tonnato and ossi bucchi. 'All this is intrinsically good,' argues Boxer, '. . . but it does seem slightly ridiculous that pesto should have become a national dish.'[2] She goes on to say that 'Our two greatest food writers, Elizabeth David and Jane Grigson . . . both wrote one or two books about English food in the end, but it came low on their list of priorities.'[3] Elizabeth is unquestionably responsible for inspiring the English to cook Mediterranean, French and Italian food with unaccustomed gusto. But to say that English food was low on her list of priorities is not entirely fair.

Right from the start, her recipes were geared to what could be done by English people in their own kitchens. Throughout her journalism, even at times when French and Italian food was uppermost in her mind and those of her editors, she was informing people about what locally grown food was in season. In this context, she rarely lost an opportunity to give her readers some simple, perfectly English ways of making chutneys and jams, and what to do with spring lamb, or a glut of apples, or herrings and mackerel. At the same time, she was pouring scorn on the 'worked-over, worried, teased-up food' purveyed by English magazines, while the English catering trade received the regular tongue-lashings it deserved. Time and time again she remarked that English cookery, like our language, is one that is remarkably open to new influences – we have been using currants and spices, rice and potatoes for so long they hardly seem foreign at all. Her point, in presenting authentic French or Italian recipes to the public, was not that our cooking should become French or Italian: it is that we should learn from their techniques and absorb their ideas, and use them to develop and enliven our own home cooking.

Elizabeth could perhaps be accused of not acknowledging the renaissance in English food that took place between the wars – although she had been inspired by Hilda Leyel, Countess Morphy and, of course, Boulestin.

From the 1960s on, she wrote more and more about English cookery, and several *Spectator* pieces were devoted to those who had written best about English food: William Verral, Eliza Acton, Mrs Beeton, Dorothy Hartley and Lady Llanover. Several more pieces were devoted to specifically English food: pears and quinces, spiced beef, Cumberland sauce. Had she written the series of books to be called 'English Cooking Ancient and Modern', they would have more than balanced – in numbers and weight – those she had written in the first half of her career. And yet, inevitably, they would have sounded different. Elizabeth never found a lyrical voice to describe England, or even Wales, in the way that she had described France and Italy: perhaps, as an Englishwoman, she was too close. When there is a glimmer of it, she seems to be evoking an England that is so far away that it no longer seems real.

Yet it was not the state of English cookery that was preoccupying Elizabeth, nor even the shop; it was her sister Diana. By the beginning of 1971, Diana's suffering had become terrible. The incessant ringing in her ears was making her life unbearable, and affected her balance: Rosalind Jenkinson remembered that when Diana came to the shop, she had to be helped down the narrow stairs. She was profoundly depressed, and now openly talking of suicide. Her eldest son Rupert, who was then in his mid-twenties, was spending a year in Nepal; he was called home and for a while she seemed more cheerful. But although Diana was comforted by the presence of her children, the peace and quiet she so desperately needed was not enhanced by having five young people and their friends around the house.

Dr Christopher Grey's anguish and anxiety about his wife's suffering was made worse for him by the fact that he, a doctor, could do so little to help; yet he was by temperament an optimist, and hoped that the crisis she was undergoing would ease in its own time. Elizabeth was more pessimistic, feeling that there was only one way out of Diana's agony. She began to neglect the shop, spending more and more time with her sister. She tried to persuade her to eat, but Diana could manage no more than chicken broth and Dr Grey was too distraught to want anything else either. When Elizabeth was not with her, Diana telephoned her perpetually. Elizabeth had become her lifeline.

On one occasion, Diana rang Elizabeth and said she had to get out of the house. She and Christopher came round to Halsey Street, and together they all went to a local restaurant. Elizabeth and

Christopher talked about their forthcoming trip to Venice: Diana had so loved it the first time that they hoped the city would work its magic on her again. Flights and hotels had already been booked. But at dinner that night Diana kept saying 'I'll never make it Liza, I'll never see Venice again.'[4]

A few days later she went down to her cottage at South Harting in Sussex, for quiet was what she needed above all. Elizabeth spent hours on the telephone, while Diana, half-crazed by the terrible noises in her head, talked and talked of suicide. She asked Elizabeth if she thought it was wrong; Elizabeth assured her that it was not wrong, just very sad. Diana was more concerned for Christopher and his old age than for her children, who were almost grown up and had their lives ahead of them. She made Elizabeth promise to look after Christopher, and would not take no for an answer when Elizabeth tried to remonstrate. Elizabeth promised, and Diana thanked her. It was the last time they spoke.

The next day, 31 March 1971, Christopher called to see Elizabeth at the shop. He told her that Diana was in a pretty bad way and he was taking no chances: he had removed all dangerous pills, and was commuting from his London practice to Hampshire every day. But Diana had made up her mind, and had already arranged how to end her life. Christopher telephoned Elizabeth again that evening, soon after she had got home from the shop. Diana had been found dead in her bedroom, a suicide note beside her. She was buried at South Harting.

Christopher was heartbroken at his wife's death, and exhausted by the emotional strain that had preceded it. Fortunately he had his children to think of, his demanding work to get on with and sympathetic friends. Within a few years he was married again, and he and his children began to spend their Christmases in the Isle of Wight, where his new wife had a house.

For Elizabeth, Diana's death was harder to come to terms with. Although their lives were so different, for many years there was a sort of complicity between Elizabeth and Diana, an understanding which Priscilla and Felicité did not share. Elizabeth also felt protective and indulgent towards Diana, whose scattiness seemed more of a lovable characteristic than a fault. The main recipe in her little booklet called *The Baking of an English Loaf* begins with the useful reminder, 'Take off your rings and leave them in a safe place.' The recipe had been written for Diana, 'whose tendency to mislay her engagement ring while cooking has caused many a household drama'. With Diana's death, Elizabeth had also lost a focus of family life, particularly when the Greys began spending their Christmases on the Isle of Wight. When friends invited her out for lunch on Boxing Day, her birthday, they noticed that she would not be drawn on what she had done the day before.

Elizabeth had stayed at Wootton for Easter after the funeral, and on 18 April she and Renée left on their regular spring buying trip to France. 'I hope Renée's old Fiat proved reliable,' wrote Peter Higgins in a brief note on her return; but it was Renée herself who, with Elizabeth in such a fragile state, proved the most reliable and sympathetic friend she could have wished for. The thank-you letter she wrote when they came back, on 3 May, is a good indication not only of Elizabeth's state of mind, but of how much she leant on Renée and appreciated her.

My darling Renée,

You will never know how much you have helped me. As you know, I didn't believe that I could manage the trip at all, and certainly with anyone but you there could have been no question of my going away. As things turned out I think you were right, and anyway the job had to be done. You have done all the work, all the planning and coping, and at the same time you have comforted me and kept me going, and provided many moments when grief was forgotten and we could both give our minds to the work we were supposed to be doing – and like every one of our journeys together this one produced what will prove to be happy memories of waterfalls and lakes and flowers and trees, nice hotels, delicious wine, even sometimes a good meal.

You must be very tired. As I well know from my sessions with poor Diana during the last weeks of her life, sustaining somebody who is in misery is totally exhausting. Your patience and understanding are not gifts for which one can exactly say thank you I suppose – I can say thank you, my love, for using them so wonderfully. Dearest Renée, I do love you very much.
Elizabeth

Elizabeth and Renée had known each other for nearly forty years, and seen each other through periods of misery and desolation. At that moment, Elizabeth must have felt as close to Renée as they had ever been. But from then on, events in the shop were to drive them not only apart, but beyond the point of forgiveness.

Another source of comfort was Ellen-Ann Ragsdale, who had joined the staff of the shop in 1971. Warm and emotional, Ellen-Ann had none of the reserve that so characterized Elizabeth and Renée; but Elizabeth took to her instantly ('I think she was amused by the fact that I had never heard of her').[5] Yet what had really brought them together was that Ellen-Ann, like Elizabeth, had recently suffered the loss of someone very close. Soon she and Elizabeth were having lunch together – 'our requiem lunches, I used to call them. Elizabeth needed someone to mourn with, to get weepie with – and I had nothing else to do. Our friendship was based on shared regret and loss, encouraged by wine and long lunches.'[6]

That summer, Elizabeth's niece Sabrina (Priscilla's elder daughter) married an officer in the Life Guards called Charles Harcourt-Smith; and many of the wedding presents, both from Elizabeth and other friends and relations, came from the shop. For Priscilla, the wedding was a moment of joy after Diana's death and at an extremely difficult and anxious time as the inheritor-in-waiting of her Uncle Roland

Gwynne's estate. In the troubled years that followed, Wootton and its future were much on Elizabeth's mind.

The estate was nothing like what it had been in her father's day. Roland Gwynne had lived in considerable style, way beyond his income. For many years before the war, when he was Mayor of Eastbourne, he had been blackmailed by his sinister butler, who knew the secret of his homosexuality. His fortunes might have recovered, had he married the very rich lady who loved him; but she grew tired of being kept at arm's length, and left him to his own devices.

The bulk of the land had been let, sold or mortgaged to finance the luxury in which he liked to receive his friends; and over the years the houses at Wootton and Folkington became seriously dilapidated. One of his nieces described walking 'down passages and through unused rooms where the walls were covered in damp and mildew and the fittings were mouldering away'.[7] The years of good living eventually caught up with Roland. He was taken off to a nursing home in Eastbourne from which he never returned, and gave his power of attorney to his lawyer.

In the late 1960s, the lawyer died suddenly leaving Priscilla – as Roland's heir – in an impossible situation. For months there was no one to administer the estate and all money was frozen, so Priscilla could not carry out the repairs that Wootton so desperately needed. The only way to raise the necessary cash was to sell Folkington Manor. 'It just didn't seem possible,' wrote the same niece. 'To us in our youth Folkington had always stood for solid strength and security.'[8]

Priscilla had moved into Wootton to look after the estate some time before Roland's death in November 1971. Soon after, Stella was moved into Wootton as well. She was miserable at losing her garden and her independence, but Priscilla insisted because she was getting so old and frail. With both Stella and Priscilla now firmly in control of Wootton, it seemed as if the long line of male heirs set down by James Gwynne had finally been sidelined.

Priscilla, who felt that Wootton was hers by right of primogeniture, certainly thought so. Elizabeth supported her firmly: 'Pris has worked so hard to restore the wreckage left by Roland,' she wrote.[9] Elizabeth had not taken any part in the revitalizing of Wootton, but she admired the energy and determination with which Priscilla set about it. Indeed Priscilla had made a real commitment to Wootton, and had sunk all her own capital into it. But if Priscilla were going to leave the house to her eldest daughter Sabrina, she would have to dissolve the complex entail set up by James Gwynne in his will. Elizabeth was thought to be the only heir intervening between Priscilla and Sabrina, and she happily signed away her right to inherit a house for which she had little attachment, in return for a lump sum from the estate.

Diana too was sent a legal document to sign, for reasons that were not entirely clear. So Christopher suggested that it might be wise to ask his brother Martin, a lawyer, to go over the papers. The result was that Martin Grey discovered that Diana's claim was every bit as strong as Elizabeth's because, in inheritance law, a person's existence is calculated from the moment of conception rather than birth. If Diana spent the normal nine months in the womb, she would have been legally 'alive' at the time of her grandfather's death – and of the four sisters, she had produced the only sons. As Martin Grey confirmed, that not only gave Diana's eldest son Rupert a strong claim to the estate but, even more inconveniently, all of Diana's sons had a potential claim if Rupert died before they did.

This revelation was completely unexpected, and plunged Diana into a difficult dilemma. She was not a grasping woman, and hated the idea of sparking off another family feud. On the other hand, she did not see why Rupert's claim should not be recognized, in the same way that Elizabeth's had. What she did insist on was that if Rupert's claim was admitted by the Wootton estate, it was to be considered a one-off settlement and he would divide the money equally between all his siblings. Diana made this clear to Rupert before she died.

However, it must also be remembered that as this problem was developing, Diana had been reduced to a very fragile emotional state by tinnitus. The idea of a family confrontation was more than she could bear, and to Elizabeth and Priscilla she stressed that she wanted no part of Wootton for herself. Elizabeth records that at the time the whole thing blew up, Diana wrote to Priscilla 'renouncing totally and unequivocally any interest in the inheritance. Of course she hadn't any right to do so, any more than I have until I receive permission from the Courts – but she didn't know that – neither did I.'[10] Yet her attitude was nowhere near so clear-cut. She never expressly forbade Rupert to proceed with the claim, and her son Johnny remembers his mother telling him that Rupert, acting for his siblings, should be compensated.

After Diana's death in 1971 Rupert pressed his claim, encouraged by his uncle and his father. The matter was settled by the Wootton estate, and the money divided equally between all the Grey children.

Elizabeth was so angry that she did not speak to Rupert for ten years. She continually maintained that Diana had never recognized Rupert's claim to Wootton, and refused to listen when Johnny and Christopher both tried to explain that Diana's feelings had been much more equivocal than Elizabeth was prepared to admit. Rupert was particularly hurt by her attitude, since his claim to Wootton had been settled in the same way as her own.

Elizabeth's attention had returned to the shop after Diana's death; but tensions between the partners and the staff had not eased, and after six years in business the shop was still failing to make a significant return.

In 1970, a man called John Smith had been brought in as general manager of Elizabeth David Ltd, in an attempt to make the shop more streamlined and, it was hoped, profitable. He knew nothing about cookery but he did know about retailing, and he stormed into the intimate atmosphere of Bourne Street like a bull in a china shop. He had a broad grin and flirted with the girls; the first thing he did was organize a stocktake. For Elizabeth, the arrival of John Smith was not merely an intrusion, it was an invasion. To her dismay he ordered the removal of some of the most beautiful things in the shop, because they had never sold; while many of the 'hideous' things that had languished for years at Vauxhall were given another chance, dusted off and put back on display.

John Smith's feeling was that since the wholesale end was the most profitable side of the business, this was where efforts should be concentrated. He also felt that the range of stock was too narrow, and should be developed to give it a broader appeal. The more business-minded of the partners agreed that this was the right direction. Elizabeth, however, fought it with every ounce of her determination. Over the next two years there was a series of quarrels, misunderstandings, threats, accusations and blunders; but they all stemmed from this fundamental disagreement in policy.

She felt that in their new emphasis on wholesale trade, the partners were deliberately neglecting the shop. In her eyes, it began to look tacky and rundown. It is hard to imagine just how passionately Elizabeth identified herself with her shop. It had been created with her taste and expertise, represented years of work and was the tangible expression of her own vision. The signs of neglect that Elizabeth saw everywhere were all the more distressing because they represented a refusal to acknowledge what she had brought to the business: not just the shop itself, but the publicity her name had generated and the loyalty her name inspired.

Renée too was finding life in the shop increasingly distressing, and in March 1972 she resigned as a working director – even though she was still a shareholder in the business, and continued to sit on the board. Elizabeth was very sorry to see her go, and sent her a little present 'with my love, and to say goodbye because what else can I say? Except that perhaps one day Sainte Foi will be good, and restore something of what has been destroyed.'[11]

A brief respite from the storm that was gathering over the shop took place in May, when Elizabeth took a trip to Denmark. The

British Food Export Council were taking part in a British trade drive (which included everything from heavy industry to food). Among the many attractions were a double-decker bus, policemen from Liverpool, a nursery garden expert, and Elizabeth David, 'culinary expert and writer, who is well-known throughout Denmark'. The Danes gave her a very enthusiastic reception and, considering how naturally wary of publicity Elizabeth was, she was very amenable. The press took photographs of the '*engelsk gastronomik skribent*' with eminent Danes and wrote respectful articles, while Elizabeth did a number of signing sessions and interviews. She also spent time each day at the English stand of the food exhibition.

The crisis in the shop reached its climax in the first week of July 1972. There was a meeting of the partners, after which Elizabeth stormed out in tears. 'I am still in a state of shock,' Elizabeth wrote to Renée on 5 July, 'over the events which took place at Bourne Street immediately succeeding our last company meeting, and at the part which you played in those events. I think that you allowed yourself to be used to create a situation which could only result in my instant departure from the shop.'

Elizabeth chose to see a situation in which Renée had 'allowed herself to be used' by the other partners; but it is far more likely that Renée was trying to tell Elizabeth, in the quietest and most tactful way, that she was going align herself with their more businesslike methods.

In fact, Elizabeth had already reached the conclusion that things had become so tense and uncomfortable that she would have to leave sooner or later. She had told April Boyes, saying that her partners were becoming increasingly difficult and that anyway it was time she got back to her writing. She then asked April whether she would come and work for her at Halsey Street, to make a proper catalogue of her collection of cookery books. 'But what about the shop?' asked April. 'Oh, they'll get on well enough without me,' she said – a casual line which scarcely reflected her sense of betrayal.[12]

All these anxieties and upheavals were compounded by Elizabeth's increasing bad health. The chronic fatigue that was a natural sequel to Diana's death did not lift. The trip to Denmark had tired her more than she cared to admit, and her legs – which had never been good – were swollen and often ulcerous. One specialist she consulted asked, 'Why do you look so much older than you are?' She knew exactly who to blame, in her letter to Renée after the partners' meeting. 'The company could certainly answer that one – it is not only personal grief which has got me into the state in which I now find myself.'[13]

Over the next few weeks Elizabeth sat and lay around the house 'like a zombie'[14] and hardly knew what to do with herself. She could scarcely imagine an existence without the shop. She saw some people from the London Museum, who were looking for objects to show in an exhibition about London in the 1930s. Elizabeth had had the idea of starting a museum of kitchen artefacts herself, and sometimes thought about it in a desultory way. When she and Renée met for lunch, her mood was profoundly bleak. Later on that summer Renée sent her a postcard from Conques of Sainte Foi, with the message 'I came to ask if she could help us – love Renée.'[15] But Sainte Foi was invoked more from sentiment than from faith in a cure for their growing separation.

April Boyes came round to the house five mornings a week, and began work on the catalogue. The bookshelves in the sitting room had long ago been filled, both vertically and horizontally. Piles and drifts of books and magazines had gradually occupied the chairs and sofas, while stalagmites of books were steadily rising on the floor. Outside in the hall, Sybille Bedford described how one had to make one's way through 'a positive trench made of books – one's shoulders touched them either side, and one had the feeling they might fall in on one at any moment'. More books were set in piles on the stairs, and in the kitchen there was a further small library. April kept asking for instructions: she did have some experience of cataloguing, but Elizabeth had been so dogmatic about how things were done in the shop that she did not want to get off on the wrong foot. Elizabeth, however, was only sporadically interested. Much of April's time was spent driving her about, to see exhibitions and go shopping, and keeping her company over long lunches.

The death of Diana and the increasing tensions at the shop had left Elizabeth with some very raw wounds. In December 1972 she had found solace at La Alfarella, where Celia Denney had just received the news that her beloved grandmother had died. 'Elizabeth and I wept companionably, a glass of local plonk to hand, a cat on each lap.'[16]

In February 1973, April drove Elizabeth and her mother to Heathrow. Stella was going on what was to be her last visit to Jamaica, and a wheelchair had been ordered to meet her at the airport. Once Stella was safely enthroned in the wheelchair, April was surprised to see how Elizabeth fussed and fretted around her mother. Stella, however, was very much enjoying all the attention and remarked, 'My dear, do you know what I feel like? I feel like the Queen of Sheba!'[17] This broke the ice for a moment and they laughed; but Elizabeth was still very much on edge.

Once they had seen Stella safely on to the plane and had got back to the car, Elizabeth dissolved into tears. 'How could I have let her go on her own? I should be going with her! How on earth is she going to manage the other end?'[18] Her mother's frailty had touched a nerve of remorse and regret that was not usually so exposed in Elizabeth.

Stella came back safely from Jamaica; but her strength was failing, and she died at Wootton on 8 June 1973. Elizabeth, who had still not got over Diana's death, was in mourning once again. The funeral took place on 13 June, and coincided with an extraordinary general meeting of the partners. Elizabeth always laid great emphasis on the date, as an example of how callous her partners were to expect her attendance.

A week or so after the funeral, Elizabeth and Doreen Thornton drove through France and Spain, and were with the Denneys at La Alfarella a week later. The main excitement was a trip that took in

Albacete and Teruel, staying overnight at the Venta de Contreras. Elizabeth, determined to put the shop out of her mind, enjoyed it all – and was particularly touched by the hospitality they received at the Venta de Contreras. They dined on *gazpacho manchego*, and the following morning, they were sent on their way with little posies of mint and carnation.

At the same time, she was still absorbing the loss of her mother. At one point she confided to Celia Denney that she had recently given Stella a little hand-wound musical box, which had got mislaid; and that in the last days of her life, her mother became almost obsessed in her determination to find it again. It was only a small detail, but to Elizabeth it seemed to have significance. Once home, she had to go to Wootton to help Priscilla and Felicité sort out Stella's things. 'It will be painful, and going to Wootton is always a terrible penance to me. I fear the inevitable squabbles.'[19]

The meeting of 13 June, which took place while Elizabeth was at her mother's funeral, formally agreed to pursue the shift the business had already made: towards wholesaleing and mail order, away from the shop. They also agreed to expand the range of their stock. On that last point, Elizabeth had been willing to compromise (in so far as she could, which was not very far). But the deliberate neglect of the shop in the interests of the wholesale and mail-order end was more than she could stand. Elizabeth said that it had declined from being 'a well-stocked, elegant, efficient and profitable unit to a rather tatty corner hardware shop. That situation is intolerable, as it affects my name and reputation, earned and built up over many years.'[20]

Yet what Elizabeth could never get over was that Renée had, on this occasion, openly aligned herself with the rest of the partners. In a way, Renée had no choice. She felt responsible not only for her own stake in the business, but that put in by her friend Rosie Peto. Renée had been persuaded that the only way to make good and build on the efforts of the past seven years was to endorse the tough decision – and she knew, as they all did, that this would probably precipitate Elizabeth's resignation.

Elizabeth did indeed resign: from the board and as a consultant, and she announced her intention of selling her shares as soon as possible and publicly severing all connection with the shop. The worst of it was that when she walked out, she had to leave her name above the door.

Had Elizabeth put herself in Renée's shoes she might have seen where Renée's interests and loyalties lay. But Elizabeth was not always very good at that. Some of her most recent behaviour – in which she had accused Renée of stealing – was so exaggerated that it is possible that her mind was affected, perhaps by some drug she had been prescribed for her legs or her blood pressure. At all events Renée's defection came as a complete shock, and it amounted to high treason. That night she sat at the kitchen table sobbing and shouting, 'How *could* they! How *could* they!' as she slammed her fists down on the table.[21] It was as if a great poisonous wound, opened first by the loss of the Guttusos and the defection of Peter Higgins, had opened up again with a vengeance.

A year or so later, Renée's friend Rosemary Peto tried to force them to make up. In an undated letter to Elizabeth she wrote, 'I can't bear it that you and Renée should be separated . . . it seems so silly – but I believe strongly that [John Smith] was the only practical money-maker of you amateur hopeless lovely idealists . . .' Elizabeth wrote back as she did to everyone who tried to make her see reason about Renée: '. . . friendship betrayed is friendship slaughtered'. Rosie persisted. 'I long to bang your heads violently together and say "You bloody silly bitches, you love each other, you are amused by each other . . . how can you allow the nonsenses of business to stand in the way of your friendship?"' Elizabeth remained adamant. Peter Higgins was forgiven, but Renée would never be.

* * * * * * *

CHAPTER NINETEEN

Baking Bread

While Elizabeth had no time for the Englishwoman's passion for cakes and biscuits, she had always been drawn to bread. One of the works that had sparked her interest was the little book called *Home Baked* by George and Cecilia Scurfield, which Leonard Russell had coaxed her into reviewing in 1956. The magical effect of yeast on flour and water, the sensual pleasure of kneading a substance as soft and springy as flesh, the smell as it baked ('even bad bread smells good in the oven'), all gave her a profound satisfaction; and a table without fresh bread, and a pat of butter, was not a table at which she would choose to eat. Bread is timeless; and made with the right ingredients, it never let her down – unlike friends, lovers, editors, business partners. As the authors of *Home Baked* had pointed out, 'the great thing about baking with yeast is the difficulty of failure'.

Back in England, she immersed herself in work. *English Bread and Yeast Cookery* is the first book on which she tried to concentrate almost full-time, precisely what she wanted to do – but it was not easy. She could not summon up the energy she had once possessed, and as her research went deeper and deeper into the subject she wondered whether she would ever emerge to complete the book. Yet the hours in libraries, the fascination of what she was learning, the endless experimentations were soured by one constant nagging thought. Her name was still above the shop in Bourne Street, and there seemed to be no way of getting it back.

Some of her friends feel that she went into the whole business with too much enthusiasm, and too little professional advice; and that had she consulted a lawyer at the time, he might have warned her of the dangers inherent in putting one's name to a company. No doubt that is true, but even if Elizabeth had thought of what had happened to John Lehmann, it is unlikely that she or her partners would have considered a different name. The shop had to be called Elizabeth David: that was what gave it its unique selling point, and an edge over the competitors that sprang up in its wake.

Her first move was to put an announcement in *The Times*, which said that 'Mrs Elizabeth David wishes it to be known that she has no personal connection with the shop trading under her name.' And yet, while supposedly trying to rebuild her life as a writer, she could not take her eyes off what was going on in Bourne Street. She continued to press her claim that she was entitled to more pay because of the work she had done on the catalogues. The partners refused, but issued new catalogues largely based on her work. They then started redistributing recipe leaflets of Elizabeth's without asking her permission; on another occasion, she wrote a stiff letter about the exorbitant prices the shop was charging for the postage and packing of her books sold through the catalogue. There was a nasty moment in the summer of 1974 when it looked as if an Australian entrepreneur might start up a line of 'Elizabeth David' cookshops in Australia, and she was advised that neither she nor her erstwhile partners in Elizabeth David Ltd could do anything about it – but this particular threat never materialized. For the next ten years Elizabeth badgered the company at regular intervals to change its name, which the company had once allowed itself to say it might 'reconsider'. Eventually it did, but not to Elizabeth's satisfaction.* In the meantime, she had to content

* In 1986, after incorporating with Peter Trier's company Clarbat Ltd, the company did change its name to The Kitchenware Merchants Ltd. Bryan Llewellyn suggested that he might be willing to surrender the name 'Elizabeth David Ltd', which was still being used for one of the subsidiaries, in return for her shares. Elizabeth flatly refused: she wanted her name back as a matter of principle, and

herself with rapping the knuckles of any hapless journalist who made the mistake of mentioning 'Elizabeth David's shop'.

Elizabeth's rage, whether it was in its creative manifestation that made her write or the destructive one that made her bitter, was never contained: it managed to spill out in a modified form into whatever else she was doing, and the anger provoked by her dealings with the shop inevitably spilled into the bread book. A draft of her announcement to the press, in which she severed all connection between herself and Elizabeth David Ltd, was written on the back of a draft of the opening page of the chapter entitled 'The Bread Factories', one of her most trenchant chapters.

In it Elizabeth admits that English bread, and particularly London bread, had been bad for at least two hundred years. She quotes Tobias Smollett, who in *Humphrey Clinker* (1771) wrote that 'the bread in London is a deleterious paste, mixed up with chalk, alum and bone ashes; insipid to the taste and injurious to the constitution'. The people of London were well aware of this adulteration, 'but they prefer it to wholesome bread because it is whiter than the meal of corn'. This ancient tradition of over-processing bread had been taken ever further after the war. In an earlier chapter entitled 'Milling', Elizabeth takes the reader through the series of government orders concerning bread. Since the war these have permitted the great bakery conglomerates to make vast profits on a flour that is so refined that – by law – it has to be 'enriched' with all the nutrients that were taken out of it in the processing. The *coup de grâce* for English bread came with the invention of the so-called Chorleywood process in the 1960s. Instead of leaving the dough to stand for up to two hours to mature, it is agitated violently in high-speed mixers

---

had no intention of paying for it in any way. To Elizabeth's fury, a new shop was opened in Covent Garden in 1986. The Kitchenware Merchants then put out a press release saying that the founding shareholders 'remain in control of the new business: Mr Peter Trier, Mr Arthur Lewis, Mrs Elizabeth David CBE, Miss Pamela Pugh and Mr Bryan Llewellyn'. The Bourne Street shop was closed down in 1989, though the one in Covent Garden is still trading.

for a few minutes, thus making an enormous saving on time and human resources. 'Of any advantage to the bread itself,' remarks Elizabeth bleakly, 'nobody has anything much to say.'[1]

She meant the book to sound as plainly factual as a serious work of history; but her indignation at the all-conquering steamed loaf, her impatience with the government that could not control it and the public who are prepared to accept it, are palpable nonetheless.

Elizabeth went into every detail of bread manufacture: from its earliest beginnings, the ovens it was cooked in, the tools that people used, how the baking of bread – and the brewing of beer, which also depended on yeast – were a focus of people's lives. She knew well enough that the past was not romantic. That while the bread they ate might have been better than it is now, people's lives were hard and the baker's was no easier. While he might be envied for being the only man in the village who could keep warm, his job was more like that of a stoker on a steamship – as hot, as dirty and often as dangerous. At the same time, there was something very comforting about the past. It posed no threat, and made no demands.

Historical research also brought her closer to Felicité, who put her bibliographical experience to use with considerable enthusiasm. She combed the most recondite catalogues for books and references, sought out obscure works from the London Library, and had an instinct for nosing out what Elizabeth would find most useful and interesting. When the bread book was published, she gave Elizabeth a tiny gold pill-box in the shape of a loaf.

Those who had accompanied Elizabeth on her research trips also deserved a present; for once Elizabeth was on the scent of something, she did not let go. Elizabeth Savage, who had worked in the Bourne Street shop, drove Elizabeth around Normandy in 1974. Towards the end of the trip, Elizabeth was bitterly disappointed to find that the bakery to which they had driven from Rouen to inspect was closed. To make matters worse, it was effectively their last day in France. Nothing daunted, Elizabeth found out where the baker lived and persuaded him to show them round his bakery. He showed them everything he could, but the whole visit was very frustrating because none of the ovens was working and no bread was being made. However, they did find another good bakery that was open: 'This is a point for English visitors to look out for,' wrote Elizabeth in the bread book. 'Don't assume, if you . . . find the nearest bakery closed, that all bakers all over France are closed that day.'[2] Elizabeth bought a sample of all the loaves they had, and back at the hotel, they were all laid out on the bed and photographed.

It was the first trip that Liz had taken with Elizabeth, and she found herself rather tense, wanting to please and get everything right. It was a feeling Elizabeth often inspired in people: the feeling that sloppiness of any kind would not be tolerated. But on that trip, Elizabeth was a wonderful companion, full of information and interested in everything – although her curiosity to try out different establishments once meant that, in the square of a large market town, they sat down in a different restaurant for each course of their lunch.

April Boyes was another companion on Elizabeth's research trips, which were never undertaken without a good picnic lunch – fresh bread, pâté, perhaps that vegetable gratin that was such a feature of Provençal picnics, the tian. The Guildhall Library was a particularly convenient spot, because near by was a pond with an overhanging bush. A bottle of white wine was attached with a piece of string (Elizabeth never packed a picnic without including a corkscrew, a stout knife and some string) to the bush and lowered into the water, while they did a morning's work; and by lunchtime it was deliciously cold. They did this on several occasions, and their bottle was never spotted or stolen.

Once installed in a library, April Boyes was astonished at the way Elizabeth could become so utterly absorbed in her work that it became the only imperative. The lengths to which she was prepared to go to get what she wanted were demonstrated when Elizabeth and April took a trip to Leicester in March 1975, where Elizabeth wanted to see the two reconstructed querns (for grinding grain) in a certain museum.

Once inside a city, Elizabeth was such an unreliable map-reader that April had to drive and navigate on that rainy day. Finally they found the museum, and Elizabeth was delighted with the querns – particularly since grain was provided, and visitors were encouraged to try them out. Seeking for more information she asked to see the director, and was told he was not in that day. She and April then did a little tour of the museum, which was deserted. Elizabeth found a door and opened it: inside some students were larking about, but seeing Elizabeth and April they quickly got back to their work. 'Where is the director's office?' asked Elizabeth in a voice of quiet authority. One of the students led the way. The door was not locked, and Elizabeth marched in with April behind her. The student looked a bit uncertain, but was dismissed with an imperious wave from Elizabeth.

Once inside, she started opening drawers and filing cabinets and generally peering around. Then she installed herself at the director's desk, moved his papers out of the way, and settled down to work. April was kept busy bringing her photographs and folders, and the piles of paper mounted on the director's table; but April noticed that one pile was being carefully put aside, consisting largely of photographs and press cuttings. April began to feel that Elizabeth's intentions towards this pile were not strictly honourable, and that she might be planning to 'borrow' them without the director's permission.

Elizabeth could work with such concentration, such total absorption in her notes that she did not notice when April surreptitiously removed the pile. First she simply moved it to another part of the desk; and then, since she was still bringing Elizabeth more documents, she removed it altogether and returned the items to their proper places.

After about an hour or so, Elizabeth decided it was time to leave. It was still raining. She got up from the desk, looked around and gave an involuntary gasp. 'Where is that pile I had here?' – 'What pile?' asked April innocently. 'You know very well what pile. Where is it?' April said everything had been put away; but that since she had made a note of everything in the pile, it would be easy to request the information and have it sent or copied. This made no difference to Elizabeth, who was shaking with fury. 'Do you realize what you have done? You have set my book back by six months.' 'But –' '*Six months.*' Elizabeth did not say a word all the way back to London; and when April let her out at Halsey Street, she got out of the car, let herself into the house and slammed the door without looking round.[3] Elizabeth came round in the end, for April's help is gratefully acknowledged in *English Bread and Yeast Cookery*.

Jill Norman had been deeply involved in the book from the start because, as she explained, 'Elizabeth needed a sounding board.' Her first books had been largely based on information already acquired, and the big Italian and French books had demanded a great deal of travelling and practical kitchen work. This was the first time Elizabeth had ever worked on a book that demanded so much scholarly research. She had never gone into a subject in such depth and detail, and she wanted to make sure that she stayed on course. As time went on and Jill's interest deepened, she gave Jill recipes to try out with the words, 'Have a look at these.' She also showed Jill each chapter in draft as she wrote it.

As the writing progressed, they made several research trips in Jill's car: to look at mills, buy flour and search out small firms who made baking equipment. On one occasion they visited Jordan's flour mill in Bedfordshire, which was then quite a small concern. Elizabeth questioned their guide with extraordinary thoroughness and concentration: as if she was trying to understand the nature of flour itself, how it behaved. She did not take many notes at the time; but once they were back in the car she would talk over what they had seen and found out.

The first of what became several journeys to Wales was to visit Jean Bolland, who had bought a cottage called Ty Isaf near Llandeilo.

It had belonged to the same family for generations, and when Jean bought it, it had no electricity or running water; but it did have a brick bread oven, which had been in continuous use since it was built. Elizabeth had first got to know Jean when she worked in the shop, which she did two days a week, commuting from Kent. She was a hearty, jolly woman, who hid a certain melancholy under her determination to live life to the full. To some she might have sounded brusque, but Elizabeth appreciated her straightforwardness, her company and the fact that she still used her brick oven for baking. Baking with Jean gave Elizabeth great pleasure, and allowed her to try her hand at the techniques she was writing about.

Had Elizabeth travelled only for reasons of work, she might not have spent so much time in Wales. She wrote that in Norfolk, Suffolk and Cambridgeshire, 'traditions of cooking and baking seem to have remained intact long after they had been destroyed in areas subjected to the upheavals of the early nineteenth century'.[4] But at the time she was working on bread, Wales was very much on her mind. It was where her father's family had originally come from, and as she grew older, she began to feel the invisible ties of her unknown ancestors more deeply. She tried to find out more about them, and trace the Welsh side of the family tree: but as Elizabeth herself admitted, 'whether [we are] descended from the Gwynnes of Taliaris or Glanbran, or from one of the numerous families of that name who once flourished in mid-Wales, nobody seems to have established'.[5]

While Elizabeth had always loved the Sussex countryside around Wootton, she had never really felt a part of its life: neither when her mother was mistress of the house, nor when Priscilla took over. Too much had gone on there for Elizabeth ever to make her peace with the place, but Wales was different. She had always been refreshed by its unspoilt beauty, and it held memories of the holidays that she and her sisters had spent there before the war. Even in the 1970s, there were still vestiges of the old way of life. The work she was doing – and baking bread in Jean Bolland's oven – brought her in touch with them.

Quite apart from these satisfactions, it was also the site of one of her favourite restaurants in the British Isles: the Walnut Tree Inn at Llandewi Skirrid. Ann and Franco Taruschio had bought the Walnut Tree in 1963. Over the years they had developed a network of local suppliers, which meant that only the freshest and best of what was in season went into Franco's cooking. What Elizabeth loved, as much as the food, was the Taruschios' hospitality in what is still essentially a pub. Elizabeth sat in the bar, at a corner table in the window, and would ask Franco to prepare something for her that was not on the menu. He always obliged: serving it in tiny portions, and arranging little samples of this or that dish which had taken her fancy or aroused her curiosity. She even enjoyed his salad: 'I ate every scrap of it,' she wrote after one salad at the Walnut Tree, 'and I think perhaps yours is the only restaurant in these islands where I would even order a salad, let alone be able to eat it.'[6]

Such were the pleasures offered by Wales that Elizabeth thought she would like to buy a little house there. The estate agents were given very strict instructions. Anything they wanted to show her must be very quiet, but within walking distance of a few homely shops. The house should also combine the utmost tranquillity, while also being within half an hour of a main-line station with frequent and direct trains to London. But while she dreamed of Wales and always yearned to go back, she would never have abandoned London altogether. She could never have lived so far from a fishmonger such as Burkett's and Mr Ducat at Harrods, let alone her family and friends.

Elizabeth was now in her early sixties. Her thick grey hair, which had been worn short for much of the previous decade, was now in a chignon at the back of her neck. Her style of dress had scarcely changed. When going out she still favoured cream silk shirts and dark jackets, but the shirts were now worn with scarves or bows at the neck, and whenever possible she wore well-tailored trousers in preference to skirts. She had never had good legs; but her hands were beautiful, and her eyes – of a colour once described as 'prunes-in-brandy' – still held their challenging glint.

In 1975, her engagement book shows that she often saw Peter Higgins. Although he had lived in Spain for many years, he still came over to England fairly regularly; and he was in London, off and on, throughout that summer. 'Higgins will be interrupting us,' Elizabeth might say to Jill as they sat working at the kitchen table in Halsey Street. He was always beautifully dressed, having come straight from some meeting in the city. Elizabeth communicated with him very discreetly, leaving messages at White's Club. Peter Higgins's messages were even more discreet: they took the form of postcards, informing Elizabeth of the dates when he would be passing through London.

It was not until the following April that Elizabeth could write 'finished last chapter of bread book'. It was a considerable relief – not only to her but to Jill. To celebrate the event, Elizabeth asked Jill to dinner: this in itself was a rarity, for she seldom entertained in the evenings any more. She cooked a dish of ham in brioche for the occasion. They talked of future books in the 'English Food Ancient and Modern' series; Elizabeth felt that she might tackle meat next.

In June 1976 the proofs of the bread book were ready. Elizabeth rented a large cottage in Portmeirion, where she and Jill went to go over them. They took it in turns to cook, bought wine from the hotel, talked a great deal and read in the evenings. Elizabeth was in an excellent mood, and was more interested in the picnics and expeditions they organized than in the task on hand. *English Bread* was an enormous book; but they had brought all the various drafts of the manuscript to check against the proofs, and Elizabeth could still rely on her extraordinary memory.

In the autumn, George Elliott drove her down to visit the Denneys, who were becoming disenchanted with the countryside around Valencia. It was still beautiful, but tourism was on the increase; and for those who had known it before the rise of 'the Benidorm factor', it was not the same. Anthony and Celia had decided to move out, and had found an old castle in Badajoz that looked promising. It was called Salvatierra, and was going to require a great deal of work. For Elizabeth, however, a period of work was over. She had finished the bread book at last, and she was much gratified that her contribution to Britain's cultural life was publicly recognized with the OBE. She had received the award on 17 February 1976 from the Queen, who asked her what she did. 'Write cookery books, Ma'am,' said Elizabeth. 'How useful,' remarked Her Majesty.[7]

In 1977, Elizabeth increased her efforts to find a house in Wales, but finding the right one was evidently going to take time. Her first trip that spring produced no likely candidates, and she was back in London in early summer. Soon after she wrote a message and a poem to John Lehmann, her first publisher, who was celebrating his seventieth birthday. She says the poem is 'unoriginal and unworthy of you, but you will know it comes from the heart of a most affectionate and loyal friend, one also much in your debt. I could say so much more – but this is a greeting, not a testimonial, so I'll leave it at that.'[8]

The poem was called 'Scrambled Eggs Variation 77'. It is perhaps longer than it should have been, and not all of it is quoted here; but is almost certainly the only recipe Elizabeth was to write in free verse.

You must first find fresh eggs laid by hens running about
In the open air and pecking on corn and other wholesome things
Not reared in a cage and crammed with pellets and fish meal
This is the most difficult part
Then you take two or three of those eggs
And a not very large lump of butter,
About half as large as one of the eggs
And a frying pan or sauté pan, seven or eight inches in diameter
You need also a fork. Salt only comes later, although that is
    against all the rules

You put the pan over low heat and melt the butter
You break the eggs straight into the pan
You beat them and fold them with the fork
For just about twenty-five seconds until they are in soft and creamy
flakes
Now you pour them out into a little dish
I forgot to say that this should be warmed –
but not too much –
Or the eggs will go on cooking and they will be spoiled.
Now you sit down and eat them, with the crunchy salt you have
put ready on the table
And pepper from a mill . . .
With a slice or two of brown bread and some good butter
You now have a feast fit for a poet.

Her next visit to Wales took place in August, where she stayed with Jean Bolland and made bread again. On 7 August her diary records that she made 'two beautiful loaves with white Mill flour'. Two days later she saw three houses, and on the 11th she records that during a picnic on the banks of the Edw they sighted a kingfisher. The next two days were spent at Ty Isaf, and more bread was baked. It seemed an idyllic holiday, even if she had not found a house; and she returned to London in good spirits to pack up the kitchen, before having it rewired and repainted.

Elizabeth had enlisted the help of her nephew Johnny Grey to put up shelves in her refurbished kitchen. He was then twenty-four, had studied architecture and was already planning to specialize in kitchen design. That autumn, he joined her house-hunting efforts in Wales. He had a car, was a willing driver and his architectural training would be put to good use on those houses where the main question was, 'Is it fixable?'

They saw a beautiful vicarage at Abergwesyn, and on the 23 September, visited what looked like a very promising cottage at Newbridge-on-Wye. The following day, with a case of red wine in the back of the car, they were on the road from Portmeirion to Builth Wells, where they had to see another cottage. Johnny was not driving fast, because Aunt Liza didn't like it; but he did notice that the roads were slippery. He urged her to put on a seat belt. There was a snort of derision: like many of her generation, Elizabeth did not believe in seat belts. Prompted by a sort of misplaced gallantry Johnny decided not to wear his either. Shortly afterwards, while taking a corner, Johnny lost control of the car. It swerved across the road and smashed into a telegraph pole. He sustained no more than a broken arm, but Elizabeth had been thrown forward and her mouth had hit the dashboard. In the silence that followed the crash, Johnny saw that she was very badly injured. There was also a sickly, vinegary smell from the bottles of wine that had smashed in the back of the car. It was about ten years before Johnny could bring himself to drink red wine again.

Elizabeth received emergency treatment locally, and on 26 September she was transferred to the Princess Grace Hospital in London. The first thing she did was to send Johnny a case of wine (white this time), and urge him not to feel guilty for what had happened. The police too had said that the accident was not his fault, but Johnny could not help blaming himself.

'I have a fractured right wrist and left elbow,' she wrote to Peter Higgins on 7 October,

> also smashed knee cap, and teeth all over the place. Johnny also has a broken arm, a bill from the PO for damaging their property and terrible misery about the damage to me. Poor boy, it was in no way his fault, just rotten luck. I fell in love with the doctor who set my arm at the local hospital but I was whisked away by ambulance to London to have my knee and elbow operated on and to get Mr Moreton [her dentist] to work on my teeth. Am lolling in great comfort in a hospital a few yards from Devonshire Place so I don't have to get out of bed

to go to Mr M., that's lucky because I can't anyway, just like you when you fell off your horse. Going down to the operating theatre is like a ride through the souk. There's a beautiful Arabian prince next door and two security guards outside. I have a lovely view of the Post Office Tower, at night it's all coloured lights, very pretty. There should be a muezzin calling to prayer on the top.

I expect I shall be here several more weeks, isn't it lucky my book was finished before I had the accident. So annoying, I just had my kitchen rewired, lovely new lights and beautiful clean paint, I was enjoying it, and Wales was lovely too. I'll be quite all right, but it's a slow business. I just long to see you my love. E.

From this letter it is obvious that Elizabeth was completely reconciled with Peter and still, from the way she is trying to sound cheerful and amusing, eager to please him. But although various friends had tried to reunite her with Renée from time to time, here she remained implacable. When Robin Fedden died that year, Elizabeth did write to Renée. But her letter of condolence, however well-meant, sounded hard and cold.

George Lassalle came to see her in hospital. He had just married his fourth wife, the publisher and novelist Caroline de Crespigny, and they were about to move to Cyprus. The weather was very cold, and George appeared wearing an overcoat with a Persian lamb collar. 'So, Vronsky, you've come,' said Elizabeth.[9]

She did not think much of the food she was given. One friend was with her when the nurse came in with her lunch, and on top of the aluminium plate cover was a piece of pitta bread. Handing it to the nurse she said, 'Please take this away and find a patient who needs a poultice. It's not good for much else.' When asked if she needed anything she said, 'Stamps, just stamps, I can never have enough of them.'[10]

*

English Bread and Yeast Cookery came out in November, while Elizabeth was still in hospital. The fact that the reviews all hailed it as a great and important work of scholarship must have done much to raise her morale. 'I doubt if anyone who reads this book,' wrote Hilary Spurling in the *Observer*, 'will ever feel quite comfortable with a supermarket loaf, whether white or wheatmeal.'[11]

Another generous review came from Paul Levy in *Books and Bookmen*. The piece begins with a paeon of praise for her work, and says that her OBE was 'a rather mingy honour for someone who has made a social and cultural revolution. Who else in recent time can be said to have changed the *habits* of so large a section of the population of an entire country? Surely she should be Damed as soon as possible.'[12]

Levy went on to point out that Elizabeth was not a crank. What she detested was the factory loaf, and what she provided was the instruction and the information required by those who were not prepared to tolerate it any longer. Elizabeth wrote Levy a note to thank him, saying he had understood exactly what she was trying to say.

Elizabeth's book was a very important milestone in the campaign for better bread, which so far had been fought on two fronts that were sometimes inimical to each other. On the one hand were the health-food lobbyists, who argued that the only wholesome flour was one made of 100 per cent stoneground wheat. On the other were the people who simply wanted bread that tastes good, as it does in other countries. Elizabeth took a sensible middle course between these two positions. She did understand the health benefits of wholewheat bread, but she did not disapprove of white flour – provided that it had not been refined and bleached of all its goodness and taste. At the same time, she had gone into the subject in such depth that every twist and turn in the story of bread legislation and the rise of the factory-made loaf was made alarmingly clear. In fact, the big concerns were already aware of this change in the air, and were beginning to turn it to their advantage. A whole new range of steamed, sliced brown loaves had appeared, promising health and nutrition, while Tesco opened their first in-store bakery in Newport in 1970. It did not take them long to notice that the smell of 'fresh' bread made their customers feel good, and thus encouraged them to spend more time in the store – and more money.

Elizabeth was still in hospital when Peter came over in December. She had needed a series of operations to mend her arm, elbow, knee and teeth. He had lunch with her on several occasions, and no doubt did much to raise her spirits; but her friends felt that Elizabeth never really made a complete recovery. The accident had taken something out of her, and she would never have the same strength and energy again. There was no more talk of buying a house in Wales.

* * * * * * *

CHAPTER TWENTY

Omelette and Ice

On 13 April 1978 Elizabeth was made Author of the Year in the Glenfiddich Awards, given annually for excellence in writing, publishing and broadcasting on food and drink. She received the prize for *English Bread and Yeast Cookery*, and in her speech of thanks, Elizabeth alluded to the recent collapse of Spillers, one of the big three milling companies in England: 'I received a card from a friend,' she announced, 'which simply said: *One down – two to go*.'[1] In the following year, the University of Essex decided to award Elizabeth an honorary doctorate. Elizabeth was particularly proud of this acknowledgement of her scholarship, and was accompanied to the ceremony by John and Veronica Nicholson. In her long black gown and mortarboard, Veronica thought Elizabeth looked rather small; but she was in great spirits, and tipped Veronica a big wink as she went up to the rostrum. In her speech, she laid particular emphasis on her debt to Veronica, who had 'nagged and bullied' her into journalism all those years ago.

English Bread and Yeast Cookery was an important part of a general drive for better bread which did then gather speed. In 1979 the *Sunday Times* launched a Campaign for Real Bread, headed by Caroline Conran and the health correspondent Oliver Gillie. Considering that its aims were to improve the variety of shop bread and make wholemeal bread available everywhere, the campaign could claim a measure of success. As the 1980s wore on, other campaigns

– for organic fruit and vegetables, and better conditions for animals, all gathered momentum. Elizabeth, almost at the end of her working life acknowledged as the best food writer of her generation, might have lent the weight of her name to those campaigns. She chose not to. Campaigning, even in print, is a very public endeavour, and Elizabeth was turning inwards.

She had become absorbed in history and research. Through Felicité, she came across two booksellers – Guy Cooper and Gordon Taylor – who had just become co-directors of the Herb Society. She wrote occasional articles for *The Herbal Review*; but what particularly interested her was the seventeenth-century still-room book of Lady Granville, which belonged to the Society's library. It contained one of the earliest English references to ice cream, and led to further research which took her into Bishop Ken's Library under the eaves of Longleat.

She first visited Longleat in June 1979, with Alan Davidson. The archivist had gone to great trouble to find samples of the handwriting and signature of Grace Granville. However, Lord Christopher Thynne (son of the Marquess of Bath) was keen that she should also see the *Pynson Boke of Cokery*, which – dated 1500 – is the only surviving copy of the first cookery book ever published in England. Elizabeth went back to Longleat again a few years later, to discuss a possible reprinting of the book with Lord Christopher. Nothing came of it, for Elizabeth felt that she could only participate if the reprinting were done to the most exacting academic standards, while the Thynnes were evidently thinking of a publication with more general appeal.

At about this time Elizabeth met an antiquarian book dealer called Stephanie Hoppen, who had a strong interest in books on food and wine. Elizabeth was particularly drawn to books compiled by the *maestri di casa* of the sixteenth and seventeenth centuries, who managed the kitchens of the most powerful families in Italy. These books were much more practical than their French equivalents, more descriptive of the food itself and the techniques of cooking. Elizabeth

also took an intense interest in Stephanie's work of compiling catalogues and bibliographies, and questioned her every reference and
assumption: 'She was always telling me to go back to the source:
whenever you're in doubt, go back to the source. She made me do
everything that much better than I would have done without her.'
Elizabeth bought several books from Stephanie, some of which cost
well over a thousand pounds: 'She loved books with such a passion.'[2]

She also became fascinated by a small, stout, handwritten book
dated 1604, which the biographer Hilary Spurling had been cooking
from for the last ten years. Elizabeth said, most emphatically, that
it ought to be published: 'she wasn't a person you said "no" to
twice', said Hilary Spurling.[3] Elizabeth was a great help in the
preparation and presentation of *Elinor Fettiplace's Receipt Book*:
when sent the notes that were to accompany the text, the five pages
of corrections and suggestions Elizabeth sent back reveal the range
of her knowledge, and the accuracy she insisted on.

Professional chef is a designation which didn't become usage until the mid
nineteenth century. Chef is an anachronism. Master cook would be the
correct designation of Robert May . . . *The Prince de Condé's chef*. Not only
an anachronism, but an error of fact. Vatel . . . was never Condé's head
cook. He was his maître d'hôtel, which in the case of a great establishment
like Chantilly, meant that he was in overall charge of organizing the supplies
. . . *Artificial colourings*. In the light – if one can call it that – of present-day
usage of the term, saffron and the rest are surely natural colourings?
Perhaps you could say additional colouring?[4]

In March 1979, Elizabeth emerged from her studies to join John
and Ellen-Ann Hopkins for a holiday in Tangier, where the Hopkinses then lived. Several years had passed since Elizabeth and Ellen-
Ann had mourned together over their 'requiem lunches', but they
had always kept in touch. Since 1977, when Ellen-Ann Ragsdale
had married the writer and novelist John Hopkins, she had often
asked Elizabeth to come and see them.

They spent a few days in southern Spain before sailing to Morocco, eating in all sorts of little restaurants and *ventas* – the smaller and more rustic the better. As usual, people were flattered by Elizabeth's boundless curiosity, and she was an appreciative guest. The only time she misbehaved was in the Marbella Club, where she ordered a consommé. It was the sort of place that pretended to a knowledge of French cuisine so Elizabeth had no qualms about sending it back with the words, 'This is horrible.' The chef took it back and the dish was presented for the second time: 'This is even worse!'[5]

As soon as she arrived in Tangier she was happy. She wrote in the morning as usual, then dressed and went exploring – usually with Ellen-Ann. She became obsessed by a green leafy vegetable she saw in the Socco Grande, the great market of Tangier. In Morocco it is called *b'khola* and John Hopkins always thought it was a kind of kale. No, said Elizabeth, it was more like a sort of Swiss chard, but not one she had ever come across before. The result was that John and Ellen-Ann were put to work trying to find out what it was, and Elizabeth would not let the subject go – she worried at it, like a terrier with a bone.

She was also fascinated by John's collection of the conical cooking pots called *tagines*, which he had built up over seventeen years in Morocco. Some had been bought in extremely remote places, in the mountains or the desert, and many were adorned with beautiful designs. When the Hopkinses moved back to London a year later, several of the tagines arrived broken and had to be thrown out. When Elizabeth heard of this she was very upset. She thought they could have been repaired, and all were worthy of being in a museum. John was quite taken aback to see how distressed she was.

The Hopkinses introduced her to the writer Paul Bowles, with whom she had one thing in common – they had been the only authors on John Lehmann's list to be retained by Macdonald, when his publishing company was forced to fold in 1954. They got on famously; and Paul Bowles's Moroccan helpmate Abdelouahid took her on a memorable day out.

Elizabeth had said she wanted to see how Moroccan bread was

made, from beginning to end. 'Abdelouahid obligingly drove her out to the countryside where Moroccan women in their colourful costumes harvest wheat with sickles. Then to the threshing floor where animals go round and round. Then to the huge watermill where the huge stone pulverizes the grain. Abdelouahid then took Elizabeth to his home so that she could watch his mother prepare the loaf. Then to the local oven where it is baked. A perfectionist and notoriously difficult to please, Elizabeth returned thoroughly satisfied.'[6]

She had not been back in London for more than a month when Elizabeth received one of the saddest letters she was ever to read in her life. Her old friend Viola Johnson, to whom she had dedicated *Italian Food*, had committed suicide in Greece. The letter she sent to Elizabeth was not so much a suicide note as a grateful farewell. 'Alas, you and I will never again sit together at a table with a bottle or two, for I have reached the end of the road . . . Goodbye, dear Liz. Thank you for your friendship, and the many good times and good laughs we have shared.'[7]

The year 1979 saw the creation of a new cookery journal called *Petits Propos Culinaires*. It was founded by Alan and Jane Davidson, who had for some time been thinking of launching such a publication. They had discussed the idea with Elizabeth, who expressed enthusiasm – the magazine would be the perfect showcase for certain pieces of research she herself had done. But the spark that got the magazine started came over lunch one day with Richard Olney.

Richard Olney was born American, but realized early on that his only natural home was France. He rapidly became an authority on French food and wine. He was also as close to being a French chef as is possible without the formal training. 'Elizabeth teased me mercilessly,' he wrote after her death, 'claiming that my cuisine and my taste in wines were much too grand for the "likes" of her.'[8]

Richard Olney had recently been appointed chief consultant for an ambitious series of cookery books planned by Time-Life Books, called *The Good Cook*. Since its American editors wanted it to be as authoritative as possible, they laid down a great many rules – one of which was that no recipe could be included that had not already been published. At lunch one day with the Davidsons, Olney was venting his rage over this particular rule, which forbade him to include one or two perfectly straightforward dishes for which no satisfactory recipe existed. The answer was, of course, to publish them himself – in *Petits Propos Culinaires*. The first issue contained an article by Elizabeth called 'Hunt the Ice Cream', and two by Olney – posing as Nathan d'Aulnay for an aubergine gratin, and Tante Ursule, for crayfish à la bordelaise. Elizabeth was to contribute several articles for *PPC*, as it came to be called, and took her position as honorary president very seriously – she had no hesitation in telling those concerned when she felt it was getting too rarefied and scholarly. 'For every ten postcards or telephone calls to us expressing pleasure or congratulation . . . there would be one telling us that we had gone off the rails.'[9]

Olney admired Elizabeth, and when she came to visit him at the Time-Life flat he used while living in London, he gave her only the simplest food: elvers in oil, scrambled eggs with truffles; but she happily joined him in the 'Montrachets, Chambertins, Lafites and Yquems that I sometimes imposed on her'.[10] On one occasion, however, Elizabeth joined him in a meal that was far from simple.

Olney's fiftieth birthday fell on 12 April 1978, when he happened to be in England staying with Lesley Marple, ex-wife of the film director John Huston. A brilliant young Californian chef called Jeremiah Tower did the cooking, Sybille Bedford chose the wines, and the guests were Richard Olney and Elizabeth. The menu was carefully noted by Sybille Bedford, along with the wines that went with it.

First they had prosciutto, with bread made by Elizabeth: with this went a bottle of Roederer Crystal Vintage Champagne 1969. Then, after a *fumet de poisson* (with a Sauvignon de St-Bris '76) they went on to the entrée, roast saddle of lamb with a sauté of spring vegetables: tiny onions, turnips and broad beans, and a chiffonade of lettuce and sorrel. This was accompanied by Château Pape-Clément '66. With the fresh goat cheese and a Saint-Nectaire they drank another bottle of Pape-Clément, this time a '61. Then came a Blanc Manger, accompanied by a Château Climens 1961.

The occasion provides another example of Elizabeth's talent for giving presents. Her gift to Olney was 'a large, heavy, oval porcelain platter – antique restaurant service – with a faded burnt-orange rim, a thread of the same colour just inside the rim. I love it. When not in use, it is always on view.'[11]

That summer, Felicité fell gravely ill. She was taken to St George's Hospital. The main cause was heart trouble; but when Elizabeth came to talk to Felicité's doctors, it emerged that they were concerned by the fact that she was alarmingly undernourished.

Felicité's habitual lack of interest in food was quite genuine, not just a way of underlining her independence from her famous sister. People who took her out to lunch or dinner noticed that she ordered the plainest and dullest things on the menu, and the pleasure she took in going out was entirely in the talk. According to John Sandoe, in whose bookshop she worked for so many years, Felicité felt the need to keep her weight down. She ate the yogurt she made herself, or bed-sit stand-bys like eggs and baked beans, or the sort of self-consciously spartan health food that Elizabeth would have had no time for – but whatever she ate, it was in tiny quantities, and as she grew older she started skipping meals altogether.

Over the years, Elizabeth had had little occasion to think about what Felicité ate. She did not notice her tiny appetite on family occasions, because her own appetite was small too. Both sisters scrupulously respected each other's privacy: neither of them encroached on the other's territory without a telephone call before-hand. But on hearing that Felicité was suffering from malnutrition, Elizabeth was profoundly shocked. Quite apart from her concern for Felicité's health, the idea that someone might find out that

Elizabeth David's sister, who lived in her house, was half-starved, was too terrible to contemplate.

She immediately concurred with the doctors' recommendation that Felicité be given rich, tempting food, in very small quantities. Elizabeth had not cooked regularly for many years, except for the fresh loaves that she loved; but now she started cooking again for Felicité. Starting with soups and broths, which were all that her sister could manage at the beginning, she moved on to tiny pâtés, rich jellies, little egg dishes, delicious morsels of fish or chicken in cream – all served in the doll's house proportions that Elizabeth herself liked. John Sandoe often drove her to the hospital, with the dishes in a basket. Felicité was very touched by her efforts, but very weak and could scarcely manage more than a mouthful.

Her stay in hospital was succeeded by a long period of convalescence in a nursing home; and although she did get her strength back, she was never quite the same again. She went back to work in the shop, but only three mornings a week to open the mail and answer the telephone. On the one hand, she could not get used to having her role in the shop so reduced; and on the other, she had become so forgetful and absent-minded that she had become more of a hindrance than a help. John Sandoe finally had to ask her to leave. Elizabeth and the rest of her family never forgave him.

The tiny basement flat in Halsey Street was empty much of the time, though it was still nominally occupied by Lesley O'Malley. Several years before, Lesley had been persuaded by her old friend Roald Dahl to buy three little cottages, side by side, in the quiet street of a village called Great Missenden in Buckinghamshire. Dahl and his wife, who lived nearby, had helped her with the purchase. Two were rented, and Lesley used the third at weekends.

When Lesley was sacked from her job in advertising at the end of the 1970s, she decided to go freelance. She spent more and more time at Great Missenden, where she now occupied two of the cottages, converted into one by her architect niece, Jane Blakemore.

Elizabeth immediately noticed that Lesley was not using her bed-sit as much as before, and let it be known that she would like the space back. This was not done as tactfully as it might have been: Lesley was deeply offended, and moved out at once. They did make it up a few years later; but for the time being a distinct coldness existed between them.

Some years before Elizabeth had given her nephew Johnny Grey his very first commission, for a new sink cabinet. He built it in the street, and installed it himself. Then, in 1983, she asked him to design a new kitchen in the basement flat. Johnny describes Elizabeth as a surprisingly easy client: she had her own very definite ideas, but was not particularly demanding because her kitchen requirements were very simple. There was no microwave, no dishwasher, no kitchen gobbler – although her cleaning lady, Jean McAuliffe, did persuade her to install a washing machine, the first there had ever been in Halsey Street.

Over the course of her life in Halsey Street Elizabeth had had a succession of cleaning ladies, most of whom left after a few months, but Jean was different. She was very retiring and sweet-natured, and Elizabeth found her easy to get on with because she never disturbed her books and papers. Her relationship with the builder was far more difficult. On the one hand, she did not like the idea of him being there at all, he was invading her space; while on the other, Elizabeth felt he had left the job before it was finished. She described him as 'a proper tease. I have to *beg* him every day to come back, and put up a plate rack or fix handles on the cupboard doors – as elusive as Higgins.'[12]

However, she was very pleased with the results. The new kitchen had more space, and more natural light than the old one. It also had a 'soft' area which was carpeted; and around the table in this space went an upholstered banquette. The cupboard and sink cabinet were made of London plane and English ash, which glowed against the pale, blue-grey paint with which she painted not only this room, but almost every other room in the house. An enormous daybed was another feature, although it would not go downstairs. Jack Andrews had to spend a morning taking out the area window so as to get it in that way. Johnny suggested that the new one should be the 'winter kitchen', while the old one remained as the 'summer kitchen'. Elizabeth liked the idea of a seasonal migration, between one kitchen and the other – but it did not turn out that way.

The door of the old kitchen was shut, as if she had shut off a part of her past. It was not locked, merely abandoned, left to its own devices, rather like the sitting room. At one point the sitting room had had a proper turnout, and a new sofa was bought. 'For a while, it was actually usable; but since she never used it, the books and papers started to pile up and soon it was unusable again.'[13] Elizabeth had four rooms at her disposal, but retreated into two of them: her new kitchen and the bedroom.

Elizabeth felt very close to Johnny, and certainly he inherited her tastes for cooking and design more than his brothers and sister. The building of the new kitchen had been a satisfying time for them both, sharing long lunches and suppers at the kitchen table. He tried to persuade her to move: the Halsey Street house was very dark, and he knew that she sometimes found it depressing: 'She, of all people, shouldn't have to live in the dark! I thought she would be much happier in a big first-floor flat with huge windows, like the ones in Cadogan Square, where she could enjoy the sun streaming in all day.'[14]

She never moved, but Johnny seemed to move out of her life. He contracted glandular fever, after which he could no longer take the late-night drinking sessions. They began to see each other less frequently, and Elizabeth began to feel slightly neglected.

In fact, she was far from neglected. Rosi Hanson took her on picnic jaunts outside London, as did Liz Savage, Jill Norman and Jack Andrews. With April Boyes she went to any number of exhibitions. Elizabeth was fascinating company in an art gallery: she looked at pictures as keys to the past, filled with the sort of information that did not appear in books. She still kept in touch with old friends like

Doreen Thornton and Sybille Bedford; though since Sybille now only liked going out for dinner while Elizabeth wanted to go out for lunch, they saw each other less frequently than before. She had not seen as much of Hugh and Judy Johnson as she used to, for they had moved to the country and had young children; but she retained a very wide circle of friends. She was particularly good at long-distance friendships, because she remembered what amused or interested the people she liked. Out of the blue would come a newspaper cutting, or an extract from a book catalogue, or an advertisement from a magazine, accompanied by a postcard from Elizabeth saying, 'I thought you might be interested.'

Similarly, her correspondents knew what would interest her. 'I currently find myself with considerably raised blood pressure,' wrote Anthony Denney from Spain, 'having just finished reading M. F. K. Fisher's *Two Towns in Provence*. . . In the Aix section she describes proudly how she was able several times to resist being told and shown the preparation of *calissons d'Aix*: her own version of the recipe then follows.'[15] For Elizabeth, who never turned down an opportunity to see how a local speciality was made, this just about summed up the difference between herself and Mrs Fisher.

One person who was very interested to meet her was the cricket commentator John Arlott, who also ran the *Guardian*'s Wine Club. They had met at some formal occasion but he wanted to know her better, and Rosi and Anthony Hanson arranged a dinner for them to meet. They were astounded by the way that Arlott was not only curious about her early life, but quite openly so. He asked her questions about her childhood, her youth, and her husband that they would never have dared ask her – and even stranger was the fact that she did not seem offended. In fact she seemed to be rather enjoying it. At one point she mentioned some uncomfortable moment in her youth and Arlott exclaimed, 'If only *I'd* been there, you wouldn't have had to go through all that!' Elizabeth was flattered and amused; but she replied, 'I think not, John. You see, I was a bolter.'

In her thank-you letter to Rosi she wrote,

I wasn't able sufficiently to deflect John from his apparent purpose of conducting a 'Face to Face' interview across the dining table, in front of an unpaid, unwilling and captive audience. It must have been boring for you two . . . On the whole I can't help thinking that it was just as well our paths didn't cross when he was a lusty – or did he say lustful – Hampshire policeman. When I said I was a Bolter he didn't get the allusion. I was thinking of Nancy Mitford's Bolter, Fanny's mother in *Love in a Cold Climate*, who was always running away from husbands and other gentlemen. John would have been very disillusioned, very quickly I fear . . .[16]

Many friends came into Elizabeth's orbit thanks to Felicité, who met them in John Sandoe's bookshop. One was Michael Day, a cheese connoisseur and wholesaler – later founder of the Huge Cheese Company – who used to swap cheese for proof copies of books at Sandoe's. When he first came to see Felicité at Halsey Street and came upstairs, she jokingly told him that the bottom half of the house was occupied by 'my terrifying sister'; but when Michael himself came to meet Elizabeth, she was not a bit frightening and they began to see each other. Michael was young and very good-looking, and Elizabeth enjoyed going out to lunch with him. She also enjoyed long evenings with him in Halsey Street, where he kept her entertained with stories of his different girlfriends.

One friend whom she met through Jane Grigson was the broadcaster and novelist Paul Bailey. In the early 1980s he was involved in a series for Radio Three called 'Third Ear', which consisted of interviews with writers: not because they had a book to plug, but simply because they were worth talking to. He had already interviewed Jane Grigson, and after the companionable lunch with Jane at which he had met Elizabeth, he tried to persuade her to be interviewed as well. Paul Bailey understood that she was very shy, and tried to make the interview he proposed sound as undemanding as possible. She would not have to say anything personal, she would be talking exclusively as a writer, and it could all be done at Halsey Street with the minimum of fuss. Elizabeth dithered and dithered – and finally said she simply couldn't, she was too terrified. Paul accepted this, with regret but with grace: he did not try and change her mind. Elizabeth was grateful for his understanding, and their friendship developed.

Two years later, in the autumn of 1982, Elizabeth was invited to take part in an edition of *The Food Programme*, presented by that veteran food campaigner and connoisseur of single malts, Derek Cooper. The programme was going to be devoted to bread, and Elizabeth was suspicious from the start. 'Who else is going to be interviewed?' she wrote on the letter of invitation. 'Don't ask me to taste any bread.' On balance, she decided to say no: she was not a natural performer. However, the producer approached Jill Norman, and she persuaded Elizabeth to change her mind. After all, Derek Cooper's programme had an excellent track record, and was widely respected.

The programme was recorded on 22 October, and got off to a bad start. Derek Cooper launched into a fulsome introduction in praise of her work, and described Elizabeth as the woman who had done more to change British attitudes to food than anyone else this century. He then turned to her and asked, 'Is that true?' There was an agonizing silence as Elizabeth sighed inaudibly, tilted her head and looked around the studio. She finally replied, 'You tell me.'

The interview never really recovered, but Derek Cooper plugged on manfully. Elizabeth answered his questions in a way that started clipped and brusque, and then died away with a hesitant 'don't you think?' She was obviously not enjoying it, and every attempt to ignite a spark in her fizzled out. When discussing the time it took to bake bread Cooper asked, 'What about women who work all day?' – 'That's their problem.' – 'What do you do when you are served terrible bread at dinner?' – 'I don't go to dinners like that.' At one point, thinking that Elizabeth had taken against him, he asked his colleague Christopher Driver to take over, hoping that perhaps he might do better. Elizabeth did not appreciate the change and was, if anything, even frostier and more monosyllabic. In despair, Cooper thought the only thing to do would be to tie up the interview as if it had ended, and keep the tape running. This was done, but Elizabeth never really loosened up. By the time she left they had hundreds of feet of tape, and by dint of a great deal of skilful splicing, the producer Joy Hatwood managed to put together something like an interview.[17] At one point, they did give Elizabeth some rice bread to try, and she made a stab at being more forthcoming. 'This is rather *damp*. . . not at all like mine . . . it's interesting . . . someone's trying, anyway . . .'[18]

The programme had been a great deal of hard work, and Derek Cooper felt it had been a disaster: 'She just couldn't play the game, and she knew it. I blame myself, I should have respected her initial refusal.' At the same time he was glad that she had been recorded because her voice is now in the BBC Archive; and the fact that people had actually heard it was so exciting that they did not notice the shortcomings of the interview. Derek Cooper recalled one listener who said what a joy it was to hear Elizabeth David, but then added 'what a pity Cooper didn't give her the chance to say more'.

Elizabeth now had two books in mind: one called *Ice and Ices*, for which the research seemed (like the bread book) to be expanding exponentially, and the other was a volume of her journalism. It was an idea suggested by Jill Norman as a way of getting her back into making books as opposed to researching. Elizabeth was enthusiastic, and for the moment, this book was known as 'Early Works'.

As far as Elizabeth was concerned, Jill was now irreplaceable: they worked together so well that she never wanted to have another editor. When Jill left Penguin in 1979 to set up on her own, Elizabeth followed her. By 1983, however, Jill had discovered that going solo had its disadvantages. She had to spend too much time on the administration of the business, and not enough on books. For these reasons she decided to maintain her independence and her list, while sheltering under the umbrella of a larger publisher who would provide services like warehousing, sales teams and distribution. In January 1984 Jill moved her list to Robert Hale Ltd.

Part of the deal was that Robert Hale acquired certain rights over Jill's list, though the sum paid by him did not reflect its value: it was a kind of insurance measure, repayable by Jill if she left the company within eighteen months. It was understood, at least by Jill, that she should retain her own imprint. Since Elizabeth was one of her most important and best-selling authors, Jill was keen to present a new book by her in the first list she produced that autumn.

This was to be 'Early Works', the collection of Elizabeth's journalism. She and Jill went through the dusty files that sat on the bottom shelf of the bookcase in the hall, where Elizabeth kept all her articles. When Elizabeth went to Uzès in February, Jill was left with the keys of Halsey Street to get on with the selection. Soon after Elizabeth came back she developed a painful skin complaint on her legs and feet. This became so bad that she had to be prescribed painkillers, and could not go out for days on end. Jill came round very often, bringing a picnic lunch, and worked at weekends too.

The pieces they gathered together included the best of the work she had done for *Vogue* and the *Spectator*; and it was Elizabeth's idea to include extracts from the little books that she had written for the shop. The pieces were, with very few exceptions, left as they stood – Elizabeth preferred to write introductory notes where necessary, rather than change them. But the book still took six months of hard work. Elizabeth decided to call it *An Omelette and a Glass of Wine*.

By mid-July, the book was in page proof. Jill and Elizabeth corrected it together, but the contract for it had not yet been signed. Elizabeth had let the matter slide because she was not entirely happy with it: under the new terms, the publisher was Robert Hale Ltd, and not Jill Norman. But John Hale (son of Robert) was pressing Jill for the contract, and Jill was reassuring. Elizabeth signed.

On Friday 13 July, Jill delivered the corrected page proofs and the contract for *An Omelette and a Glass of Wine* to John Hale. She then set about clearing her desk, since she was going on holiday the next day. At the end of the afternoon, John Hale came in and gave her a letter. It told her that she had been dismissed. 'I was so astounded I couldn't take it in; I think I just carried on with what I was doing.'[19]

It was not until she returned from holiday that reality sank in. Jill was barred from entering the building – even to retrieve her own filing cabinets. These contained the contracts, correspondence and work-in-progress of her authors, and all the papers relating to her backlist. She was told that all her papers were now the property of Robert Hale Ltd, including her name, which she was no longer allowed to use as a publishing imprint. Among the assets seized were a great many draft chapters of *Ice and Ices*, and the hardback rights of the 'Elizabeth David Classics': a collective title that, iron-ically, covered the books that Elizabeth had extricated from Mac-donald with so much difficulty.

Elizabeth was appalled by what had happened. She felt that Jill had been sacked so that Hale could get his hands on her list, and that she herself had been tricked into giving him two books that she had always wanted Jill to handle. They saw a great deal of each other over the next few weeks: not only for mutual support, but to think about what could be done. The only hope was to go to law but it is a fact of life that large companies can afford lawyers, while individuals very often cannot.

Elizabeth was particularly concerned about the draft chapters of her ice book. On several occasions she demanded their return; and when finally they were returned to her, in mid-September, it was obvious that the papers had been photocopied: they were out of order, and all the paper clips had been removed.

Thus Elizabeth had publishers very much on her mind when, on 30 September, she attended Ellen-Ann Hopkins's fortieth birthday

party at the Quat' Saisons restaurant in Oxford (this was before
Raymond Blanc had moved into his Manoir). She found herself at
a table with three people: the writer and publisher Jeremy Lewis,
the American publisher Jerry Epstein and Clare Astor. These three
had, by surreptitiously changing the place cards, contrived to sit
next to each other; but they did not know her.

Jeremy Lewis described the occasion in his memoir *Kindred
Spirits*. As yet unidentified, Elizabeth appeared as

a white-haired woman in her sixties, whose elegance and rather washed-out
beauty was sadly upset by an unhappy expression and the abstracted air
of someone who would obviously prefer to be somewhere else . . . Clare –
eager to make her feel at home, and worried in case she was baffled by the
menu – began, in the kindest of ways, to translate the various items on
offer and explain, very slowly, what they tasted like. Far from showing
gratitude for a helping hand, our dinner companion looked unhappier than
ever; and when – unwisely, perhaps – I revealed that I was in publishing,
she embarked on a tirade against the iniquities of publishers, and how
shockingly she had been treated by a particular firm.[20]

Lewis had charitably put Elizabeth in her sixties; she was in fact
seventy, and the situation she found herself in was a terrible
replay of what had happened with *Italian Food* thirty years before.
Through no fault of her own, she had fallen into the hands of a
remarkably unsympathetic publisher. In the revised page proofs of
Omelette, Jill's name was removed from the title and credits pages.
This revised proof was hurried through and circulated to the press
before being sent to Elizabeth. She immediately hired a lawyer,
and Robert Hale Ltd were obliged to put back the original dust
jacket and alter the tampered proofs. Hale then had the nerve to
deduct £400 for 'excess proof corrections' from her first royalty
cheque.

An Omelette and a Glass of Wine delighted Elizabeth's legion of
fans. In the *TLS* Jane Grigson praised it for including all the dishes
most closely associated with her (spiced beef, salted Welsh duck,

syllabub), as well as all her pet hates (fake mayonnaise, Bird's custard, the rise and flop of the quiche). She also pointed out that 'Mrs David has been more to us, I think, than Mrs Beeton was to aspiring Victorians.'[21]

She did not mean so much to the novelist Angela Carter, who as a food critic was a notoriously loose cannon. She distrusted any woman whose books sent other women 'back to the stove' and loathed anything that smacked of Upper Class Writing. 'An enthusiasm for the table, the grape and the stove itself is characteristic of the deviant subsection of the British bourgeoisie that has always gone in for the arts with the diligent enthusiasm of (as they would put it) "the amateur in the true sense of the word". This class is more than adequately represented by Mrs Elizabeth David.'[22] Yet even Carter could tell the difference between the oh-so-civilized Mrs David and the pretentious, slurping foodie culture which seemed to have infiltrated everything. 'Piggery triumphant,' fumed Carter, 'has invaded even the pages of the *Guardian*.'[23]

The economic boom of the eighties had ushered in the age of the yuppies: the young upwardly-mobile professionals, who had money to burn on designer clothes and designer food. Their attitude to life was summed up by the character of Gordon Gecko in the film *Wall Street*, who proudly pronounced that 'Greed is good.' Triumphant piggery was in the air. It was also on the minds of both the above-mentioned reviewers, because *An Omelette and a Glass of Wine* had appeared at the same time as a book that was being celebrated, disputed and deplored in equal measure: *The Official Foodie Handbook*, by Ann Barr and Paul Levy.

The *Handbook*'s time had come, as its authors were well aware: 'Foodism is glamorous, Foodism is fun. "I am a Foodie" is as proud a boast as the old Roman citizen's "Civis Romanus sum" . . . What they both mean is "I am a winner". Eating is a vocation worth devoting your life to.'[24] It aimed to inform as well as amuse, and much of it is based on considerable research. But it was seen as a successor to the Sloane Ranger books, and it was taken as a bluffer's guide to the latest social craze.

From the days when Elizabeth had started writing, when food was not a topic of conversation, fashion had gone to the opposite extreme. Now it was not only acceptable to talk about food, one could show off one's knowledge. It was permissible to ask the waiter whether the salmon was farmed or wild, to ask which side of Lucca the olive oil came from, and to thrill with excitement on being told that the baby broad beans had just come into season. Yet there was something fake, pretentious about it all: in the word of the moment, 'pseud'. The real food and wine experts hated the word, for it lumped them together with pretentious cookery writers, duff wine buffs and the prancing TV chefs.

Elizabeth had always disliked Paul Levy, a dislike which he traces back to his early days on the *Observer*. When he became the food correspondent in 1980, he was hailed as an innovator and heaped with prizes because his pages talked about food in an intelligent way without getting clogged up with recipes. 'I didn't know about the articles she had written twenty years before in the *Spectator*, but when *Omelette and a Glass of Wine* came out I realized that on several occasions I had written about precisely the same things – Madame Barattero, truffles . . . I can imagine what she thought: plagiarism. It's not uncommon – I sometimes feel I've been ripped off, too.'[25]

Elizabeth never found out that Paul Levy had initiated the campaign to award her the Fellowship of the Royal Society of Literature, to which she had been elected in 1982. Michael Holroyd, who was on the council, was her official champion and the council had voted for her unanimously. Among all her honours it was the one that gave her the most satisfaction and pleasure; but knowing that she owed it to Levy would have taken a lot of gilt off the gingerbread.

She did like Ann Barr, who had once been her sub-editor when she worked for Hugh Johnson on *Queen*. When she heard that Barr and Levy were going to collaborate on the *Foodie* book she warned Barr against him and said 'Miss Barr, you'll never pull it off.'[26] They did pull it off: the book did not have quite the impact of the Sloane Ranger books, but it became a best-seller nonetheless.

The success of a book that, to Elizabeth, represented the worst aspects of the eighties food culture was galling enough; but that she was included in the 'Foodies Who's Who' was unforgivable. Derek Cooper's name was not included because he had told Levy that if his name appeared in the book he would sue. Elizabeth wished she had done the same – but it was too late now. *The Official Foodie Handbook* came out when she was still boiling with anger and indignation over what she had been subjected to with Robert Hale; and in a pattern that was now becoming familiar, her hatred boiled over and fixed on another object. Paul Levy became her *bête noire*, and in order to account for the fact that her friend Ann Barr was co-author, she persuaded herself that Levy had somehow conned Barr into doing the book with him.

Her only revenge was to review the book. The cartoonist Mark Boxer, who was then editor-in-chief of the *Tatler*, persuaded Elizabeth to write it for him. It appeared in February 1985, entitled 'Scoff Gaffe'.

She began with what they had written about her. There was no Ministry of Information in occupied Greece during the war; it was in Cairo that she had been librarian, not Alexandria; and she had never, at any time, been married to a Lieutenant Colonel in the Bengal Lancers. The real criticism, however, was deeper. 'To be sure they are skilful enough in the arts of toadying to their public and providing it with a little giggle at itself, but the meaning of satire in the true sense eludes them. Their truly awful brand of teasy jocularity isn't any kind of substitute.'

Mark Boxer was delighted with this corruscating review, and asked Elizabeth to write for the *Tatler* on a regular basis. She was very fond of Boxer, who knew how to handle her and never messed about with her copy; but there was another reason for taking up journalism again. She had spent a lot of money in legal fees.

Jill's dismissal from Robert Hale Ltd. the year before had shocked the publishing world. Jane Grigson and Kit van Tulleken, an editor at Time-Life, launched a campaign to gather funds for Jill's legal costs, to which a great many authors and almost all the publishers in London contributed. The case went to independent arbitration in April 1985. Jill's plea of unfair dismissal by Robert Hale Ltd was upheld, and Hale was not allowed to hold on to her name as an imprint; but all Jill's backlist was deemed the property of Robert Hale Ltd. Only two books were returned to Jill: one of them was *An Omelette and a Glass of Wine*.

With the help of her solicitor Clifford Harris and the firm of Payne Hicks Beach, Elizabeth had managed to wrest the ice book and the 'Elizabeth David Classics' from Robert Hale; but Hale had not let them go without huge compensation payments for loss of expected revenue. This was in part borne by the publisher Dorling Kindersley, for whom Jill was now working.

Paul Levy, well aware of Elizabeth's dislike of him, never wavered from his profound admiration of her. He was not the only person who felt she deserved to be made a Dame: so did the writer and editor Drusilla Beyfus and, surprisingly enough (in December 1978), the *Guardian*. In their different ways, they all tried to do something about it. The result was that in the 1986 New Year's Honours, Elizabeth was made a Companion of the British Empire. Peter Higgins wrote, 'A rather belated communication to congratulate you on HM The Queen's birthday present. It is agreeable to know that someone sees that merit is recognized.'[27] Elizabeth was then plunged into the problem of what to wear. Her legs were now so bad that she never wore skirts any more, but at the same time it would never do to wear trousers to Buckingham Palace. She compromised with a long skirt, and set off for the palace on 7 March with Jill Norman and Kit van Tulleken. Once there, she found that she was the only woman not wearing a hat. Elizabeth received the CBE from the Prince of Wales, who mentioned in passing that 'My wife loves Italian food.'[28]

A few days later, Felicité was taken to the Cromwell Hospital. Once again, the trouble was her heart, but there was little that could be done and she was sent home a few days later. On 20 March she had a stroke: 'I found her sitting on her bed,' wrote Elizabeth to Celia Denney, '. . . fully dressed and obviously expecting to go out, but unable to speak . . . She was making frantic efforts to make herself understood. It was terribly distressing.'[29]

For four days she fought to make a recovery, and her speech did begin to come back. But 'on the morning of the 24th when I took her papers up there was no sound of early morning news on her radio. She was lying dead, half in and half out of bed.'[30]

One of the first people Elizabeth rang was Stephanie Hoppen, who had by that time become a close friend. Stephanie recalled that Elizabeth was 'like a child, she was so devastated'.[31] She was also in urgent need of emotional support. 'I don't yet know what I will do in this house without her . . . although we lived such different lives we were each dependent on the other for many things. She was really a very remarkable person . . . She was sixty-eight and she didn't really have a lot of luck in her life. But she was happy during the shop years, and must have encouraged scores and scores of people to read . . . Gerald always says, "Felicité educated me." '[32]

Stephanie accompanied Elizabeth to the funeral at Folkington. 'I sat beside her in the pew because she insisted, though it was reserved for family . . . Elizabeth could not bring herself to go to the burial itself, but afterwards we went back to Wootton for the reception. I knew almost nobody there, but Elizabeth clung to my arm . . . It was strange because I had always seen her as such a confident person, but she would not let me go out of her sight for a second. It was as if she dreaded being left alone with her family.'[33]

Felicité was buried in the same ground as her parents and her infant brother. Rupert Grey noticed a handsome old man milling among the guests, who stood out because of his tan. Rupert did not recognize him; but during the service the stranger, who was standing behind him, whispered, 'I made love with Felicité on the Downs in the summer of 1942.' 'Who are you?' asked Rupert. The man replied, 'Peter the Pole.' Rupert wanted to talk to him again, but by the time the service had ended, Peter the Pole had vanished.[34] But it was good to know that he had not forgotten her, and had come to her funeral.

Felicité's death sank Elizabeth into a profound, silent grief. When she did talk, she seemed almost unable to believe that her sister was dead. She had never understood how much she relied on Felicité; not just as a friend and sister, but as someone who kept her in touch with the outside world and as a friendly presence in the house. It felt oppressively big, and Elizabeth had never felt so desolate.

As the weeks went by, the grief turned into a depression and Elizabeth began to suffer from chest pains. She was frightened that she might be developing lung cancer. X-rays established that she had nothing to fear on that account, but the doctors suspected that she might be suffering from tuberculosis – of which her brother-in-law Christopher Grey had died in 1982. She was admitted into hospital, and Stephanie, who accompanied her, was asked to sign in as Elizabeth's next of kin. Stephanie was reluctant but Elizabeth urged her to get on with it, implying that it really didn't matter who signed.

Elizabeth was put under very heavy sedation, and was receiving drugs for TB which, apparently, put a very heavy strain on the liver. At the same time, the hospital was also allowing her wine. The combination of alcohol and these powerful drugs began to undermine not only her health, but her mind.

Stephanie Hoppen was on holiday when her ex-husband, Richard Leech, telephoned her to say that he was seriously worried about Elizabeth, who seemed desperately ill. Stephanie flew back at once, though by the time she reached London she fully expected to discover that Richard had been exaggerating and that Elizabeth was not as ill as he had made out. However, as soon as she saw Elizabeth she realized that things were even worse. 'She was wandering, completely and utterly out of it – she didn't recognize me.'[35] Stephanie immediately sought out the matron and Elizabeth's doctor, who were obviously very worried about her but seemed to have no idea what was wrong – perhaps cancer, perhaps a brain tumour? They did not know. One of the consultants who was looking after her definitely felt that alcohol was the main culprit, and he had already said that he would no longer treat her if she went on drinking. The fact that Elizabeth had had a succession of doctors over the past few years complicated matters, for no one was really certain of her medical history. Their only solution was to give her more and more drugs.

It was obvious to Stephanie that whatever was wrong with Elizabeth, she was getting no better where she was. She therefore arranged for her to be transferred to King Edward VII Hospital for Officers (Sister Agnes). There was a good deal of resistance from the first hospital, but Stephanie used her authority as 'next of kin'.

Elizabeth arrived at Sister Agnes's on 8 September. All the medication she had been on was stopped, and she was not allowed any wine. Almost immediately she began to recover, but the lack of wine made her very angry. She said King Edward's was as strict as a boarding school, and she was furious with Stephanie for transferring her – 'It was the only time she ever shouted at me.'[36] Many of Elizabeth's friends and family, however, felt that Stephanie had saved Elizabeth's life by moving her when she did.

As the days passed and Elizabeth came out of the fog of drugs, her anger turned from Stephanie and King Edward's to the hospital she had been in previously. She was distressed, frightened and furiously angry at the way she had been treated. The loss of memory upset her most, and the idea that things had been done to her without her consent. Elizabeth came out of hospital on 26 September, having been in for almost three months. She needed a long rest, preferably in the sun.

As soon as she could be moved, Gerald Asher arranged for her to go and stay with him. He lived in a warm, sunny place where Elizabeth always felt happy and well: California.

* * * * * * *

CHAPTER TWENTY-ONE

Brave New World

Elizabeth had already been to stay with Gerald Asher in San Francisco on a number of occasions. After Asher Storey & Co. stopped trading in the summer of 1970, Gerald moved to New York and then, in 1974, to San Francisco where he settled with his two sons. He continued working in the wine business, and wrote regularly for *Gourmet Magazine*.

He had first persuaded Elizabeth to come and visit him in the spring of 1981, which was quite a feat in itself, for Elizabeth did not like the idea of America. Only two years before, when her nephew Johnny had told her excitedly that he was going to the United States, Elizabeth's reaction was 'Why on earth do you want to go there? What a waste of time.'[1] Gerald Asher had evidently been very persuasive, for Elizabeth did start contemplating the idea, but she was nervous of undertaking such a long journey alone. Hugh Johnson had encouraged her. But what finally made up her mind to take up the invitation was that her Californian friend Chuck Williams was in London at the time, and she could travel to San Francisco with him. Chuck Williams was the director of one of the largest cooking equipment stores in California. Over the years, Elizabeth had often helped him with names of suppliers, and she occasionally wrote little pieces for the magazine which accompanied his catalogue.

At that stage Elizabeth could still get about, and on that first visit Gerald Asher showed her as much of California as he could. They drove north to see the redwoods, south to Big Sur and into the

Napa valley to visit the vineyards. Elizabeth was enchanted by San Francisco: a place where fresh fruit and vegetables were not only abundant, but as beautifully presented as in France or Italy. As for the restaurants, fresh bread, good salad, real espresso coffee and cheerful service were taken for granted from the cheapest to the most expensive. The San Franciscans enjoy food and take it seriously: 'The latest restaurant,' observed Asher, 'is of more interest in San Francisco than the latest movie.'

Perhaps the biggest surprise of all was that Elizabeth, whose books had never really taken off in the States, was something of a celebrity. Her photograph, blown up to poster size, hung in the back of Chuck Williams's shop. Alice Waters, whose restaurant Chez Panisse was considered the purest expression of West Coast or Californian cuisine, always maintained that Elizabeth David was the greatest influence on her cooking. Not only that, she and her partners had come together over her books and she attributed a large part of the restaurant's success to the fact that they had held firmly to her principles. Chuck Williams, Alice Waters and Gerald Asher had spread the word and works of Elizabeth David, and in California they fell on remarkably fertile soil.

When Asher decided to take Elizabeth to Yosemite National Park, he did not worry about the lack of good restaurants on the way. They would just have to eat in a hamburger bar: 'It would have done her good, and amused her.'[2] Alice Waters had another idea. To thank Elizabeth for everything she meant to her, Alice prepared a picnic: the ultimate, fantasy picnic. The food included roast quails, herb salad, plus three different bottles of Zinfandel wine, each decanted and re-stoppered. She hunted down beautiful old linen, found just the right glasses, packed everything lovingly into huge baskets. Perhaps the most generous part of this gift was that Alice herself left Gerald and Elizabeth to enjoy it alone, which they did: on a perfect afternoon in May, by the side of the San Pedro Lake.

They spent the night in a hotel in the Yosemite mountains, and woke the next morning to six inches of snow. Then they drove back to San Francisco through the relics of California's history. Many of the old ghost towns are now firmly on the tourist track; but in Mendocino they found a shop crammed with old records of the 1930s, and in Murphys, another Gold Rush town, they discovered an ice-cream parlour which had, behind the store, the remains of a nineteenth-century above-ground ice-house. At that time, ice, cut from the Alpine Lake and stored in blocks weighing 50–100lb, was bought by householders in 25lb blocks which cost 3 cents a pound in June which rose to 12 cents in August.

It was on another trip to San Francisco that Elizabeth, following her nose, arrived at a modest eatery which served tea and grilled sandwiches. There was no proper kitchen: the food was cooked over mesquite wood, on a grill on wheels that stood out in the alley. Elizabeth could not stay to lunch; but she talked to the owner-cook, Billy West, and noted the name of his little enterprise: the Zuni Café.

Elizabeth went to the Zuni Café as often as she could, taking Gerald and other friends of his. Before long, thanks to her enthusiastic endorsement, everyone on the food scene was talking about the Zuni Café. The place took on bigger premises, installed ventilators and wood-burning stoves, and went from strength to strength; but no matter how crowded and fashionable it became, there was always a place for Elizabeth when she came to San Francisco.

Elizabeth returned year after year, between 1981 and 1990. Sometimes in the spring, sometimes in the fall, she would come and stay for one month or even two, depending on Gerald's work schedule. She loved the markets, and the second-hand bookshops. Asher remembers how out of a whole bank of books she could pick out just the one that was of interest, and talk about it as she caressed and turned it over in her hands. There was a Lebanese shop which she loved, because it contained things she had not seen since she was in Cairo: the leathery sheets of dried apricot that is softened to make a drink called *amar-el-din*, and little implements for gouging out courgettes before stuffing them.

When Elizabeth came to California in the autumn after Felicité's death, she was still very weak from her long stay in hospital. She spent a month in bed before she was strong enough to get up and about, but after that her spirits soared. She enjoyed the occasional visit to her favourite restaurants, the afternoon drives, the not-too-strenuous outings Gerald arranged to entertain her. An exhibition of jewellery by Lalique she found particularly fascinating. Some of the pieces were so large and elaborate that it was hard to work out how they would have been worn at all. She went back to see it several times.

The only worry was just how much of her time in hospital was a complete blank. She was appalled to find out that she had no recollection whatever of certain friends having come to see her, and feared that the medication she had been given had wiped out great chunks of her memory.

Gerald Asher's apartment was on the sixteenth floor of a building set high on a hill. It looked out over the Bay and the Golden Gate Bridge, and the views from the dining room were particularly fine; but Elizabeth always preferred to eat in the kitchen. Almost everything in the kitchen had been bought at her shop, and reflected her taste. They would talk at the kitchen table as she stroked his cats, while he cooked a fritatta or a risotto. Gerald knew how to awaken her appetite, merely by putting a fresh loaf, a few olives and a thick slab of butter on the table.

On one of her visits, Gerald hoped to arrange a meeting with the celebrated writer M. F. K. Fisher. Gerald wanted to meet her, and Mrs Fisher was keen to meet Mrs David. But when Gerald proposed it to Elizabeth, she was far from enthusiastic. 'Gerald,' she said, 'what on earth would we two old women have to talk about?'[3] Elizabeth did not want to see many people, preferring to be left in peace; so Gerald accepted few invitations, and chose the guests he invited to dinner with special care. 'She always wanted to know about who was coming, and why they were being asked. It was difficult for me because there were many here who wanted to meet her, and I must have given the impression that I wanted her all to myself.'[4] So the evenings passed quietly, often with a rented movie. Sometimes a recent one, such as *Amadeus* and *The Last Emperor*, or one of the old Garbo films she was so fond of. *Citizen Kane* was another favourite, which Gerald thought they must have watched at least half a dozen times.

Within hours of her arrival, the bed looked exactly like her own in Halsey Street. On a tray were her pens and scissors, plus the little wooden-handled Opinel knife that she never travelled without. The rest of the bed soon vanished under piles of books, newspapers and magazines, marked with little yellow stickers, with her annotations and exclamations carefully written out in green ink. Beside the bed was a thermos of black coffee and a cup, at which she sipped occasionally. More black coffee arrived early in the morning, with toast and tropical fruits. The room she was given was ample and comfortable. It looked east; and on clear days, sunlight streamed in all morning.

To return to the cold, dank air of London in November 1986 was particularly depressing, even though she felt better and stronger in herself. Jean and Liz Savage saw to it that she came back to a warm house with fresh sheets and flowers. Yet Halsey Street, silted up with books, cardboard boxes full of files and papers, smelling faintly of electric fires (she had never installed central heating) must have seemed particularly cramped and dingy after California. It also brought back just how painfully she missed Felicité: at that time, Elizabeth could barely hear her sister's name without weeping.

A few days later, she saw her nephew and godson Steven Grey, who was over from Australia. Steve had never had much in common with his Aunt Liza, and was seventeen before he discovered that she was his godmother. But rather to his surprise, she was beginning to warm to him. He was a happy-go-lucky character, with that raffish, irreverent charm she had found so attractive in her youth. He seemed to enjoy a long evening spent chatting over the wine as much as she did, and he made her laugh with his wild Australian stories. When he had given up hope of any food, she leaned over her chair and peered into the oven. Out came a few little potatoes cooked in a *diable*, and a piece of salmon baked in tinfoil.

Her nephew Johnny, with his love of cooking and kitchens, had always seemed to be her natural heir; but Johnny was rather out of favour. In 1984, while Elizabeth and Jill were locked in battle with Robert Hale Ltd, he had married. Johnny and his wife Rebecca moved out of London and soon after, they had their first child. On top of all this Johnny was trying to get his business established, and looking after his sister Christabel who was a diagnosed schizophrenic. Emotionally, he could not cope with Elizabeth as well.

Johnny arranged to have lunch with her in London. She was obviously in a bad mood, and feeling resentful of what she saw as his neglect. A different character might have expressed these feelings with more sadness than anger, and so given Johnny the chance to talk about the changes and upheavals in his own life. But that was not Elizabeth's way: if she felt wronged, she had to draw first blood. Before they had even sat down at the table she announced, 'I'm leaving all my money to Steve.' To which Johnny indignantly replied that what she did with her money was her own business, and no concern of his. They made it up, and became close once more in the final years of her life; but Elizabeth's testamentary plans were never referred to again.[5]

About a year after Felicité's death, Elizabeth fell down the stairs of Halsey Street. Once again she was back in hospital. The bone was just beginning to mend when, in May, she slipped on the bathroom floor again and fractured another bone. Fortunately the Lister was a friendly hospital and Elizabeth rather enjoyed being looked after, and occupied her time on an illustrated edition of *Italian Food*. She managed to buy or borrow a small fridge. This was kept well-stocked with half-bottles of white wine ordered from Anthony Hanson's firm of Haynes, Hanson & Clark, and the foie gras and smoked salmon brought by the steady procession of friends and well-wishers. Antonio Carluccio used to bring her delicious baskets of food from his restaurant.

She emerged from hospital and resumed her normal life; but she stopped all but the simplest top-of-the-stove cooking, because she did not trust her brittle bones to support her any longer. She lived on Roka cheese biscuits, omelettes, Parma ham and the occasional delivery of oysters or smoked salmon. Otherwise, there were restaurants: the Kundan in Horseferry Road, the Phoenicia in Abingdon Road and the Hilaire in the Brompton Road. She visited this last restaurant with Richard Olney, when Simon Hopkinson was the chef. He was very pleased to be to told that she was there, and asked whether she would be willing to try some of his shrimp consommé. 'Here we go again,' grumbled Elizabeth, who did not like the ritual of the chef's specials being trotted out for her to taste; but on this particular occasion, the shrimp consommé was so good that she asked for another bowl. When Simon Hopkinson moved to Bibendum in 1987, that soon became a favourite too. There was a dish of aubergines he made, a variation of the Turkish *Imam Bayeldi*, which she ordered time after time. Soon Hopkinson was taking her out to dinner; the evening always started with a bottle of wine in the kitchen at Halsey Street.

Elizabeth's work on ice and ices had been in progress since she had finished *English Bread and Yeast Cookery*, and was still not finished. She took great pleasure in describing the elaborate feasts of the Medici and the Sun King, the sherbets of Persia, and the painstaking work of the Italian and French confectioners in creating everything from iced drinks to iced creams and sorbets. By careful research into contemporary recipes, she also conjures up an idea of what the earliest ices would have tasted like. Like her Gwynne forebears, she was fascinated by technology: of ice gathering, ice houses, iceboxes, ice pails, and the leaden moulds and *bomba*s into which the iced confections were pressed. Perhaps the greatest attraction of the work lay in the way that so many legends and conflicting accounts had grown up around the development of ices; these she was determined to unravel so as to reveal, with incontrovertible scholarship, the facts. It is not an unhappy book. Rich in anecdote and curious detail, it even includes little stories from her own past: the ices from Gunter's on a summer afternoon at the Open Air Theatre, and the barman in Darjeeling shaking ice-less martinis for her and Tony as they gazed out towards the Himalayas. Yet this is a book she wrote for herself. She set out into this frozen, sunlit landscape for her own reasons, without particularly caring whether readers would follow her or not.

Because Elizabeth herself had been so reticent, the crystallizing of her image into an icon went a few steps further. In January 1987, Radio 4 broadcast an appreciation of her work by Melissa Bakewell called *A Matter of Taste*, with contributions from, among others, Jane Grigson, Prue Leith, Michel Roux and (the late) John Lehmann. One person described it as 'a premature obituary'.[6] All the distinguished food writers and cooks interviewed had placed her work on such an Olympian level that the impression was hard to avoid. Two years later, a similar piece was put together for *Woman's Hour*. Even Elizabeth could not object to this sort of attention; but she was annoyed, almost frightened, when untrue stories about her came into circulation. She knew that these stories were like ticks: once established in print they were difficult to dislodge, and tended to grow bigger.

Some years before, Jilly Cooper had put together an anthology of women's writings and sayings with the gruesome title of *Violets and Vinegar*. Introducing a piece by Elizabeth, Jilly Cooper wrote:

'During her first flush of popularity, when the whole of the middle classes were trying out her recipes for daubes and coq au vin, a friend went to interview her and was invited to stay for dinner. He was totally enchanted by her lack of pretension. She matched him drink for drink for several hours, then, muttering that she'd better do something about dinner, went off and threw two partridges into the oven, and returned to match him for several hours more until the partridges were burnt to a cinder!'[7]

In a letter to Hugh and Judy Johnson Elizabeth explained that she had been obliged to share her meal with the journalist in question, because he simply would not leave. 'When I wrote to Jilly Cooper that her story was a complete fabrication, that the occasion had been lunch and not dinner, that there aren't too many partridges around in mid-August [when the interview took place] and I was wondering whether to reach for Lord Goodman or Sir David Napley, she replied saying she thought it was *such* a lovely story, she admired me *so* much, and the story showed how human I was, just like other people. You can't win . . .'[8]

In December 1988 Elizabeth received a letter from Nick Lander, who had been part-owner of a restaurant called L'Escargot. He was married to the writer and broadcaster Jancis Robinson, and they were putting together a series of food programmes for Channel 4 television. Nick Lander said that he would like to make a programme about her. It would be an attempt to put Elizabeth and her writing into a historical context; to look at the British diet before her books were published, and again after their impact.

Both Nick and Jancis were warned that Elizabeth was notoriously difficult to interview, and that she would probably refuse outright; but there was nothing to be lost by asking, and they were blessed with beginners' optimism. Although Jancis Robinson was an experienced presenter, this was the first time that she and her husband had produced a television programme.

To their astonishment, Elizabeth did not turn down the idea. She had her misgivings, and wondered why anyone should be interested in seeing her on television; but she liked the thought of a programme that would reaffirm her own work, at a time when the fashion in food was all nouvelle cuisine on octagonal plates. Jancis Robinson's approach to food and wine was exactly in line with Elizabeth's, and Jancis feels that she had an added advantage in being a wine writer. 'If I had been a food writer,' she explained, 'I expect I would have put my foot in it before now . . . but she was more lenient with wine writers, because she didn't know so much about the subject.'[9] The programme would be firmly restricted to her writing, and it would all take place at her favourite restaurant – the Walnut Tree at Llandewi Skirrid.

Over the first half of 1989, Elizabeth saw a lot of the Landers. They had friends in common such as the Hansons, Gerald Asher and Hugh and Judy Johnson; and she felt happy and stimulated in their company. They talked of the programme, and she particularly looked forward to seeing Ann and Franco again at the Walnut Tree Inn. A date for filming was set for 17 July. About a week before, Elizabeth got cold feet. She never threatened to pull out, but she was obviously considering ways of escape. For Nick and Jancis, who had made a considerable commitment to the programme, it was a very nasty moment; but they succeeded in reassuring her.

'Remember that no "performance" is expected of you,' wrote Jancis on 12 July. 'There are no time constraints. We can nip, tuck and destroy the tape at any point. The aim is to take you to see some old friends in a jolly nice place. You and I will talk over a glass of wine as we would do anyway and hope that some snippets of our conversation will make interesting television.'

Early on the morning of 17 July, Jill Norman accompanied Elizabeth in a hired car on the three-hour journey to Wales. The cameras started rolling the minute Elizabeth arrived at the kitchen door of the Walnut Tree, leaning heavily on Jancis, who was already there to meet her. Elizabeth was given a chance to rest, as the make-up artists powdered her nose and did her hair. The first part of the interview was the 'set-up lunch', in which Jancis and Elizabeth talked over a glass of wine and a dish of stuffed zucchini flowers. Elizabeth was disappointed that they were not allowed to sit at the table by the bar which she habitually occupied. For technical reasons they had to be in the dining room, at a table with a brown cloth. Elizabeth made it clear that she did not like tablecloths unless they were white, and she particularly hated brown ones; but the director was adamant. Not only that, he had put the camera on tracks so it could zoom in and out of her plate or her face, which made her profoundly uneasy. 'You could see the stress building up in her face as the filming progressed,' said Ann Taruschio.

When the filmed lunch was over they went out into the garden, for a real lunch with Ann and Franco. Elizabeth and Jancis, now released from the formality of interview on camera, enjoyed this a great deal more: it was a beautiful day, and by the end of the meal they were thoroughly relaxed. Then they returned indoors to another setting, and the camera was set up again to take the final part of the interview. Elizabeth was doing her best to 'perform' in so far as she was able, but by now she was tiring. The long silences were evident, and she obviously resented some questions more than others. At one point, Jancis admired the fact that Elizabeth had written her first four books in five years, and asked how she had done it. Elizabeth fidgeted impatiently, gazed over her shoulder, and when she leaned forward there was a dangerous glint in her eyes. 'Why does anyone write books?' 'For money?' ventured Jancis. Elizabeth looked at her as a teacher might look at an inattentive schoolgirl who had finally got the right answer.

The film, entitled *A Matter of Taste*, was due to be broadcast on Elizabeth's birthday: Boxing Day 1989. As the time drew nearer, Jancis wrote a piece in *The Listener* to publicize it. To Jancis, this was a straightforward publicity exercise, designed to arouse interest in the programme. To Elizabeth, it was a violation – made worse by the fact that other papers had picked up the story. She wrote an outraged letter to Jancis that went through several drafts, saying that when she had agreed to do the programme, 'I did not bargain for also being the subject of vulgar and insensitive journalism nor for finding myself bounced around every magazine and newspaper in the country. I suppose I have only myself to blame for breaking my rule of not giving interviews . . . I should have known all this could only end in tears.'[10]

One might imagine that Elizabeth resented being cast as an elusive wild animal while Jancis played David Attenborough, but it is not that to which she was objecting. Elizabeth's tone is that of a well-brought up gentlewoman who only expects to read her name in the papers in the hatched, matched and dispatched columns of *The Times* and the *Daily Telegraph*. She expected to be treated as such, even though she had been a journalist and a writer all her life.

She never spoke of the programme itself, and never watched it. When Jean McAuliffe said, 'I saw you on the telly last night, Mrs David,' Elizabeth made no answer. Many of her friends were saddened. The television camera in close-up exaggerated her age and emphasized the slightly slumped muscles to one side of her face, which had never fully recovered from the cerebral haemorrhage she had suffered twenty-five years before. This had the effect of slurring her words, and some people even reached the conclusion that she was drunk. This was not the case. According to Jancis Robinson, she consumed no more than she would normally have done at lunch with friends.

A letter from Jane Grigson must have offered much more comfort. 'Of course I wanted to appear in the Jancis Robinson programme,' she wrote.

> You know well how I have always admired you, been in awe of you, and been well aware of how much I owe you in a personal way. I was not happy about the programme. It did not emphasize your intellectual standing as a scholar, or your wonderful eye for a painting. You belong to that notable group of people that I got to know when I first met Geoffrey in the fifties, people of first-class minds who tried to share their knowledge with the rest of the population. It was an extraordinary time, all those TV programmes and good books about archaeology and painting. Geoffrey always said it took a first-class mind to popularize a subject . . . You opened a new world to us, not just the world of the Mediterranean, but a mental world as well as a sensual one.[11]

The letter must have been all the more moving to Elizabeth, who suffered the deaths of so many friends and relatives during this time, because Jane herself was dying of cancer. 'I'm going to try the Bristol Cancer Clinic for a week in March. It's a blend of raw carrots, meditation, counselling and visualization. At times I can see it will be difficult keeping a straight face, but people who've been say it's well worth going . . . Just as long as they don't expect me to go to that place in Mexico where you have to give yourself *coffee enemas* every four hours. That would be no laughing matter.'[12]

In late 1989, shortly before *A Matter of Taste* was broadcast, Elizabeth received a letter from George Lassalle in Cyprus. They had always been in touch, and he was often grateful for her advice on his cookbooks.* He now wrote to explore the possibility of writing her biography. 'Dear Liz, please don't immediately fall down and break a leg with shock, but there it is. I can do it well, I want to do it and it would give me a marvellous year's work.'[13] The answer came back swiftly: 'Dear George, I can't stop you writing a biography of me – I'm sure you have ample material – but please don't expect me to cooperate.'[14]

The spectre of a biography was bad enough; but the idea that posterity had a right to her papers was intolerable. One of her American friends had written to urge her to leave her archive to some academic institution, implying that failure to do so would be an act of irresponsibility. This had infuriated Elizabeth to such an extent that she had begun throwing out her papers there and then. April Boyes had arrived to find her outside, in her dressing-gown, stuffing file after file into her dustbins. April persuaded her to come indoors and calm down over a cup of coffee. The mood passed, and Elizabeth took no further steps to destroy her archive.

At the same time, as she grew older, she sensed that a biography

---

* On one occasion he wrote to thank her 'for saving me from the exploding pizza and the seed cake gaffe' (letter of 5.11.75), but his proof-reading skills had been of use to Elizabeth in the past. In her first book she described an Arab soup called *melokhia*. She also gave its name in Latin and Greek, but owing to an unfortunate misspelling, the Greek word read 'masturbation'. Luckily, George caught this slip before the book went into print.

would eventually be written. Through Paul Bailey Elizabeth had met Jeremy Round, a young writer who had joined the *Independent* as its food correspondent in 1986. His pieces had turned Elizabeth into a regular reader of this recently launched newspaper, for Round's blows against the adulterated, the overpriced, the over-packaged and the over-hyped were always well aimed and extremely funny. Paul and Jeremy had taken Elizabeth out to lunch one day when the subject of biography came up, and Elizabeth turned to Jeremy and said, 'If anyone writes my biography, I hope it's you.'[15] Elizabeth became very fond of Jeremy. Perhaps the little yellow stickers that occasionally appear in her archive, with comments that could only be of interest to a biographer, were addressed to him. But Jeremy Round died in 1989, aged thirty-two, before the idea was ever seriously mooted.

In the spring of 1990 she went to San Francisco again. She always dreaded coming back, and this time she returned to find that Jane Grigson was dead. It was a bitter blow, closely followed by another. Her niece Christabel Grey, then in her thirties, had committed suicide by jumping off the cliffs at Beachy Head.

Christabel's tragedy was all the more poignant because she had been a particularly gifted and beautiful child. The onset of schizophrenia had happened at the time of her mother's death, eighteen years before. Since then her mental condition had deteriorated steadily, but the note Christabel left before she killed herself shows that when she took the decision to end her life her mind was clear. Christabel had been Elizabeth's godchild, the sole daughter of her favourite sister. In fits and starts Elizabeth had tried to help her, encouraging her interests and giving her little secretarial jobs from time to time; but as her nephew Johnny remarked, 'Liza couldn't cope with mental illness. Some people can, but she simply couldn't.'

At the end of the month there came another blow: Anthony Denney died at Salvatierra, on 30 April 1990. Celia rang to tell her, and Elizabeth wrote to her soon afterwards. 'Ever since your sad telephone call – somehow I knew what you were going to say – you have seldom been out of my thoughts . . . at Salvatierra Anthony will always be with you. For that matter he will forever be sitting beside you in the car, jeep whatever – saying there's a right turn now or that's a no–entry street – You made such a happy life for Anthony. Truly, I wonder if he had ever been really happy, before he met you.'[16]

Of the four Gwynne sisters, only Elizabeth and Priscilla remained alive. They had been close in their youth, and Priscilla had had a part in Elizabeth's culinary education; she was also a skilled and enthusiastic cook in her own right. But although they exchanged bottles of olive oil at Christmas, they had drifted apart with the years; and Michael Day, who knew them both, thought it sad that they should only see each other at funerals. He arranged a dinner for Elizabeth and Priscilla at the Colony Club, hoping it would revive a certain sisterly warmth; but it did not quite work out like that. Priscilla was in a cheerful and sparkly mood, but she devoted all her attention to Michael. Elizabeth was rather disgruntled by the way Priscilla was hogging the limelight; but she liked the food, and complimented John King, who came out of the kitchen to meet her.

This was not out of politeness. Elizabeth had always set herself the highest standards; and while she was generous in her praise to any friend who cooked for her, professional chefs were expected to get things right. On one occasion, Jancis Robinson remembered taking Elizabeth to a smart new restaurant where she ate a dish of 'wild' mushrooms. Elizabeth might have kept her opinions to herself, had not the chef emerged to be introduced; but instead of the praise he was expecting, Elizabeth tore a strip off him – beginning with the fact that the mushrooms he had served her were certainly not wild.

The deaths of others could not help but remind Elizabeth of her own frailty. 'Right leg won't work,' Elizabeth wrote in her diary on

8 September; and a few days later, just as she was about to get into a taxi with Jill Norman outside Sally Clarke's restaurant in Church Street Kensington, she tripped and fell. She was helped up, and the taxi took her straight to the Lister. The break was bad and her leg took a long time to heal, and once again, she was prescribed a drug that caused her considerable alarm. To a friend she wrote, 'It was lucky for me that you came in on Friday. If you hadn't heard me – and I hadn't heard myself jabbering like an ape . . . I'd have been in a box by now . . . I'm pretty certain the new heart medication was the cause.'[17] She was home before Christmas, but from now on she could not move without a stick.

A little fridge was installed in her bathroom, so that she should not have to go all the way down to the kitchen; and although she still went out from time to time, she was more or less bed-bound by the time Jenny Lo moved in to the top flat in the summer of 1991. Jenny Lo was Chinese, as discreet and reserved a character as Elizabeth herself. She was going through a painful divorce at the time, and Elizabeth was very sympathetic.

Jenny used to bring Elizabeth her post and the papers before she went out to work. Sometimes they would fall into conversation. Elizabeth talked about how she had started cooking, her nephews, her days at Ménerbes and the Greek islands. Olivia Manning's Balkan and Levant Trilogies, collectively called *Fortunes of War*, had been dramatized for television. It was while they were talking about it that Elizabeth mentioned that 'something of me is in those books', and recalled her Cairo life with Tony. They also talked about food writers. She rated Jane Grigson very highly indeed, and approved of Delia Smith: no great stylist, but someone whose understanding of cooking was based on solid principles and experience.

Jean McAuliffe came to clean every morning, accompanied by her little daughter Carly. When Jean had first taken on the job in the early 1980s, she had explained that she could not come without the child, who was then only two years old. Elizabeth had been very uneasy about Carly at first, fearing that she would upset things or pull them about. But Carly never did cause any trouble, and as she grew older Elizabeth became very fond of her. Sometimes Elizabeth would ask Carly to take something downstairs or pass her a hairbrush, and for these little services, at the end of the week, Elizabeth would solemnly tip the child a pound.

Elizabeth was fastidious about her clothes and her immediate surroundings, and visitors to the house remember the faint smell of Penhaligon's Bluebell scent that hung in the air. Jean concentrated on the bedroom, kitchen and bathroom, for the boxes of files, the books and magazines, and the piles of paper had taken over to such an extent that cleaning the rest of the house was almost impossible; Elizabeth did not seem to mind. (There were corners of Halsey Street that had remained untouched for years: when the house was cleared it was found that pigeons were nesting in the cistern of the downstairs lavatory, which had been out of use since Elizabeth filled it with all the pots and pans she had brought back from Egypt.) So when the washing and cleaning and ironing was done, Jean also spent time keeping Mrs David company. They talked about the great 'ifs' in history, particularly those of the Tudor and Stuart periods. They were both great fans of Pepys, and told each other a lot of cat stories too.

In mid-May 1992, Elizabeth suffered a stroke. Jean came in to find her on the floor, and managed to get her up into a chair. Elizabeth was conscious but her speech was impaired, and she had lost the use of one arm. From then on she had nurses round the clock, and a stream of family and friends came to see her. To several of them she said, 'I'm going to beat this thing'; but Liz Savage remembers one of the doctors saying to a nurse, 'We are not here to cure her, just to make her comfortable.'

Gerald Asher came over from Paris as soon as he could. He described her last evening, with himself and Liz Savage, as 'much like any other, except that she couldn't move very much'.[18] Liz remembers Gerald sitting on Elizabeth's bed, making her laugh, trying to persuade her to eat. Propped up on the pillows, Elizabeth announced that she needed 'a bottle of good Chablis', and Gerald brought up some caviar which she told him he would find in the fridge. She was surprised that he did not pick up an allusion to Sir Philip Sidney. She told him to look it up, since she might have misquoted Sir Philip's famous last line: as he lay dying on the battlefield, Sir Philip gave the water he was offered to a wounded foot soldier with the words 'Thy necessity is yet greater than mine.'

'I pulled the *Chambers Biographical* off the shelf. "It doesn't help much," I told her. "There's nothing here about a glass of water." We were both still wondering about Sir Philip Sidney's glass of water when I kissed her before leaving.'[19] Gerald and Liz left before twelve: the night nurse was there, but Liz still regrets that she did not stay the night as she sometimes did. Liz was woken by the telephone at two o'clock, on the morning of Friday 22 May. Elizabeth David was dead.

The funeral took place at St Peter's ad Vincula, Folkington, on 28 May. It was a cloudy day, but the bluebells were out, glimmering through the woods. The little church was filled to bursting, the floral tributes were stupendous. And among the wreaths and baskets of lilies and blue iris, and the violets she loved, someone had left a loaf of bread, and a bunch of herbs tied up in brown paper.

* * * * * * *

Epilogue

In her lifetime, Elizabeth was often tagged 'the doyenne' or 'grande dame' of cookery writers – to her intense irritation. 'I would thank you *not* to use that phrase,' she said with some asperity to an American journalist who had come to interview her. 'I know it means something different in America, but in England it suggests some ghastly old dragon who's stamping about with an ebony stick.'[1]

Poor Elizabeth. As soon as she was dead, such phrases larded almost every tribute and obituary that appeared in the British press. For *The Times* she was 'the doyenne of cookery writers', for the *Daily Telegraph* she was 'the grande dame of the kitchen'. The *Observer* hailed her as a 'household goddess', while the *Yorkshire Post* called her 'a latter-day Mrs Beeton'. She was the saviour of English cooking, and her pen inspired a thousand cooks. 'It is no exaggeration to say that for middle-class British people of the second half of the century she did more to change their way of life than any poet, novelist or dramatist of our time,' wrote Richard Boston in the *Guardian*.

All agreed that Elizabeth David had changed British cooking for ever, although it is hard for anyone not familiar with pre-war English attitudes to food to understand just what an impact she had made. In France and Italy it is taken for granted that food is one of the greatest pleasures in life, that one should take time and trouble to find the best ingredients one can afford, that shoddy compromises with margarine and stock cubes are unnecessary. In the England of the 1950s and 60s, this message – as championed by Elizabeth – had had all the power of startling novelty.

Her influence crossed the Atlantic. Every American cookery writer was familiar with her work; the *New York Times* wrote that 'Dozens of young chefs who have brought glory to American cooking over the last two decades are indebted to Mrs David. Alice Waters, often described as the mother of contemporary American cooking, considers Mrs David her greatest inspiration.'[2]

Ironically, the biggest side effect of the revolution started by Elizabeth David came with the proliferation of cookery programmes on television. The food writer Nigel Slater wondered whether a young, unknown cookery writer with original ideas would even get into print in today's market. 'Some of our greatest cookery classics sell just a few hundred copies a year . . . whereas a troop of all-singing, all-dancing clowns with a daytime cookery television slot may sell a quarter of a million.'[3]

Elizabeth's last book, *The Harvest of the Cold Months*, never aspired to become a best-seller, if only because the subject of ice and ices was too specialized for her regular readership. Elizabeth nevertheless wanted to see it in print. In the last years of her life, she realized she would never finish the manuscript herself and asked Jill Norman to take on the task. 'The trouble was that the book had grown without a structure,' said Jill. 'There was no logical flow. It was a collection of essays really, and images of ice and snow in different cultures at different times.' The book was published in 1994, two years after Elizabeth's death.

Elizabeth's memorial service took place at St Martin-in-the-Fields, on 10 September 1992. It was a sunny day, and the church was filled with the scent of white flowers, arranged in great pyramids by Stephanie Hoppen. There had not been more than a brief announcement in the press, but the church was packed with chefs and restaurateurs, food critics, cookery writers and wine writers – not to mention a great throng of family and friends. Leslie French, who had played with her at the Open Air Theatre, remembered her poise. In a letter read out by Sally Clarke, Alice Waters spoke of the gratitude she felt to Elizabeth and recalled the fantasy picnic she had made for her in California. Hugh Johnson observed that she 'combined the writing of an angel with a certain celestial invisibility, made your heart beat faster, turned you (or at least me) into an adoring fan with a sentence, and into a disciple with a paragraph'. Gerald Asher remembered her sitting in his kitchen in San Francisco, looking intently at a slab of butter on a white dish. 'How beautiful,' she had said.

Everyone that day had their own memory of Elizabeth and what she had meant to them; but the best expression of it came from Sally Clarke, who with Simon Hopkinson and Martin Lam, gave a celebratory picnic in her memory for friends and family after the service. In a perfect world it should have taken place on a sunny hillside, with a river near by in which to cool the wine. But although the Nash Room of the Institute of Contemporary Arts in the Mall can hardly be described as a pastoral setting, it looked beautiful nonetheless. The fireplace had been decorated with great garlands of hops and brambles and rowan berries, and on the long tables stood flower pots, some containing artichokes, some filled with fresh herbs. In between were little white bowls of olives, radishes, butter, and loaves of cornmeal and rosemary bread. At each place was a menu, rolled up with a sprig of rosemary held together with twine: rosemary for remembrance.

The rest of the meal was set out on round tables spread with blue-and-white gingham picnic cloths: *bocconcini* with basil leaves, marinated lentil and goat-cheese salad, tarts of spinach and gruyère, baby beetroots and chives, Piedmontese peppers, spiced aubergine salad, grilled tuna with red onion and beans, and a *salade de museau*. With it the guests drank a Macon Prissé 1991 and a Morgon Château Gaillard 1991. The sun streamed in through the tall windows. It was a profoundly happy and convivial meal. Everyone there understood that the best way to remember Elizabeth, then as now, was at a table with wine and talk and friends.

* * * * * * * *

336

Notes and Sources

EDP: Elizabeth David Papers; AC: Artemis Cooper.
Unless otherwise stated, all quotations from ED's published works
are taken from the Penguin edition current in 1999.

CHAPTER ONE: *The Gwynnes*
Main source: 'My Father's
Family', an unpublished memoir
by Katharine Ayling (daughter of
Nevile Gwynne) 1980. Also
'Wootton Manor', *Country Life*,
7 April 1955.

1. ED to Mr Shah of Nabarro &
   Co, 4.8.74.

CHAPTER TWO: *The Gwynne
Girls Grow Up*
1. Obituary of Stella Gwynne by
   Lord Archie Gordon, *The
   Times* 18.6.73.
2. EDP: draft letter to Pelham
   Maitland, undated, spring
   1974.
3. *Eastbourne Chronicle*, 12.9.14.
4. Lady Anne Brewis in
   conversation with A.C.
5. ibid.
6. *French Provincial Cooking*, p. 32.

7. *Kitchens and Their Cooks*,
   Smallbone, summer 1989.
8. ibid.
9. *French Provincial Cooking*,
   p. 279.
10. 'A la marinière', *An Omelette
    and a Glass of Wine*, p. 86.
11. *Kitchens and Their Cooks*,
    Smallbone, summer 1989.
12. EDP: draft of a letter to Mrs
    Bazell, McEvoy's daughter,
    undated; written after a visit to
    an exhibition of McEvoy's
    work at the Morley Gallery,
    Feb./Apr. 1974.
13. *Eastbourne Chronicle*, 18.10.24.
14. Barbara Doxat, letter to AC,
    25.8.97.
15. *French Provincial Cooking*,
    p. 279.
16. Jill Norman in conversation
    with AC.
17. EDP: undated draft of 'Point
    de Venise', *c.* 1963.

18. 'Remembering Aunt V': piece written by ED for Jessica Douglas-Home, biographer of Violet Gordon Woodhouse.
19. ibid.

CHAPTER THREE: *Paris and Munich*

1. EDP: undated letter from Stella Gwynne.
2. *French Provincial Cooking*, p. 24.
3. ibid. p. 23
4. EDP: undated letter from Stella Gwynne.
5. EDP: analysis by A. Dreyfus Hirtz, Paris, 24.2.31.
6. *An Omelette and a Glass of Wine*, p. 86.
7. *French Provincial Cooking*, p. 24.
8. 'Better Ways of Eating Fish', *Harper's Bazaar*, August 1955.
9. Undated letter from Stella.
10. Letter, in German and English, from 'Lalt' to EG.
11. ibid.

CHAPTER FOUR: *Acting it Out*

1. EDP: draft of a letter to Pelham Maitland, undated, spring 1974.
2. Queen Mary's diary, 11 May 1932; quoted by gracious permission of HM The Queen.
3. EDP: undated letter to the journalist Suzy Benghiat, 1985.
4. EDP: undated draft of a letter to Joan Hickson, *c*. April 1989.
5. ibid.
6. EDP: draft of undated letter to Mrs M. P. Silverman.
7. EDP: undated letter from Stella Hamilton, autumn 1933.
8. Doreen Thornton in conversation with AC.
9. Leslie French, speech at ED's memorial service, St Martin-in-the-Fields 10.9.92.
10. ED interviewed by Nancy Mills, *Daily News* (U.S.), 18.6.80.
11. *Harvest of the Cold Months*, p. 351.
12. 'Survival', *Spectator*, 28.6.63.
13. ibid.
14. ibid.
15. Ambrose Heath, *Good Food*, Faber & Faber 1932, p. 75.
16. 'Having Crossed the Channel', *Wine and Food*, spring 1965.
17. Letter to AC from Aileen Gibson Cowan, 27.10.98.

18. Doreen Thornton in conversation with AC.
19. Roger Ellis in conversation with AC.
20. Letter from Frances Harper to AC, 10.5.98.
21. Letter from ED to Frances Harper, 24.1.86.
22. ibid.
23. *French Provincial Cooking*, p. 234.
24. EDP: draft of a letter to Frances Fedden, early 1992.
25. [Charles] Gibson Cowan, *The Voyage of the Evelyn Hope*, Cresset Press 1946, p. 11.
26. EDP: ED's memoir of Sir Jasper Ridley.

CHAPTER FIVE: *Norman Douglas*
1. *The Voyage of the Evelyn Hope*, pp. 11–38.
2. ibid.
3. ibid.
4. ibid.
5. ibid.
6. ibid.
7. ibid.
8. Patrick Leigh Fermor in conversation with AC.
9. Mark Holloway, *Norman Douglas*, Secker & Warburg, 1976, pp. 424–9.
10. 'Have It Your Way', *An Omelette and a Glass of Wine*, p. 122.
11. ibid.
12. ibid.
13. op. cit., p. 123.
14. *The Voyage of the Evelyn Hope*, p. 59.
15. op. cit., p. 57.
16. 'Have It Your Way', *An Omelette and a Glass of Wine*, p. 120.
17. ibid.

CHAPTER SIX: *The Loss of the Evelyn Hope*
1. *The Voyage of the Evelyn Hope*, pp. 61–106.
2. ibid.
3. ibid.
4. ibid.
5. ibid.
6. ibid.
7. ibid.
8. Norman Douglas to EG, 23.9.40.
9. 'Pudding and Pickles', *Spectator*, 24.11.61.
10. ibid.
11. ibid.
12. ibid.
13. *The Voyage of the Evelyn Hope*, p. 158.
14. Robin Fedden to EG, 28.11.40.

15. Charles Gibson Cowan, personal log, 16.11.43.

CHAPTER SEVEN: *Alexandria*
1. EDP: draft of a letter to Frances Fedden, early 1992.
2. EDP: draft of 'Two Cooks', *Wine and Food*, 1951.
3. Elizabeth to Charles Gibson Cowan, 16.10.41.
4. EDP: draft of 'Two Cooks', *Wine and Food*, 1951.
5 Undated letter from Max Bally to EG.
6. EDP: draft of a letter to Frances Fedden, early 1992.
7. Elizabeth to Charles Gibson Cowan, 8.10.41.
8. Elizabeth to Charles Gibson Cowan, 9.12.41.
9. ibid.
10. ibid.
11. ibid.
12. ibid.
13. Elizabeth to Charles Gibson Cowan, 18.3.42.
14. EDP: draft of a letter to Frances Fedden, early 1992.

CHAPTER EIGHT: *Tony David*
1. Roger Eland in conversation with AC.
2. Christopher Kininmonth, *Frontiers*, Davis Poynter, 1971, p. 9.
3. George Lassalle, *The Fish in my Life*, Macmillan, 1989, pp. 27, 28.
4. EDP: unpublished article in MS (Anastasia, Suleiman).
5. J. M. Richards, *Memoirs of an Unjust Fella*, Weidenfeld & Nicolson, 1980, p. 180.
6. EDP: unpublished article in MS (Anastasia, Suleiman).
7. ibid.
8. 'Fast and Fresh', *An Omelette and a Glass of Wine*, p. 22.
9. Josette d'Amade in conversation with AC.
10. ibid.
11. Elizabeth to Charles Gibson Cowan, June 1942.
12. Telegram dated 12.8.43.
13. Two undated letters from Elizabeth to Charles Gibson Cowan, August 1943.
14. EDP: Tony David to EG, 15.6.44.
15. ibid.
16. EDP: letter from Tony David, 28.5.44.

17. EDP: letter from Tony David, undated.
18. EDP: letter from Tony David, 29.5.44.
19. EDP: letter from Tony David, 25.5.44.
20. EDP: letter from Tony David, 8.7.44.
21. EDP: letter from Tony David, 20.7.44.
22. EDP: letter from Tony David, 24.7.44.
23. EDP: letter from Tony David, 8.8.44.
24. Jenny Lo in conversation with AC.
25. Olivia Manning, *The Levant Trilogy*, Penguin Books, 1982, pp. 457–8.

CHAPTER NINE: *Indian Interlude*
1. Veronica Nicholson in conversation with AC.
2. *Spices, Salt and Aromatics in the English Kitchen*, p. 161.
3. *Summer Cooking*, pp. 214–15.
4. EDP: undated letter from Eddie Gathorne-Hardy.

CHAPTER TEN: *Back in Blighty*
1. 'Look to Your Tables', *Spectator*, 2.3.62.
2. Doris Lessing, 'The Roads of London', *Granta: Ambition*, summer 1997, pp. 54–5.
3. Marguerite Patten O.B.E., *The Victory Cookbook*, Hamlyn 1995, p. 10.
4. 'Fast and Fresh', *An Omelette and a Glass of Wine*, p. 24.
5. 'John Wesley's Eye', *An Omelette and a Glass of Wine*, p. 19.
6. ibid.
7. EDP: untitled, perhaps unpublished piece.
8. 'John Wesley's Eye', *An Omelette and a Glass of Wine*, p. 19–20.
9. Letter from Caroline Lassalle to AC, 22.9.96.
10. 'John Wesley's Eye', *An Omelette and a Glass of Wine*, p. 20.
11. EDP: early draft of piece entitled 'How it All Began', *Spectator*, 1.2.64 (re-named 'John Wesley's Eye' by ED, and reprinted in *An Omelette and a Glass of Wine*).
12. 'John Wesley's Eye', *An Omelette and a Glass of Wine*, p. 21.
13. EDP: early draft of 'How it All Began'.
14. ibid.

15. George Lassalle, *The Adventurous Fish Cook*, Macmillan 1976 p. 52.
16. EDP: early draft of 'How it All Began'.
17. EDP: letter from George Lassalle, undated; first part of letter lost.
18. EDP: unpublished piece (cars/holidays) undated.
19. EDP: Stella Hamilton to Tony, undated, mid-November 1947.
20. EDP: draft of petition for divorce, July 1958.
21. ibid.
22. Neville Phillips, in conversation with AC.
23. EDP: petition for divorce, July 1958.

CHAPTER ELEVEN: *Mediterranean Food*
1. EDP: undated letter from Veronica Meagher, 1949.
2. Anne Scott-James in conversation with AC.
3. EDP: letter from Herbert Joseph, 2.2.49.
4. Frances Spalding, *Dance Till the Stars Come Down: a Biography of John Minton*, Hodder & Stoughton, 1991, p. 106.
5. Introduction to *A Book of Mediterranean Food*.
6. Letter from ED to Lady Sibell Rowley, undated.
7. EDP: Peter Higgins to ED, 17.1.49.
8. Johnny Grey in conversation with AC.
9. Johnny Grey, *The Art of Kitchen Design*, Cassell, 1994, pp. 53–4.
10. Veronica Nicholson in conversation with AC.
11. Lady Sibell Rowley in conversation with AC.
12. Veronica Nicholson in conversation with AC.
13. Elizabeth Nicholas, *Sunday Times*, 4.6.50.
14. John Chandos, *Observer*, 18.6.50.
15. EDP: O.W. Darch to ED, 23.6.50.
16. EDP: letter from Lawrence Durrell, June 1950.
17. EDP: draft of a letter to Patricia Siddall of Penguin Books, February 1963.
18. Veronica Nicholson in conversation with AC.
19. EDP: undated letter to John Lehmann.
20. EDP: letter from John Lehmann, 2.10.50.

21. EDP: letter from Stella Hamilton, 9.8.51.
22. Doreen Thornton in conversation with AC.
23. ibid.
24. ibid.
25. EDP: letter from Hamish Erskine, September 1951.
26. 'The Cooking of Provence', *Harper's Bazaar*, June 1955.
27. EDP: letter from George Lassalle, 4.7.51.
28. EDP: letter from Jane Stockwood to ED, 5.6.51.
29. EDP: letter from Stella Hamilton 27.7.51.

CHAPTER TWELVE: *Italian Food*
1. EDP: letter from J. C. Hall, 19.10.51.
2. John Lehmann, *The Ample Proposition*, Eyre & Spottiswoode, 1966, p. 151.
3. EDP: Italian notebooks, 1952.
4. EDP: letter from John Lehmann, 22.5.52.
5. EDP: undated letter from Derek Hill.
6. EDP: Italian notebooks, 1952.
7. ibid.
8. ibid.
9. *Italian Food*, p. 123.
10. EDP: Italian notebooks, 1952.
11. ibid.
12. ibid.
13. *Italian Food*, p. 169.
14. EDP: letter from John Lehmann, 24.6.52.
15. EDP: draft of an undated letter to Renato Guttuso.
16. EDP: draft to Michael Rubinstein of her dealings with Macdonald.
17. *Italian Food*, Introduction to the first Penguin edition.
18. ibid.
19. EDP: draft of 'Grabbies', which appeared as 'How Publishers Like to Have Their Cake and Eat It', *Tatler*, October 1985.
20. ibid.
21. ibid.
22. ibid.
23. 'Is Butter Better?', *Daily Express*, 21.6.54.
24. Introduction to the first Penguin edition.
25. Olivia Manning, *Jerusalem Post*, 12.11.54.
26. EDP: draft of a letter to Anthony Denney, spring 1965.
27. EDP: letter from ED to Lynette Hunter, 27.2.89.
28. Eunice Frost in conversation with AC.

CHAPTER THIRTEEN: *Friends, Editors and Other Enemies*

1. EDP: draft of a letter to Nicholas Serota, 19.11.91.
2. EDP: list of bequests attached to ED's will.
3. Veronica Nicholson in conversation with AC.
4. EDP: letter from Anthony Hunt, *House and Garden*, 27.11.53.
5. Introduction to *An Omelette and a Glass of Wine*, pp. 16–17.
6. *Sunday Times*, 9.11.58.
7. *Sunday Times*, 2.9.56.
8. Ernestine Carter, *With Tongue in Chic*, Michael Joseph, 1974, pp. 85–6.

7. EDP: letter from Avis de Voto, 8.2.58.
8. Simon Hopkinson and Lindsey Bareham, *The Prawn Cocktail Years*, Macmillan, 1997, p. 137.
9. EDP: deposition for divorce, 14.7.58.
10. Doreen Thornton in conversation with AC.
11. EDP: draft of letter to Jean LeRoy of the *Sunday Times*, May 1959.
12. EDP: letter to Audrey Withers, 6.7.59.
13. ibid.
14. Doreen Thornton, *Standard-Triumph Review*, No. 10, 1959.

CHAPTER FOURTEEN: *On the Road in Provincial France*

1. EDP: piece on cookery book illustration.
2. EDP: undated letter (*c.* late sixties) to Sybille Bedford.
3. Doreen Thornton in conversation with AC.
4. 'Golden Delicious', *An Omelette and a Glass of Wine*, p. 83.
5. EDP: pocket diary, 3.1.58.
6. EDP: undated letter from Roald Dahl.

CHAPTER FIFTEEN: *The Year of Betrayal*

1. 'French Cooking in England', in *French Provincial Cooking*, p. 17.
2. EDP: letter from Lawrence Durrell, autumn 1956.
3. EDP: draft of 'Grabbies', which appeared as 'How Publishers Like to Have Their Cake and Eat It' in *Tatler*, October 1985.
4. EDP: short piece on connections with Michael Joseph.

5. EDP: draft of an introduction to *French Provincial Cooking*.

6. *Daily Worker*, 8.12.60.

7. EDP: letter to Neil Hogg, 29.11.69.

8. ibid.

9. Katharine Whitehorn, 'The Compleat Imbiber: A Profile of Cyril Ray', *Wine* Magazine, Christmas 1973.

10. EDP: letter to Ailsa Garland, on resignation from *Vogue*, October 1960.

11. EDP: Daniel S. Watson, Lahore, 8.11.61.

12. Anthony Hanson, 'Personal Memories of Elizabeth David', speech given at the PEN Club, June 1998.

13. EDP: Iain Hamilton to ED, 2.7.62.

14. EDP: draft of a letter to the management of Walls.

15. EDP: letter to Mme Noëlla Audas, 6.10.62.

16. Hugh Johnson in conversation with AC.

17. EDP: draft of an article for *Wine and Food* on William Verral.

18. EDP: letter from Leslie Nye, undated, *c.* October 1962.

19. EDP: draft of a letter to Peter Higgins, undated.

20. EDP: draft of a letter to Eunice Frost of Penguin Books, February 1963.

21. ibid.

22. EDP: letter to Lesley O'Malley from Tangier, 24.3.63.

23. ibid.

CHAPTER SIXTEEN: *Farewell to P.H.*

1. 'Points de Venise', *Spectator*, 14.6.63.

2. EDP: letter from Sybille Bedford, 9.7.63.

3. EDP: draft of a letter to Sybille Bedford, 8.9.63.

4. Sybille Bedford in conversation with AC.

5. ibid.

6. ibid.

7. ibid.

8. EDP: letter from Julia Child, undated, 1963.

9. *Spectator*, 18.10.63; reprinted in *An Omelette and a Glass of Wine*, p. 280.

10. 'Golden Delicious', *Spectator*, 10.1.64; reprinted in *An Omelette and a Glass of Wine*, p. 83.

11. Annotation by Gerald Asher to Anthony Hanson's 'Personal Memories of Elizabeth David',

speech given at the PEN
Club, June 1998.

CHAPTER SEVENTEEN: *The Shop*
1. 'Para Navidad', *Nova*, July
   1965; reprinted in *An
   Omelette and a Glass of Wine*,
   p. 94.
2. Letter to Anthony Denney,
   13.7.64.
3. ibid.
4. EDP: letter to Mrs A.
   Mather, 26 March 1965.
5. EDP: draft letter to Anthony
   Denney, spring 1965.
6. EDP: drafts of letters to
   Anthony Denney, 1965.
7. Peter Trier in conversation
   with AC.
8. EDP: drafts of letters to
   Anthony Denney, 1965.
9. ibid.
10. Jill Norman in conversation
    with AC.
11. 'Garlic-presses are Utterly
    Useless', *Tatler*, February
    1986.
12. Drusilla Beyfus, *Telegraph
    Magazine*, November 1965
13. EDP: draft letter to Jane
    Grigson, March 1988.
14. Michael Zyw, letter to AC,
    5.6.98.

15. Sybille Bedford in
    conversation with AC.
16. Letter from Celia Denney to
    AC, 3.5.99.
17. April Boyes in conversation
    with AC.
18. EDP: draft of a letter to an
    unnamed correspondent.

CHAPTER EIGHTEEN: *Salt and
Spice*
1. 'Bruscandoli', in *An Omelette
   and a Glass of Wine*, p. 107.
2. Introduction to *English Food:
   A Rediscovery of British Food
   from before the War*, by
   Arabella Boxer, Hodder &
   Stoughton, 1991, p. 1.
3. op.cit., p. 13.
4. EDP: draft of a letter to
   Pelham Maitland, *c*. 1974.
5. Ellen-Ann Hopkins in
   conversation with AC.
6. ibid.
7. Katharine Ayling, 'My
   Father's Family', unpublished
   memoir, 1980, p. 287.
8. ibid., p. 291.
9. EDP: draft of a letter to
   Christopher Grey, *c*. March
   1974.
10. ibid.
11. EDP: letter to Renée, 29.5.72.

12. April Boyes in conversation with AC.
13. EDP: to Renée, 5.7.72.
14. EDP: to Renée, 27.7.72.
15. EDP: postcard from Renée Fedden, 2.9.72.
16. Letter from Celia Denney to AC, 14.1.99.
17. April Boyes in conversation with AC.
18. ibid.
19. Letter to Anthony and Celia Denney, 14.6.73.
20. EDP: letter to Mr Crowe, June 1973.
21. George Elliott in conversation with AC.

CHAPTER NINETEEN: *Baking Bread*
1. *English Bread and Yeast Cookery*, p. 195.
2. ibid., p. 364.
3. April Boyes in conversation with AC.
4. *English Bread and Yeast Cookery*, p. 172.
5. EDP: draft letter to Lynn Hughes, 14.7.87.
6. EDP: draft of a letter to Franco Taruschio, 29.11.80.
7. Jill Norman in conversation with AC.

8. EDP: draft of a letter and poem to John Lehmann, *c.* May 1977.
9. Letter from George Lassalle to AC, 28.7.96.
10. Jack Andrews in conversation with AC.
11. Hilary Spurling, *Observer*, 18.12.77.
12. Paul Levy, *Books and Bookmen*, Jan. 1978.

CHAPTER TWENTY: *Omelette and Ice*
1. *Daily Telegraph*, Peterborough column, 14.4.78.
2. Stephanie Hoppen in conversation with AC.
3. Hilary Spurling in conversation with AC.
4. EDP: notes on typescript of *Elinor Fettiplace's Receipt Book*, edited by Hilary Spurling (Salamander Press and Penguin Books, 1986).
5. Ellen-Ann Hopkins in conversation with AC.
6. John Hopkins, *The Tangier Diaries 1962–1979*, Arcadia Books, 1997, p. 239.
7. EDP: letter from Viola Johnson, 2.4.79.

8. Jill Norman, ed., *South Wind through the Kitchen*, Michael Joseph, 1997, p. 1.

9. *Petits Propos Culinaires*, 41, p. 8. Tribute to ED.

10. Jill Norman, ed., *South Wind through the Kitchen*, p. 1.

11. Letter from Richard Olney to AC, 6.5.99.

12. EDP: draft of a letter to Sybille Bedford, undated.

13. Jill Norman in conversation with AC.

14. Johnny Grey in conversation with AC.

15. EDP: letter from Anthony Denney, 18.4.86.

16. Letter to Rosi Hanson, 15.7.82.

17. Derek Cooper in conversation with AC.

18. Recording of *The Food Programme*, with ED, 22.10.82.

19. Jill Norman in conversation with AC.

20. Jeremy Lewis, *Kindred Spirits: Adrift in Literary London*, HarperCollins, 1995, pp. 233–4.

21. Jane Grigson, *Times Literary Supplement*, 21.12.84

22. Angela Carter, 'An Omelette and a Glass of Wine and Other Dishes', *London Review of Books*, vol. 7, no. 1.

23. ibid.

24. Ann Barr and Paul Levy, *The Foodie Handbook*, Ebury Press, 1984, p. 7.

25. Paul Levy in conversation with AC.

26. Ann Barr in conversation with AC.

27. EDP: letter from Peter Higgins, 22.2.86.

28. Jill Norman in conversation with AC.

29. Letter from ED to Celia Denney, 4.4.86.

30. ibid.

31. Stephanie Hoppen in conversation with AC.

32. Letter from ED to Celia Denney 4.4.86.

33. Stephanie Hoppen in conversation with AC.

34. Rupert Grey in conversation with AC.

35. Stephanie Hoppen in conversation with AC.

36. ibid.

CHAPTER TWENTY-ONE: *Brave New World*

1. Johnny Grey in conversation with AC.

2. Gerald Asher in conversation with A C.

3. ibid.

4. ibid.

5. Johnny Grey in conversation with A C.

6. EDP: Nick Lander, letter to ED, 29.12.88.

7. *Violets and Vinegar, an Anthology of Women's Writings*, ed. Jilly Cooper and Tom Hartman, George Allen & Unwin, 1980, p. 103.

8. Letter to Hugh and Judy Johnson, 28.2.85.

9. Jancis Robinson in conversation with A C.

10. Draft of an undated letter to Jancis Robinson.

11. EDP: letter from Jane Grigson, 16.1.90.

12. ibid.

13. EDP: letter from George Lassalle, 15.12.89.

14. EDP: draft of a letter to George Lassalle, 24.12.89.

15. Paul Bailey in conversation with A C.

16. EDP: draft of letter to Celia Denney.

17. EDP: letter to Ellen-Ann Hopkins, November 1990.

18. Gerald Asher, Obituary of ED, *Independent*, 25.5.92.

19. ibid.

Epilogue

1. Nancy Mills, *Daily News*, 18.6.80.

2. *New York Times*, 10.6.92.

3. Nigel Slater, *Waterstone's Magazine*, Winter/Spring 1997.

Selected Bibliography

Ayling, Katharine, 'My Father's Family', unpublished memoir, 1980

Boulestin, Marcel, *Having Crossed the Channel*, Heinemann, 1934

Boxer, Arabella, *Arabella Boxer's Book of English Food*, John Curtis at Hodder & Stoughton, 1991

Burnett, John, *Plenty and Want: A Social History of Diet in England from 1815 to the Present Day*, Routledge, 3rd edn, 1989

Barr, Ann and Levy, Paul, *The Foodie Handbook*, Ebury Press, 1984

Chaney, Lisa, *Elizabeth David: A Biography*, Macmillan, 1998

Cooper, Artemis, *Cairo in the War 1939–1945*, Hamish Hamilton, 1989

Cowan, [Charles] Gibson, *Loud Report*, Michael Joseph, 1938; *The Voyage of the Evelyn Hope*, Cresset Press, 1946

David, Elizabeth

  A Book of Mediterranean Food: first published John Lehmann, 1950; revised editions 1955, 1958, 1965, 1988; new introduction 1991

  French Country Cooking: first published John Lehmann, 1951; revised editions 1958, 1966

  Italian Food: first published Macdonald & Co., 1954; revised editions 1963, 1969, 1977, 1987

  Summer Cooking: first published Museum Press, 1955; revised edition 1965

  French Provincial Cooking: first published Michael Joseph, 1960; revised editions 1965, 1967, 1970

Spices, Salt and Aromatics in the English Kitchen: first published Penguin Books, 1970; revised editions 1973, 1975

English Bread and Yeast Cookery: first published Allen Lane, 1977

An Omelette and a Glass of Wine: first published Jill Norman at Robert Hale Ltd, 1984

Harvest of the Cold Months: first published Michael Joseph, 1994

Douglas-Home, Jessica, *Violet: The Life and Loves of Violet Gordon Woodhouse*, Harvill Press, 1996

Grey, Johnny, *The Art of Kitchen Design*, Cassell, 1994

Grigson, Jane, *Good Things*, Michael Joseph, 1971; *English Food*, Macmillan, 1974

Hardyment, Christina, *A Slice of Life: The British Way of Eating since 1945*, BBC Books, 1995

Hartley, Dorothy: *Food in England*, Macdonald, 1954

Holloway, Mark, *Norman Douglas*, Secker & Warburg, 1976

Lasalle, George, *The Fish in My Life*, Macmillan, 1989

Leyel, Mrs F. C, and Hartley, Olga, *The Gentle Art of Cookery*, Chatto & Windus, 1925

Norman, Jill, *South Wind through the Kitchen: The Best of Elizabeth David*, Michael Joseph, 1997

Patten, Marguerite, *The Victory Cookbook*, Paul Hamlyn, in association with the Imperial War Museum, 1995

Spurling, Hilary, *Elinor Fettiplace's Receipt Book*, The Salamander Press, in association with Penguin Books, 1986

Index

ED stands for Elizabeth David

Abdelouahid 294–5
Aberdeen and Temair, Countess of 10
Adair, Robin 139–40
Alexandria
  ED in during war 84–5, 90, 91–4
Anastasia (Alexandrian cook) 86
Anderson, Diana 57
Andrews, Jack 300
Angela (Maltese cook) 52, 55
Arlott, John 301–2
Art of Simple French Cooking, The
  (Watt) 213
Asher, Gerald 336
  and ED's last evening 332–3
  in San Francisco 315, 316, 319–20
  and sardines 220–1
  and wine 217, 230, 231
Astor, Mrs David (Clare) 307
Auchinleck, Gen. Sir Claude 93, 95, 117
Ayling, Katharine (née Gwynne) 6, 53

Bailey, Paul 302–3, 329
Bakewell, Melissa 323
Baking of an English Loaf, The
  (booklet) 250, 264
Balfour, David 101
Bally, Max 89
Barattero, Mme 199, 309
Barette, Mme 29–30, 198
Barr, Ann 309–10
Barrington, Bill 25

Bastard, Algernon 146
Baxter, Walter 184, 187
Beaumes de Venise 230–1
Bedford, Sybille 227–9, 246–7, 271,
  296, 301
Beeton, Mrs 214, 231
Benckendorff, Count Constantine 41, 49
Beyfus, Drusilla 245, 311
Blakemore, Jane 298
Blow, Detmar 8–9
Bolland, Jean 281–2, 286
Bologna 172
Book of Mediterranean Food, A 87,
  139–45, 151–4, 239
  agreement to publish by John
    Lehmann 143–4
  appreciation of and success xiv, 153
  illustrations 144, 152
  initial rejections from publishers 142
  Penguin edition 180–1, 181–2, 222
  publication and reviews 151–2
  use of other authors in 141
Boston, Richard 334
Boulestin, Marcel 46, 140, 163, 231, 261
Bowles, Paul 176, 294
Boxer, Arabella 260–2
Boxer, Mark 310–11
Boyes, April 247, 248, 270, 271–2,
  279–81, 300, 328
bread book see English Bread and Yeast
  Cookery

Brien, Alan 215
British Food Export Council 270
Brownhill, Doreen *see* Thornton,
    Doreen
Butterworth, Marian *see* Thomas

Cadec, Madame 237–8, 239, 240–41
Carels, John 2
Carlisle, Earl and Countess of 119–20
Carluccio, Antonio 322
Carroll, Sydney 42
Carter, Angela 308
Carter, Ernestine 139, 192–3, 204–5
Carter, John 139, 141
Catsaflis, Renée *see* Fedden, Renée
Cecil, Vera 12, 21
Chancellor, Robin 142
Chandos, John 152
Charcuterie and French Pork Cookery
    (Grigson) 251
Child, Julia 230
Clarke, Sally 336
Classic French Cuisine, The (Donon) 213
Clifford, Alexander 99
Cohen, Chapman 47
Collins, Alex 237
Colquhoun, Archie 169
Conran, Caroline 291
Conran, Terence 238, 243
Cookery in Colour (Patten) 213–14
Cookery and Household Management
    (Beeton) 214
Cooper, Derek 303–4, 310
Cooper, Jilly 323–4
Cooper, Guy 292
Costa, Margaret 247
Crespigny, Caroline de 288
Cumberlege, Mike 63, 82, 86, 89, 90,
    117
Cumberlege, Nancy 63–4
Cunard, Nancy 66

Dahl, Roald 201, 298
Daily Express 177–8, 191
Daily Telegraph 216, 217–18

Daintrey, Adrian 180, 188
d'Amade, Josette 104–5
Daniels, Anthony 189
David, Anthony (Tony) (ED's
    husband) 156–7
  army career 108–9
  background 107–8
  death 253–4
  ED's feelings for 112, 114, 125,
    137–8
  filing for divorce by ED 146, 203
  involvement in setting up club
    135–6
  leaves Indian army 133
  love for ED 109–10, 114, 125,
    145–6, 203
  marriage and honeymoon 111–14
  moves to Spain 183
  posted back to India 117, 118
  strains in marriage 136–7
David, Beatrice 107–8
David, Elizabeth (née Gwynne)
  Food and Cooking 127–9, 159
    attitude towards 149
    auction of kitchen contents xiii–xv
    in Cairo 103–4
    dealing with rationing 126–7
    first cookery books 44–6
    first introduction to French
      cooking and seafood 29, 31
    influence of Boulestin 46
    influence of Norman Douglas 66–7
    kitchens and utensils 147–8, 149,
      162, 299–300
    learning to cook 38, 43–5, 79
    loss of sense of taste 231
    love of olive oil 246
    making pickles in Syros 80
    in Morocco 223–4
    photographs of food 195
    shop venture *see* Elizabeth David
      Ltd
    taste in wine 172, 217, 229, 247,
      296, 333
    testing of recipes 151, 175, 189

David, Elizabeth – *cont.*

Early Years

birth and christening 11

childhood and upbringing 12, 14,
15–16, 18–19

debutante and presentation at
court 32–3, 35–6

and father's death 21, 23

holidays 23–5

lack of affection shown by mother
14, 15, 23, 24

love of reading 16

memories of Wootton 26–7

in Munich 32, 33, 36

nursery food 16–18

in Paris and attending the
Sorbonne 29–31

platonic relationship with older
man 33–4

portrait by McEvoy 20–1

relationship with Aunt Violet 25,
26

relationship with cousin Anne 18,
24

relationship with father 7, 14–15

relationship with sisters 15

running away 18–19

schooling 22–3, 28

tea with mother 19

Personal Life

ancestry and family background
1–9

appearance and dress style xv, 51,
283–4

attachment to Wales and visits to
54–5, 282–3, 285, 286

attitude towards children 48, 130,
186–7, 210

attitude towards money 31, 44,
59, 134

attributes 29–30

awarded CBE and OBE 24, 285,
289, 311–12

awarded honorary doctorate from
University of Essex 291

book collection and love of books
xvi, 271–2, 293

car accident and injuries sustained
287–8, 290

and cats 15, 211

cerebral haemorrhage 225–6, 231,
327

characteristics xvii–xx, 30–1,
99–100, 109

circle of friends 184, 187–8,
300–3

daily routine 189

and death of ex-husband 253–4

death and funeral 333

and death of mother 273

and death of sister Diana 263–4

and death of sister Felicité 312,
313, 320

deterioration of marriage and
divorce 136–7, 145–6, 151, 203

diet in later years 322

and drinking 225, 231–2, 314

early married life 114–15

entertaining 189–90

flats in London 43–4, 46, 54

fragility in later years 321, 330–1

and Halsey Street 134, 136–7, 183

handwriting analysis 30–1

interest in history 292

interviews of 245, 246, 303–4

job as 'showroom second' for
Worth 55–6

London life after return from
India 125–6

marriage and honeymoon 113–14

memorial service 335–6

obituaries 334

and painting 28, 36

painting collection 188–9

in Ross-on-Wye 130–1

and Rupert Grey's claim to
Wootton 268

stroke 332–3

television programme on 324–7

theatre career 37–9, 41, 42–3

David, Elizabeth – *cont.*
  on Tory Island 203–4
  Relationships and Friendships
    Anthony Denney 235, 236–7
    Charles Gibson Cowan *see* Gibson
      Cowan
    Diana (sister) 262–3
    Doreen Thornton 42, 64–5, 175,
      204, 225, 301
    Edward Marjoribanks, 35
    Felicité (sister) 184–5
    George Lassalle 100–1, 110,
      129–30
    husband *see* David, Anthony
    mother 36, 37, 51, 272
    Norman Douglas *see* Douglas,
      Norman
    Peter Higgins *see* Higgins, Peter
    Peter Laing 92, 93–4, 96–7, 100,
      124, 169
    Priscilla (sister) 64, 187
    Renée Fedden *see* Fedden, Renée
    Stanford Holme 38, 41, 42
    Sybille Bedford 227–9, 301
  Second World War
    in Alexandria 84–5, 86, 87, 90,
      91–3, 94
    in Athens 77–8
    in Cairo 94–5, 100, 101–3
    escape from Crete 82–3
    in France 62–3, 68, 70
    internment in Italy 72–6
    leaving of Corsica for Giglio 71–2
    leaving of France for Corsica
      68–9, 70–1
    leaving of Syros for Crete due to
      bombing 82
    running of reference library in
      Cairo 98–9, 124
    in Syros 78–81, 124
  Travels
    buying trips in France for shop
      241, 253, 254–5, 264
    Capri 161, 163, 165
    Corsica 57

Denmark 269–70
Egypt 53–4
France 56–7, 154
French travels in *Evelyn Hope*
  60–3
India 118–23
Italy 164–72, 172–4
Malta 51–2, 54
Ménerbes (France) 156–60
research trips to France 197–200,
  205–7, 278–9
San Francisco 316–20, 329
Sardinia 171–2
Spain 235–7, 272
Tangier 293–5
Venice 167, 169–70, 256–7
Writing Career 155
  attributes xv
  'Author of the Year' in
    Glenfiddich Awards 291
  awarded Fellowship of the Royal
    Society of Literature 309
  begins to write in Ross on Wye
    131–2, 133
  booklets written for shop 250
  contribution to *Sunday Times
    Travel Guide to France* 153–4
  and *Daily Express* 177–8, 191
  and *Daily Telegraph* 216, 217–18
  and editors 140, 192–3
  and English food 261–2
  enhancement of reputation 209
  and *Go* 153
  and *Harper's Bazaar* 139–40, 154,
    155, 159, 190–1, 194
  and *House and Garden* 190–1, 194
  influence and impact of xv,
    334–5
  influence on other writers 250–2
  little books 250
  and Macdonald publishers *see*
    Macdonald
  and *Nova* 239
  opinion of own 179
  and *Petits Propos Culinaires* 296

David, Elizabeth – *cont.*
  reviews of books 151–2, 178–9,
    213, 289
  and Robert Hale publishers
    305–6, 307, 311
  and *Spectator* 214–15, 218, 220,
    221, 227, 230, 232, 236, 261
  and *Sunday Dispatch* 216
  and *Sunday Times* 191–3, 204–5
  and *Tatler* 310–11
  upsetting of food industry 218
  visit to sardine cannery in Nantes
    219
  and *Vogue* 194–7, 198, 200, 202,
    215–16
  Wine and Food articles 220
  see also individual books
David, Ivor 107
Davidson, Alan 252, 295
Davidson, Jane 295
Day, Michael 302, 330
Denmark ED's trip to 269–70
Denney, Anthony 194–5, 195–6, 205,
    206, 215, 284–5, 301
  background 195
  death 329–30
  and design of shop 238, 241, 242
  engagement to Celia 248
  relationship with ED 235, 236–7
Denney, Celia (née Royde-Smith) 247,
    248, 272, 329
Douglas, Norman 89, 122, 141, 165
  in Capri 161
  death 164
  and ED's marriage 115
  and food 66
  forced to leave Italy 64
  influence of on ED 66–7, 124
  letters to ED 70–1, 76–8
  relationship with ED 64–5, 68–9,
    164
Dried Herbs, Aromatics and Condiments
    (booklet) 250
Ducat, Mr 216
Durrell, Eve (née Cohen) 101, 107

Durrell, Lawrence 85, 99, 101, 153,
    209

Eland, Roger 99, 252
'Elizabeth David Classics' 306, 311
Elizabeth David Ltd. 240–50, 275–6
  attempts by ED to change its name
    after her departure 275–6
  buying trips in France 241, 253,
    254–5, 264
  design 242–3
  ED working in 243–5, 247, 248
  mail-order and wholesale 249–50
  naming of 242
  opening 243
  plans for 237–9
  premises and stock 240–1
  resignation and severance of all
    connections with by ED 274,
    276
  staff 247–8
  tensions and growing crisis between
    ED and partners 249, 253,
    68–9, 270, 272, 273
Ellis, Roger 49–50, 130
English Bread and Yeast Cookery 275,
    277–8, 284
  ED receives award for 291
  importance of in campaign for better
    bread 289–90, 291–2
  publication and reviews 289
  research for 279–82
English Potted Meats and Fish Pastes
    (booklet) 250
Epstein, Jerry 307
Erskine, Hamish St-Clair 150, 157, 158
Evelyn Hope, The Voyage of the, 60–63,
    72–3

Fedden, Frances 58, 86, 186–7, 247,
    248
Fedden, Renée (née Catsaflis) 91, 94–5
  background 88–9
  buying trips to France with ED
    254–5, 264

Fedden, Renée – *cont.*
  on ED's marriage 114
  falling out with ED over shop 271,
    272, 273, 274, 288
  friendship with ED 88, 89, 91,
    264–5
  marriage 94
  resignation from shop 269
  and Rosie Peto 254
  and shop 238, 249, 253, 270
Fedden, Robin 81, 85, 88, 89, 101, 126,
    254
  death 288
  marriage 94
  relationship with ED 53–4, 57–8
Fisher, M.F.K. 301, 319
Florence 166–7
Folkington Manor 2–3, 8, 266
Food Programme 303
Fortunes of War (Manning) 102,
    115–16, 331
France
  ED's buying trips 253, 254–5, 264
  ED's research trips 197–200, 205–7,
    278–9
  visits to by ED 56–7, 154, 156–60
Freeman, Denis 126, 136–7, 142, 156
French Country Cooking 156, 159,
    161–3
French, Leslie 42, 335
French Provincial Cooking 198, 208–9,
    211–13
  dedication 212
  illustrations for 212
  publication by Michael Joseph 211–
    13
  reception 213
  research trips for 197–9
Frost, Eunice 181, 222, 239
Furness, Professor Robin 90

Garland, Ailsa 215
Gathorne-Hardy, Eddie 101, 117, 122
Gautier, Théophile 141
Gentle Art of Cookery, The (Leyel) 44, 45

Gibson Cowan, Leonard (Charles)
  in Athens 77–8
  background 46–7
  ending of relationship with ED 83,
    85
  French travels in *Evelyn Hope* 60–3,
    67–8
  internment in Italy 73–5
  joins *Samothrace* as bosun 87–8
  Loud Report 46, 47, 58
  relationship with ED 47–9, 54, 58,
    63, 67, 70, 105–7
  teaching job in Syros 78, 79
  theatre career 42, 47, 52
  and *The Voyage of the Evelyn Hope*
    60, 82–3, 88, 105, 204
  ED's reactions to 105, 204
Gillie, Oliver 291
Gilmour, Ian 215
Glenfiddich Awards 291
Go 153
Goldsworthy, Mrs 250
Good Food (Heath) 45–6
Goodwin, Dorothy and Teddy 51, 53,
    85
Gordon, Dudley 11
Gould, Cecil 126
Grace, Aunt *see* Palmer, Grace
Graham, Antonia 247
Granville, Lady (Grace) 292
Grey, Christabel 321, 329
Grey, Diana (née Gwynne) 129–30
  birth 11
  character 49
  early years and schooling 15, 22
  and ED's marriage 114
  holiday in Venice with ED 256–7
  living with Benckendorffs 41, 49
  marriage 91, 125, 186
  relationship with ED 262–3
  relationship with Roger Ellis 49–50
  rift with Aunt Violet 125
  suffering from tinnitus 256, 258, 262
  suicide 35, 263
  and Wootton 267–8

Grey, Douglas 135, 256
Grey, Dr Christopher 91, 125, 186,
    256, 262, 263, 267, 313
Grey, Johnny 148, 149, 186, 286–7,
    299, 300, 321, 329
Grey, Martin 267
Grey, Rupert 96–7, 262, 267, 268
Grey, Steven 320–1
Grigson, Geoffrey 251
Grigson, Jane 251, 252–3, 260, 302,
    307–8, 311, 323, 327–8, 329
Guttuso, Renato 169, 170, 171, 178,
    222
Gwynne, Agnes (née Anderson) (great
    grandmother to ED) 1, 2
Gwynne, Diana (sister) see Grey,
    Diana
Gwynne, Dorothy (aunt) 2, 3, 12, 20
Gwynne, Evelyn 2
Gwynne, Felicité (sister)
    attitude towards food 185
    birth 11
    bookselling career 156, 200–1, 211
    character 155, 185
    death and burial 312–13
    during Second World War 127, 155
    early years and schooling 15, 22, 25–
        6, 41
    and ED's bread book 278
    ill-health 297
    relationship with ED 184–5
    stroke and death 312
    suffering from malnutrition 297–8
    typing of ED's articles 155, 156
Gwynne, James (grandfather) 1–2,
    3–4, 6, 7, 11, 12, 20
    will 7–8, 11, 20, 22, 267
Gwynne, John (great grandfather) 1
Gwynne, Kathleen (cousin) see Ayling
Gwynne, May (née Purvis)
    (grandmother) 2, 3, 11
Gwynne, Nevile (uncle) 2, 3, 4, 6, 7,
    12, 13
Gwynne, Priscilla (sister) see Longland,
    Priscilla

Gwynne, Reginald (uncle) 2, 4
Gwynne, Roland (uncle) 2, 3, 12, 20
    awarded DSO during First World
        War 13–14
    dissipating of inheritance 22
    and Folkington 8, 11, 266
    in nursing home 266
    relationship with Stella 39
    upbringing 3
    and Wootton 40
Gwynne, Rupert (father) 2, 3, 4–6
    affair with Vera Cecil 11–12, 21
    death and funeral 21
    early years 2–3
    education and career 4–5
    and father's will 20
    marriage 6, 7
    political career 7, 11, 13, 20
    weak heart 5, 19–20
    and Wootton 8
Gwynne, Stella (née Ridley) (mother)
    135, 266
    and antiques 50, 134, 135, 187
    appearance and dress style 10, 39
    attitude towards Charles Cowan 48,
        51
    death 272
    and death of Edward Marjoribanks
        35
    end of marriage to Hamilton and
        move back to England 50
    feud with Violet Gordon
        Woodhouse 12, 26
    finances 32
    first husband's affair 12
    first husband's death and after 22
    first marriage 6, 11
    and First World War 13
    and James Gwynne's will 11
    lack of affection shown towards
        daughters 14, 15, 23, 24
    and painting 28
    personality and talents 10, 14
    relations with Rupert's family 12
    relationship with ED 36, 37, 51, 272

Gwynne, Stella – *cont.*
  relationship with Roland 39
  second marriage to John Hamilton
    and move to Jamaica 40
  Wootton 22, 39
Gwynne, Violet *see* Woodhouse, Violet
  Gordon

Habitat 238–9
Haines, Arthur Lett 187–8, 189, 223
Hale, John 305, 306
Hamilton, Iain 218
Hamilton, Major John 40, 50
Hamlyn, Paul 214
Hammond, Nicholas 82
Hanson, Anthony 217, 325
Hanson, Rosi 247, 300, 325
Harcourt-Smith, Charles 265
Harcourt-Smith, Sabrina (née
  Longland) 26, 265–6, 267
Harper, Frances 56
Harper's Bazaar
  ED's articles 139–40, 154, 159,
    190–1, 194
Harris, Clifford 311
Harris, Katherine 36
Harrods 216, 236
Harvest of the Cold Months, The 304,
  306, 322–3, 335
Harvey, Captain Eric 176, 177
Harvey, Wilfred 176
Heath, Ambrose 45–6
Hebdon, Peter 212
Herbert Joseph 142
Henry, Mr and Mrs Rex 223–4
Herbal Review, The 292
Hickson, Joan 38
Higgins, Kathleen (née Dunn) 150
Higgins, Peter 119, 146
  affair and relationship with ED 149,
    150–1, 160, 174, 203, 210–11,
    212
  and Anne Holland-Martin 225,
    232
  background 118, 149–50

ED keeps in touch with 284
  ending of affair with ED 232–3
Higgins, Rupert 149
Hill, Derek 166, 178, 203
Hodgkin, Eliot 188
Hodson, Harry 205
Hogg, Douglas (1st Viscount
  Hailsham) 21–2
Hogg, Neil 89, 213
Hogg, Quintin 22
Holland-Martin, Anne (née Fane) 225,
  232
Holme, Stanford 37–8, 39, 41, 42
Holme, Thea 37
Holroyd, Michael 309
Home Baked (Scurfield) 275
Hope-Nicholson, Felix 159
Hopkins, Ellen-Ann (née Ragsdale)
  248, 265, 293, 294, 306–7
Hopkins, John 293, 294
Hopkinson, Simon 322
Hoppen, Stephanie 292–3, 312,
  313–14
Hotel du Midi 199–200
House and Garden 190–1, 194
Hunt, Anthony 191
Hunter, Barbara (later Doxat) 46

India
  ED in 118–23
Inglis, Brian 215, 218
Italian Food 167, 175
  and American market 201–2
  commissioning of 164
  illustrations 169–70, 178, 222–3
  Penguin editions 172, 179, 222
  publication and reception of 178–9
  reaction to by Macdonald publishers
    176–7
  success 179
  wine chapters 172
Italy
  ED in 164–72, 172–4
  food in 163
  wine 172

'Janet' 128–9
Jasper, Uncle *see* Ridley, Jasper
Jenkinson, Rosalind 247, 262
Johnson, Arthur 164, 165, 178
Johnson, Hugh 219–20, 301, 336
Johnson, Judy 301
Johnson , Viola 164–5, 178, 230, 295
Joseph, Anthea 211, 212
Joseph, Michael 211
Josipi 78, 79, 80

Keik, Ian 211
Kemsley, 1st Viscount 153
Kenney-Herbert, Colonel 119, 258
King, John 330
Kininmonth, Christopher 100
Kinross, Patrick 101, 117
Knopf, Alfred 201
Korchinska, Maria 41
Kyriacou (Greek cook) 86, 87

Laing, Peter 92, 93–4, 95–6, 96–7,
    100, 115, 124, 169
'Lalt' 33–4
Lampson, Miranda 109
Lander, Nick 324, 325
Lane, Allen 181
Lassalle, George 132, 328
    affair with ED 100–1, 110, 129–30
    marriages 187, 288
Leech, Richard 313
Lehmann, John 154, 156, 180, 222, 242
    closure of company 176
    ED's poem for 285–6
    and *Italian Food* 163, 170
    and *Mediterranean Food* 142–3,
        143–4, 144–5
Leigh Fermor, Patrick 100, 118, 190
Leith, Prue xiv, 323
Léontine (Parisian cook) 29, 32
Lessing, Doris 126
Levin, Bernard 215
Levy, Paul 289, 309, 310, 311
Lewin, Patrick 136
Lewis, Jeremy 307

Leyel, Hilda 44, 45, 55, 231, 259, 261
Llewellyn, Bryan 240, 241, 249
Llewellyn, Daphne 109, 110
Llewellyn, Hermione *see* Ranfurly
Llewellyn, Owen 107–8
Lo, Jenny 331
Longland, Priscilla (née Gwynne) 90–1
    birth 11
    daughters 125
    early years and schooling 13, 15, 22,
        24
    ED's visits to Malta to see 51–2, 54
    end of marriage 151
    engagement and marriage 39, 40–1
    and marriage of daughter Sabrina
        265
    relationship with ED 64, 187, 330
    and Wootton 266–7
Longland, Richard Barnes 39, 40–1,
    51, 151
Longleat 292
Loud Report (Gibson Cowan) 46, 47, 58
Lyall, Archie 164
Lyon 199
Lyttelton, Alfred 11

McAuliffe, Carly 331–2
McAuliffe, Jean 299, 331–2
McConnell, Kathleen 96
McDermott, Gracie 203–4
Macdonald (publishers) 201, 224
    and *Italian Food* 176–7, 179–80, 181
    losing of Guttuso illustrations 222,
        224, 232
    and *Mediterranean Food* 181–2
McEvoy, Ambrose 20–1
McPherson, Kenneth 161
Mafalda (cook, Capri) 165
Manning, Olivia 101–2, 115, 179, 331
Margaret, Princess 250
Marjoribanks, Edward 35
Marple, Lesley 296
Mary, H.M. Queen 36
Mastering the Art of French Cookery
    (child) 230

Matter of Taste, A (Radio 4 broadcast) 323, 328
Mayer, Tony and Thérèse 157
Meade, Antonia 32
Meagher, Veronica *see* Nicholson, Veronica
Mediterranean Food see Book of Mediterranean Food, A
Menasce, Georges de 94, 114
Middle Eastern Food, A Book of (Roden) 251–2
Midleton, Countess of 32, 35
Milan 167–8
Minton, John 144, 152, 156, 222
Montgomery, General Bernard 95
Moorehead, Alan 99
Morny, Patrick de 183–4
Morphy, Countess 44, 55, 231, 261
Morris, Cedric 188, 189
Murchie, Joyce 184, 187, 247
Museum Press 142, 180

Nash, John 188
Nerina, Zia 172
New Writing 142–3
Newnham-Davis, Lt Col. 141, 146
Nicholas, Elizabeth 151–2, 153
Nicholson, Major John 151, 224
Nicholson, Veronica (nee Meagher) 190, 291 and ED's writing 139–40, 145 in India 118–19, 121 marriage 151 relationship with ED 136, 224
Nijinsky, Vaslav 137
Norman, Jill xvi, xvii, 243–4, 258, 284, 300, 304–5
  and Robert Hale 306, 311
  editing of ED's books 239–40, 281, 304
Nova 239

Observer 251
Official Foodie Handbook, The (Levy and Barr) 308, 310
olive oil 246

Olney, Richard 295–6, 297
Olympia Food Fair (1956) 192
O'Malley, Kate 187
O'Malley, Lesley (née Pares) 126, 183–4, 225, 298–9
Omelette and a Glass of Wine, An xvi, 304, 305–6, 307–8, 309, 311
Open Air Theatre (Regent's Park) 42
Oxford Repertory Theatre 37–9

Palmer, Anne (ED's cousin) 18, 23, 38–9, 41, 122–3
Palmer, Grace (née Ridley), Viscountess Wolmer, Countess of Selborne (aunt to ED) 10, 18, 23, 40, 41–2
Palmer, Roundell Cecil (Viscount Wolmer), 3rd Earl of Selborne (uncle to ED) 18, 21
Parma 170
Parrish, Walter 224
Patten, Marguerite 127, 174, 213
Penguin 180–1, 222, 239
Perrier, M, chef at Hôtel du Midi 199–200
'Peter the Pole' 313
Petits Propos Culinaires 295–6
Peto, Rosie 249, 254, 273, 274
Phillips, Neville 126, 136–7, 142
Piccini, Giulia 166
Pugh, Pam 240, 249, 253, 254
Purnell 176

Ragsdale, Ellen-Ann *see* Hopkins, Ellen-Ann
Ranfurly, Hermione, Countess of (née Llewellyn) 109, 114–15
Ray, Cyril 215, 232
Renny, Juliet 212
Recipes of All Nations (Morphy) 44
Richards, Jim 104
Richardson, Judith 161, 187
Ridley, Katharine 24
Ridley, Grace *see* Palmer, Grace
Ridley, Jasper (son of uncle Jasper) 117

Ridley, Sir Jasper (uncle to ED) 23, 37, 38, 58–9
Ridley, Nathalie 23
Ridley, Stella *see* Gwynne, Stella
Ridley, 1st Viscount 6
Robert Hale Ltd (publishers) 305–7, 311
    dismissal of Jill Norman from 306
Robinson, Jancis 324
Roden, Claudia 251–2
Round, Jeremy 329
Rowe, Vivian 213
Rowley, Lady Sibell (née Lygon) 145, 151, 224, 225
Rowley, Michael 145, 151
Royal Society of Literature 309
Royd-Smith, Celia *see* Denney, Celia
Rubinstein, Michael 232
Russell, Leonard 153, 191

San Francisco 316–20
San Remo 168
Sandoe, John 200, 297, 298
Sardinia 171–2
Savage, Elizabeth 248, 278–9, 300
Scott, Paul 180, 201, 211
Scott-Ellis, Jim 111
Scott-James, Anne 139, 140–1, 194
'Scrambled Eggs Variation 77' 285–6
Scurfield, George and Cecilia 275
Seafish of Tunisia (Davidson) 252
Selborne, 3rd Earl and Countess of, *see* Palmer
Slater, Nigel 335
Smart, Lady (Amy) 54, 102
Smart, Sir Walter 54, 102
Smith, Arnold 95
Smith, Delia 331
Smith, John 268–9
Smith, Reggie 102, 126
Smollett, Tobias 277
Spectator
    ED stops writing for 232
    ED's articles for 214–15, 218, 220, 221, 227, 230, 232, 236, 261

Spencer, Bernard 101
Spices, Salt and Aromatics in the English Kitchen 259–60
Spurling, Hilary 289, 293
Stark, Freya 99, 178–9
Strachey, Julia 132, 143
Suleiman xvii, 103–4
Summer Cooking 121, 160, 178, 180, 240
Summers, Romney 90, 157, 158
Sunday Dispatch 216
Sunday Times
    Campaign for Real Bread 291
    ED's articles for 191–2
    interview with ED 246–7
    relationship between ED and Ernestine Carter 192–3, 204–5
    resignation of ED 205
    series on French markets 204, 206
Sunday Times Travel Guide to France 153–4
Syllabubs and Fruit Fools (booklet) 250
Syros
    bombing of by Germans 82
    ED's life in during war 78–81, 124

Taruschio, Ann and Franco 179, 283, 326
Tatler 310–11
Taylor, Gordon 292
Telegraph magazine 245
Thomas, Marian 29, 43, 46, 48, 55, 91
Thomas, Peter 91
Thornton, Colin 175, 204
Thornton, Doreen (née Brownhill) 48, 56–7, 157, 272
    accompanies ED on French trips 133, 198, 205, 207
    first impression of ED 42
    friendship with ED 42, 64–5, 175, 204, 225, 301
Thynne, Lord Christopher 292
Tollemache, Denis 25
Tory Island 203, 204
Tower, Jeremiah 296

Trier, Jenny 238, 240, 249
Trier, Peter 238, 241, 249
Trust House Hotel's catering manual
   132–3
Tulleken, Kit van 311
Turin 173
Twining, Herbert 1

University of Essex 291

Venice
   ED's visits to 167, 169–70, 256–7
Verona 167
Verral, William 231
vinegar 'mother' 245
Vogue
   ED's articles 194–5, 198, 200, 202,
      215–16
   'Food at Its Best' series 196, 198
Voto, Avis de 202
Voyage of the Evelyn Hope, The
      (Cowan) 61, 82–3, 88, 105, 204

Walnut Tree Inn 179, 283, 325
Waters, Alice 317, 335, 336
Watt, Alexander 213

Waugh, Evelyn 145, 179
West, Billy 318
White, Sir Matthew 6–7
Whitehorn, Katharine 214, 215, 232
Willert, Paul 187
Williams, Chuck 316, 317
Wine and Food 219–20
Wine and Food Society 219
Withers, Audrey 194–5, 196, 197, 204,
      215
Woodhouse, Gordon 4
Woodhouse, Violet Gordon (née
      Gwynne) 2, 3, 4, 5, 24–5
   character 25–6
   feud with Stella 12, 26
   men friends 4, 25
   musical talent 3
   rift with Diana 125
Wootton house 8–9, 266

Yannaki 78, 79, 80

Zoppi, Signor 167
Zuni Café 318
Zwy, Lesley 246
Zwy, Michael 246